A Teacher's Source Book for Mathematics in Classes 6–8

MAKING MATHS MEANINGFUL

A Teacher's Source Book for Mathematics in Classes 6–8

Jamie York

First published in the United States of America
by Jamie York Press, Boulder, Colorado in 2009
www.JamieYorkPress.com
First published in the UK in 2016
by Floris Books, Edinburgh,
adapted from the 2015 American edition
Second printing 2022

© 2009 Jamie York
UK edition © 2016 Floris Books

All rights reserved. No part of this book may be
reproduced in any form with the written permission of
Floris Books, Edinburgh
www.florisbooks.co.uk

British Library CIP Data available
ISBN 978-178250-318-7
Printed in Great Britain
by Bell & Bain Ltd

Contents

Introduction	11
Maths Curriculum Topics	29
Class Six Arithmetic	**33**
The world of numbers	33
Division	36
Fractions	40
Decimals	43
Business maths main lesson	47
Other topics	54
Class Six Geometry	**59**
The basics	59
Geometric drawing	61
Spirals	68
Advanced constructions	71
Area	72
Class Seven Arithmetic	**74**
The world of numbers	74
Measurement	75
Percents	76
Ratios	80
A new type of number: irrational numbers	85
Word problems	90
Class Seven Algebra	**93**
Formulas	94
Positive and negative numbers	96
Expressions	97
Equations	98
Algebraic word problems	100
Class Seven Geometry	**101**
Area	101
Geometric drawing	102
The pentagon and the golden ratio	109
Angle theorems and proofs	113
Pythagorean Theorem	116
Other topics	119
Class Eight Arithmetic	**120**
Number bases	121
The world of numbers	129
Percents and growth	131
Dimensional analysis	136
Proportions	141
Class Eight Algebra	**144**
Expressions	144
Equations	145
Class Eight Computers	**148**
Computer memory and ASCII code	148
Computer algorithms	149
Class Eight Geometry	**151**
Mensuration (areas and volumes)	151
Area	151
Volumes of solids	155
Surface area	158
Stereometry	163
Loci	178
Curves generated from loci problems	179
Appendix	**195**
Drawings	196
Advanced topics	205

Wonder of number	218
Tables and handouts	236
Assessment tests and maths skills	255
Suggested reading	**260**
Glossary	**261**
Special symbols used in this book	266
Index	**267**

Introduction

About this book

Who is this for?
While most of my teaching experience is within the Waldorf school system, the curriculum presented here can be effectively used by any teacher wishing to bring meaningful, age-appropriate material to their students. The explanations in this book are also useful for parents (or tutors) who are helping their children in a maths class that uses the curriculum laid out in this book.

While most of the material is not overly difficult, much of it is foreign, even for conventional maths teachers. In writing this book, I have assumed that the reader may be weak in maths. I hope that with some effort, even the most difficult topic is understandable.

A word of caution
This book should not be viewed as a recipe for teaching mathematics in a Waldorf school. Indeed there is no such recipe. This book is merely a resource that reflects the opinions of the author. There are other opinions as well that may also be called 'Waldorf'.

The reader (presumably a teacher) should not simply follow instructions or carry out a plan just because it is stated in this book. As always, it is the teacher's job to develop the inner sense of what is right at a particular moment for the class and to create an effective lesson. It is ultimately the teacher's love and creativity that will bring the material alive for the students. No book can give this to the teacher.

Things to keep in mind regarding this book
- You can't cover all of this! I have never, with any class, covered all the material listed in this book. How much material is covered will depend upon the teacher, the class, and the amount of time available. Obviously, it is important not to rush through the material for the sake of getting through the curriculum.
- *Main lessons and ongoing classes.* Some of the material presented here assumes familiarity with the Waldorf lesson structuring, known as main lessons (which are three or four-week intensive blocks of up to two hours every day) and ongoing classes (which continue several times a week throughout the whole year). In Waldorf schools, we typically introduce a completely new topic in the main lesson and then work on developing skills in the regular ongoing classes.
- *Order of topics.* The topics in this book are arranged by class, according to subject area. It is not intended that a teacher should cover the topics in the order that they appear in this book. Teachers using my workbooks may find it best to cover topics in the order that they appear in the workbooks. Some topics don't appear in the workbooks at all.

Workbooks, other books and website
The following *Making Maths Meaningful* workbooks are available from Floris Books.
- *A Student's Workbook for Maths in Class 6*
- *A Student's Workbook for Maths in Class 7*
- *A Student's Workbook for Maths in Class 8*

These school workbooks are an integral part of our maths curriculum. While our workbooks largely focus on standard skill development, they also provide mathematical experiences and give the students a feeling of discovery. The workbook packs come with an answer sheet for teachers.

There are further workbooks and teachers' source books (Classes One to Five, and high school) from Jamie York Press in the United States, as well as *Fun with Puzzles, Games and More!* The maths puzzle and game book is intended as a resource in order to supplement the normal classroom material and provide for that 'something different'.

The website *www.JamieYorkPress.com* shows full-colour photos of children's main lesson book pages, free downloads of a variety of practice sheets, and access other resources related to *Making Maths Meaningful* books. You can also contact us there with questions and comments.

Acknowledgments and permissions

Thank you to Nettie Fabrie and Wim Gottenbos for many of the ideas included in the introduction.

Drawings in this book have been reprinted with permission from the following:

The Geometrical Foundation of Natural Structure, by Robert Williams, Dover Publications, 1979.

Geometric Drawing and the Waldorf School Plan, by H. von Baravalle, Rudolf Steiner College Press.

Platonic and Archimedean Solids, by Daud Sutton, Walker & Company, 2001.

Today's challenge

The maths tightrope
In teaching mathematics, perhaps like no other subject, we find ourselves walking a tightrope. If we step a bit to one side, a sizable portion of the class becomes perplexed and overwhelmed. If we correct ourselves to the other side, the quicker students get bored and the class as a whole doesn't progress enough. For many teachers, each step along this tightrope brings up unpleasant memories from their own childhood.

As Waldorf teachers, we are aware that the teaching of maths is more than just an intellectual exercise. Rudolf Steiner, the founder of Waldorf education, spoke of the importance of 'permeating the soul with mathematics in the right way' and how a healthy relationship to mathematics can benefit the student's later spiritual development.

Certainly, maths in a Waldorf school is viewed differently and taught differently. Yet, the problems we face are often the same as in the mainstream. How can we do better?

The list

If people believe that maths should always be practical, then it stands to reason that skill development would become the primary focus. Over time this has degenerated into a horrifically long list of skills that are supposedly necessary for our students to move to the next level. Such a list manages to put pressure on teachers at all levels of education. They fear that if they don't get through the entire list, then their students won't be prepared. We are led to believe that this list is getting longer and longer, and more and more daunting. Such an over-emphasis on skill development is boring or overwhelming (or both) for many students, as well as for the teacher.

I believe that basic skills are important, but the list of topics needed to move forward is not horrifically long; it is actually quite manageable. I also believe there is much more to maths than just learning skills. With so much emphasis going toward the mastery of a long list of skills, some of the more interesting aspects of mathematics become neglected.

Why this curriculum?

Previous to when I began teaching at Shining Mountain Waldorf School in 1994, my experiences as a mathsteacher had been fairly typical. I taught out of a textbook, and it was expected that my class would complete the majority of that book.

When I arrived at Shining Mountain and was given the task of teaching middle school maths, I was surprised to find that there were no textbooks, and that very little existed in terms of a maths curriculum guideline. I was expected to create my own materials. This newfound freedom was both exciting and daunting. I proceeded to research what was happening at other Waldorf schools regarding the maths curriculum. I spent a great deal of time creating my own worksheets. My original question ('What should I teach?') was soon transformed into 'What topics would best help in developing the thinking and imagination of my middle school students?'

This book is intended to share with others what I have discovered and developed during this journey.

Being a Waldorf teacher

All teachers have a tremendous responsibility to oversee the development of the children in their class. Additionally, all Waldorf teachers have a great deal of freedom in deciding what to bring into the classroom. They do not rely on textbooks; instead each child creates their own book for every main lesson.

It is important that we, as Waldorf teachers, are the authors of what comes into the classroom. It needs to be clear to us why we do what we do. We shouldn't just blindly do something because it's what everyone else does. We need to feel it's right for the students in front of us. In this way we take ownership of the curriculum.

What is maths?
All of this leads to an important question: What is maths, really?

Why does our modern educational system have such difficulty teaching maths effectively? A significant part of the problem is that we don't really understand what maths is. And then comes the shocking realisation: We aren't actually teaching *real* maths.

Much of the focus of mainstream mathematics curricula today seems to be to cram as much material into the students' heads as possible. This emphasis on learning 'maths skills' is often at the expense of understanding the maths behind the maths. Students just want to be fed a formula or be told how to follow some procedure blindly in order to 'solve' the problem. In summary, *most people think that maths is a collection of blind procedures to be used to solve meaningless problems.*

In contrast, I believe that it is critically important for students to understand the maths behind the maths, to realise that maths isn't something that's 'out there somewhere', but rather that maths is one of those things that makes us human.

We want our students to experience maths as an adventure, and to feel that maths is a profoundly human endeavour.

Meaningless maths
What is society's view of maths? Maths is often not seen as meaningful in and of itself. A widespread belief is that 'good maths' must be practical and useful. It then follows that the main reason to study maths is that it can be useful for some other purpose or subject. All of these attitudes toward maths can make it challenging to teach maths in a meaningful way.

I believe that practical applications of maths can be helpful, but I also feel that there is a higher purpose to learning maths.

What is the higher purpose of teaching maths?
Maths teaches us how to *think*. We want our students to be able to think for themselves, think analytically, and we hope that their thinking is heart-felt and imbued with imagination.

Character development. Maths teaches students discipline, perseverance, patience and how to deal with mistakes. For many students, maths teaches them how to work through struggle.

Combating cynicism. In today's world, our youth can easily come to believe that things are meaningless and without purpose. Cynicism is a pervasive social disease today. By teaching maths in the right way, we can show our students that the world is true and is filled with awe and wonder.

Spiritual and moral development. Steiner talks about the importance of maths as part of the students' future spiritual development:

> The student of mathematics must get rid of all arbitrary thinking and follow purely the demands of thought. In thinking in this way, the laws of the spiritual world

flow into him. This regulated thinking leads to the most spiritual truths.*

Maths is human. Not everything we teach has to be practical. Maths, like music, drama, painting and literature, is an art. Through these subjects, a true education teaches us what it means to be human.

Imagination and maths

In today's society, imagination is associated largely with fantasy and not viewed as very 'useful'. It is therefore not surprising that in mainstream education, the development of the child's imagination can be considered unimportant. In contrast, Waldorf education holds that the development of the child's imagination is a central aspect of developing the whole child.

In terms of the teaching of maths, imagination can be woven into the lessons, not just by telling compelling stories, but also by showing students that maths is a fascinating and creative human endeavour. In this way, maths can be a springboard for thinking flexibly and creatively.

Imagination is more important than knowledge. Knowledge is limited. Imagination encircles the world (Albert Einstein).

Thoughts on teaching maths

What makes a student good at maths?
As teachers, we all hope our students will become good at maths. But to realise this we

---
* Rudolf Steiner, *The Spiritual Ground of Education*, lecture of Aug 21 1922, (CW 305), Steinerbooks 2004.

need to fully understand what maths is, and what it isn't. So now we ask: what are the key attributes that enable a student to become good at maths? Here is my short list:

- *Striving to understand deeply.* We want our students to understand the concepts they encounter. Good maths students are never satisfied with going through a procedure without understanding what they are doing.
- *Asking good questions.* Good maths students are curious, and wonder 'what if …?' They question why something is true, and they become skillful at articulating questions.
- *Making mistakes.* Contrary to what many people think, mistakes are an important part of learning maths. Good maths students don't let mistakes discourage them. In fact, mistakes can motivate students to find the truth and make mathematical discoveries. We want our students to become comfortable with making mistakes and to learn from their mistakes.
- *Attitude and work ethic.* This includes many things, such as enthusiasm, determination and discipline. Good maths students persevere through their challenges; they are determined to succeed.

All of the above shows how our students learn many life lessons through studying mathematics. (And, yes, the same may be said about the proper teaching of other subjects as well.)

What makes a good maths teacher?
Many class teachers feel under-confident in their own maths skills and, in some cases,

have had traumatic experiences with maths when they were in school. Often, this results in the teacher developing an antipathy towards maths. However, if such teachers can find a way to rise above their antipathy toward maths, then they may find joy in maths, which can result in bringing maths lessons to the students with wonderful enthusiasm.

This is what I feel makes a good maths teacher:
- *Enthusiasm for learning maths.* For many teachers, this amounts to finding a new relationship to maths. How wonderful it can be to find out that maths can be interesting and rewarding!
- *Ability to present the material effectively.* This is the art of teaching.
- *Adequate preparation time* for the maths lessons. With everything that is demanded of the class teacher, there often isn't enough time left to prepare adequately for the maths lessons.
- *A healthy relationship to the students.* This helps create a safe and comfortable learning environment for the students.

Teaching the 'big topics'
The 'big topics' in middle school maths are fractions, decimals, percents, ratios and (simple) algebra. Our students should have these topics mastered before entering the upper school. There are two common mistakes made with these big topics.

The first is to do too much too soon. The topic may have been introduced in a wonderful and effective way, but if we build too much on the new foundation then many of the students may drown. The second mistake is not enough follow-up and review. This often happens with percents, for example. It is introduced and practised (perhaps too much!) in Class Six, and then the students might never see it again.

So how should percents be done? It should be introduced in a wonderful Class Six main lesson – not too much – and kept very simple. Then, one year later, the topic is reviewed and deepened – again being careful that it isn't too much. And then, once again, it is put to sleep. Now the stage has been set for going into depth in Class Eight. A similar three-step plan can be followed with any 'big topic'. If we want the students to learn something well and permanently, then we need to create a 'dance' between introducing, deepening, practising, sleeping and reviewing.

Separation of form and number
It is helpful to think of *form* (pure geometry) as having its roots in the physical/material world, and *number* as having its roots in the non-physical world of pure thought. In education today, form and number are often blended together. This can lead to unnecessary confusion.

There certainly are times when it is appropriate and helpful to integrate numbers into a geometrical topic. For example, geometric figures become associated with numbers and algebraic formulas in the study of measurement (e.g. area and volume). However, we also need to find ways for our students to experience 'pure geometry' without attaching formulas and numbers. Waldorf Schools do this in Class One with form drawing, and then continue working with 'pure geometry' with subjects (not typically taught in the mainstream) such as geometric drawing and loci (in middle school), and projective geometry in the upper school.

Likewise, using geometrical pictures can be helpful when teaching pure number topics. But we have to be careful, especially when introducing these topics (e.g. fractions, percents, etc.). Physical pictures or manipulatives can appear to make it easier in the beginning for a student to seemingly comprehend a topic, but this may not lead easily to a true understanding of the concept. Fractions aren't just pizza, but later we can point out that dividing a pizza is one way to see a fraction. Similarly, we can give students a pictorial view of the percentage of water in a glass, but only once the students have sufficiently grasped the idea that percents represent a fraction of a hundred.

The major themes for maths
- *Classes 1–4:* Developing a sense of number. This is also when the arithmetic facts should be mastered. These early classes are not about the mastery of written procedural skills (e.g. long division, adding fractions, etc.).
- *Classes 5–6:* Consolidating skills. We consolidate skills that were introduced in earlier classes and develop mastery with written procedural skills (e.g. long division, adding fractions, etc.).
- *Classes 7–9:* Developing abstract thinking. Students start to develop confidence in their thinking.
- *Classes 10–12:* Developing logical, analytical, synthetic thinking. 'Real maths' and independent thinking can all really take off at the end of the upper school as students begins to find thier own identity and destiny.

Two types of topics:
Skills and mathematical experiences
As teachers, we sometimes think that the students are supposed to 'learn' everything that we teach – that everything should be learned, tested, and retained. However, that's not true. It can be helpful to consider that maths topics can be divided into two categories: skills (i.e. material that needs to be mastered) and mathematical experiences.

Skills (a topic that needs to be mastered). Here the teacher needs to create a dance between introducing, deepening, practising, sleeping and reviewing. The bigger the topic, the greater the number of times it needs to be put to sleep, and then later reviewed. It is quite typical to introduce a skills topic one year, but not to have the students reach mastery until the next year, or the year after.

Mathematical experiences. With a 'pure' mathematical experience, there is often no expectation that the students remember the topic or learn it as a skill. Examples of such topics include puzzle problems, 'Wonder of number' topics, number bases (Class 8), and a variety of geometric topics. We teach these topics because they stretch our students' minds, teaching them to think mathematically, and they engender enthusiasm and wonder for maths.

The three myths of maths
- *Myth 1:* Only people born with maths ability can become good at maths.

In reality, hard work can help develop maths ability. A student in the upper school who is seen as being strong in maths might very well have once struggled with maths.
- *Myth 2:* Confusion is bad.

In reality, confusion is part of learning maths. Every time we learn a new topic in maths, we must go through a period of confusion as we gain clarity.
- *Myth 3:* Forgetting is bad.

In reality, forgetting is an important part of learning. In fact, for important topics, you need to forget it three times in order to learn it permanently!

Four steps towards maths trauma
1. *Confusion.* Everyone experiences confusion when learning maths.
2. *Struggling.* Most students struggle with maths at least occasionally.
3. *Frustration.* Many students get frustrated with maths.
4. *Shutting down/trauma.* Some students shut down and become 'maths traumatised'.

One of the jobs of the teacher is to guide the students through the challenges they encounter in school and in life. In today's world, our children are often shielded from discomfort; they come to expect that things should be easy. They have little patience. It is therefore not surprising that so many children have little tolerance for confusion and struggle. If we compound this with a variety of emotional issues, then we can see how important it is for us, as teachers, to coach these students through these challenges.

What makes maths meaningful?
For starters, no workbook or textbook (not even this one) can make maths meaningful. Only the teacher can make maths meaningful and inspire the students. Here are some ideas to help make maths meaningful:
- *Make it developmentally appropriate.* The question should not be: 'Are the children able to learn this material now?', but rather: 'Are the children developmentally ready for this material?'
- *Work with questions.* Does the topic at hand answer a real question that lives within the student? It is quite meaningful for the students when they are able to answer a question that they have been living with.
- *Allow for depth.* The tendency in the mainstream is to teach too many topics. This leads to superficiality. By covering a topic in depth, we allow thinking to develop more effectively.
- *Challenge the students.* Every student should be challenged appropriately. The teacher needs to ensure that the level of challenge is manageable and allows for the students to feel successful.

- *Transform struggle into success.* The greatest feeling of success doesn't come from doing something easy. It comes from working through struggle and accomplishing something that had seemed rather impossible.
- *Offer interesting material.* Engaging the students in the material is an important part of the art of teaching. Practical applications can make the material interesting to the students. But often a good puzzle, or a new type of problem, can catch the students' interest, as long as it is presented in the right way.
- *Provide the historical context.* It makes it quite meaningful for the students to realise that they are living and breathing the same thoughts that the greatest minds in history have also struggled with.

What to do when things aren't going well…

- *Relax.* Parents are often fearful. This gets through to the students and pressures the teacher, who in turn becomes fearful and anxious. Try not to have your teaching driven by anxiety and fear.
- *Parent communication.* Speak to parents, in parent evenings, and individually. Parents need to understand clearly what you are doing and why, especially if it is different than the norm. Parents need to be well informed. They need to know what their child has achieved and what their child needs to work on.
- *Ask yourself: 'Why am I doing this?'* The answer shouldn't be: 'Because that's how everyone does it'. We should have a real pedagogical answer that we can give to our parents, our colleagues and ourselves.
- *Give it a rest.* Re-evaluate what you're doing. Doing more isn't necessarily helpful. Maybe if a particular topic is put to rest for a month or two – or even until next year – then the class will really absorb it better at that later time.
- *Make sure that the timing is right.* When should we introduce a certain topic? The question shouldn't be 'How soon can I do it?' but rather, 'Is this the developmentally appropriate time to bring this topic?' Live into where the students are developmentally. If it seems that many of the students aren't ready for something, then it may be wise to listen to that instinct. When in doubt, wait!
- *Remember your role.* Remember that one of the most important roles of the maths teacher is as 'maths coach' – to help these students through their emotional maths issues.

Perfectionism and fear of failure

Some students have a tendency towards perfectionism. Often, it is one of the stronger students in the class. Perfectionists want life to be rhythmical and predictable. When faced with a task, they need to be confident that they can do it well.

The trouble is that maths often violates these rules. Confusion and learning to overcome your struggles is an important part of doing maths. To some degree, especially in middle school and above, maths is about facing the unknown and figuring out how to solve unfamiliar problems. To a perfectionist, this can be is threatening.

Things become further complicated as the student enters adolescence, becomes more self-aware, and maths becomes even more unpleasant and scary. Such a student may eventually just give up on maths. Why? Because it is less painful to give up than it is to put forth effort and, in the end, perhaps fail anyway. This is known as 'fear of failure'.

So what can we do as teachers? Once again, our role as a coach is critical. And this is bigger than just maths. We need to look for situations where they feel they can't succeed, but we know they can. Such a situation could be having a role in a class play, climbing a mountain, riding a bicycle (or a unicycle!), or solving a particularly daunting maths problem. They think they can't, and we know they can. At the right time, and in the right way, we need to gently push them into these situations. Our role is to coach them through their challenges and to help ensure their success. And once they succeed, celebrate! After that, we can build on this success. In this way, the student's confidence is slowly built up, and, over time, the student becomes more comfortable with the challenges that life presents and hopefully becomes more open to learning maths.

Support for learning

Meeting the needs of students with learning challenges can take a good deal of time and energy. In general, we can always expect to have a few students who are somewhat behind the rest of the class. It is especially important for the teacher to know where each one of these students is at, to understand why there is an issue, and to have a plan of how to move forward.

Individual coaching often makes a huge difference, but all of this shouldn't fall on the shoulders of the class teacher. The class teacher should ask the remedial teacher for help early on. Some students with remedial needs can be behind the rest of the class for years, but then they can 'wake up' to maths as late as Class 8 (especially if we are able to work with the situation effectively).

Confidence is an important factor. The student needs to know that his teacher believes in him. The student shouldn't feel that he is doing 'dumbed-down maths'. If the student (or the class as a whole) is behind or has certain holes in his knowledge, then we still should find ways to bring the current material to him.

All too often, students who are labeled as being 'behind' are then made to spend extra time working on basic skills (e.g., fractions). This strategy often backfires; it can be rather discouraging to keep working on things that you should have learned years ago. Instead, it may be best to offer puzzles (but not too difficult) and new class-level material – anything to get them excited about maths and to engender a feeling of confidence and enthusiasm.

What about old material that hasn't been adequately learned? First of all, we need to carefully consider what is really necessary. No student needs to master all previously covered material in order to move forward. Once the student is past Class Six, an emphasis on long multiplication and long division, as well as work on the arithmetic facts, is usually not productive. We need to carefully choose which previously covered skills to work on, and then strategise when – in small, manageable doses – to work them into the current class-level material.

Additionally, we need to be careful not to allow fear to set in with us, the student, or the parents – fear exacerbates the situation. We need to work productively with the parents of a student with remedial needs. Clear communication with parents is critical. This includes having a written record (as a school document) of the student's progress and a written record of any modifications in the student's program.

Depending upon a school's resources, it may not be feasible to keep a student with serious learning challenges in the school. Sometimes, in spite of our own emotional attachments to the student, we have to admit that we can't meet a student's needs.

Practical advice

How much algebra?
In a Waldorf school, the basic fundamentals of algebra are presented in a three-week main lesson block in Class Seven. After this, the subject is 'put to sleep' for up to a year, allowing the students to digest this important step before building on it. This is in direct contrast to the normal approach to algebra, which gives an initial introduction to algebra, and then immediately builds on this not-yet-firm foundation.

While I recognise that schools can feel pressured to give their Class Eight students a full year of algebra – and each school needs to decide about this for themselves – I feel strongly that the bulk of algebra belongs in Class Nine, when developmentally children are most ready for it. The goal is to have the students enter the upper school saying, 'I love algebra, and I'm good at it!' Too much algebra in Class Eight is likely to be overwhelming for many of the students, and dampen their enthusiasm for this important subject.

The algebra curriculum during the middle school years should not have priority over other material. At the very least, it is necessary to review the algebra covered in Class Seven during Class Eight. However, any algebra topic that is not covered in Class Eight, will be covered as part of a standard Class Nine algebra course. In contrast, most of the topics listed here under geometry and arithmetic should be covered by the end of Class Eight, as it is generally not part of upper school curricula.

Should classes be divided into faster and slower?
Many schools split the middle school maths regular ongoing classes according to ability level. The argument is that this improves the teacher-student ratio, thereby allowing struggling students to receive more individual attention. It is also argued that it allows the more advanced students to go faster.

While I can understand both sides of this debate – and each school must decide about it according to its own situation – I am personally opposed to splitting the maths classes in middle school.

First of all, the maths curriculum in the middle school, as outlined in this book, is generally not sequential. In other words, success in one topic does not depend on the success of a previous unit. This allows students to recover from a unit in which they did poorly.

Secondly, if the classes were divided starting in Class Six or Seven, the students would be 'put in a box' that would be difficult to get out of. Middle school is the time that the students 'wake up' in their thinking – and some students 'wake up' later than others. I have seen many students who struggled at the start of Class Seven, but then 'woke up', worked hard, and ended up entering the upper school very strong.

Having the whole class together is definitely more of a challenge for the teacher. It requires better classroom management skills, better organisation, and a conscious effort to meet the needs of a more diverse class (i.e., finding ways to challenge those students who need to be challenged, and supporting those students who are struggling). But I feel that it can be well worth it!

Group work
In my maths classes – Classes 6 to 12 – I have the students spend a significant amount of time working in groups. I assign the groups (of two or three students) carefully. Sometimes, a stronger student may help a classmate to understand a problem. However, this doesn't always work out because the weaker student may rely too much on his stronger classmate. More often, I group students together with similar ability and skill level. It may even be that the weakest two or three students are together, in which case I have to spend more time with that group than the others.

Mental arithmetic
In our modern technological world, it may seem that the ability to work with numbers in your head is no longer necessary. I disagree. Mental arithmetic is an important skill to be developed from Class One up through the middle school. If practised regularly in the classroom, mental arithmetic strengthens the students' sense of number, challenges their memory, increases their ability to focus, and develops general cognitive capacities. The use of calculators weakens the students' ability to do mental arithmetic. We therefore discourage the use of calculators before Class Eight.

By 'mental arithmetic', I am referring to doing calculations in your head without writing down the work. Mental arithmetic can be worked on in a variety of ways, including orally with the whole class, or individually on paper (e.g. arithmetic facts practice sheets). Another aspect of mental arithmetic, which many students love, is maths tricks. I have listed all of these maths tricks in Appendix D.

Repetition and review!
Waldorf education seems to be the antithesis of dull, repetitive rote learning. We tend to be strong at introducing things in an interesting and imaginative way, but often there is not enough repetition and drill when it is needed. The end result can be that our students don't retain what we've taught them – they can't remember how to do fractions; they don't have their multiplication facts down; and they are very slow at doing simple arithmetic. It shouldn't be this way. The teacher needs to systematically integrate repetition and review into the lessons in order to strengthen the students' skills. And here's the added bonus…if the teacher wants the students to remember something, then briefly reviewing the concept every day, maybe even for just one minute, will make it possible for the students to learn and remember it without having to practise as much.

What is the purpose of homework?
My views on homework have shifted dramatically over the past few years.

As parents and teachers, we are led to believe that homework has great value. Homework is supposedly necessary in order to develop strong maths skills. Parents want their children to become strong students; they believe that a good amount of regular homework will prevent their children from falling behind. We are told that students need good 'homework habits' in order to be prepared for upper school. In a variety of ways, teachers often feel pressured to give homework. After all, if we didn't give homework, our parents and colleagues would think that we don't take academics seriously.

All of this is problematic. Homework is problematic.

Maths homework tends to make students hate maths. It widens the 'ability gap' in the class. The stronger students can do their homework independently, but the weaker students – mentally exhausted after a full day of school – can't manage to complete a homework assignment successfully on their own at home.

Good work habits can be developed in school. If we make sure that there is adequate time set aside during the school day for maths, then all 'homework' can be done in school.

All of this does not mean that homework should never be given. But it does mean that whatever homework we give should serve a real purpose. Perhaps the guiding question should be: 'Will this homework assignment further their love and enthusiasm for learning?' When homework goes too far – and I believe that more than an hour of homework (in total, for all subjects) on a given night is too much in the middle school – then it inevitably dampens the students' natural enthusiasm for learning.

And, after all, don't we wish our students to have a healthy life outside of school?

Arithmetic facts

Knowing the arithmetic facts – the basic ability to add, subtract and multiply (like 8 – 3 or 6 × 8) – has nothing to do with how 'smart' a student is. In reality, a lack of confidence often causes students to do poorly in maths during their middle school and upper school years. This lack of confidence often starts from them not knowing their arithmetic facts, which makes them think that they must be bad at maths, and in the end it can turn into a self-fulfilling prophecy.

There is a fairly narrow window – the centre of which is Class Three – for learning the arithmetic facts. It is much more difficult to learn these facts by heart after Class Four. So how can we reach our goal of having all of our students learn their arithmetic facts by heart by the end of Class Three? The real key to achieving this goal is working systematically and creatively with the children starting in Class One. To help in this effort, we have prepared arithmetic facts sheets that can be used in Classes 3 to 6. These sheets can be downloaded for free from *www.JamieYorkPress.com.*

If a student hasn't learned the facts by Class Six, then it is probably best to identify and work on the few facts that haven't been properly learned. This should be done *daily* by using flashcards (just for those facts) for several months. This flashcard work should then be continued even after these facts have been learned, in order to ensure that they are retained. But remember – it is quite possible to become good at maths even if the facts aren't solid.

Word problems

At times, word problems are held up as being more important than they really are. Some say that word problems show how maths can be useful in the real world, and that word problems help to develop problem-solving abilities. Neither is necessarily true. In truth, many students (especially in the upper school) quickly learn to hate word problems; they shut down as soon as they see a word problem.

There are many different types of word problems, and many levels. It is helpful to keep in mind that the analytical thinking abilities needed for true problem solving only really blossom toward the end of the upper school.

My point here is not to say that word problems should be avoided until upper school. Word problems should be brought into the classroom, starting in Class One, through stories and images. But we should be very careful! We need to keep in mind the pedagogical purpose of word problems. Word problems – if well chosen – can show how mathematics can appear in our everyday lives. We need to carefully consider how to bring word problems to the class in a way that isn't traumatising. Keep it simple, and make it fun!

Calculators

I first allow my students to use calculators in the middle of Class Eight, when many of the calculations by hand can be overly tedious. In the upper school, calculators are used more and more each year.

Computers
I do a brief unit on computers in an effort to meet the needs of Class Eight students who have a hunger for knowledge of the modern world as they prepare to enter the upper school. I believe that actual work with computers should be delayed until the upper school. In order to begin to understand about how computers store information, I do a unit on *number bases* and *ASCII code*, which gives a basic picture of how computer memory works.

One aspect of what I am proposing here – teaching about computer programming – is quite different from what is done in a typical Waldorf school. I call this unit *algorithms*; it is the 'thinking' behind the computer.

I have the students experience the thought process of computer programming without getting on a computer. Essentially, the students get to see algorithms, written in English, which are similar to computer programs.

Will our students be prepared?

Preparation for upper school and university maths
Often we hear parents who worry about their children's maths say, 'Will our children be prepared?' We may then ask, 'Prepared for what?' Usually the anxiety is regarding preparation for the next step – whether this next step is to be middle school, upper school or university.

It is an interesting exercise to ask a group of parents who have this question – and perhaps the anxiety as well – what they think it would look like to have their children well prepared in maths for the 'next step'. Surprisingly, when brought in this way, parents won't usually speak of the necessity for their child to learn a long list of maths skills, nor will they say how important it is that their child be ahead of other students.

I believe that there are three critical ingredients that our students need in order to be prepared for their next step in their maths education – be it middle school, upper school or college.

1. *Enthusiasm for learning.* If our students are truly enthusiastic about learning maths, this naturally leads to interest in the material, and a motivation to do excellent work.
2. *Mathematical thinking.* This means different things at different class levels. If we can effectively develop true mathematical thinking in our students, they will be able to think analytically and problem solve as adults in the world.
3. *Basic maths skills.* Yes, skills are important! However, the list of essential skills needed for the next step isn't as daunting as we are often led to believe. The list is relatively short and is quite manageable.

What maths skills are really needed?
Maths educators often agree that there is too much of an emphasis on procedural skills in maths education today. They say that we need to find more time to develop problem-solving

skills and creative thinking capabilities. Yet many teachers complain that there is never enough time for these 'extras'. We can begin to feel that there is an overwhelming amount of material that the students must learn, and, if they don't learn it all, they won't be ready for the next step. As stated above, the actual list of necessary skills is relatively short. (The lists below are simply intended as benchmarks in two-year intervals. Any skill listed under a certain year may very well be mastered a year earlier.) *Skills needed by the end of:*

Class Four: Arithmetic facts learned 'by heart', and a *sense of number*.

Class Six: The four processes. Fractions. Decimals. Measurement. Estimating.

Class Eight: Percents. Ratios and proportions. Basic algebra (not too much!). Area and volume. Dimensional analysis (i.e., unit conversions).

Preparation for life

There is much more to education than preparing our students for maths in middle school, upper school, or college. Patrick Bassett, the head of the National Association of Independent Schools, asks the question, 'What are the skills and values that will be necessary for students to succeed and prosper in the twenty-first century?'

In order to answer this question, Bassett refers to several sources, including: a Harvard-based study; the government's commission on education; a think tank for higher education; the academic testing industry; public opinion surveys; Tony Wagner's *Seven Survival Skills;* and Howard Gardner's book, *Five Minds for the Future*. What Bassett finds is a surprisingly high degree of congruence between these very different sources.*

In the end, Bassett's list of six skills and values needed for the twenty-first century is:

1. *Character.* This includes a variety of qualities, such as empathy, integrity, resilience courage, etc.
2. *Creativity.* Later in life, this quality manifests itself as adaptability and developing an entrepreneurial spirit.
3. *Critical thinking.* This includes problem solving, the ability to analyse information (filtering, analysis and synthesis), questioning what you are 'told' in the media, and thinking for yourself.
4. *Communication.* The emphasis here is public speaking. In today's information world of media and computer screens, children (and adults) are losing their ability to speak articulately.
5. *Team work.* Working together productively and collaboratively has become more important than ever.
6. *Leadership.* Today, perhaps more than ever, the world is in need of inspirational leaders who have strong values, and the courage and will to 'stand up for the good'.

I believe that the above six skills and values speak for the strength (and need) of Waldorf education.

* Patrick Bassett, Demonstrations of Learning for 21st Century Schools, *Independent Perspective* (Journal), Fall 2009.

Tips for success in maths

(for students in Classes 7–12)

Below are some thoughts to keep in mind as you strive to become the best maths student you can be.

- *Three goals:* maths skills, mathematical thinking, and enthusiasm. The time you spend working on maths problems will develop your maths skills. Focusing in class, following the teacher's thought process and working through challenging problems will all help to develop your mathematical thinking capacities. Perhaps it is most important to find ways to keep yourself enthusiastic about learning. After all, if you are excited about learning, then everything is more enjoyable and you will make better progress.
- *Things to avoid.* Avoid or minimise the memorisation of formulas and blindly following procedures.
- *Understand deeply.* Good maths students are never satisfied with going through a procedure without understanding what they are doing. Always question why something is true, and never be satisfied until you understand it deeply.
- *Make lots of mistakes.* Contrary to what many people think, mistakes are an important part of learning maths. There is great value in becoming comfortable with being wrong and making mistakes. Learning from your mistakes is a critical part of becoming a good maths student.
- *Organise your work.* You need to be able to follow your own work, but it doesn't have to be perfectly neat. Do hand calculations (fractions, multiplication, etc.) off to the side, or on a separate scratch sheet, but be sure to label it in case you need to find a mistake later.
- *Short term vs. long term.* Don't fall into the trap of quickly getting through assignments just to get them done, or learning things superficially for an upcoming test. Take the time to learn things deeply. This will save you time in the long run, and lead to greater success.
- *Be present.* Be fully present in class at all times. Every minute you spend in maths class is an opportunity to learn. Before the start of each maths class, tell yourself that your goal is to get as much out of class as possible.
- *Ask questions.* Asking good questions is an important skill to develop in order to become a successful student. Find the courage to ask questions in class even if you are afraid of what others might think.
- *Keep up.* Ask yourself every day if you understand the material. Try to clear up any confusion now, even if there is no test on the horizon. By keeping up on a day-to-day basis, you will not need to panic just before the test.
- *Follow up.* When you get a problem on an assignment wrong be sure to follow up – find out why you got it wrong, and figure out how to do it correctly. When you

encounter something that you don't know how to do, make a note of it, and get your questions answered.
- *Be determined.* You learn maths best when you get confused and then work through that confusion. Struggle and frustration are part of doing maths. Never get discouraged; get determined!
- *Responsibility.* Take responsibility for your own learning. Find the inner motivation to do your work for yourself – not for your teachers or your parents. By the time you graduate from upper school, you should be fully independent.
- *Maths and life.* You will notice that most of the above tips can be applied to other subjects and other areas in life. We learn much about life by learning maths. If maths (and life) were always easy, we would miss out on important opportunities for personal growth.

Maths Curriculum Topics

Class Six

Arithmetic (75%)

The World of Numbers: Mental arithmetic & maths tricks; casting out nines; exponents & roots; divisibility; prime factorisation.

Division: Division and fractions; long division; why long division works; short division; checking answers.

Fractions: Thorough review; the relationship between fractions, decimals & division; comparing fractions and decimals; compound fractions.

Decimals: Thorough review; converting between fractions and decimals; repeating decimals; converting repeating decimals to fractions.

Business maths and percents: Introduction to percents; determining the percent of a given number; determining a percentage; percent increase and decrease; profit, commission & tax; simple interest; discount; loss; rate of pay; unit cost; temperature conversion formulas; business formulas; line graphs; pie charts.

Other topics: Conversion between imperial and metric system; word problems (rates); statistics; introduction to ratios; significant digits; currency exchange rates.

Geometry (25%)

General concepts: Circle and polygon terminology; angle measure; the three dimensions.

The basic constructions: Copying a line segment; copying an angle; bisecting a line segment; bisecting an angle; construction of perpendicular lines; construction of a parallel line; division of a line into equal parts; construction of regular polygons (square, hexagon, etc.).

Spirals: Equiangular spirals; the Archimedean spiral.

Advanced constructions: Rotations of circles; the limaçon and the cardioid; the hierarchy of quadrilaterals; knot and interpenetrating polygons; the 24-division with all its diagonals; the King's Crown.

Area: Areas of rectangles, squares, and right triangles.

Maths main lesson blocks

1. Business maths (including percents, formulas, and graphs).
2. Geometry (geometric drawing).

Maths ongoing classes

These meet three times per week (one of which is for 'homework').

Class Seven

Arithmetic (50%)

The world of numbers: Mental arithmetic & maths tricks; divisibility; roots.

Measurement: Review of the metric system.

Percents: Finding the base; strange percents; compound interest; calculating the percentage of increase or decrease.

Ratios: The three thoughts; the two forms; reciprocals of ratios; proportion of the whole; similar figures; direct and inverse proportion.

Irrational numbers: The ratio in a square; the ratio in a circle (π); repeating decimals; rational & irrational numbers; the square root algorithm (optional).

Other topics: Puzzle problems with doubling; word problems (rates).

Algebra (20%)

Basic ideas: Basic goals; the importance of form; an introductory puzzle; history; terminology.

Negative numbers: A careful introduction; combining positive and negative numbers; rules for multiplication and division.

Expressions: Simplifying expressions.

Formulas: Gauss's summing formula; car rental formula; Galileo's law of falling bodies; Euclid's perfect number formula.

Equations: An equation as a puzzle; solving equations by 'guess and check'; the golden rule of equations; solving equations by balancing.

Algebraic word problems: An introduction to algebraic word problems.

Geometry (30%)

Area: Shear and stretch; areas of parallelograms, trapeziums, and non-right triangles.

Geometric drawing: Geometric division; star patterns; triangle constructions (optional).

The pentagon & the golden ratio: Construction and properties of the pentagon; the golden ratio; the golden rectangle & golden spiral; the golden triangle.

Angle theorems & proofs: Theorems arising from two parallel lines cut by a transversal; angles in a triangle add to 180°; angles in other polygons; angle puzzles; theorem of Morley; theorem of Thales.

The Pythagorean theorem: Visual proofs; Pythagorean triples; calculating missing sides of triangles.

Other topics: Perspective drawing, various other drawing exercises.

Maths main lesson blocks

1. Algebra (intro to the basics – not too much!).
2. Geometry (geometric drawing, areas, theorems up to the Pythagorean theorem).

Maths ongoing classes

These meet four times per week (one of which is for 'homework').

Class Eight

Arithmetic (45%)

Number bases: Ancient number systems; expanded decimal notation; scientific notation; octal; base-five; base-sixteen (hexadecimal); base-two (binary); arithmetic in various bases; converting between binary and hexadecimal.

The world of numbers: Square root algorithm; Pythagorean theorem.

Percents & growth: Four ways to find the base; increase/decrease problems; exponential growth; the exponential growth formula; the rule of 72.

Dimensional analysis: The two methods; Review converting between metric and imperial units; converting units for rates; converting areas and volumes; density.

Proportions: Shortcuts for solving (moving along diagonals, cross-multiplying); solving word problems with proportions; rate problems.

Algebra (10%)

Expressions: The laws of exponents; fractions & negatives.

Equations: Order of operations; evaluating expressions; distributive property; equations with fractions; 'strange solutions'; converting repeating decimals into fractions.

Computers (5%)

Computer memory & ASCII code: Bits and bytes; decoding binary codes.

Computer algorithms: Writing algorithms using English; the prime number algorithm; an algorithm for addition; an algorithm for long division, the square root algorithm.

Geometry (40%)

Mensuration: Baravalle's proof of the Pythagorean theorem; area of a trapezium; Heron's formula; the area of four types of triangles; area of a circle; portions of circles; volume & surface area of solids (box, prism, pyramid, cylinder, cone, sphere, octahedron, tetrahedron); Archimedes' ratio; tricks with dimensions.

Stereometry: Types of polyhedra; Platonic solids; the transformation of solids; orthogonal views; duality; Archimedean solids; the stretching process; the Archimedean duals; constructing paper model; close-packing; Euler's formula; imagination 3-D transformation exercises.

Loci: Curves generated from loci problems (a circle, two parallel lines, two concentric circles, a perpendicular bisector, two angle bisectors, parabola, ellipse, hyperbola); alternative definitions; conic sections; curves in movement, the curves of Cassini.

Maths main lesson blocks
1. Number bases and Loci.
2. Geometry (mensuration and stereometry).

Maths ongoing classes
These meet four times per week (one of which is for 'homework').

The year for strengthening skills
While there are new topics to be introduced in Class Six maths, much of the year is an important review, or a furthering of material introduced in earlier years. The challenge is to weave in the review in such a way that there is always something new. The practice sheets in our Class Six workbook include a fair amount of review problems. If your students enter Class Seven feeling that division, fractions, and decimals are all 'easy', and they are excited about learning maths, then you have succeeded.

A continual theme through the year is the sense of number and the interrelationship between division, fractions, decimals, and percents. Fractions play the central role. The key is that division, decimals, and percents can all be thought of as a fraction.

The order of topics
The order in which topics are introduced in my workbook is as follows:
- the four processes with fractions and decimals.
- long division (incl. repeating decimals), reducing fractions, casting out nines, short division.
- mixed numbers and improper fractions, exponents.
- converting decimals to/from fractions.
- estimating, square roots, divisibility, unit cost.
- metric measurement, formulas.
- converting repeating decimals to fractions.
- factors and prime numbers.
- angle measurement.
- prime factorisation, basic percents.
- mean/median/mode, pie charts.
- area and perimeter.
- percent increase and decrease, tax rate, discount, profit and loss, rate of pay.
- converting to/from percents, ratios, speed.
- line graphs, foreign exchange rates.
- compound fractions.

Class Six Arithmetic

The world of numbers
Mental arithmetic

See sections on *Mental arithmetic* and *Arithmetic facts* in the Introduction (pp. 22, 24).

Begin every class, throughout the whole year, with either a speed sheet or mental arithmetic.

Maths tricks

Cover *Class 6 maths tricks* (see Appendix).

Introduce one every other week and keep the tricks fresh by including them in mental arithmetic throughout the year.

In general, the idea in Class Six is not so much to explain why each maths trick works, but instead to use them to build the students' calculating skills and to increase their confidence. These tricks will also develop their sense of wonder for numbers.

New multiplication facts to be memorised

* indicates optional

```
   13 ×  2 =  26
   13 ×  3 =  39
   13 ×  4 =  52
*  13 ×  5 =  65
   13 × 13 = 169

   14 ×  2 =  28
   14 ×  3 =  42
*  14 ×  4 =  56
*  14 ×  5 =  70
   14 × 14 = 196

   15 ×  2 =  30
   15 ×  3 =  45
   15 ×  4 =  60
   15 ×  5 =  75
   15 × 15 = 225

   16 ×  2 =  32
   16 ×  3 =  48
   16 ×  4 =  64
*  16 ×  5 =  80
   16 × 16 = 256

   18 ×  2 =  36
*  18 ×  3 =  54
*  18 ×  4 =  72
*  18 ×  5 =  90
   18 × 18 = 324

   25 ×  2 =  50
   25 ×  3 =  75
   25 ×  4 = 100
   25 ×  5 = 125
   25 ×  6 = 150
*  25 ×  8 = 200
   25 × 25 = 625
```

Casting out nines

A must do! Lots of fun!

Normally, we check a multiplication problem to see if it is right simply by redoing the problem. This is problematic for two reasons: it is time consuming, and we are likely to make the same mistake again.

Casting out nines allows us to quickly check our answer after doing a multiplication problem.

Example: The key is to realise that the arrows

represent summing the digits (e.g., with 7296: 7 + 2 + 9 + 6 = 24):

```
    7296    →      24    →     6
  ×  376    →      16    →   × 7
   43776                       42
   51072                       ↓
   21888                       6
 2743296    →      33    →     6
```

If the **bold** results aren't the same, then there is a mistake in the multiplication.

A short cut for summing the digits is to cast out all groups of digits that add to nine, or multiples of nine. Thus, with the answer 2,743,296: the first two digits (27), the next three (432), and then the 9, are all cast out, leaving just the 6 as the result. With practice, this is very quick!

Exponents and roots

Introduce exponents and roots using only numbers and simple examples. Do not use variables.

Examples:

$3^4 = 3 \times 3 \times 3 \times 3 = 81$

$10^3 = 1000$

$2^5 = 32$

$(0.02)^3 = 0.000\,008$

$(\frac{2}{5})^2 = \frac{4}{25}$

$(4\frac{1}{2})^2 = (\frac{9}{2})^2 = \frac{81}{4} = 20\frac{1}{4}$

$\sqrt{25} = 5$

$\sqrt{1{,}000{,}000} = 1000$

$\sqrt{12{,}100} = 110$

$\sqrt{160{,}000} = 400$

Have the students calculate the powers of two as high as they can go. You may want to have them check their answer with every exponent increase of 10 or 20 (see Appendix, *Powers of two table*, p. 231, for a listing of the powers of two up to 2^{100}).

The students should memorise the following powers:

$2^3 = 8; \; 2^4 = 16; \; 2^5 = 32; \; 2^6 = 64; \; 2^{10} = 1024$

$3^3 = 27; \; 3^4 = 81$

$4^3 = 64; \; 4^4 = 256; \; 4^5 = 1024$

$5^3 = 125; \; 5^4 = 625$

Optional ones:

$2^7 = 128; \; 2^8 = 256; \; 2^9 = 512$

$3^5 = 243; \; 3^6 = 729$

$6^3 = 216; \; 7^3 = 343; \; 8^3 = 512; \; 9^3 = 729$

Divisibility rules

A number is evenly divisible (that is, without a remainder):

by **2** only if it is even.

by **3** only if the sum of the digits is divisible by 3. The nice thing here is that we can cast out threes or groups of digits adding to multiples of three (3, 6, 9, 12, etc.). For example, with 65,387 we can immediately cast out the 6 and 3 because they are divisible by 3, and then we can cast out the 8 and 7 because they add to 15. This leaves us with just the 5, which is not divisible by 3, so we conclude that 65,387 is not evenly divisible by 3.

by **4** only if the last two digits are divisible by 4. For example, 6,380,716 is evenly divisible by 4, because it ends in 16, which is evenly divisible by 4.

by **5** only if the number ends in a 5 or a 0.

by **9** only if the sum of the digits is divisible by 9. Again we can cast out nines in order to check divisibility for 9 quickly. If we cast out nines and are left with nothing in the end, then the number is evenly divisible by nine. For example, for 71,284 we cast out the 7 and 2 and then cast out the 8 and 1 and we are left with just a 4, so the whole number is not evenly divisible by nine.

On the other hand, with 2,381,697 we cast out the 8 and 1, the 6 and 3, the 2 and 7, and the 9, leaving us with nothing. Therefore, we can conclude that 2,381,697 is evenly divisible by nine.

by **10** only if the number ends in a 0.

Practise using the divisibility rules to reduce large fractions.

Example: Reduce $\frac{132}{420}$

We recognise that both the denominator and numerator are evenly divisible by 4 and 3. So after dividing both the denominator and numerator by 4 and 3 we get an answer of $\frac{11}{35}$.

Example: Reduce $\frac{54}{126}$

Dividing both the denominator and numerator by 2 and 9 gives an answer of $\frac{3}{7}$.

Example: Reduce $\frac{14175}{14850}$

Dividing both the denominator and numerator by 9 gives us $\frac{1575}{1650}$, then dividing by 5 gives $\frac{315}{330}$, then dividing by 5 again gives $\frac{63}{66}$, and then finally dividing by 3 gives our answer of $\frac{21}{22}$.

Prime factorisation

Don't use factor trees. While factor trees work, students often don't understand them and are puzzled about what the final prime factorisation is by looking at the tree.

The best method is to keep breaking down any non-prime number into the product of two more numbers until there are only prime numbers left. The students need to realise that each step in the process is equal.

Example: Find the prime factorisation of 700.

There are several routes to the answer. Below, we show two different ways to arrive at the same answer. Remember that each step represents a different way to express 700 as a product of numbers.

$700 \to 7 \times 100 \to 7 \times 2 \times 50 \to 7 \times 2 \times 5 \times 10$
$\to 7 \times 2 \times 5 \times 5 \times 2 \to 2 \times 2 \times 5 \times 5 \times 7$
$\to 2^2 \times 5^2 \times 7$

$700 \to 25 \times 28 \to 5 \times 5 \times 28 \to 5 \times 5 \times 14 \times 2$
$\to 5 \times 5 \times 7 \times 2 \times 2 \to 2 \times 2 \times 5 \times 5 \times 7$
$\to 2^2 \times 5^2 \times 7$

Example: Find the prime factorisation of 208.
(Answer: $2^4 \times 13$)

Example: Find the prime factorisation of 12,375.
(Answer: $3^2 \times 5^3 \times 11$)

Class Six Arithmetic

Least common multiples (LCM) and *greatest common factors* (GCF) *(optional)*. Simple cases can easily be done in your head, such as:

Find the LCM and GCF of 12 and 8.

The LCM is 24 and the GCF is 4.

For larger numbers, it is useful to use prime factorisation in order to determine LCMs and GCFs. Build up to problems like:

Find the LCM and GCF of 29,040 and 207,900.

The prime factorisation for 29,040 is
$2^4 \times 3 \times 5 \times 11^2$,
and for 207,900 is
$2^2 \times 3^3 \times 5^2 \times 7 \times 11$.

The GCF is what is in common for both, therefore: $2^2 \times 3 \times 5 \times 11$, which is 660.

The LCM includes everything from both (without duplicating), therefore:
$2^4 \times 3^3 \times 5^2 \times 7 \times 11^2$, which is 9,147,600.

Common denominators for 'ugly' fractions.

Example: $\frac{5}{3024} + \frac{11}{576}$

The prime factorisation of 3,024 is $2^4 \times 3^3 \times 7$ and the prime factorisation of 576 is $2^6 \times 3^2$, therefore the common denominator (LCM) is $2^6 \times 3^3 \times 7$ (which is 12,096).

The first fraction must have its denominator and numerator multiplied by 2^2 (or 4), and the second fraction by 3×7 (or 21). This gives an answer of

$$\frac{5 \times 4}{12096} + \frac{11 \times 21}{12096} = \frac{251}{12096}.$$

Division
Division and fractions

Think of division as a fraction.

Reduce before dividing (See Appendix, *Class 6 maths tricks*, p. 236).

Example: $804 \div 44$

$804 \div 44$ becomes $\frac{804}{44}$ and is then reduced to $\frac{201}{11}$. The division problem has been made easier. We now can divide 201 by 11, to get an answer of $18\frac{3}{11}$.

Example: $108 \div 48$

This is reduced (by dividing top and bottom by 12) to $9 \div 4$, which is $2\frac{1}{4}$.

Making the divisor easier.

Think fractions! There are two ways to make the divisor easier:

- Move the divisor's decimal point all the way to the right.
  Example: $30.17 \div 0.035$ becomes $30,170 \div 35$ since we multiply numerator and denominator by 1,000, or move the decimal point three places.
- Chop off ending zeros by moving the decimal point, which is initially invisible, to the left.
  Example: $173.6 \div 800$ becomes $1.736 \div 8$ since we divide numerator and denominator by 100, which is the same as moving the decimal point two places to the left.

Long division

Vocabulary

The *dividend* is the number that is being divided by the *divisor*. The *quotient* is the answer.

```
                   324  ← Quotient
    Divisor →  5 ⟌ 1620  ← Dividend
```

Normal long division

Practise lots of normal long division problems with divisors up to 4 digits.

Don't leave a remainder. Students should leave their answers either as mixed numbers or as decimals.

Example: The answer for 58 ÷ 5 can be given either as 11⅗ or as 11.6.

How do we know if a digit in the answer is too small? If, at any point during the process, a remainder (before bringing down the next digit) is equal to or larger than the divisor, then you know that the previous digit in your answer was too small. Have students find this error:

```
          161
    47 ⟌ 7990
         -47
          329
         -282
           47
          -47
            0
```

Why long division works

Few people really understand why long division works. Giving the students an understanding of why it works, helps take the mystery out of it, and helps to develop their thinking.

The key to understanding long division is to realise that what we are really doing is figuring out how many times the divisor can be taken out of the dividend.

With long division, we are removing a multiple of the divisor from the dividend, looking at what is left, then removing more multiples of the divisor from that, and continuing until no more divisors can be taken out of what is left. Our answer is the sum of all the multiples that have been removed.

Consider this example: 112,182 ÷ 42 (answer is 2,671)

Normally our work looks like this:

```
            2671
    42 ⟌ 112182
         -84
          281
         -252
           298
          -294
             42
            -42
              0
```

Fully-written, it looks like this:

```
            2000 + 600 + 70 + 1  =  2671
    42 ⟌ 112182
         -84000
          28182
         -25200
           2982
          -2940
             42
            -42
              0
```

Looking at our 'fully-written' version, we can understand what long division really does. Remembering that what we are trying to figure out is how many 42s can be taken out of 112,182, we start by taking out 2,000 42s (= 84,000), which leaves us with 28,182. We then remove 600 42s (= 25,200) from that, which gives us 2,982 left over. From that we remove 70 42s (= 2,940), resulting in just one 42 left over. Our final answer is the total number of 42s that have been removed, which, in this case is 2000 + 600 + 70 + 1, or 2671.

It is important for the students to understand that long division is just a shorter way of writing our 'fully-written' method.

It is also important to understand that while long division is restricted to working out the answer one digit at a time, and that each of those digits must be correct, that our 'fully-written' method is not restricted in this way. For example, instead of removing 2,000 42s, followed by 600 42s, followed by 70 42s and then finally one 42, we can (somewhat randomly) first remove 1500 42s, and, from what's left over, we could next remove 800 42s, and then 120 42s, and then 240 42s, and lastly 11 42s, and the result would be the same!

```
            1500+800+120+240+11   =  2671
       42 ⌐112182
          − 63000
            49182
          − 33600
            15582
          −  5040
            10542
          − 10080
              462
          −   462
                0
```

Making difficult division problems easier by rounding

This should be done in Class Five.

Students should be able to quickly estimate how many times the divisor goes into a remainder (at any point during the process) with reasonable accuracy. It is very important for students to practise this. It increases their speed for doing long division and develops a flexible sense of numbers.

A key example: 293,346 ÷ 387

It is important for the students to understand the following reasoning.

They should immediately round the divisor to 400, and then they can ignore the ending zeros. Therefore, the first question that they should be asking themselves with this problem is: How many times does 4 go into 29? instead of: How many times does 387 go into 2,933? Since 4 goes into 29 seven times, we can make a fairly good guess that 387 goes into 2,933 also seven times. We continue the long division problem in the normal way: writing the 7 above the house (as the first digit in our answer), then multiplying 7 times 387 to get 2,709, and subtracting that from 2933, to get 224. Since 224 is less than 387 (our divisor), we know that 7 wasn't too small. Now we bring down the 4 and combine that with our remainder to get 2,244. The problem now looks like this:

```
               7
       387 ⌐293346
          − 2709
            2244
```

Normally, people would now ask themselves: How many times does 387 go into 2,244? but it is much easier to ask: How many times does 4 go in 22? The answer to this question is 5, which tells us that 387 probably goes into 2,44 five times also. So we write the 5 down next to the 7 (as the next digit in our answer), multiply the 5 by 387 to get 1,935, then subtract that from 2,244 to get a remainder of 309, and bring down the 6. After all this, our problem now looks like this:

```
         75
387 ) 293346
     -2709
       2244
      -1935
        3096
```

Once again we ask the easier question, not how many times does 387 go into 3,096, but rather, how many times does 4 go into 31? (Notice that we said 31 because 3,096 rounds up to 3,100.) Now, we ought to think that 4 goes into 31 seven times, but it is almost eight times. In fact, because we had initially rounded 387 to 400, then we should have a sense that our estimate of how many times 387 goes into 3,096, could possibly be 8 instead of 7. But we can't be sure.

If we first tried 7, and multiplied 7 times 387 to get 2,709, and subtracted that from 3096 then we would get a remainder of 387, which tells us that we could have one more 387 out of 3,096 – in other words, 8 instead of 7. It turns out that 8 was our correct answer for the third digit is 8. The final result is shown with an answer of 758.

```
         758
387 ) 293346
     -2709
       2244
      -1935
        3096
       -3096
           0
```

Short division *for single digit divisors*

This should be introduced in Class Three or Four.

Example: 58,741 ÷ 7 (leave answer as a mixed number).

Step 1: 7 goes into 58 eight times with a remainder of 2.

$$
\begin{array}{r}
8 \\
7\,)\,5\;8\,^27\;4\;1
\end{array}
$$

Step 2: 7 goes into 27 three times with a remainder of 6.

$$
\begin{array}{r}
8\;3 \\
7\,)\,5\;8\,^27\,^64\;1
\end{array}
$$

Step 3: 7 goes into 64 nine times with a remainder of 1.

$$
\begin{array}{r}
8\;3\;9 \\
7\,)\,5\;8\,^27\,^64\,^11
\end{array}
$$

Step 4: 7 goes into 11 once with a remainder of 4. We then put this remainder over the divisor, thereby forming the fractional part of the mixed number.

$$
\begin{array}{r}
8\;3\;9\;1\;{}^4\!/_7 \quad \text{answer} \\
7\,)\,5\;8\,^27\,^64\,^11
\end{array}
$$

Class Six Arithmetic

Checking answers by multiplying.
Check answers also when the answer is a mixed number.

Example: Checking the answer to the above problem: 8,391 × 7 + 4 → 58,741 correct!

Fractions

Give a few fraction problems on every assignment throughout the Class Six year. They need to get to the point that doing anything with fractions is easy.

Review from Classes Four and Five

Fractions aren't just pizza!
It's OK to show a couple 'pizza problem' examples, but it needs to be pointed out that this is just one application in the real world for the concept of fractions. Be sure not to over-emphasise the pizza image, or to say 'in order to understand fractions, we just need to picture a pizza.'

Fractions are part of the whole.
The denominator tells us how many parts the whole has been divided into, and the numerator tells us how many of those parts are present.

Example: With $5/8$ we have divided the whole into 8 equal parts and we have 5 of those parts.

This helps to answer the following questions. It is helpful to give a few different examples to illustrate each one. For example, using $3/4 = 6/8$, we can show how it can be applied to a group of 24 people, or to a sum of money (like £24), or to a block of cheese.

- Why is $3/4 = 6/8$? Eighths are half as large as fourths. So, it follows that $6/8$ represents twice as many parts that are half as large as $3/4$, and if we take twice as many things that are half as large, then we have not changed the amount.
- Why is $2\,3/4 = 11/4$? The two wholes (from $2\,3/4$) can also be divided into fourths, thereby producing 8 fourths. Combining these 8 fourths with the 3 fourths (from $2\,3/4$) gives us 11 fourths, or $11/4$.
- Why do we need a common denominator to add or subtract fractions? Using $2/5 + 3/7$ as an example, we should point out that in the same way that we can't (directly) add together £2 and €3, we also can't add together 2 fifths and 3 sevenths. And just as we could convert the pounds into euros and then add that result to 3 euros to get an answer, we can convert one fraction or (in this case) both fractions so that they will have the same size parts, and then we can add them. The common-sized part for $2/5 + 3/7$ is 35ths, so we change both fractions to these common-sized parts (denominators) and get $14/35 + 15/35$, giving us an answer of $29/35$.
- How can we think of doubling $3/8$? We can either double the number of parts (the numerator), which gives us $6/8$ for an answer, or we can make the size of the parts (the denominator) twice as big – so instead of eighths we have fourths, and our answer is $3/4$.
- How can we think of taking half of $4/5$? We can either take half the number of parts, which gives us $2/5$ for an answer, or we can

make the size of the parts twice as small – so instead of fifths we have tenths, and our answer is 4/10.

Reducing fractions (or simplifying)
Give reducing fractions as practice problems, such as:

Example: Reduce $\frac{810}{4455}$

We can see that the top and bottom are both divisible by 9 (see *Divisibility rules*, p. 34). After dividing both the top and bottom by 9, we get $\frac{90}{495}$. Then we divide by 5 to get $\frac{18}{99}$. Lastly we divide by 9 to get a final answer of $\frac{2}{11}$.

Reducing fractions gets naturally mixed in with most fraction problems as it is expected that all answers with fractions should be in reduced form.

Fractions are division
The bar in a fraction is a division sign; therefore a fraction is an 'undone' division problem.
Example: 37/3 is really the division problem 37 ÷ 3, which is 12⅓.

A fraction over a fraction is actually the same as a fraction divided by a fraction. The short cut is to take the denominator, flip it, and multiply by the numerator. Students need to see this frequently for it to sink in completely.

Example: $\frac{5/8}{3/4}$ is the same as 5/8 ÷ 3/4.

This then becomes 5/8 × 4/3, giving a final answer of 5/6.

'Of' means multiply
Example: What is 3/7 of 28?
This is really 3/7 times 28.
Therefore we do 3/7 × 28/1 = 12.

Mixed numbers

Practise converting improper fractions into mixed numbers and back.
Example: What is 34/5 as a mixed number? (Answer: 6⅘).
Example: What is 7⅔ as an improper fraction? (Answer: 23/3).

Multiplying and dividing mixed numbers
You need to first convert them to improper fractions.
Example: $2\frac{4}{5} \times 3\frac{1}{3}$

A common mistake is to multiply separately the 2 and 3 and then the 4/5 and the 1/3, giving a wrong answer of $6\frac{4}{15}$. Instead, we get the correct answer by first converting to improper fractions:

$2\frac{4}{5} \times 3\frac{1}{3} \rightarrow \frac{14}{5} \times \frac{10}{3} \rightarrow$

cross cancelling $\rightarrow \frac{14}{1} \times \frac{2}{3} \rightarrow \frac{28}{3} \rightarrow$

our answer is 9⅓.

Class Six Arithmetic

Adding and subtracting mixed numbers

It's not necessary to convert them to improper fractions.

Example: With $5\frac{2}{3} + 3\frac{1}{4}$, first add 5 and 3, then add $\frac{2}{3}$ and $\frac{1}{4}$, giving a result of $8\frac{11}{12}$.

Mixed numbers are best for final answers (for instance, for word problems).

Comparing fractions and decimals

Sometimes fractions are easier than decimals.

Example: Calculate $85 \div 7$ both as a (repeating) decimal and as a mixed number.

As a fraction, we get $12\frac{1}{7}$, and as a decimal, we get $12.\overline{142857}$.

Example: Calculate $450 \div 1.875$ (decimal) versus $450 \div 15/8$ (fraction).

The first is found by doing long division. The second is $\frac{450}{1} \times \frac{8}{15}$. Both give an answer of 240.

With decimals it's easy to compare the size of two numbers. With fractions, it may not be so obvious.

Example: Which is larger (and by how much): $\frac{13}{35}$ or $\frac{3}{8}$?

We see that the two fractions have a common denominator of 280 (which is 35 times 8).

$\frac{13}{35}$ then becomes $\frac{104}{280}$ and $\frac{3}{8}$ becomes $\frac{105}{280}$.

Therefore we can say that $\frac{3}{8}$ is larger by $\frac{1}{280}$.

Compound fractions

Build up to problems like these:

Example: Simplify $\dfrac{\frac{3\frac{1}{2} - 1\frac{2}{3}}{2\frac{2}{5}}}{2\frac{7}{10}}$

Converting to improper fractions makes the numerator $7/2 - 5/3$, which becomes $11/6$.

The denominator is $\frac{12}{5} \div \frac{27}{10}$, which simplifies to $\frac{8}{9}$. We now have $\frac{11}{16}$ over $\frac{8}{9}$, which is also $\frac{11}{6} \div \frac{8}{9} \to \frac{11}{6} \times \frac{9}{8} \to \frac{33}{16}$ so the answer is $2\frac{1}{16}$.

Example: Simplify $\dfrac{2\frac{1}{3} - \frac{\frac{1}{2} + \frac{1}{3}}{2} - \frac{1}{4} \times \frac{1}{3}}{\frac{1}{2 - 4/5} + 1}$

Starting with the middle of the numerator, we simplify $1/2 + 1/3$ to $5/6$.

$5/6$ over 2 can be seen as $5/6 \div 2/1$, which is $5/12$. Simplifying the other parts of the numerator leads to the whole numerator becoming $7/3 - 5/12 - 1/12$, which simplifies to $22/12$, or $11/6$. Now working on the denominator, we simplify $2 - 4/5$ to $6/5$. We now have 1 over $6/5$, which is the same as $1/1 \div 6/5$, which becomes $5/6$.

The whole denominator is this number plus 1, which makes it $11/6$, which happens to be the same as the whole numerator, therefore leading to a final answer of 1.

Example: Simplify $\dfrac{2}{2 - \dfrac{2}{2 - 1/2}}$

In the small denominator we have $2 - 1/2$, which is $3/2$. We now have 2 over $3/2$, which is $2/1 \div 3/2$, which becomes $4/3$.

The whole denominator is now 2 – 4/3, which becomes 2/3.

The entire fraction is then 2 over 2/3, which becomes 2/1 × 3/2, which gives a final answer of 3.

Example: Simplify $\dfrac{3}{3 - \dfrac{3}{3 - 1/3}}$

Following the same procedure as the problem above, we get an answer of 1 3/5.

Example: Simplify $\dfrac{3}{3 - \dfrac{3}{3 - \dfrac{3}{3 - 1/3}}}$

Plugging in the answer of the previous problem into this problem, we get 3 over 3 – 1 3/5.

3 – 1 3/5 simplifies to 1 2/5, which is 7/5. The whole fraction is now 3 over 7/5, which gives an answer of 15/7 or 2 1/7.

Decimals
Review from Class Five

General concepts
A decimal is a fraction with a special denominator (10, 100, 1000, etc.)

Example: Think of 0.37 as $\dfrac{37}{100}$ which is 37 parts, where each part is one-hundredth of the whole.

Reading decimals: 0.34 should be said as thirty-four-hundredths (*not* point three four). This reinforces the connection between decimals and fractions. In Class Seven and Eight, reading 'point three four' is OK.

Arithmetic with decimals
Do lots of practice using the four processes with decimals.

Multiply and divide by 10, 100, 1000, etc. (see Appendix, *Class 6 maths tricks*, p. 236). This must be done with ease.

Fraction to decimal conversions

Convert fractions into decimals by dividing.

At first, only do examples that don't result in repeating decimals. Later give examples that result in repeating decimals (see *Repeating decimals,* below). In each case, we divide the numerator by the denominator.

Examples: $\dfrac{3}{8} \to 0.375$; $\quad \dfrac{5}{16} \to 0.3125$;

$\dfrac{31}{40} \to 0.775$

Memorise the following key fraction/decimal conversions:

Note: A line over decimal places means that those digits repeat. (i.e., $5.3\overline{72}$ means 5.3727272…)

1/2 = 0.5	1/5 = 0.2
1/3 = $0.\overline{3}$	2/5 = 0.4
2/3 = $0.\overline{6}$	3/5 = 0.6
1/4 = 0.25	4/5 = 0.8
3/4 = 0.75	
1/6 = $0.1\overline{6}$	1/9 = $0.\overline{1}$
5/6 = $0.8\overline{3}$	2/9 = $0.\overline{2}$
1/8 = 0.125	4/9 = $0.\overline{4}$
3/8 = 0.375	5/9 = $0.\overline{5}$
5/8 = 0.625	7/9 = $0.\overline{7}$
7/8 = 0.875	8/9 = $0.\overline{8}$

The trick for elevenths, and twentieths

The students don't need to memorise the following fraction to decimal conversions for the 11ths and the 20ths, but should be able to do it easily in their head.

Elevenths: Multiply the numerator by 9, and make that product repeat itself.

Give the students a few examples (e.g. ³/₁₁; ⁷/₁₁; ⁸/₁₁) and see if they can discover the trick for themselves!

Example: Convert ⁴/₁₁ into a decimal.

Instead of dividing 11 into 4, we can just multiply 4 times 9, giving a result of $0.\overline{36}$.

Twentieths: Multiply the numerator by 5, and place that after the decimal place, without repeating.

The nifty short cut here is to 'think 5p', because 5p (or 5c) is worth ¹/₂₀ of a pound (or euro). For example, ⁷/₂₀ is thought of as 7 5p, which is 35p, or £0.35.

Example: Convert ¹¹/₂₀ into a decimal.

We multiply 11 times 5, giving a result of 0.55.

Decimal to fraction conversions

Simply make a fraction with 10, 100, 1000, etc. in the denominator and then reduce.

Example: What is 0.075 as a fraction?

This is $\frac{75}{1000}$ which reduces to $\frac{3}{40}$.

Repeating decimals

For additional ideas on repeating decimals see Appendix, *Questions regarding repeating decimals,* p. 205.

Emphasise that a division problem starts to repeat when a remainder is encountered for the second time.

Even though any division problem will eventually repeat or end, you should make sure that the division problem is worked out ahead of time, so that the number of digits that repeat is manageable.

How to determine the number of digits that will appear under the repeat bar

(For the teacher only.) It is useful to know this, so that when a division problem is given with an answer as a repeating decimal, you can know how difficult the problem is, based upon what the divisor is.

Recall that any division problem can be looked at as a fraction whereby we divide the numerator by the denominator. Assuming the fraction that we're given is already reduced, we can say the number of digits that will appear under the repeat bar depends only on what the denominator (divisor) is.

The following list shows how many digits repeat (fall under the repeat bar) given various denominators:

- The following denominators lead to decimals that end **without** repeating. (Notice that the prime factorisation of each one consists only of powers of 2 and 5. See

Prime factorisation, p. 34.):
2, 4, 5, 8, 10, 16, 20, 25, 32, 40, 50, 64, 80, 100

- The following denominators lead to decimals that repeat every **one** digit. (Notice that the prime factorisation of each one has one or two 3's, and any amount of 2's or 5's.):
3, 6, 9, 12, 15, 18, 24, 30, 36, 45, 48, 60 ...

- These denominators lead to decimals that repeat every **two** digits:
11, 22, 33, 44, 55, 66, 88, 99...

- These denominators lead to decimals that repeat every **three** digits:
37, 74, 111... and 27, 54 (not 81).

- These denominators lead to decimals that repeat every **four** digits:
101, 202, 303 ... and 1111, 2222 ...

- These denominators lead to decimals that repeat every **five** digits:
41, 82, 123 ... and 271, 542 ...

- These denominators lead to decimals that repeat every **six** digits:
7, 14, 21... and 13, 26, 39...
also 143; 259; 297; 351; 407; 481.

- These denominators lead to decimals that repeat every **seven** digits:
239, 478 ... and 4649, 9298 ...

- These denominators lead to decimals that repeat every **eight** digits:
73, 146 ... and 137, 274 ...

- These denominators lead to decimals that repeat every **nine** digits:
81, 162 ... and 333,667 (really!)

Example: $8 \div 37 \rightarrow 0.\overline{216}$
Example: $173 \div 808 \rightarrow 0.214\overline{1089}$
Example: $39 \div 64 \rightarrow 0.609375$ (doesn't repeat)

- Denominators that have just one digit repeated multiple times give an answer with the same number of digits under the repeat bar (except for sevens). For example, if we divide 273,956 by 88,888, then we know that the answer will have 5 digits under the repeat bar because with 88,888 there is only one digit (an eight), and it repeats itself five times.

With these examples, we do long division and divide the numerator by the denominator:
Example: $871 \div 111 \quad \rightarrow 0.\overline{7839}$
Example: $179 \div 444 \quad \rightarrow 0.40\overline{315}$

Division problems with repeating decimals

Do many of these! These can be done as straightforward division problems, or as problems that convert fractions into decimals.

Notice how each one has a number of digits repeating that is consistent with the rules stated directly above.

Example: $10 \div 13$ (or $\frac{10}{13}$) $\rightarrow 0.\overline{769230}$

Example: $21 \div 88$ (or $\frac{21}{88}$) $\rightarrow 0.238\overline{63}$

Example: $133 \div 54$ (or $\frac{133}{54}$) $\rightarrow 2.4\overline{629}$

Example: $53 \div 81$ (or $\frac{53}{81}$) $\rightarrow 0.\overline{654320987}$

Converting repeating decimals to fractions

This topic stretches and develops the Class Sixer's thinking in an age-appropriate way. It also helps the students to develop an appreciation of how numbers work.

This topic is revisited in Class Eight, when the students learn how to use algebra to convert repeating decimals into fractions, and in Class Ten, when they study repeating decimals as an infinite series.

Fractions with 9, 99, or 999, etc. in the denominator
See Appendix, *Class 6 maths tricks*, p. 236). Give the students a few of these problems converting the fractions into repeating decimals, and they should be able to quickly see the pattern.

Practise many conversion problems in both directions (both by converting fractions into repeating decimals and repeating decimals into fractions) such as:

Example: $\frac{7}{9}$ ↔ $0.\overline{7}$

Example: $\frac{37}{99}$ ↔ $0.\overline{37}$

Example: $\frac{13}{999}$ ↔ $0.\overline{013}$

Example: $\frac{2503}{9999}$ ↔ $0.\overline{2503}$

Fractions with 90, 900, 990, 9900, 9990, etc. in the denominator.
These are slight variations to the above problems.

To avoid unnecessary complications, make sure that the number of digits in the numerator is no more than the number of nines in the denominator.

The students should be able to discover for themselves that the number of nines in the denominator indicates the number of digits that will repeat in the answer, and the number of zeros in the denominator indicates how many zeros will be between the answer's decimal point and repeat bar.

Practise many conversion problems in both directions, such as:

Example: $\frac{7}{90}$ ↔ $0.0\overline{7}$

Example: $\frac{37}{990}$ ↔ $0.0\overline{37}$

Example: $\frac{37}{9900}$ ↔ $0.00\overline{37}$

Example: $\frac{19}{9990000}$ ↔ $0.0000\overline{019}$

General conversions of repeating decimals into fractions
This is fairly complicated and difficult for the students, but in the end, it is quite rewarding.

The idea is to determine the fractional equivalent of the repeating part and the non-repeating part separately, and then to add the results together for a final answer.

Example: Convert $0.31\overline{6}$ into a fraction.

Separating the two parts, we know that 0.31 is $\frac{31}{100}$ and that $0.00\overline{6}$ is $\frac{6}{900}$ as a fraction.

$0.31\overline{6}$ can therefore be written as $\frac{31}{100} + \frac{6}{900}$.

Getting common denominators and adding these two fractions gives us $\frac{285}{900}$ which reduces to a final answer of $\frac{19}{60}$.

Example: Convert $0.147\overline{72}$ into a fraction.

Separating the two parts, we know that 0.147 is $\frac{147}{1000}$ and that $0.000\overline{72}$ is $\frac{72}{99000}$ as a fraction (don't reduce it!). Getting common denominators and adding these two fractions gives us $\frac{14625}{99000}$ which reduces to a final answer of $\frac{13}{88}$.

Example (challenge): Convert $0.028\overline{4653}$ into a fraction.

Separating the two parts, we know that 0.028 is $\frac{28}{1000}$ and that $0.000\overline{4653}$ is $\frac{4653}{9999000}$ as a fraction. Adding these two fractions gives us $\frac{284625}{9999000}$ which reduces (by dividing top and bottom by 25, then 5, then 9, and then 11) to a final answer of $\frac{23}{808}$.

Business maths main lesson

(Including percents, formulas and graphs)

A few thoughts on this main lesson

If planned carefully, this three-week main lesson can include an introduction to percents, business maths, formulas (algebra) and graphs.

In order to teach this main lesson on business maths (economics), I recommend reading Ernst Schuberth's book, *Mathematics Lessons for the Sixth Grade*.

What is listed here is too much to cover in one main lesson, and therefore much of the material on percents will need to be continued in the ongoing class.

Keys to success for percents

Emphasise that *a percent is a special fraction* with 100 in the denominator. Also emphasise that the big advantage of percents is that we can easily convert from a decimal into a percent by moving the decimal point over two places (e.g. 0.71 = 71%). This is because we are converting the decimal into a fraction that has 100 in the denominator, so we are essentially multiplying the numerator and denominator by 100, which moves the decimal point two places.

Keep it simple! If you do too much with percents in Class Six, the students will not be able to take it all in. The goal here is to lay the foundation which can then be built upon in the next two years.

Practise lots of problems that can be done fairly easily in the head; avoid percent

Class Six Arithmetic

problems that require difficult calculations until Class Seven or Eight.

Save strange percents (e.g. 200%, 12.53%, 0.04%) for Class Seven.

Use formulas only well after the concepts have been introduced, allowing the students to first develop a good sense for percents.

Do not rely on pictures (e.g. imagining a cylinder that is 80% full) in order to help the students understand percents.

See also *Separation of form and number* in the Introduction (p. 16).

Whenever students get stuck they should remember that a per*cent* is simply the number of parts per one hundred (*cent*), and then retry doing the problem.

Represent some answers to problems graphically (with a bar graph or pie chart).

Percent to fraction conversions
To be calculated and then memorised

$1/100 = 1\%$ $1/2 = 50\%$
$1/50 = 2\%$ $1/3 = 33\frac{1}{3}\%$
$1/25 = 4\%$ $2/3 = 66\frac{2}{3}\%$
$1/20 = 5\%$ $1/4 = 25\%$
                       $3/4 = 75\%$

$1/10 = 10\%$
$3/10 = 30\%$ $1/5 = 20\%$
$7/10 = 70\%$ $2/5 = 40\%$
$9/10 = 90\%$ $3/5 = 60\%$
                       $4/5 = 80\%$

$1/6 = 16\frac{2}{3}\%$
$5/6 = 83\frac{1}{3}\%$
$1/8 = 12\frac{1}{2}\%$
$3/8 = 37\frac{1}{2}\%$
$5/8 = 62\frac{1}{2}\%$
$7/8 = 87\frac{1}{2}\%$

Determining a certain percent of a given number

I teach three different ways to do this. The students should use the easiest method, which varies depending on the problem.

Looking at it as a division problem (most important!)

This method of changing a percent problem into a division problem only works for these percents:

    50% (we divide by 2);
    33⅓% (we divide by 3);
    25% (we divide by 4);
    20% (we divide by 5);
    10% (we divide by 10);
    1% (we divide by 100).

Example: What is 25% of 320?

Recognising that 25% is ¼, we rephrase the question as 'What is ¼ of 320?', which is really 320 ÷ 4, which gives us an answer of 80.

Converting to a fraction and multiplying
Example: What is 80% of 350?

Since 80% is $\frac{4}{5}$, we get $\frac{4}{5} \times \frac{350}{1}$ which is 280.

Converting to a decimal and multiplying
Example: What is 31% of 62?

$0.31 \times 62 \to 19.22$

Don't over-emphasise this process; students could end up blindly using it for all percent problems.

Especially make sure that students don't use this method for ones that can be done more easily using one of the two above methods, such as 25% of 320.

Determining a percentage

Have the students practise lots of these. In order to determine a percentage, the students should think of a fraction.

It is important for the students to learn all three of the following methods, as it helps to develop speed and mental agility. They should use the easiest method, which varies depending on the problem.

The fraction is (or reduces to) something that they have memorised the percentage for
Example: 240 is what percent of 400?

$\frac{240}{400}$ reduces to $\frac{3}{5}$ which is 60% (⅗ = 60% should be memorised.)

The fraction can easily have its denominator changed to 100
Example: 7 is what percent of 25?

We multiply the top and bottom of $\frac{7}{25}$ by 4, which gives us $\frac{28}{100}$ which is 28%.

The fraction is first converted into a decimal by dividing the numerator by the denominator
This method is always possible but often slower. Students should only use it when the previous two methods aren't feasible.

Example: 270 is what percent of 2400?

$\frac{270}{2400}$ reduces to $\frac{9}{80}$ and dividing 80 into 9, we get 0.1125, which is 11.25%.

Example: On a 75-question test, Fred answered 62 questions correctly. On a 70-question test, John answered 59 questions correctly. Who got a higher percentage correct?

Fred got $\frac{62}{75}$ of the test correct, which is $82\frac{2}{3}\%$ or $82.\overline{6}\%$ correct, and John got $\frac{59}{70}$ correct, which is $84\frac{2}{7}\%$ or $\approx 84.3\%$ correct. Therefore, John got a higher percentage correct.

Percent increase and decrease problems

Increasing or decreasing a number by a certain percent
Start with very simple problems, and then build up to problems like these:

Example: What is 430 increased by 20%?

20% of 430 is 430 ÷ 5, which is 86. We then increase 430 by 86 to get an answer of 516.

Example: What is 60 decreased by 15%?

Since 15% of 60 is 9, we decrease 60 by 9 to get an answer of 51.

Calculating the percentage of increase or decrease

These types of problems (e.g. going from 16 to 20 is what percentage increase?) should be saved for Class Seven, after the students have had some time to 'digest' their introduction to percents in Class Six.

Profit, commission and tax

Profit, commission and tax are all percent increase problems (see above).

Example (Profit): If Bill makes chairs at cost of £36, including parts and labour, what must his selling price be if he wants to make a 30% profit?

30% of 36 is £10.80, which is his profit on each chair. So he should sell each chair for £36 + £10.80, which is £46.80.

Example (Commission): If an estate agent makes a commission of 2% when he sells a house, then how much money does he earn if he sells a house for £348,000?

2% of £348,000 gives him a commission of £6960.

Example (Tax): If a bicycle in a shop is marked at £260 excluding VAT (tax), then what must you pay if the tax rate is 17%?

17% of £260 is £44.20, which is the amount of tax. The total price is £260 + £44.20, which is £304.20.

Interest

Comparing simple interest and compound interest

Simple interest is not what is done with most bank accounts, therefore it should be taught from a historical perspective. For example, it could be pointed out that a long time ago money lenders gave out loans on the basis of simple interest, because it made the calculations easier. At some point later, it was decided that simple interest wasn't fair, and therefore compound interest came into being.

Example: To show the difference between simple and compound interest, imagine that John has a loan for £500 at 10% simple interest, and that Sue has a loan for £500 at 10% interest compounded annually. Each loan is for two years

With both Sue and John, they will owe £50 in interest after the first year. The difference comes in the second year. Because John's loan is simple interest, the interest for the second year is based only upon the amount of the initial loan – so he will owe £50 interest again for the second year. Sue's loan, on the other hand, is determined differently. Compounded interest means that the interest is calculated based upon the total current debt at that point, which is the initial loan plus any interest accrued up to that point. Therefore, the interest that Sue owes for the second year is calculated by taking 10% of £550 (which is

500 + 50), which means that she owes £55 in interest for the second year.

Therefore, at the end of the two years, John will owe £100 in interest, and Sue will owe £105 in interest.

Calculating simple interest
Students should first be able to do simple interest problems without the formula. Later they learn how to use the formula (see *Business formulas*, overleaf). This helps them to understand that the formula isn't just some mysterious thing; it expresses something that they already know, but in the language of algebra.

Example: Kate agrees to lend £800 to Jeff at 5% simple interest. How much interest will Jeff need to pay to Kate after 4 years?

The interest for a single year is 5% of £800, which is £40. After four years, Jeff will owe 4 × 40 = £160 in interest.

Calculating compound interest should be delayed until Class Seven.

Discount and loss

Discount and loss problems are really percent decrease problems (see *Percent increase and decrease problems*, p. 49).

Example: If a clothing store is offering a sale of 35% off all its marked prices, then what is the new discounted price of a jacket that was originally marked at £119?

35% of £119 is a discount of £41.65, giving a new price of £119 − £41.65, which is £77.35.

Rate of pay

Note: 'per' means 'for each', and in a word problem it is a division symbol.

Example: How long does it take Sue to earn £2,000 if she is paid £12.50/hr, and she works 25 hrs/week?

We divide 2,000 by 12.5 to find that it takes 160 hours to earn £2,000. To get the number of weeks, we see that 25 goes into 160 six times with 10 hours left over. Therefore our answer is that in order for Sue to earn £2,000 she must work 6 weeks and 10 hours.

Example: What is the hourly rate of pay for someone who has an annual salary of £44,940 per year, given a 35-hour workweek and four weeks of holiday annually?

Working 48 weeks per year and 35 hours per week means that they work a total of 1,680 hours per year. Dividing 1,680 into £44,940 gives an hourly wage of £26.75 per hour.

Example: If Morgan gets paid £4.50 per hour for babysitting, then how much does he earn babysitting for 3 hours and 20 minutes?

20 minutes is ⅓ of an hour, so we do: £4.50 × 3⅓, which is £4.50 × ¹⁰⁄₃ and gives an answer of £15.

The unitary method and unit cost

These are good problems for the students to practise frequently, and to get good at. The method is used for determining the cost of items sold at a certain cost per unit.

Example: If 7 pens cost £3.64, then how much do 12 pens cost?

The 'unitary method' requires us to first

calculate the unit cost. With this example we divide £3.64 by 7, giving us a unit cost of £0.52 per pen. 12 pens then cost 12 × £0.52, which is £6.24.

Example: If in America 2½ pounds of cheese costs $10.98, then what is its unit cost per pound, and per ounce?

The cost per pound is $10.98 ÷ 2.5, which is $4.39/lb. The cost per ounce is thus divided by 16, which is about 27.5c/oz.

Temperature conversion formulas

Done in ongoing classes this serves as an introduction to formulas before the business maths main lesson. The Fahrenheit scale is used in the United States of America, and was commonly used in Britain until recently. I don't explain why these formulas work – they are perhaps a bit 'magical', giving the students a sense of the power of formulas. This changes during the business maths main lesson, when the business formulas (see Business formulas, below) show that formulas express something we are already familiar with.

It helps to relate the two temperature scales by thinking of a thermometer that has both Fahrenheit and Celsius. At the freezing point of water we see that 32°F = 0°C. From there, every increase of 5°C is exactly equal to an increase of 9°F, as can be seen on the thermometer on the left. This also sheds light on where the above formulas come from.

C°	F°
35	95
30	86
25	77
20	68
15	59
10	50
5	41
0	32

$$C = \frac{5}{9}(F - 32) \qquad F = \frac{9}{5}C + 32$$

Avoid problems that deal with negative numbers (e.g. 10 degrees below zero) until Class Seven.

Example: 30°C is what in Fahrenheit?

Putting 30 into C in the second formula, we get F = 9⁄5 (30) + 32, which gives an answer of 86°F.

Business formulas

Formulas serve as an introduction to the concept of a variable, and give the students a brief glimpse into the thinking behind algebra.

Before introducing each business formula, the students should first be able to easily do each problem without using a formula. This helps them to understand that the formula isn't just some mysterious thing; it expresses something that they already know, but in the language of algebra. Otherwise, the students will just use the formulas blindly, without a real understanding of what they are doing.

Rate of pay

$P = R \times T$

where P is the amount of pay, R is rate of pay and T is time.

Simple interest

$I = P \times R \times T$

where I is the amount of interest owed, T is the number of years, P is the principle (or size of loan) and R is percent tax rate expressed as a decimal or fraction.

Example: Using the same example as in *Calculating simple interest*, above: Kate agrees to lend £800 to Jeff at 5% simple interest. How much interest will Jeff need to pay to Kate after 4 years?

$P = 800$; $R = 5\%$, which is 0.05 as a decimal; $T = 4$. Therefore $I = 800 \times 0.05 \times 4 = £160$.

Price after tax

$F = B + (B \times R)$

where F is final price, B is base price, and R is percent tax rate expressed as a decimal or fraction.

Example: How much do you have to pay for a shirt priced at £28 without tax, if there is 20% tax?

The base price (B) is 28, and the tax rate (R) is 0.2. Therefore, we do: $F = 28 + (28 \times 0.2)$, which means that the final price is £33.60.

Discount price

$F = B - B \times R$

where F is final price, B is base price, and R is discount rate expressed as a decimal or fraction.

Example: What is the price of a bike that was originally marked at £320, if it is on sale at a 30% discount?

The base price (B) is 320, and the discount rate (R) is 0.3. Therefore, we do: $F = 320 - (320 \times 0.3)$, which means that the final price is £224.

Perhaps cover some other business related formulas, as well.

Graphs

It is best not to spend too much time on graphs, since much of it is rather intuitive. Do only a few exercises, but make sure that they are done effectively. Examples of graphs from current newspapers and magazines can be helpful.

Pie charts

See the Class Six workbook for a few good examples.

Line graphs

See the Class Six workbook for a few good examples.

A good page for a main lesson book

Have the students make a pie chart that shows how their time is spent during the day.

To the nearest ¼ hour, each student should record how their time is spent during the day. The day should be divided into around eight activities (e.g. eating, sleeping, studying, in school, etc.).

Convert the times into percentages out of 24 hours.

Determine the number of degrees that each activity will take out of 360° in the pie chart.

Make the pie chart using a protractor. Label each section with the activity and its percentage.

Other topics

Metric system

In Britain when measurement is taught in Class 4, the imperial measures (foot, pound, etc.) are shown to be a standardisation of earlier human measures (like hand, foot, etc.). While the imperial system is not taught at all in state schools, it can be briefly reviewed every year, as some parts are still in use (like miles in Britain), and the United States uses the same measures as imperial (except that their capacity measures are different). Teaching both systems also gives the students agility in maths.

Definitions

Give imaginative definitions only. NO calculations! These definitions need time to digest before doing calculations in Class Seven.

A *metre* is the approximate height of a 4-year-old.

A *centimetre* is the approximate length of a fly There are 100 centimetres in a metre.

A *millimetre* is the approximate diameter of a poppy seed. There are 10 millimetres in a centimetre, and 1,000 millimetres in a metre.

A *kilometre* is 1,000 metres. Measure a kilometre from the school to some landmark to give the children a sense of the length of a kilometre.

A *litre* is the volume of water in a large water bottle.

A *millilitre* is the approximate volume of a large drop of water. It is the result of dividing a litre into 1,000 parts.

A *kilogram* is the weight of a large block of cheese. It is also the exact weight of a litre of water.

A *gram* is the weight of a large pill. It is also the weight of a 'nibble' of cheese – the result of taking a thousandth of a one-kilogram block of cheese.

A *milligram* is the weight of a tiny spec that you get if you take a large pill or a nibble of cheese that weighs 1 gram and divide it into 1,000 pieces. It is perhaps a 'nibble' of cheese for an ant!

Developing a sense for metric

As the metric system does not originate from centuries of usage, but is a logical, thought-out system, it helps to estimate the size of units.

Length. Estimate the length of things (e.g. the room, pencil, someone's height) and then use a ruler or tape measure to check how good your guesses were.

Volume. Estimate the volume of things (e.g. cup, bucket, etc.) and then check your answer by measuring (e.g. using a graduated cylinder or a measuring cup).

Weight. Estimate the weight of things (e.g. person, pencil, rock, etc.) and then check your answer with a scale.

Word problems

See comments on *Word problems* (p. 24) in the introduction.

General word problems

Give word problems that practise a variety of things from the topics listed above, while trying to have the students develop their intuitive sense of when it is necessary to multiply and when to divide.

Example: 120 minutes is how many seconds? (120 × 60 = 7,200 seconds)

Example: 210 minutes is how many hours? (210 ÷ 60 = 3½ hours)

Rate of speed

In Class Six, give only a brief introduction that uses simple problems. Much more is done with rate of speed problems in Class Seven.

Introduce this topic first by only doing problems that find the distance given a certain speed and an amount of time. After they have really grasped these types of problems, then you may introduce problems that find the speed or the time.

It may help some students to draw diagrams for some of these problems.

Example: How far does Hank bike in 5½ hours if he averages 18 km/h?

Solution 1: Given that he goes 18 km every hour, we can say that after 5 hours he goes 90 km, and in the next half hour he goes another 9 km, for a total of 99 km.

Solution 2: We realise that we need to multiply 18 by 5½, which gives us our answer of 99 km.

Example: What is the average speed of a plane that goes 3,600 km in four hours?

Speed is given in kilometres per hour (km/h), so we ask ourselves how many km the plane goes every (one) hour. Since it goes 3,600 miles in 4 hours, it makes sense to say that it goes ¼ as far in 1 hour. So we divide 3,600 by 4 to get an answer of 900 km/h.

Example: How long does it take a train to go 350 km if it is traveling 70 km/h?

Given that the train is going 70 km every hour, we can picture the train going 140 km in two hours, and then 210 km after three hours. It then hopefully becomes clear that we must divide 350 by 70, giving an answer of 5 hours.

Word problems in business maths
see *Business maths*, p. 47.

A key strategy

Change 'ugly' numbers into something easier.

Ugly numbers can turn an otherwise simple problem into confusion for many students, so much so that they might not have the slightest idea even of what operation (e.g. multiply, divide, etc.) to perform. The strategy is to change the ugly numbers into something much simpler and then to do the problem with the easier numbers. We can then ask ourselves, 'What calculation did we perform for the easier problem?' and then apply the same process to the original problem.

Example: How far does Hank bike in 5 hours and 15 minutes if he averages 19.6 km/h?

We change the problem to something with much easier numbers, such as: 'How far does Betty bike in 3 hours if she averages 20 km/h?' Many students can readily determine that the answer to this easier problem is 60 km. They should then ask themselves, 'What did I do with the easier problem – did I multiply or divide?' They can see that they multiplied with the easier problem, and therefore it follows that they must also multiply with the original problem. Therefore, the answer is 5 hours 15 minutes times 19.6 km/h, and since

Class Six Arithmetic

15 minutes is 0.25 hours, the calculation that we actually do is 5.25 × 19.6, which gives us an answer of 102.9 km.

Ratios

The basic idea

Ratios and fractions are very similar, but there are important differences. In general, we can say that a ratio compares the size of two quantities or numbers.

If we say that the ratio of water to flour in a recipe is 5 : 4, we read this as 'five to four', and it means that for every five units of water there are 4 units of flour.

In Class Six, only do a brief introduction to ratios with simple examples that use whole number form. Much more detail will come over the next two years.

Example: What is the ratio of boys to girls in a class with 15 boys and 12 girls?

The ratio of 15 : 12 is reduced to 5 : 4.

Example: What is the ratio of the heights of two buildings if one is 36 metres tall and the other is 24 metres tall?

The ratio of 36 : 24 is reduced to 3 : 2.

Statistics

This topic should be covered briefly.

Averaging

The *arithmetic mean* is what we normally think of when we think of 'average'. We calculate the arithmetic mean by adding up all the scores and then dividing by the number of scores.

The *median* is the score that is in the middle, which is also the 50th percentile. We simply put all the scores in order (i.e. from smallest to largest), and then the median is the score that falls exactly in the middle. Half the scores are higher than (or equal to) the median, and half the scores are lower than (or equal to) the median. If there is an even number of scores, then the median is halfway between the two middle scores.

The *mode* is the score that occurs most frequently It is possible to have more than one mode.

Example: Find the mean, median and mode of the ages of a group of ten people with these ages:

18, 12, 72, 25, 13, 12, 16, 13, 12, 14.

The mean is the sum of all the ages (207) divided by 10, which is 20.7. The median is the middle score, so we list the ages in order as 12, 12, 12, 13, 13, 14, 16, 18, 25, 72. Since there are an even number of scores, there are two scores (13 and 14) that fall at the middle of this order, making the median halfway between the two, which is 13.5. The mode is the most common score, which is 12.

Question: In 2000, the mean annual income for Americans was $31,000 and the median income was $22,000. Why is the mean income in the U.S. greater than the median income?

The mean income is greater because a small segment of the population is very wealthy and 'throws off the curve'. For example, if a small village has only ten people, and nine of them earn $10 per hour and the tenth makes $1,000 per hour, then the mean income would be $109 per hour and the median income would be $10 per hour.

For this reason, the median income is generally considered to be a better indicator of what the average person is earning.

Significant digits (*or significant figures*)
The number of significant digits for a number is equal to the number of digits in the number, without the ending and beginning zeros.

Example: 2,300,000 has two significant digits. 0.000408 has three significant digits.

Often when doing calculations in science and maths, we cut off the answer after a certain number of digits, especially when using decimals. One reason for this is that the initial given number is often only accurate to a couple of significant digits, and so it doesn't make sense to say that our final answer is accurate to more significant digits.

Example: If Sue ran 3.25 km in 12 minutes 32 seconds, then what was her average speed (in metres per second)?

12 minutes 32 seconds is 752 seconds, and this number, as well as the distance, both have three significant digits. Therefore our answer should be rounded to three significant digits. The average speed is 3,250 m ÷ 752 sec ≈ 4.321808511 m/s, which gets rounded to 4.32 m/s.

Currency exchange rates
I usually do these problems at the end of the year in my ongoing class, if time allows. These are good problems because they challenge the students and help to develop their thinking in a way that is appropriate for Class Six. They also get the students to work on division and multiplication, and give them a glimpse of how financial institutions make money through trading.

The latest exchange rates are easy to find online.

The example below is probably too complicated to present to Class Six students. I include it here in order to help the teacher understand how exchange rates are actually done. In particular, the idea that selling dollars for 1.39 dollars per pound is the same as selling dollars for 0.719 pounds per dollar, is rather confusing (see the explanation, below). I simplify things somewhat for the students, and only give one exchange rate. See my Class Six workbook for good examples of problems.

Example (for the teacher only): National Westminster Bank in London posts its exchange rate for the dollar as: *selling dollars* for 1.39 dollars per pound, and *buying dollars* for 1.54 dollars per pound. In New York on the same day, Citibank's exchange rate for the pound was listed as: *selling pounds* for 1.56 dollars per pound, and *buying pounds* for 1.37 dollars per pound.

First, we must realise what the rates mean. At first glance, it seems that the London bank is selling for less (1.39) than they are buying (1.54), and that it must be losing money. This becomes a bit less confusing once we realise that it is arbitrary whether their rates are listed

Class Six Arithmetic

57

in terms of dollars per pound or pounds per dollar. In other words, the London bank could have just as well listed their rates as: *selling dollars* for 0.719 pounds per dollar (which is 1 ÷ 1.39), and *buying dollars* for 0.649 pounds per dollar (1 ÷ 1.54).

For example, if the bank is buying $20 dollars from an American tourist in London, then it could do the calculation as 20 × 0.649, instead of what it actually does, which is 20 ÷ 1.54. The result is the same either way (ignoring any negligible difference due to rounding), and the tourist would walk away with £12.98.

Secondly, we should keep in mind that the words 'selling' and 'buying' specify whether the bank is buying or selling the foreign currency. Of course, with every currency exchange, the bank is buying one currency and selling the other. Therefore, the selling dollars rate for the London bank (1.39 $/£) is basically the same as the buying pounds rate for the New York bank, because in both cases the bank is selling dollars and buying pounds at the moment the money is exchanged between the bank's teller and the customer.

Problems: Assuming no extra costs (e.g. commission, tax, etc.), then:

(a) At National Westminster Bank, how many pounds will you get for $500?
(b) At Citibank, how many pounds will you get for $500?
(c) At National Westminster Bank, how many dollars will you get for £80?
(d) At Citibank, how many dollars do you need to give in order to receive £200?
(e) What is National Westminster Bank's profit if one person changes $1,000 into pounds and then another person purchases this $1,000?

For each problem, we must first answer two questions:

(1) Is the bank buying or selling the foreign currency?
(2) Should we multiply or divide by the given rate?

Answers (to each of the above problems):

(a) The bank is buying dollars. We divide 500 by 1.54 for an answer of £324.68.
(b) The bank is selling pounds. We divide 500 by 1.56 for an answer of £320.51.
(c) The bank is selling dollars. We multiply 80 by 1.39 for an answer of $111.20.
(d) The bank is selling pounds. We multiply 200 by 1.56 for an answer of $312.00.
(e) First the bank buys $1,000 for £649.35 (1000÷1.54), and then they sell the $1,000 for £717.42 (1000÷1.39). They have made a profit of £68.07.

Class Six Geometry

This is a great main lesson block to start the year with. It can nicely share a main lesson with maths review.

Julia Diggins' book, *String, Straightedge and Shadow*, gives a great, readable summary of the history and thinking of Greek geometry.

The basics

Basic geometry terminology
Don't have the students write down or memorise definitions. Familiarity is the idea here.

Give examples for each of these: *Point, line, line segment, plane, polygon, parallel, perpendicular*.

Supplementary angles are angles that together form a straight line equaling 180°.

Two lines that are *perpendicular* form 4 *right angles*.

Vertical angles are opposite angles formed when two lines intersect. Vertical angles are always equal.

Angle measure
With a circle, an angle that has its rotation from its centre going completely around is 360°.

A hexagon is specially related to the circle because a compass set to the radius of the circle goes around the circle *exactly* six times. This allows the hexagon to be divided into six equilateral triangles.

Develop a good feeling for angle measurement. Students should be able to look at an angle and give a good estimate of how many degrees it is.

Have a student stand, point directly forward and then jump up and spin to see how many degrees they can turn in the air.

Example: What does a 360° turn mean? A 720° turn? A 270° turn? A 540° turn?

Using a protractor
Do constructions given specific angle measures in order to practise using a protractor.

Example: Construct a triangle that has two angles equal to 98° and 34°, and then find the measure of the third angle. (48° is what they should get, but a degree or two off is acceptable. This is because the number of degrees in a triangle is 180°, which is learned in Class Seven.)

Polygon terminology
The *perimeter* is the distance around the outside of a figure.

An *equilateral* figure has sides that are all congruent (equal).

An *equiangular* figure has angles that are all congruent.

A *regular* figure is both equilateral and equiangular.

Two *congruent* figures are identical in shape and size.

Two *similar* figures have the exact same shape, but they are different in size – one is an enlargement of the other.

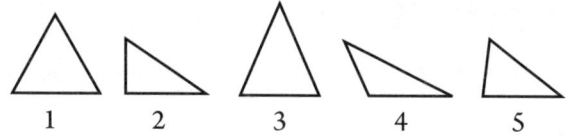

Types of triangles
1. An *equilateral triangle* has three congruent sides and three congruent (60°) angles. It is regular.
2. A *right triangle* has one 90° angle.
3. An *isosceles triangle* has two congruent sides and two congruent angles.
4. An *obtuse triangle* has one angle greater than 90°.
5. An *acute triangle* has all its angles less than 90°.

A *scalene triangle* has three sides all of different length (Shown in drawings 2, 4 and 5.)

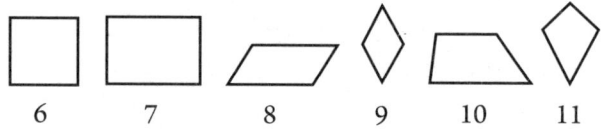

Types of quadrilaterals (four-sided polygons)
6. A *square* has four right angles and all its sides are congruent. It is regular.
7. A *rectangle* has four right angles, and its opposite sides are congruent. It is equiangular.
8. A *parallelogram* has opposite angles congruent, and opposite sides are both parallel and congruent.
9. A *rhombus* (i.e. diamond) is equilateral, and opposite angles are congruent.
10. A *trapezium* has one pair of parallel sides.
11. A *kite* has two pairs of adjacent sides that are congruent.

Introduce *polygons with more than four sides*: Pentagon (5), Hexagon (6), Heptagon (7), Octagon (8), Nonagon (9), Decagon (10), Dodecagon (12).

Circle terminology
Radius, diametre, circumference
An *arc* is a portion of the circumference of a circle.
A *chord* is a line segment that connects two points on a circle (line *b* in the drawing).
A *secant* is a line that passes through a circle (line *d* in drawing).
Two geometrical objects are *tangent* if they just touch one another at one point without actually crossing. (Line *c* is tangent to the circle in the drawing.)

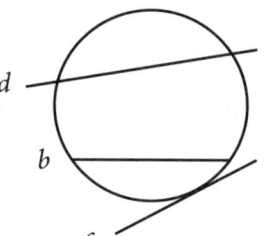

The three dimensions
This is just a brief introduction. Be careful not to make this too abstract

What is one-dimensional?
Lines and curves are one-dimensional.
If you are hiking on a trail, then you are moving one-dimensionally (even if you are going around curves and up mountains) because you can only go forward or backward along the trail.

One-dimensional objects have only length, and we measure their distance (metres, feet, etc.).

What is two-dimensional?
Surfaces and flat figures are two-dimensional (e.g. a meadow, a hexagon, the surface of the earth).

If you are sailing on the open seas, or walking in a field, you are moving two-dimensionally, because you can move forward/backward and left/right.

Two-dimensional objects have both length and width, and we measure their area (square metres, square feet, etc.).

What is three-dimensional?
Almost everything in the physical world is three-dimensional (e.g. a sphere, a box, a person, the earth).

If a bird is flying through the air, or a fish is swimming through the sea, it moves three-dimensionally, because it can move forward/backward, left/right and up/down.

Three-dimensional objects have length, width and height (or depth) and we measure their volume (cubic metres, cubic feet, litres, etc.).

Geometric drawing

Tips for doing geometric drawings
- Geometric drawings require great care and precision.
- High quality compasses and sharp pencils are essential.
- Any colouring or shading-in needs to be done thoughtfully, so that it emphasises, rather than distracts from, the key features of the form.
- Mostly, the students should learn to do each drawing by watching the teacher do the constructions on the board. Doing it in this way is a good exercise for the students in following instructions (and good practice for the teacher in giving clear instructions too!).

The basic constructions

It is very important for the students to develop competence in doing these basic constructions.

While there may be multiple ways to accomplish a construction, only one is offered for each case below.

The drawings below are only intended to help the teacher learn each construction while reading the instructions. These drawings are smaller, lacking in colour and generally significantly different from what the students should do. The students' work in their main lesson books should be beautifully done, without labelling points with letters, and should include colour and shading in. The teacher needs to be clear about their expectations.

Copying a line segment

Instructions (for the teacher only): The intention is to copy line segment *AB* onto line *CD*.

Make sure that *CD* is longer than *AB*. Set the compass's width equal to *AB*. Put the needle of the compass on *C*, and mark an arc that passes through line *CD* at point *E*. *CE* is now equal in length to *AB*.

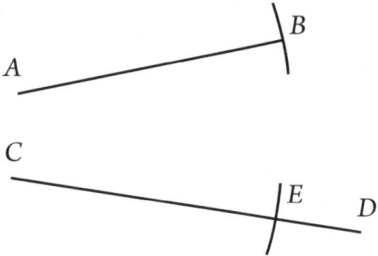

Copying an angle

Instructions (for the teacher only): The intention is to copy angle *ABC* onto line *DE*.

Set the compass at a width that is a bit less than the shortest of the line segments *AB*, *BC* and *DE*. Using this width of the compass, draw an arc with the needle at *B* that passes through both *AB* (at *X*) and *BC* (at *W*), and then draw an arc with the needle at *D* that passes through *DE* at *Y*. Place the needle at *W* and adjust the compass so that it reaches to *X*, and then draw a short arc through *X*. Keeping this width of the compass, draw an arc, with the needle at *Y*, that crosses through the previously drawn arc at point *Z*. Angle *ZDY* is now equal to angle *ABC*.

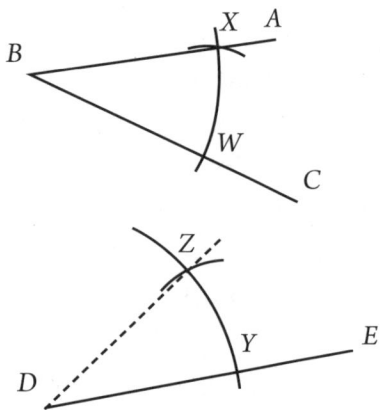

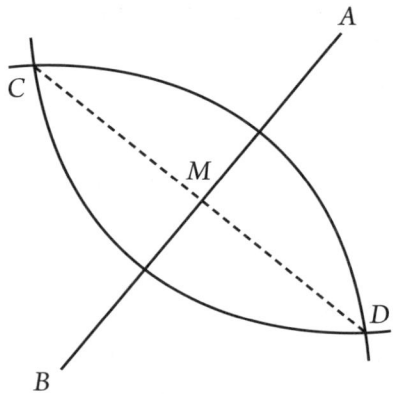

Bisecting a line segment

(and construction of the perpendicular bisector)

Instructions (for the teacher only): The intention is to bisect the line segment *AB*, and to draw a perpendicular bisector through it.

Set the compass width so that it is a bit more than half the length of *AB*. Using this compass width, draw two arcs, one with the needle at *A* and the other with the needle at *B*, so that they cross one another in two places – at points *C* and *D*. *CD* is the perpendicular bisector of *AB*, and *M* is the midpoint of *AB*. This same technique is used to bisect an arc.

A Teacher's Source Book for Mathematics in Classes 6 to 8

Bisecting an angle

Instructions (for the teacher only): The intention is to bisect angle *ABC*.

Set the compass width a bit less than the shorter of *AB* and *BC*. Draw an arc, with the needle at *B*, that passes through *AB* at *D*, and passes through *BC* at *E*. Now draw two arcs, both with the same compass width, with the needle at *D* and then at *E*, so that the two arcs cross inside angle *ABC* at point *F*. The line *BF* is the desired bisector of the angle *ABC*. Notice that this will still work if the two arcs are made to intersect 'outside' (in this case, to the left of) the angle.

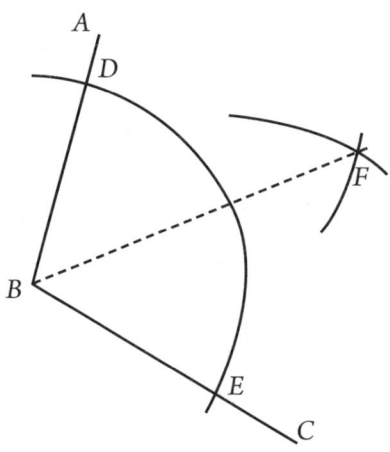

Constructing a perpendicular line through a point on that line

Instructions (for the teacher only): The intention is to construct a line perpendicular to *AB* that passes through *X*, which is a point on *AB*.

First, draw two arcs, each one using the same compass width and with the needle at *X* – one arc passing through *AX* at *C* and the other passing through *XB* at *D*. Now lengthen the compass somewhat and draw two long arcs – one with the needle at *C* and the other with the needle at *D*, such that they cross each other at points *E* and *F*. Line *EF* is the desired line; it passes through *X* and is perpendicular to *AB*.

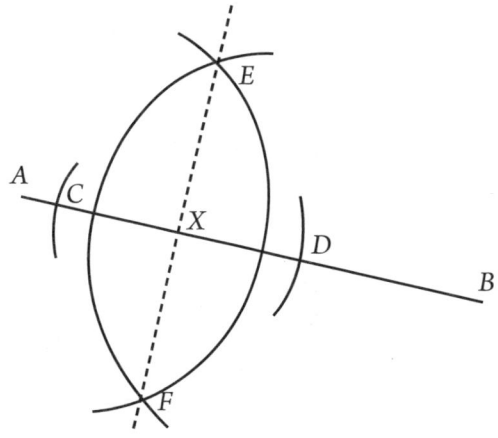

Constructing a perpendicular line through a point not on that line

Instructions (for the teacher only): The intention is to construct a line perpendicular to *AB* that passes through *X*, which is *not* on *AB*.

First, set the compass width a bit longer than the distance that *X* is from line *AB* and then draw an arc, with the needle at *X*, that passes through *AB* in two points, *C* and *D*. Now draw two long arcs, both using the same compass width, one with the needle at *C* and the other with the needle at *D*. They should cross each other at *X* and at another point *E*, which is on the other side of *AB* from *X*. Line *EX* is the desired line – it passes through *X* and is perpendicular to *AB*.

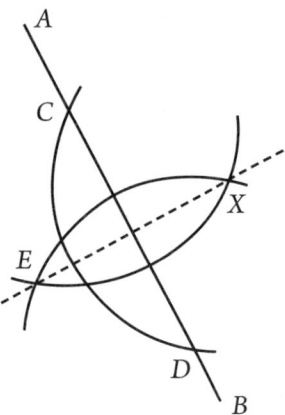

Constructing a parallel line
Instructions (for the teacher only): The intention is to construct a line that is parallel to *AB* and that passes through *X*, which is not on *AB*.

Draw line *AX* significantly beyond *X*. Set the compass width so that it is a bit shorter than *AX*, and draw an arc, with the needle at *A*, that passes through both *AB* at *D* and *AX* at *C*. Using that same compass width, draw an arc, with the needle at *X*, that passes through both the extended line *AX* (at *E*) and the line (not yet drawn) that passes through *X* and is parallel to *AB*. Now, adjusting the compass width, draw a short arc, with the needle at *C*, that passes through *D*, and then using the same compass width, draw an arc, with the needle at *E* that crosses, at point *F*, the arc that was drawn earlier that passed through

E. The line *XF* is the desired line – it passes through *X* and is parallel to *AB*.

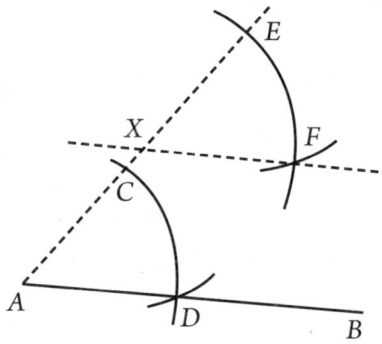

Dividing a line segment into equal parts
Instructions (for the teacher only): The intention is to divide *AB* into *n* equal parts. (In the drawing, *AB* is divided into 5 parts, so *n* is 5.)

Choose a point *C* such that *AC* is somewhat longer than *AB* and angle *BAC* is approximately 45° (but this angle could be anything). Using a compass width that is about one-*n*th as long as *AB*, draw short arcs that cross *AC* with equally long steps, first with the needle at *A*, crossing *AC* at *L*, then with the needle at *L* and crossing *AC* at *M*, then with the needle at *M* and crossing *AC* at *N*, etc., until *N* steps along *AC* are produced. We now have *n* equal steps along *AC* such that segments *AL*, *LM*, *MN*, and so on, are all equal. From the last point (*P*) where an arc crosses *AC*, draw a line to *B*. This is line *PB*. Now draw lines from each of the other points on *AC* so that they are each parallel to line *PB*, and cross line *AB*. We have now divided *AB* into *n* equal segments.

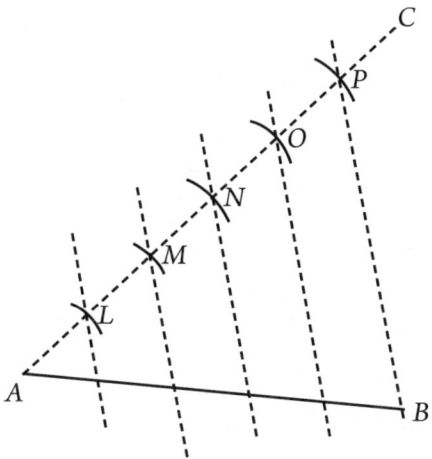

Constructing an equilateral triangle, given one side

Instructions (for the teacher only): The intention is to construct an equilateral triangle that has each side equal in length to *AB*.

Set the compass width equal to *AB*. Place the compass needle first on point *A* and draw an arc upward, then do the same with the compass needle on point *B*. The apex of the triangle (point *C*) is where these two arcs intersect. Finish the triangle by connecting points *A* and *C*, and connecting points *B* and *C*.

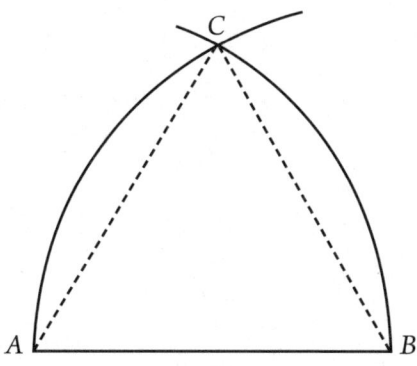

Constructing a square, given one side

Instructions (for the teacher only): The intention is to construct a square that has each side equal in length to *AB*.

Extend *AB* past *A* to *N*, and then mark point *M* on *AB* such that the length of *NA* is equal to the length of *AM*. Adjust the compass so that it is somewhat wider than *AB* and draw two arcs – one with the needle at *N*, and the other with the needle at *M*, so that they intersect vertically above *A*, at point *C*. Line *AC* is now perpendicular to *AB*. Set the compass width equal to *AB* and draw an arc, with the needle at *A*, so that it crosses line *AC* at point *D*. Using the same compass width, draw two more arcs: one that is horizontally to the right of *D*, with the needle at *D*, and a second arc that is above *B*, with the needle at *B*. These two arcs cross at point *E*. Finish the square by connecting the four points *ABED*.

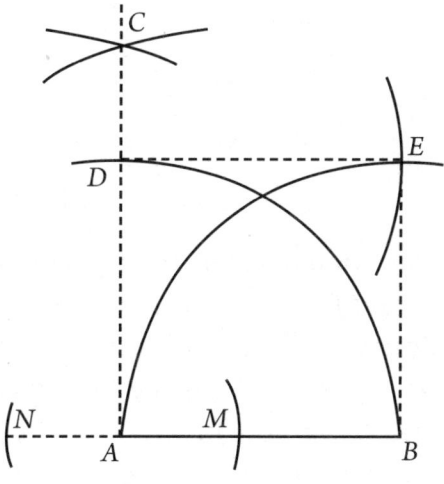

Constructing a hexagon, inside a given circle

Instructions (for the teacher only): The intention is to construct a regular hexagon inside the given circle.

Draw diameter AB passing through the centre of the circle, X. Then set the width of the compass equal to the radius of the circle, and draw one arc with the needle at B, which crosses the circle at points C and D, and another arc, with the needle at A, which crosses the circle at points E and F. The desired hexagon is AFDBCE.

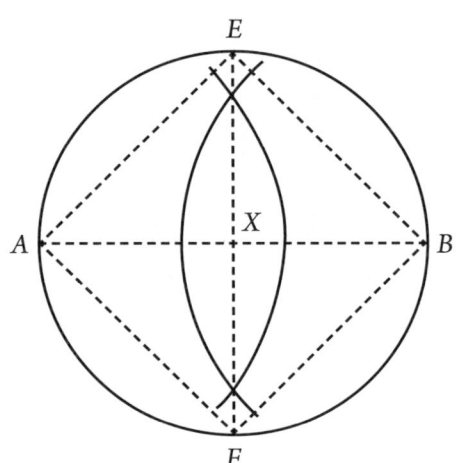

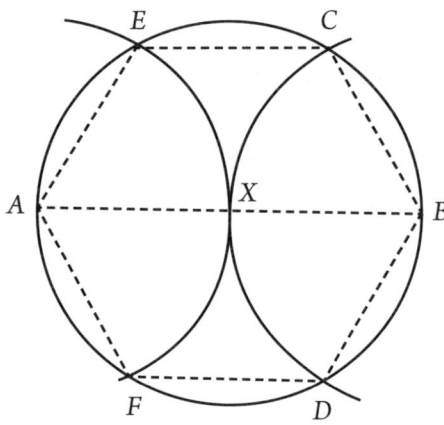

Constructing a triangle, inside a given circle

Instructions (for the teacher only): The intention is to construct an equilateral triangle inside the given circle.

Draw diameter AB passing through the centre of the circle. Set the compass width equal to the radius of the circle, and draw an arc, with the needle at A, that passes through the circle in two places, labeled C and D. The desired triangle is BCD.

Constructing a square, inside a given circle

Instructions (for the teacher only): The intention is to construct a square inside the given circle.

Draw diameter AB passing through the centre of the circle, X. Construct the line that is perpendicular to AB passing through X and crossing the circle at E and F. The desired square is AFBE.

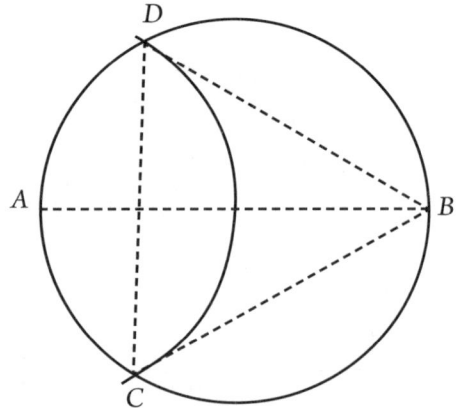

Constructing an octagon, inside a given circle

Instructions (for the teacher only): The intention is to construct a regular octagon inside the given circle.

Start by constructing the square *ABCD* inside the circle, as described above. We now only need to bisect two of the right angles formed by *AC* and *BD*. To do this, set the compass width equal to the radius of the circle and draw two short arcs, with the needle at *B* and then at *D*, that are vertically above the needle. Next, draw a long arc, with the needle at *C*, that passes through the centre of the circle, and then intersects the two short arcs (just drawn) at points *X* and *Y*. Draw lines *XM* and *YM*, and extend them so that each one intersects the circle in two places. We now have the eight equally spaced points along the circle that are needed to draw the octagon.

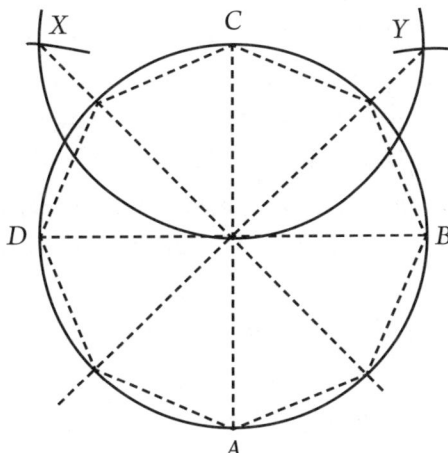

The 12-division of the circle
(Constructing a dodecagon)
Instructions (for the teacher only): The intention is to construct a dodecagon (12-gon) inside the given circle.

Locate the six points (*A*, *B*, *C*, *D*, *E*, *F*) of the hexagon inside the given circle (with centre *M*) as described above. Now, set the width of the compass to a bit less than the diameter of the circle. We only need to bisect three out of the six central angles (e.g. angle *AMB*) in order to locate the six additional points needed for the dodecagon.

We do this by drawing two arcs – one with the needle at *B* and the other with the needle at *C* – by having the compass reach over the centre of the circle. These two arcs cross each other at point *Y*. Then, with the same compass width, draw two shorter arcs – one with the needle at *A* and the other with the needle at *D* – that cross the two previously drawn arcs at *X* and *Z*, respectively. We can now locate six new points on the circle by extending *XM*, *YM* and *ZM* to form diameters of the circle so that they each cross the circle in two places. This gives us the twelve points on the circle that are needed to draw the dodecagon.

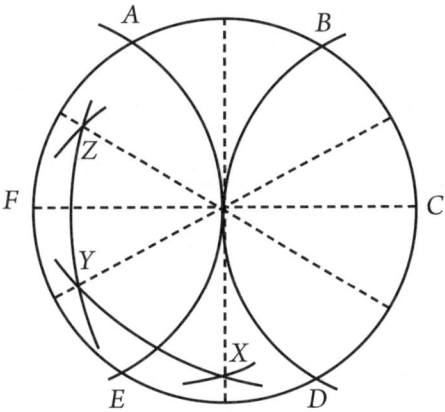

Class Six Geometry

The 24-division of the circle
(Constructing a 24-gon)
Instructions (for the teacher only): The intention is to construct a 24-gon inside the given circle.

We start here with the 12-division of the circle as described above. Using that same method, we set the width of the compass to a bit less than the diameter of the circle and draw arcs, with the needle at each one of the 12 points on the circle, where the compass reaches over the centre of the circle. It is only necessary to draw arcs from 7 of the 12 points on the circle, but in the drawing shown here I have done all 12 arcs. This gives us added accuracy for drawing the 6 diameters of the circle, since we now have three points with which to draw each diameter, rather than just the required two points. These 6 diameters give us 12 more points on the circle. We now have the 24 points along the circle that are needed to draw the 24-gon.

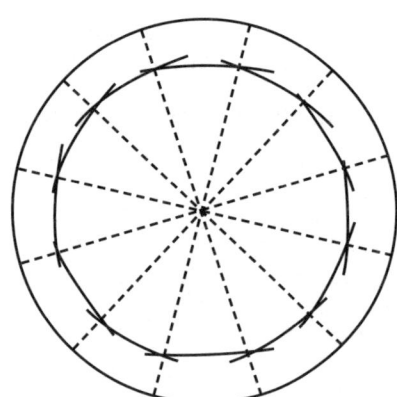

Spirals
The central idea here (as with most of this main lesson block) is to learn about these forms through the experience of drawing, and not to analyze them. In Class Six, students can make observations about the forms of the spirals (e.g. how does an equiangular spiral look different from an Archimedean spiral?). In Class Ten, we investigate the mathematical properties behind these differences that we observed in Class Six.

The equiangular spiral
(also known as a logarithmic spiral)
Construction (from the 12 division of a circle): Construct 12 points on the circumference of a circle (see *Constructing a dodecagon*, p. 67). Erase all construction lines.

Lightly draw 6 diameters by connecting all opposite points.

Start the spiral by lightly drawing a line segment from one of the 12 points on the circle that is perpendicular to a neighbouring radius (use a right-angled drawing triangle in order to save time). From that point lightly draw another line segment that is again perpendicular to the next radius. Continue lightly drawing line segments in this manner thereby creating a spiral in toward the centre of the circle (see drawing at right). Finish by darkly drawing a smoothly curved spiral over the light line segments.

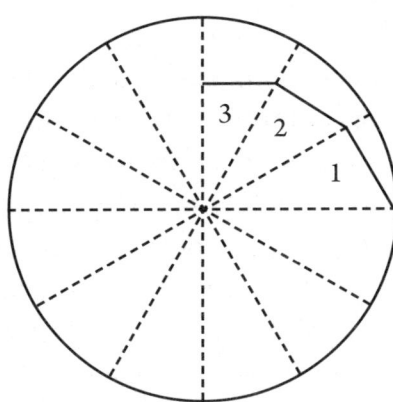

The beginning of the equiangular spiral construction

Interesting questions:
Why is this called an *equiangular spiral*?
This spiral can be seen as a series of progressively smaller, *equiangular* (similar) right triangles.
How can these triangles be seen in movement?
Each triangle moves into the position of the next triangle by rotating it about the centre of the spiral (e.g., triangle 1 moves to triangle 2, and triangle 2 moves to triangle 3). As each triangle is rotated, it is shrunk down enough so that it 'fits' into the next position.
Can we produce a spiral by using types of triangles other than right triangles?
Yes, (almost) any triangle will work, as long as the triangles are all similar and they are rotated about the centre of the circle and shrunk down as needed.
How many triangles does it take before the spiral reaches the centre?
Infinitely many.

Does the spiral actually ever reach the centre? That depends on how you look at it. This interesting question is addressed in Class Ten.

It is good to have different students start out with a different number of points on the circle (6, 8 or 24) so that the resulting spirals can be compared.

Good examples of equiangular spirals that appear in nature are rams' horns, sunflowers and nautilus shells.

Geometric progressions and the equiangular spiral

(For the teacher only.) A *geometric progression* is a type of growth (or shrinking). In Class Ten, geometric growth is analyzed mathematically, and it is shown that each step in the sequence is a certain percentage larger than the previous step (e.g. with 200, 220, 242, 266.2... each step is a 10% increase of the previous). Other names for this mathematical behavior are *geometric growth, exponential growth* or *constant percentage growth*. An example of this is a bank account with monthly compounded interest – it increases each month by the same percentage.

On the other hand, an *arithmetical progression* is where each number in the progression is increased by the same amount (e.g. 4, 7, 10, 13, 16...). None of this is mentioned in Class Six. The students simply make drawings that show geometric progressions, and then make observations about those drawings.

Class Six Geometry

Other ways to construct an equiangular spiral

Formed with inscribed regular polygons
(See Appendix, *Equiangular spirals*, p. 196, for drawings).

Nested octagons
Start by carefully drawing an octagon in a circle (see *Constructing an octagon*, p. 67). Connect the midpoints of each side thereby forming another smaller octagon. Continue in this manner, drawing one octagon inside another as far as possible. It is amazing how beautifully the students can shade in this drawing. Look at the drawing in the Appendix, p. 196, for an extraordinary example of how to shade in nested octagons.

Do three more drawings starting with a hexagon, a square and a triangle. Notice how the spirals from the different drawings approach the centre at different rates.

Joining the quarter-points of the sides of the squares
See Appendix, *Equiangular spirals*, p. 196. Draw a large square, and as you go around the perimeter of the square in one direction, mark points at one-quarter the length along each side. Connect these four new points in order to create a new, slightly smaller square. Continue making new, smaller squares in this manner, so that the squares are all rotating in one direction as they get smaller. Shade in spirals as shown in the drawing in Appendix A.

The spiral of Archimedes
Draw a line across and slightly below the middle of the page, and mark equal distances (perhaps ½ cm) out from the centre along that line. Using the midpoint of that line as the centre, lightly draw circles with radii that get progressively longer (e.g. ½ cm, 1 cm, 1½ cm, etc.) by using the distances that have just been marked on the line. Now, mark twelve evenly spaced points around the perimeter of the largest circle, and then lightly draw six diameters by joining the six pairs of opposite points. Finally, carefully draw the Archimedean spiral by starting from one of the twelve outside points and move inward, such that each step goes to the point of intersection of the next smaller circle and the neighbouring radius.

Notice that how quickly the spiral comes in to the centre of the circle is determined by the spacing of the circles and the number of circles. Therefore, using the twelve-division of the circle (as suggested above), and spacing the circles ½ cm apart, will result in a spiral that goes around exactly 2 full times before reaching the centre *if there are 24 circles*. This would require the outer-most circle to have a radius of 12 cm, which may be too big to fit on the paper. Drawing only 18 circles would result in a spiral going around 1½ times. Another option, which was used for the original of the drawing below, is to draw 36 circles that are 3 mm apart, resulting in a spiral that goes around exactly 3 times, and has a radius of 10.8 cm.

Make observations about how the Archimedean spiral is different from an equiangular spiral, including the most important difference: the Archimedean spiral clearly reaches the centre, and the equiangular spiral needs an infinite number of rotations about the centre before it reaches the centre.

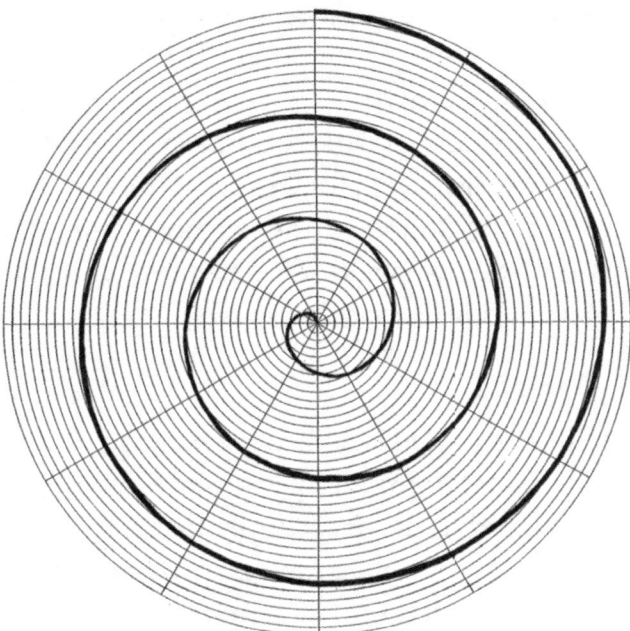

The drawing has been reduced in size

Advanced constructions
Rotations of circles
See Appendix, p. 197, for drawing. Notice with the page titled *Rotations of circles* in Appendix A, that the three drawings on the left are exactly the same as the drawings on the right, but the drawings on the right have been shaded-in.

Construction: Look at the drawing in Appendix A. With each of the drawings on the left side, you start with a 24-division of a circle (shown as a dotted circle in the drawing). Erase the construction lines, but keep the 24 points. Then use each of these 24 points as the centre to draw a circle. The difference between the three types of drawings is that the top drawing has its 24 circles with a much larger radius than the original circle, the middle drawing has its 24 circles with radii that are equal to the original circle, and the bottom drawing has its 24 circles with radii equal to half the original circle.

The limaçon and the cardioid
See Appendix, p. 198, for drawing. This drawing can be used to demonstrate how a curve can metamorphose.

Construction: Have the students start with a circle in the centre of the paper that has a radius of approximately 5 cm. Using a compass (or a protractor), do a 24-division of the circle, and then mark the 24 points on the circle with a pen. Erase everything except for the 24 points. Now each student is assigned a special point, called the cusp. Some students' cusp should be outside the circle (anywhere from 1 to 5 cm above the top of the circle); others should be inside the circle (anywhere from 1 to 3 cm below the top of the circle); a couple of students should have their cusp on the top of the circle; and one student should have a cusp at the centre of the circle. The students create their limaçon by placing their compass needle, in turn, on each one of the 24 points of the circle, and, for each one, they adjust their compass in order to draw a circle that goes through the cusp. The resulting curve is a limaçon, and should be carefully traced with a coloured pencil. The various results should then be displayed at the front of the classroom so that the students can observe how the limaçon becomes transformed as the cusp moves from the centre of the construction circle toward the edge of the circle, and then to the outside of the circle. (See Appendix, *The metamorphosis of a limaçon*, p. 198, for drawing.)

A *cardioid* is the special case of a limaçon when the cusp is located on the construction circle. In the drawing in Appendix A, the cardioid (meaning 'heart-shaped') is the drawing on the lower right.

A *cardioid* can also be generated by tracing a fixed point on a circle as it rolls around another circle of equal radius. There is a children's art toy, called a spirograph, which I used as a child that does something similar to this.

The hierarchy of quadrilaterals
See Appendix, p. 199, for drawing. This drawing is a wonderful example of how order can emerge from chaos.

Draw a large irregular (random) quadrilateral. Connect the midpoints to form a parallelogram. Bisect the parallelogram angles to get a rectangle. Bisect these angles to get a square.

Knots and interpenetrating polygons
See Appendix, p. 200, for drawing. With these drawings, it may be best to simply let the students see an example and have them figure out how to do it. Then let them come up with different knots and interpenetrations of their own.

The 24-division with all its diagonals
See Appendix, p. 201, for drawing. This drawing is very simple in concept, but requires much care and time.

You should see rings of circles expanding outward from the centre and fading.

The king's crown
See Appendix, p. 201, for drawing. This drawing starts again with the 24-division of the circle, and includes most of the diagonals from only two of the 24 points. Students love to colour this drawing in a variety of ways.

Area
Students should be able to picture square units (square centimetres, square metres, etc.).

What does it mean to say that a room has an area of 90 square metres? Students should be able to picture that a room 10 m by 9 m (or another room 6 m by 15 m) would be covered by a total of 90 one-metre by one-metre squares.

Don't introduce the shorthand way of writing square metre (m^2) until Class Seven or Eight, since students often think of this as an exponent for the number (e.g. making 7 m^2 incorrectly into 49 m).

Do areas of squares, rectangles and right triangles only. Have the students do drawings to show that the areas 'work'. Include rectangles that have fractional dimensions.

Example: What is the area of a right triangle that has a base of 3 metres and a height of 2 metres?

The area is half that of the rectangle it sits in. We can also see how the pieces of squares can be put together to form whole squares. Therefore the area equals ½ × 3 × 2, which is exactly 3 square metres.

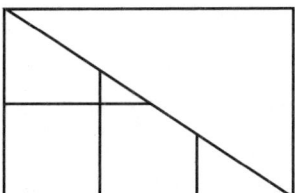

Example: What is the area of a rectangle that is 4½ cm by 3⅓ cm? Construct an accurate drawing that demonstrates this.

We can quickly see that we have 12 complete squares. Then the 2 half-squares can be added to form one square, as can the 3 third-squares. We are left with 1 half square, 1 third square, and 1 sixth-square (½ × ⅓), all of which nicely combine to form one whole square. The total area is therefore exactly 15 square cm.

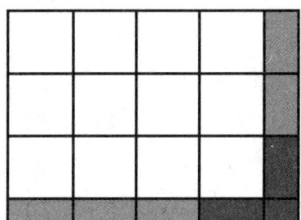

Example: What is the area of a rectangle that is 2⅔ metres by 3¼ metres? Construct an accurate drawing that demonstrates this.

We can quickly see that we have 6 full square metres (6 × 1 = 6). Then the 3 two-third-squares can be added together to form 2 square metres (3 × ⅔ = 2). The 2 quarter-squares combine to form a half square metre (2 × ¼ = ½), and the remaining rectangle (⅔ by ¼) has an area of ⅙ of a square metre (⅔ × ¼ = ⅙). Now we add the parts to get 6 + 2 + ½ + ⅙ = 8 4/6 = 8⅔ square metres.

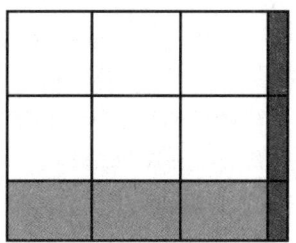

Class Seven Arithmetic

The importance of Class Seven
Class Seven is an important year academically. This is the year when students start to develop abstract thinking (through algebra, physics, essay writing, etc.). It is relatively common for a student to enter Class Seven fairly weak in maths, but then to 'wake-up' during Class Seven, and, in the end, to enter the upper school quite strong in maths.

The order of topics
The Class Seven workbook allows students to practise their skills with most of the topics listed here, with a few exceptions (e.g. puzzle problems) The order of the units in the workbook is:
1. Arithmetic review
2. Measurement
3. Ratios part I
4. Percents
5. Ratios part II
6. Pay rate, speed, etc.
7. Geometry
8. Square root algorithm (optional)
9. Algebra (for the algebra main lesson)

Review Class Six
Especially review fractions, decimals and division (see Class Six arithmetic, p. 33). Integrate review into new material, as feasible.

The world of numbers
Maths tricks
Review Class Six maths tricks (see Appendix, p. 236).

Do the Class Seven maths tricks (see Appendix, p. 238). Introduce perhaps one new trick each week, and work on practising new ones with old ones during mental arithmetic. (See Introduction, *Mental arithmetic,* p. 23.)

Divisibility rules
Review Class Six divisibility rules, p. 34, and then do these as well:

A number is evenly *divisible by* 6 only if it is divisible by both 2 and 3.
   Example: 577,368 is evenly divisible by 6 because it is divisible by both 2 and 3.

A number is evenly *divisible by* 8 only if the last 3 digits are divisible by 8. This is because it will evenly divide into any number of thousands.
   Example: 8,736,104 is *not* evenly divisible by 8 because the last three digits aren't divisible by 8.

A number is evenly *divisible by* 12 only if it is divisible by both 4 and 3.
   Example: 57,481,932 is evenly divisible by 12 because it is divisible by both 4 and 3.

A number is evenly *divisible by* 11 only if the difference of the sums of every other digit is evenly divisible by 11.

Example: With 6,273,905, we get one sum by adding the digits 6, 7, 9 and 5 to get 27. The other sum comes from adding the digits 2, 3 and 0, which gives 5. The difference of the two sums is 27 − 5, which is 22. And since 22 is evenly divisible by 11, then we can say that the original number 6,273,905 is also evenly divisible by 11.

Example: With 378,543 both sums are equal to 15, making the difference equal to zero. Since zero is evenly divisible by 11, then we can say that 378,543 is also evenly divisible by 11.

Example: With 68,479, the two sums are 19 and 15, which have a difference of 4. Therefore, we conclude that 68,479 is not evenly divisible by 11.

Roots

Review Class Six square roots.

Do also cube roots, fourth roots, etc., such as:

Example: $\sqrt[3]{125} = 5$ (because $5 \times 5 \times 5 = 125$)

Example: $\sqrt[4]{81} = 3$ (because $3 \times 3 \times 3 \times 3 = 81$)

Example: $\sqrt[3]{1000} = 10$

Example: $\sqrt[10]{1024} = 2$

Measurement

Review

Metric system from Class Six. Especially review visualising how big each metric unit is. (See Class Six, *metric system*.)

The imperial system can be briefly reviewed, including length (miles, yards, feet, inches), weight (stone, pounds, ounces) and volume (gallons, pints, fluid ounces). Also practise a few conversions.

The metric system

Spend a good amount of time on this unit, so that the students become very confident operating in the metric system.

The metric stairs. Early on in the unit, I give the students the metric stairs, which can help the students figure out how many places the decimal point should be moved for a given conversion problem. The idea is that every step up or down the stairs results in a move of one position of the decimal point.

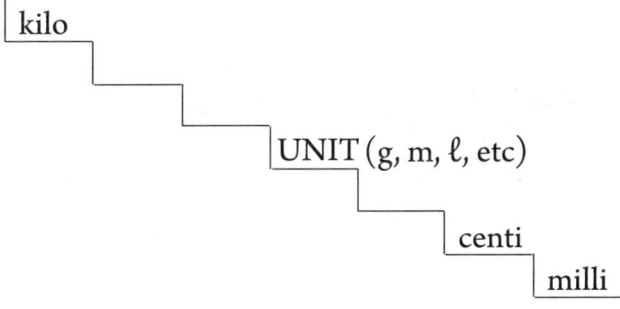

Example: 5,700 cm is equal to how many km?

Rather than have the students memorise any particular procedure (like moving up the stairs means moving the decimal point to the left), I try to have the students understand the following reasoning.

We are going from centi up to kilo, which is 5 steps on the metric stairs. This means that we need to move the decimal point 5 places. The only question now is whether to take 5,700 and move the decimal point to the right or to the left. So the possible answers are 0.057 km (after moving the decimal point to the left) or 570,000,000 km (after moving the decimal point to the right). The students should picture all these distances. Is 5,700 cm the same as 0.057 km or the same as 570,000,000 km? It should be obvious after a bit of thought that 570,000,000 km, which is actually far greater than the distance to the sun, is not reasonable. Therefore, the only reasonable answer is that 5,700 cm is equal to 0.057 km.

Emphasise to the students that they should always check their answer to see if it is reasonable. For instance, with the above example, if they moved the decimal point the wrong way, they should realise that 5,700 cm is not even close to being equal to 570,000,000 km.

Practise doing lots of conversions that remain in a given system, such as:

Example: How many inches are in 6 yards? (Answer: 6 yards = 18 feet = 216 inches)

Example: How many gallons are in 200 fluid ounces? (Answer: 200 fl oz = 10 pt = 1¼ gallon)

Example: How many kilograms are in 18 grams? (Answer: 0.018 kg)

Example: How many milligrams are in 23.6 kilograms? (Answer: 23,600,000 mg)

Practise simple conversions between metric and imperial measures.

Percents

Review Class Six percents and business maths and cover any material that was not covered in Class Six.

Finding the base

The 'base' is the number that we are taking the percentage of – usually it is the larger number.

Example: With the statement '3,500 is 70% of 5,000', the base is 5,000.

Example: With the statement '800 decreased by 25% is 600', the base is 800.

Example: With the statement '60 increased by 8% is 64.8', the base is 60 (which is *not* the larger number).

Also see Class Eight percents, *Four ways to find the base*, p. 131.

Finding the base for an increase/decrease problem is delayed until Class Eight.

Easier ones

Sometimes finding the base (larger number) is quite easy.

Example: 36 is 25% of what number?

Since 36 is ¼ of the number we are looking for, we can say that the number must be 4 times greater than 36, which gives us an answer of 144.

Thinking of inverses

Up until now, we have usually been required to find the percentage of a larger number. Now we are going the other way around. In essence, we are doing inverse operations.

This method is only introduced here in Class Seven. Much more is done in Class Eight.

Example: Here, we will play with the fact that 38 equals 8% of 475. We can either be given 475 and be asked to find 38, or be given 38 and be asked to find 475. Specifically, the two questions are:

Question A (finding the smaller number): What is 8% of 475? (This is the normal percent question.)

Using decimals: We do 475 × 0.08 to get an answer of 38.

Using fractions: We do $\frac{8}{100}$ × 475 to get an answer of 38.

Question B (finding the larger number): 38 is 8% of what number? (This is the inverse of Question A.)

Using decimals: We do 38 ÷ 0.08 to get an answer of 475. (This is the inverse of the first solution above – we *divide* by 0.08 instead of *multiplying* by 0.08.)

Using fractions: We do $\frac{100}{8}$ × 38 to get an answer of 475. (This is the inverse of the second solution above – we multiply by $\frac{100}{8}$ the reciprocal, instead of multiplying by $\frac{8}{100}$.)

Trickier ones

It is good to practise each of the above two types of solutions for finding the base. (Another method, which uses more advanced algebra, is introduced in Class Eight. See Class Eight percents, *Four ways to find the base*, p. 131.)

Example: 12 is 80% of what number?

Using decimals: Using the fact that 80% is 0.8, we can say that since 12 is 0.8 times the number we are looking for, then the inverse thought is: the number is 12 *divided by* 0.8. Therefore, our answer is 12 ÷ 0.8, which is 15.

Using fractions: Using the fact that 80% is ⁴⁄₅, we can say that since 12 is ⁴⁄₅ of the number we are looking for, then the inverse thought is: the number must be ⁵⁄₄ of 12. Answer: ⁵⁄₄ × 12 = 15.

Example: 60 is 90% of what number?

A common error is to reason that since 60 is 90% of the number that we are looking for, then that number (call it *x*) must be 10% more than 60. Since 10% of 60 is 6, we would get an answer of 60 + 6 = 66. The fault with this reasoning is that while 60 is 10% less than *x*, *x* is not 10% more than 60. Along those same lines, 75 is 25% more than 60, but 60 is only 20% less than 75! This idea is further investigated in Class Eight.

The correct solution uses the method from the solution shown above using fractions, we see that 90% is ⁹⁄₁₀. Therefore we multiply 60 by ¹⁰⁄₉ (the reciprocal of ⁹⁄₁₀). Alternatively, using the method from the first solution, we divide 60 by 0.9. Either way, the answer works out to 66⅔.

Strange percents

Example: What is 3¼% of 3000? (0.0325 × 3000 = 97.5)

Example: What is 12.52% of 60? (0.1252 × 60 = 7.512)

Example: What is 0.06% of 2100? (0.0006 × 2100 = 1.26)

Example: What is 250% of 18? (2.5 × 18 = 45)

Compound interest

Review Class Six interest (p. 50), including the 'John and Sue' example

Only do interest compounded annually. Don't use the formula $P = P_0(1 + r)^t$ until Class Eight.

Give an example that demonstrates the difference between simple and compound interest.

Example: Calculate the balance after 5 years of two accounts, each one with a beginning investment of £600 and 10% interest; the only difference being that one account has simple interest and the other has interest compounded annually.

Simple interest: Each year earns the same interest, which is £60. So after 5 years £300 has been earned, and the ending balance is £900.

Compound interest: The interest earned in the first year is £60, giving a balance of £660. The second year earns £66 interest and ends with a balance of £726. The third year earns £72.60 interest and ends with a balance of £798.60. The fourth year earns £79.86 of interest and ends with a balance of £878.46. The fifth year earns £87.85 (rounded) of interest and ends with a balance of £966.31.

Calculating the percentage of increase or decrease

When calculating the percentage of increase or decrease, we think of it as the fraction:

$$\% \text{ increase} = \frac{\text{amount of increase}}{\text{starting point}}$$

$$\% \text{ decrease} = \frac{\text{amount of decrease}}{\text{starting point}}$$

Make sure that the students can understand why this idea is true: 75 is 25% more than 60, but 60 is 20% less than 75.

In order to calculate the percentage of increase (or decrease), the students should answer these three questions:

1. What is the amount of increase (or decrease)?
2. What is the starting point (i.e. the number that we started at)?
3. The amount of increase (or decrease) is what percentage of the original amount?

Example: What percentage increase is it going from 350 to 420?

Answering the above three questions, we get: (1) The amount of increase is 70. (2) We started at 350. (3) We ask 70 is what percentage of 350? The answer to this is the fraction $\frac{70}{350}$ which reduces to $\frac{1}{5}$, which is 20%. Our final answer is that going from 350 to 420 is a 20% increase.

Example: What percentage decrease is it going from 320 down to 208?

Answering the above three questions, we get: (1) The amount of decrease is 112. (2) We started at 320. (3) We ask: 112 is what percentage of 320? The answer to this is the fraction $\frac{112}{320}$ which reduces to $\frac{7}{20}$, which is 35%. Our answer is that going from 320 down to 208 is a 35% decrease.

Example: If a bike shop purchases a bike wholesale at £300 and then sells it retail for £372, then what percent profit does it make?

Answering the above three questions, we get: (1) The amount of increase is £72. (2) We started at £300. (3) We ask 72 is what percent of 300? The answer is 24%.

Example: If a shirt that is on sale was originally £24 and is now marked at £20.40, what is the discount given as a percent?

Answering the above three questions, we get: (1) The amount of decrease is £3.60. (2) We started at £24. (3) We ask: £3.60 is what percent of £24?

This we picture as $\frac{3.60}{24}$. We can then divide 24 into 3.6, which gives us 0.15. Alternatively, we can convert $\frac{3.6}{24}$ into $\frac{36}{240}$ which then reduces to $\frac{3}{20}$ and multiplying the top and bottom by 5 gives us $\frac{15}{100}$. Either way, we get 15%.

Example: What is 200 increased by 10%, then decreased by 10%?

It is *not* 200! Instead, 200 increased by 10% is 220, and 220 decreased by 10% is 220 minus 22, which is 198.

Challenge Problem!

(a) John bought a new car for £39,000 and then sold it for £20,000 two years later. What percent loss is this?

(b) Over those two years, what was the total operating cost and the cost per km given that he spent £750 per year on insurance, £450 annually on repairs and maintenance, an average of £220 monthly for interest payments, £850 annually for other costs (parking, tolls, tax, etc.) and drove it 20,000 km per year? (Use 8 ℓ/100 km for petrol usage, and £1.20/ℓ for the cost of petrol.)

(c) Given the answer from part b, how much did it cost him, in total, when he drove to Birmingham and back on a trip covering a total of 200 km?

(d) What percent of the total operating cost was petrol? (Rounded to three significant digits.)

(a) The amount of decrease is £19,000, and from £39,000 it is approximately a 48.7% loss.

(b) The total amount of petrol used is 40,000 km ÷ 8 ℓ/100 km is 40,000 × 8 ÷ 100, which is 3,200 ℓ. At £1.20/ℓ, 3,200 ℓ costs £3840. Combined with £19,000 depreciation costs (drop in the price of the car), £1,500 for insurance, £900 for repairs, £5,280 for interest, and £1,700 for other costs, gives us a total cost for the two years of £32,220. Lastly, we divide this cost by 40,000 km and conclude that it cost John approximately £0.81/km per mile to drive his car.

(c) The 200 km trip costs 0.81 × 200, which is £162.

(d) Since the total cost of driving was £32,220, the cost of petrol (£3,840) was 11.9%.

Ratios

Ratios are a central theme for the year. This unit needs to be done before the geometry main lesson, and before the physics main lesson.

Review Class Six ratios (p. 56).

Key ideas

- The amount doesn't matter; the essence of ratio is the relationship between the two amounts.
- Ratios have no units.

The ratio of two people's heights is the same whether measured in the metric or imperial system.

Example: John's height is 7 feet 4 inches, which is 224 cm. Sam's height is 4 feet 7 inches, which is 140 cm. Find the ratio of their heights, using both measurement systems.

First, using their heights as given in feet and inches, we convert to inches, which gives us 88 in and 55 in. This is a ratio of 8:5. Now redoing the problem by using their heights given in centimetres, we reduce the ratio 224 : 140, by dividing by 8, to the *ratio* 8 : 5. These ratios are the same, thereby showing that no matter how we measure their heights, the ratio of their heights is the same.

Likewise, if the ratio of Mary's to Jane's salary is 5 : 4, it means that for every £5 that Mary makes that Jane makes £4. Notice that if Mary and Jane instead were paid in an equivalent amount of a different currency (e.g. dollars) then the numbers associated with their individual salaries would be changed, but the ratios of their salaries with respect to each other would still be 5:4.

Ratios of more than two things

Ratios can be used to compare three or more numbers.

Example: If there are 12, 15, 15 and 20 students, respectively, in four classes, then we can say that the ratio of the four classes is 12 : 15 : 15 : 18, which reduces to 3 : 5 : 5 : 6.

The three thoughts of a ratio

These three thoughts, associated with any ratio given in whole number form, get to the essence of the meaning of a ratio.

Example: What does the ratio $J : K = 4 : 3$ mean?

One way to think of this is: the ratio of Jim's money to Kevin's money is four to three. (Alternatively, we can think of it as a ratio of Jim's height to Kevin's height.) Immediately, we should be able to see that Jim has more money than Kevin. We can then list the three thoughts associated with this ratio as:

- $4K = 3J$ (4 times Kevin's money is equal to three times Jim's money.)
- $K = ¾J$ (Kevin has ¾ as much as Jim.)
- $J = ⁴⁄_3 K$ (Jim has ⁴⁄_3 as much as Kevin.)

Example: If the ratio of Jim's money to Kevin's money is 4 : 3, then what does Jim have if Kevin has £270?

Looking at the above example, the third thought ($J = ⁴⁄_3 K$) is the most helpful. This tells us that Jim's money is ⁴⁄_3 of Kevin's. So we do ⁴⁄_3 times 270 to get a final answer of £360.

Example: If the ratio of Mary's height to Nancy's height is 5 : 7, then how tall is Mary if Nancy is 161 cm?

The three thoughts associated with this ratio are:
- $5N = 7M$ (5 times Nancy's height is equal to 7 times Mary's height.)
- $M = ⁵⁄_7 N$ (Mary's height is ⁵⁄_7 of Nancy's height.)
- $N = ⁷⁄_5 M$ (Nancy's height is ⁷⁄_5 of Mary's height.)

Of the above three thoughts, the second one is the most useful. This tells us that Mary's height is ⁵⁄_7 of Nancy's height. Our answer is therefore ⁵⁄_7 of 161 (since Nancy is 161 cm tall), which works out to 115 cm.

The two forms for a ratio

Any ratio can be expressed either as two whole numbers, or as a decimal. A good deal of time will need to be spent on this, so that the students can work equally well with either form, and so that they can convert one form into the other.

Whole number form

This form is what was introduced in Class Six, and is expressed in terms of two whole numbers. It is best to make sure that the answer is reduced, just as we would reduce a fraction. For example, a ratio of 15 : 12 reduces to 5 : 4.

Decimal form

This form is expressed in such a way that the first number is a decimal, and the second number is *always* equal to one. The ratio 5 : 4 is equivalent to 1.25 : 1 in decimal form.

Example: If there are 560 cars and 320 bikes in a certain town, then what is the ratio of cars to bikes?

The answer can be expressed in either form:

Whole number form (done by reducing the fraction $\frac{560}{320}$ to $\frac{7}{4}$)   C : B = 7 : 4

Decimal form (done by dividing 560 by 320 or by dividing 7 by 4)   C : B = 1.75 : 1

Example: Convert the ratio 19 : 4 (which is in whole number form) into decimal form.

We divide 19 by 4 to get 4.75, and therefore our answer is 4.75 : 1.

Example: Convert the ratio 2.4 : 1 (which is in decimal form) into whole number form.

Our goal is make the ratio into two whole numbers. We can do this most easily by multiplying both 2.4 and 1 by 10, thereby giving us a ratio of 24 : 10, which then reduces to 12 : 5.

The two thoughts of a ratio (in decimal form)
These two thoughts, associated with any ratio given in decimal form, get to the essence of the meaning of a ratio.

Example: What does the ratio $J : K = 1.2 : 1$ mean?

We can tell by looking at the ratio that J is slightly bigger than K. No matter if J and K represent heights, or money or anything else, the two thoughts are:

$J = 1.2 \times K$ (J is 1.2 times bigger than K)
$K = J \div 1.2$ (K is 1.2 times smaller than J)

Reciprocals of ratios
Finding the reciprocal of a ratio that is expressed as a fraction is simple – just reverse the ratio.

Example: If a rectangle has a base of 16, and a height of 10, then we can say that the ratio of the base to the height is $B : H = 8 : 5$, or we could say that the ratio of the height to the base (which is the reciprocal of the first ratio) is $H : B = 5 : 8$. Quite simple!

Finding the reciprocal of a ratio that is expressed as a decimal is trickier.

Example: Again, using a rectangle that is 16 by 10, we can divide 16 by 10 to get a ratio of $B : H = 1.6 : 1$. The reciprocal of this ratio is found by dividing 10 by 16, which gives us the ratio $H : B = 0.625 : 1$.

Example: Find the reciprocal of the ratio $A : B = 1.8 : 1$.

We think of it as the fraction $\frac{1.8}{1}$ and then flip it to get $\frac{1}{1.8}$. Lastly, we convert this to a decimal by dividing 1.8 into 1, giving an answer of $B : A = 0.\overline{5} : 1$.

Alternatively, we first change the ratio to whole number form $18 : 10$, then reduce to $9 : 5$. The reciprocal of this is $5 : 9$, and then changing $5/9$ into a decimal gives us a final answer of $B : A = 0.\overline{5} : 1$.

Proportion of the whole
If the whole of something is divided into two parts, we can consider not only the ratio of these two parts, but we can also determine what proportion each part is of the whole, and use this to solve problems.

Example: Mrs Smith's class has 21 students, and the ratio of girls to boys is $3 : 4$. How many in the class are boys, and how many are girls?

Since 3 out of every 7 students are girls, we can say that $3/7$ of the whole class is girls. Likewise, we can say that $4/7$ of the whole class is boys. So to get the number of girls we take $3/7$ of 21, which gives us 9 girls. Similarly, the number of boys is $4/7$ of 21, which gives us 12 boys.

Example: If a litre of milk is completely poured into two jugs in a ratio of $5:3$, then how much is in each jug?

The ratio tells us that $5/8$ of the whole litre is in one jug, and $3/8$ is in the other. Since a litre is 1,000 mℓ, we get $5/8$ of $1,000 = 625$ mℓ in one jug, and $3/8$ of $1,000 = 375$ mℓ in the other.

Example: How can £540 be split between three people in a ratio of $2 : 3 : 4$?

The ratio tells us that the three people get

²⁄₉, ³⁄₉ and ⁴⁄₉, respectively, of the whole £540, which results in £120, £180 and £240.

Similar figures
- Similar figures have the same shape. We can make one into the other by putting it into a (perhaps imaginary) photocopier and enlarging or shrinking it.
- All the angles in similar figures are the same.
- The lengths of the sides of similar figures are in equal ratios.

Solve problems that find a missing side from two similar rectangles, or two similar triangles.

Do these problems *without* using algebra (algebra is used to solve proportions in Class Eight).

Start with easy problems, like the following:

Example: What is the length of a rectangle if its height is 8 cm, and it is similar to a rectangle that measures 6 cm by 3 cm? (Assume that the length is greater than the height.)

With the second rectangle, we can see that the length is twice the width. Since the rectangles are similar, we can say that the first rectangle's length is also twice its height. Therefore, the answer is that the length is 16 cm.

The problems are then made more complicated by having answers that turn out to be fractions, but the logic is exactly the same.

Example: What is the length of a rectangle if its height is 7 cm, and it is similar to a rectangle that measures 5 cm by 4 cm?

Here, we are looking for the length of the first rectangle, so we look at the second rectangle and ask, 'the length is how much of the height?' We see that the length is ⁵⁄₄ of the height. Therefore the length of the first rectangle must also be ⁵⁄₄ of its height (which is 7), leading us to an answer of ⁵⁄₄ × ⁷⁄₁, which is ³⁵⁄₄, or 8¾ cm.

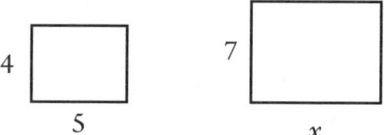

Shadow problems

By using similar triangles, find the height of something tall, by measuring the length of its shadow, and the height of something short (e.g. a ski pole), and the length of its shadow.

Example: Find the height of a tree if the length of its shadow is 25 m, and a ski pole held vertically next to the tree is 1.2 m tall and has a shadow 1.65 m tall.

It is helpful to first draw two triangles, where the vertical and horizontal sides represent the height and shadow length of the two objects. The key is to realise that the two triangles are similar, and therefore that the ratio of the two sides is the same with both of the triangles.

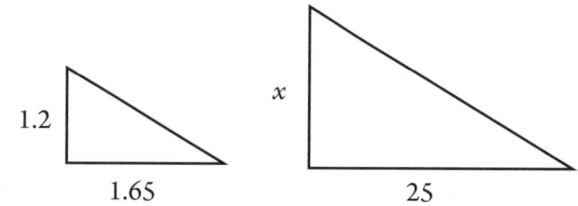

Since the ratio of the sides of the triangle created by the ski pole is 1.2 : 1.65, which (multiplying both by 100 and dividing by 5 and again by 3) simplifies to 8 : 11, we know that the ratio of the sides of the triangle created by the tree must be the same. Since the height of the ski pole is $8/11$ of its length, the height of the tree must be $8/11$ of the length of its shadow. Therefore its height is $8/11$ times 25, which is $\frac{200}{11}$, or approximately 18.2 m.

Direct and inverse proportions

Speed, time and distance

Speed and time are inversely proportional

Example: If Jeff biked to school on Monday in 20 minutes, then how long did it take on Tuesday to bike to school if he went $4/5$ as fast?

Since speed and time are *inversely proportional*, we can say that biking $4/5$ as fast means that it took $5/4$ (the reciprocal of $4/5$) as long. Therefore, the answer is $5/4$ times 20, which is 25 minutes.

Speed and distance are directly proportional

Example: If Cathy went on a 56 km bike ride on Wednesday. How far did she go on Thursday if she rode for the same amount of time but went $7/8$ as fast?

Since speed and distance are directly proportional, we can say that biking $7/8$ as fast means that she goes $7/8$ as far (using the same fraction). The answer is then $7/8$ of 56, which is 49 km.

String length and frequency (from Class Seven physics)

The ratio of two string lengths is the reciprocal of the ratio of their frequency

In mathematics, we say that the string length and the frequency are inversely proportional. This means that if one thing goes up (e.g. if the length of the string gets longer), then the other (e.g. the frequency) must go down. This is consistent with our experience of string instruments – a longer string makes a lower pitch (frequency).

Example: If a C string (90 cm long) on a cello has a frequency of 256 Hz, and you press your finger at the 60 cm mark (which is a G – the fifth note above C), then what is the frequency of the resulting note? (Hz stands for 'hertz' and means vibrations per second.)

The ratio of the string lengths of the two notes is G : C = 60 : 90 = 2 : 3, which means that the length of the string for the G note is $2/3$ as long as the length of the string for the C note. Now we know from the above stated rule that the ratio of their frequencies will be the reciprocal of the ratio of the string lengths. Specifically, the ratio of the frequencies of the two notes must therefore be G : C = 3 : 2 (which is the reciprocal of 2 : 3). Therefore the G note has a frequency that is $3/2$ of the frequency of the C note $256 \times 3/2 = 384$ Hz.

The law of the lever
(from Class Seven mechanics)
To balance a seesaw, the ratio of the weights is the reciprocal of the ratio of the distances to the centre of the fulcrum (the balance point).

For example, if the ratio of the weights of the left side to the right side is $L : R = 3 : 2$ then the ratio of the distances to the fulcrum is $L : R = 2 : 3$. This can be expressed as:

The weights of two objects on a seesaw are inversely proportional to their distances away from the fulcrum.

As a formula, this is: $W_L : W_R = D_R : D_L$ or $W_L \times D_L = W_R \times D_R$ (W is weight, D is distance.)

Experientially, if two children are trying to balance a seesaw, and the heavier one weighs ³⁄₂ as much as the lighter one, then the heavier one must sit ⅔ as far from the fulcrum as the lighter one

Example: If a boy, who weighs 25 kg, is sitting 1.8 metres away from the fulcrum of a seesaw, how far from the fulcrum must a girl, who weighs 20 kg, sit in order that the seesaw is balanced?

The girl is ⅘ of the boy's weight, so she must sit ⁵⁄₄ as far away ⁵⁄₄ × 1.8 = 2.25 m.

A new type of number: irrational numbers

The ratio of a diagonal to a side of a square
Guessing the ratio
Start by drawing a square on the board and ask the students to guess what the ratio of the diagonal to the side of the square might be. Certainly, they should be able to see that it is less than 2 : 1 (i.e. the diagonal is less than twice the length of the side). They might guess that it is 3 : 2 or 5 : 3. The best (very lucky!) guess would be 7 : 5.

The great Pythagorean crisis
One of the central tenets of the school of Pythagoras was that the gods had made the world so that it was imbued with harmony and perfection. Perfect ratios were a key theme. For example, in music, they knew that the ratio of two notes an octave apart was 2 : 1, and that if the notes were a fifth apart, then the ratio was 3 : 2.

Similarly, they believed that any two lengths were commensurable, meaning that they could be expressed as an exact ratio in whole number form. For example, with a rectangle that measures 2½ by 4¼, the ratio of the length to the width can be expressed as 17 : 10, which means that 17 times the width is exactly equal to 10 times the length.

Yet the square – one of the most fundamental geometrical forms – did not yield such a simple ratio. No one could determine exactly what the ratio of the diagonal to the side of a square was. Then, after much effort to find

Class Seven Arithmetic

this elusive ratio, someone within the school proved that no such ratio could possibly exist – that no matter how big the two numbers in the ratio were, there was no way to exactly express the ratio in whole number form.

This discovery was so horrifying to them that it was forbidden to leak the secret outside of their school. As one version of the story goes, one person did leak it, was found out and was then drowned!

This marked the discovery of a new type of number, which was so disturbing that it is known still today as an irrational number.

A further study of the Pythagorean school and the 'irrational crisis' is done in Class Ten.

The four ratios of a square
Given that x is the length of the side of a square and d is the length of its diagonal, we can express the ratio of these two lengths in one of four ways:
- $d : x \approx 7 : 5$
- $x : d \approx 5 : 7$
- $d : x \approx 1.414 : 1$
- $x : d \approx 0.707 : 1$

(0.707 comes from dividing 1.414 into 1, and also happens to be half as big.)

Practise calculating the diagonal or the side.

Example: Find the length of the side of a square that has a diagonal of 21 cm.

Using the above ratios we can get the answer by doing any of the following: $x \approx 21 \div 1.414$, or $x \approx 21 \times 0.707$, or $x \approx 21 \div 7/5$ or (the easiest method) $x \approx 21 \times 5/7$. Each answer is close to 15 cm.

π – the ratio in a circle

π is the ratio of the circumference to the diameter of *any* circle.

$c : d = \pi : 1$

Have the students precisely measure various circles and calculate this ratio (in decimal form). They should measure a fairly large circle in order to minimise error and get better results. If they have done this well (and without anyone telling them a value for π) then they should get 3 point something – perhaps 3.08, or 3.12 or 3.19.

The impossibility of measuring
It is interesting to have a class discussion about why the answers to the above experiment weren't all the same. It seems puzzling, since we know that all circles are similar and should therefore have the same ratio of circumference to diameter. The reason for the variation in our answers is that it is impossible to measure anything perfectly. Ultimately, there is no such thing as a perfect circle, *except in our minds*. Therefore, with the most accurate machines and tools, making the best circles possible, and measuring the diameters and circumferences with the greatest accuracy, we can get better values for this ratio, but they still won't be perfect.

Archimedes method for calculating π
It should be briefly mentioned that Archimedes was the first one to invent a method for calculating π with as much accuracy as desired. His method had nothing to do with measurement – Archimedes' circle was only in his mind, and he figured out how to calculate π through thinking alone. While his method could be continued indefinitely, the calculations were very tedious. He went as far as being able to conclude that π is between $3^{10}/_{71}$ and $3^{10}/_{70}$, which, in terms of decimals, is the equivalent of saying that π is between 3.1408 and 3.1429. (Further study of Archimedes' method is done in Class Ten.)

Since Archimedes, there have been several people that have calculated π to greater accuracy using his method. Today, computers are programmed using similar methods to calculate π to several billion decimal places. But they still can never get an exact value for π, because it is an irrational number – it will never end and never repeat.

Decimal approximations for π
Just as it is impossible to *exactly* express the ratio in a square (diagonal : side), so, too, is it impossible to *exactly* express the ratio of the circumference to the diameter of a circle (π) – it is *irrational*! It can be expressed approximately as a decimal, but it will never repeat or end. (π to the 10,000 decimal places can be found at www.math.utah.edu/~pa/math/pi.html) Here it is to 60 decimal places:

$\pi \approx$ 3.141 592 653 589 793 238 462 643 383 279 502 884 197 169 399375 105 820 974 944 ...

Fractional approximations for π

$\dfrac{22}{7}$ $\dfrac{355}{113}$ $\dfrac{52{,}163}{16{,}604}$ $\dfrac{104{,}348}{33{,}215}$ $\dfrac{833{,}719}{265{,}381}$

$\dfrac{5{,}419{,}351}{1{,}725{,}033}$ $\dfrac{80{,}143{,}857}{25{,}510{,}582}$

The four ratios of π (as opposed to thinking of π as only 3.14)
- $c : d \approx 3.14 : 1$
- $d : c \approx 0.318 : 1$
- $c : d \approx 22 : 7$
- $d : c \approx 7 : 22$

(0.318 comes from dividing 3.14 into 1)

Calculating the circumference or diameter
Avoid using the formula $c = \pi \times d$ until Class Eight.

In Class Seven, all answers should be given as approximate decimals or fractions. In Class Eight, answers can be given in terms of π (e.g. 8π).

To calculate a circumference or diameter, the students should use one of the four ratios given above. Although any of the four ratios can be used for any given problem, often one of them will be the easiest, and this will vary depending upon the problem. Using different methods will produce answers that are slightly different, because they are all based on approximate, but different, values for π. The students should become adept at using each ratio; this helps to develop flexibility in their thinking.

Class Seven Arithmetic

Save calculating the area of a circle ($a = \pi \times r^2$) for Class Eight.

Example: What is the circumference of a circle that has a diameter of 14 m?

Here, we notice that 14 is divisible by 7, so it is easiest to use the ratio $c : d \approx 22 : 7$, which tells us that $c \approx \frac{22}{7} \times d$, and since $d = 14$, we do $\frac{22}{7} \times \frac{14}{1}$, giving us an answer of 44 m. (Notice that this is easier than doing this the typical way of multiplying 14 by 3.14.)

Example: What is the diameter of a circle that has a circumference of 330 m?

With this problem, the ratio $d : c \approx 7 : 22$ is the easiest one to use, since it is the diameter that we are trying to find and we notice that 330 and 22 are both divisible by 11. This ratio tells us that $d \approx \frac{7}{22} \times c$, and since $c = 330$, we do $\frac{7}{22} \times \frac{330}{1}$, which, after cross cancelling by 11, gives us $\frac{7}{2} \times \frac{30}{1}$, and a final answer of 105 m. (Notice that this is much easier than dividing 330 by 3.14.)

Example: What is the diameter of a circle that has a circumference of 20 m?

Here, it is easiest to use the ratio $d : c \approx 0.318 : 1$, since it is the diameter that we are trying to find. This ratio tells us that $d \approx 0.318 \times c$, and since $c = 20$ we do 0.318×20, which gives us an answer of 6.36 m. (Note that this is *much* easier than the typical way of dividing 20 by 3.14. Be sure to emphasise this!)

Example: What is the circumference of a circle that has a diameter of 8 m?

Here, I would tend to use the typical method of multiplying 3.14 by 8, which is using the ratio $c : d \approx 3.14 : 1$, and gives us an answer of 25.12 m. If we had used the fractional approximation for π ($c : d \approx 22 : 7$), we would have gotten an answer of $^{22}/_{7} \times 8 = 25^{1}/_{7}$ in. The students will ask which answer is correct, and it is important for them to understand that both are acceptable, but neither answer is exactly correct because we cannot say *exactly* what the value for π is. We can only approximate π, and therefore our answers can only be approximations.

Repeating decimals

What are the possibilities when we convert a fraction into a decimal by dividing the numerator by the denominator? We know that in order to get an exact answer we need to keep going until the remainder repeats or becomes zero. How long do we need to go until a division problem will repeat or end? Will it necessarily ever repeat or end? Why? See Appendix, *Questions regarding repeating decimals* (p. 205), for answers and explanations to these questions and more.

The two laws of repeating decimals.
- Every fraction (with whole numbers in the numerator and denominator) is exactly equal to a decimal that either repeats or ends. In other words, if we divide the numerator by the denominator, it will eventually repeat or end.
- When a fraction is converted into a decimal, the most number of digits that can possibly appear under the repeat bar is one less than the number in the denominator. For example, 5/7 is equal to $0.\overline{714285}$, which has 6 digits (one less than the denominator) under the repeat bar.

Irrational numbers

A *rational number* is any fraction with whole numbers in both the numerator and denominator. Given the above laws of repeating decimals, we can also say that a rational number is a repeating or ending decimal.

Have the students use the guess and check method in order to calculate decimal values for $\sqrt{5.29}$ and $\sqrt{30}$ (see Appendix, *The square root algorithm, method 1*, p. 206). They should discover that $\sqrt{5.29}$ is exactly equal to 2.3, but that they can't get an exact value for $\sqrt{30}$. ($30 \approx 5.4772255750516611345696978 2800 802…$)

Ask the questions, 'How far do we need to go until we are finished calculating $\sqrt{30}$?' and 'What is the exact value of $\sqrt{30}$?'. The answer to these questions is that there is no exact decimal value for $\sqrt{30}$ and we can *never* finish it no matter how far we go!

Irrational numbers are studied in detail in Class Nine and Ten, but here in Class Seven, the following points should be emphasised:
- An irrational number is a number that cannot be expressed exactly as a decimal, or as a fraction.
- An irrational number is an unending, non-repeating decimal.
- A square root that doesn't work out evenly (e.g. $\sqrt{30}$) is one type of irrational number.
- A calculator gives an approximation of the value of any irrational number, like $\sqrt{30}$, as would a computer that could calculate its value to one million decimal places.

The square root algorithm (optional)
Comments for the teacher
This unit, if done at all, needs to be done towards the end of the year.

This unit is *very* challenging for both the students and the teacher, but very rewarding, if done well.

An algorithm (a word derived from al-Khwarizmi's name) is a step-by-step procedure that you follow in order to do something. The word 'algorithm' is associated today mostly with computers. A computer program is an algorithm.

The square root algorithm is something that used to be taught in schools before the invention of the calculator. It allows someone to calculate the square root of a number to as many decimals as desired (e.g. $\sqrt{43} \approx 6.557$) in a manner similar to long division. Simply follow the proper procedure, and you'll get the answer – even if you don't understand how it works.

The goal here is not only to teach the students how to calculate square roots, but, more importantly, to bring the students to an understanding of *why* the square root algorithm works.

Much of the content here is taken from Ernst Schuberth's book *Introduction of Advanced Arithmetical Operations in Class Seven at Waldorf Schools*. I believe that teaching the square root algorithm, as Schuberth suggests, meets the Class Seven perfectly – with their thinking awakening, a sense of wonder for number and a desire to do something really challenging.

See Appendix for a detailed lesson plan outline for teaching the square root algorithm (p. 206).

Word problems

Don't do algebraic word problems except, perhaps, for a couple during the algebra main lesson (see Class Seven Algebra, *Algebraic word problems*, p. 100).

Non-algebraic word problems. Do longer, more complex word problems than previous years, but be sure not to make them too difficult, thereby causing the students to get frustrated.

Measurement word problems
Example: Given 50 people and 21 litres of juice, how much juice (in mℓ) is there per person?

21 ℓ is 21,000 ml. Dividing 21,000 by 50, we get 420 ml per person.

Pay rate and speed problems
Review rate of pay and speed problems from Class Six.

In Class Seven, a good deal of time should be spent on rate of speed problems.

Give problems that help develop their intuitive sense of when to multiply and when to divide.

Example: Beth cycled from her house to school covering 5.4 km in 11 minutes. What was her average rate of speed in km per hour?

Since average speed is total kilometres divided by total hours, we need to think of the time in hours, which here is $\frac{11}{60}$ of an hour. The speed is therefore $5.4 \div (\frac{11}{60})$, which works out to $29\frac{5}{11}$ km/h.

Example: If a train leaves Inverness at 7:53 and averages 75 miles per hour, at what time does it arrive at Newcastle, 240 miles away?

The travel time is $240 \div 75 = 3.2$ hours, which is $3\frac{1}{5}$ hours. One-fifth of an hour ($\frac{1}{5} \times 60$) is 12 minutes, so the total travel time is 3 hours 12 minutes, which puts the train at Newcastle at 11:05.

Average speed equals total distance divided by total time.

$$\text{Average speed} = \frac{\text{total distance}}{\text{total time}}$$

Example: If Jill bikes 5 km to her friend's house at a rate of 20 km/h, and then returns at a rate of 10 km/h, then what was her average rate of speed for the whole trip?

This is tricky! Most people think that the average speed must be halfway between 10 and 20, which is 15 km/h. That's incorrect because she spent more time going 10 km/h than going 20 km/h; the average rate for the whole trip must be less than 15 km/h. To calculate the average speed we figure that it took her ¼ hour to get to her friend's house, and ½ hour to get back. Average rate of speed is *total distance* divided by *total time*, so we get 10 ÷ ¾, which is ⁴⁰⁄₃, or 13⅓ km/h.

Compound rate problems
These optional problems involve two moving objects. They are very challenging for the students, but very rewarding if taught well.

Example: Jane leaves home at 10:15 jogging at 8 km/h. If Sue leaves the same house at 10:35 on her bike at 18 km/h, when, and how far from home, will she catch up with Jane?

We start by figuring out how far ahead Jane is at the moment that Sue leaves. We get this distance by multiplying the rate (8 km/h) times the time (20 minutes, or ⅓ of an hour), giving us ⁸⁄₃, which is 2⅔. We now know that Jane is 2⅔ km ahead at the moment that Sue leaves.

The real key to solving this problem is realising that once Sue starts out, the gap between them (initially 2⅔ km) is closing in at a rate of 10 km/h (the difference of their speeds). So the real question becomes 'At a rate of 10 km/h, how long does it take this gap of 2⅔ km to close in?'. The answer to this is found by dividing 2⅔ by 10, giving a result of ⁴⁄₁₅ of an hour, which is 16 minutes. Therefore Sue catches up with Jane after 16 minutes, or at 10:51. To determine how far from home they meet, we calculate how far Sue went, which is done by multiplying her rate (18 km/h) times her elapsed time (⁴⁄₁₅ of an hour), resulting in an answer of 4.8 km from home.

Example: A slow train leaves Bigtown toward Smallville (545 km away) at 1:20 pm going 70 km/h. At 1:50 pm another (slower) train leaves Smallville heading for Bigtown at 50 km/h. At what time, and how far from Bigtown, do they pass one another?

We first calculate that when the second train leaves, the first train is 35 km along the way, so at that moment the trains are 510 km apart. They are approaching each other at a rate of 120 km/h (the sum of the two speeds). We then calculate that the initial gap of 510 km (which is closing at 120 km/h) completely closes (when the trains meet) in 510 ÷ 120 = 4¼ hours. The trains therefore meet at 6:05 pm. The second train has thus traveled 212.5 km (4¼ × 50), and they therefore meet 332.5 miles away from Bigtown.

Class Seven Arithmetic

Another very clever way to do this problem is by using ratios. Once the second train has started (and the trains are 510 km apart), it can be said that because the ratio of their speeds is 5 : 7, then the faster train must cover 7/12 of the 510 km, and the slower train must cover 5/12 of it. The rest follows fairly easily and yields the same answer that we found above.

Class Seven Algebra

Basic goals

Even though the subject matter may not be that different, the Waldorf approach to teaching algebra is quite different to that found in the mainstream. What makes the Waldorf approach to algebra so unique – and very powerful – is this Class Seven algebra main lesson. The crucial foundation of algebra (up to solving basic equations) is presented here in one main lesson and then no more algebra is done until Class Eight, thereby giving the children time to 'digest' the material before we build on it. In the mainstream, the basic foundation is introduced, and then there is usually no pause before introducing new topics.

Keep in mind that our goal is to have our students enter high school feeling confident about their ability to do algebra, even if this main lesson is basically all of the algebra that they ever see in middle school. *Do not cover too much material during this main lesson.* It is vital that *every* student completes this main lesson feeling very confident in their ability to do algebra, and that this foundation for future years of algebra study is solid.

With all this in mind, it is possible to accomplish your basic goals in a brief two-week main lesson. If time is especially short, I have even taught one three-week main lesson that combines algebra with geometry. If this is done, the 'heady' topic of algebra is nicely complemented with the drawing aspect of the geometry lesson (See Introduction, *Algebra*, p. 21).

The importance of form

It is crucial for students to develop good work habits. Since this is their first experience with algebra, form and organisation are actually more important than getting the problem correct. All the steps for the solution to each problem need to be written down neatly. Above all, the students must be able to follow their own work. Developing good habits now will really pay off in the years to come.

History of algebra

The roots of algebra go back to the Greeks, but it was the Arabs who developed the basis of algebra between 650 and 850 AD.

In the early 800s, the Abbasid Empire, perhaps the largest empire in the world at that time, was under the rule of the caliph (king) Al-Ma'mun (813–833) who was very interested in mathematics and astronomy. He collected many of the classic works from the Greeks, Jews, Hindus and other cultures from around the world. He then established his school, the House of Wisdom in Baghdad, and invited the greatest scholars in his empire to join it.

Muhammad ibn Musa al-Khwarizmi was one of the mathematicians who joined the House of Wisdom. He came from the city of Khiva in Amudarya, which was just south of the Aral Sea in what is now Uzbekistan.

Al-Khwarizmi wrote a book around 825 AD called (roughly translated) *The Science of*

Equations. Little, if anything, from the book was original. What made the book so great was that it was a collection of all the algebra known at that time (especially from Greece and India), and it was written in a way that people could fairly easily understand. It was translated into Latin 300 years later and it made a big impact on the mathematicians of Europe. Today, we call al-Khwarizmi the Father of Algebra.

The book had none of the algebra notation that we take for granted today. It was written out in words, in paragraph form, like any ordinary book. Problems and their step-by-step solutions were written in normal language. Most of our basic modern mathematical notation weren't developed until the 1400s and 1500s. For instance, writing '+' to mean adding two numbers was first used in Germany in 1489. Negative numbers were not even accepted (e.g. as solutions to equations) until the 1600s.

Algebra has developed into a powerful universal language that allows people to communicate complex mathematical thoughts in a simple and concise form.

Terminology

Equations have an equal sign and are solved.
Expressions have no equal sign and are *simplified* or *evaluated*, but not solved.
With the equation $5x - 6 = 2x + 12$
x is a *variable*.
There are four *terms*: $+5x, -6, +2x, +12$.
5 and 2 are both *coefficients*.
−6 and +12 are both *constants* because they are not attached to any variable.

Formulas

Review formulas from Class Six.
Review temperature conversion formulas from Class Six.

$$C = \frac{5}{9}(F - 32) \qquad F = \frac{9}{5}C + 32$$

Now problems can be given that result in negative numbers.

Example: 13°F is what in Celsius?
By putting 13 into F in the first formula, we get $C = \frac{5}{9}(13 - 32)$. This then becomes
$C = \frac{5}{9}(-19)$, or $C = \frac{5}{9} \times \frac{-19}{1}$ giving an answer of $-10\frac{5}{9}$°C, or approximately $-10\frac{1}{2}$°C.

Gauss's formula for summing a sequence of numbers

$$S = \frac{n}{2} \times (F+L) \quad \text{or} \quad S = n \times \frac{F+L}{2}$$

S is the total sum, n is the number of numbers, F is the first number, L is the last number.
Tell the story of Carl Friedrich Gauss (1777–1855). He was one of the greatest mathematicians ever. When Carl was 9 or 10 years old, his teacher (Herr Büttner, in a poor school in Braunschweig, Germany) gave the class the assignment to sum all the numbers from 1 to 100 (i.e. $1 + 2 + 3 + 4 + 5 + \ldots + 100$) in order to keep the students busy. Carl did the prob-

lem in his head almost immediately, wrote the answer on his slate, handed it in and then sat with his hands folded while the rest of the students worked diligently and the teacher looked at him scornfully. When the teacher finally went through the stack of slates, Carl was the only one to have the correct answer: 5,050. Carl realised that he could add the numbers in pairs: 1 + 100, and then 2 + 99, and then 3 + 98, etc. He saw that this sequence really consisted of 50 pairs of numbers, each pair adding to 101. He then simply multiplied 50 times 101 to get 5,050.

Gauss's formula (above) helps us to quickly calculate the sum of a sequence of numbers. (A sequence is a list of numbers that increase by the same amount each step.)

Example: Find the sum of the sequence 13, 17, 21 … 53.

We need to add 13 + 17 + 21 +…+ 53. Instead of adding up this list one number at a time, we use the formula, and get:

$$S = 11 \times \frac{13+53}{2} \rightarrow S = 11 \times \frac{66}{2} \rightarrow S = 11 \times 33$$

which is 363.

It is a bit tricky figuring out what n (the number of numbers in the sequence) is. We can do this most easily by writing down all the numbers in the list until we get to 53, and we then count to see that it is the 11th number in the sequence. We could also follow this reasoning: because the third number (21) is two steps of four above the first number (13). We can determine which position 53 is in the list by asking initially how many steps of four is 53 above 13. We see that 53 is 40 greater than 13, so we can say that 53 is ten steps of four greater than 13, which makes it the 11th number in the sequence, just as the third number (21) was two steps of four above 13.

Cost of renting a car

Example: Nifty Car Rental charges €35 per day and 4 cents per km. What would be the cost for a car that is rented for one week and driven a total of 550 km?

The formula here is: $C = 35 \times d + 0.04 \times k$

where C is the cost, d is the number days and k is the number of km.

Putting 7 into d, and 550 into k, we get:

$C = 35 \times 7 + 0.09 \times 550 \rightarrow C = 245 + 49.5$

giving us a final answer of €294.50.

Galileo's law of falling bodies
$$d = 4.9 \times t^2$$

Where d is the distance in metres, and t is the time in seconds.

The formula gives the distance travelled by a dropped object (assuming no air resistance).

Example: A rock is dropped out of a plane. How far does it fall after 10 seconds?

We put 10 into the formula, and get $d = 4.9 \times 10^2$. We must first square 10 (which is 100), then multiply by 4.9 to get a final answer of 490 metres.

Class Seven Algebra

Euclid's perfect number formula
$$P = (2^{(n-1)}) \times (2^n - 1)$$
Review perfect numbers from Class Five or Six.

n is a whole number. Beginning with $n = 2$, this formula produces all the even perfect numbers (P), with the condition that $(2^n - 1)$ must be a prime number.

Using Euclid's formula
Show that the formula generates 6 and 28 as the first two perfect numbers (which we knew from Class Six).

Using with $n = 2$, we get $(2^{(2-1)}) \times (2^2 - 1)$, which is $2^1 \times 3$, giving us an answer of 6.

Using $n = 3$, we get $(2^{(3-1)}) \times (2^3 - 1)$, which is $2^2 \times 7$, giving us an answer of 28.

Have the students determine the next few perfect numbers. They should be able to come up with the third, fourth and fifth perfect number fairly easily, but finding the sixth and seventh ones is somewhat challenging.

The difficulty is determining, for a given value of n, whether $(2^n - 1)$ is definitely prime, which would mean that it produces a perfect number. It is helpful to give the students the following hint:

It happens to be, that for all values of n less than 20, that the values of $(2^n - 1)$ that aren't prime have either 3, 5 or 7 as factors. The only exception to this is for $n = 11$ where $(2^n - 1) = 2{,}047$, which isn't prime. Its only factors are 23 and 89 (e.g. $23 \times 89 = 2{,}047$).

The first 7 perfect numbers* are: 6; 28; 496; 8,128; 33,550,336; 8,589,869,056; 137,438,691,328.

For more details, See Appendix, *Euclid's formula for perfect numbers*, p. 223.

Positive and negative numbers

A careful introduction
Be careful how negative numbers are introduced. Negative numbers should be introduced in terms of *pure number*.

Don't rely on pictures or a number line in order to help the students 'understand' negative numbers.

A number line, or even a picture of a mountain and valley below sea level, misguides the students into thinking that negative numbers can be represented physically. The essence of negative numbers, however, is freed from physical space.

See *Separation of form and number* in the introduction (p. 16) for the reason why an over-emphasis on such a picture isn't good.

Introduce the concept of negative numbers by asking, 'Is it possible to have less than nothing, or less than zero?' The answer is: yes. Money is one example.

---

* Note that '1' is not considered to be a perfect number for the same reason that it isn't considered to be a prime number: it is the basis of all numbers. '1' can't be said to have any 'genuine' factors because to get '1' we didn't have to multiply by anything.

Combining positive and negative numbers
A new perspective

18 − 3 is now looked at as combining positive 18 with negative 3, instead of subtracting 3 from 18. The result, of course, is 15 either way you look at it.

Compare combining positive and negative numbers to how a bank account works.
- A positive number means that we are making a deposit into our bank account.
- A negative number means that we are writing a cheque, and therefore subtracting from our bank account.

Example: Simplify 13 − 20 + 3 − 12 − 5

This is looked at as first depositing £13, then writing a check for £20, then making a deposit for £3, then writing a check for £12, and, lastly, writing another check for £5. The final balance is £21 overdrawn, which is −21.

Back-to-back signs.
Example: 8 − (−5) becomes 8 + (+5) (Taking away a negative is the same as adding a positive), which is 13.

Example: These are all the same: 8 − (+5); 8 + (−5); 8 − 5 (The answer is 3.)

Multiplication rules
Pos × Pos → Pos
Neg × Pos → Neg
Pos × Neg → Neg
Neg × Neg → Pos

Division rules
Pos ÷ Pos → Pos
Neg ÷ Pos → Neg
Pos ÷ Neg → Neg
Neg ÷ Neg → Pos

Do lots of practice with positive and negative numbers using all four processes.

Examples: Find each:
(a) −5 + 13 [8]
(b) −4 × 7 [−28]
(c) −12 − (−19) [7]
(d) −48 ÷ −6 [8]

Expressions

Simplifying expressions
Law of any order

You can change the order of the terms that are being added or subtracted. This is more commonly known as the commutative property of addition, such as:

Example: Simplify 4 − 3 − 11 + 12 − 14

We can group the negatives together and the positives together, by changing the order, to get: 4 + 12 − 3 − 11 − 14. Now we combine the two positives to get 16 and combine the three negatives to get − 28. So our expression is now: 16 − 28, which gives a final answer of −12.

Combining like terms
Example: Simplify $3k − 16f + 7 + 5k − 21$

We combine the two 'k' terms and the +7 and −21 to get the answer $8k − 16f − 14$.

Class Seven Algebra

Fractions and decimals as coefficients and constants

Example: Simplify $\frac{2}{5}x - \frac{1}{2} - \frac{1}{3}x + \frac{2}{3}$

Combining $\frac{2}{5}x$ and $-\frac{1}{3}x$ results in $\frac{1}{15}x$. And $-\frac{1}{2}$ combined with $\frac{2}{3}$ is $\frac{1}{6}$. Therefore, our answer is $\frac{1}{15}x + \frac{1}{6}$.

Use an arrow to show the progression of steps with equations when working from left to right.

Example: Solve $5x - 2 = 3x + 8$

It is best to show the work so that the steps are under one another. But if it is necessary to work from left to right, then an arrow can be used to show the progression from one step to another:

$5x - 2 = 3x + 8 \rightarrow 5x - 3x = 8 + 2 \rightarrow 2x = 10 \rightarrow x = 5$

Do not connect the steps with more equal signs because it is harder to read.

Equations

An equation is a puzzle

The goal is to find a value (or values) that we can put into the equation in order to make the equation work, or balance. If we plug the solution into the equation, then both sides of the equation will have the same value, thereby showing that the solution works.

An introductory puzzle

The following puzzle is a nice way to introduce the idea of an equation.

We use a scale to represent the equation $3x + 9 = 5x + 2$. First, we place 9 equal weights and 3 bags on the left side of the scale, where each bag is hiding the solution (3½ weights) inside it. We also place 2 weights and 5 bags (with each bag again hiding 3½ weights) on the right side of the scale. The scale should balance. Each bag represents the variable (or unknown). The students should be told that all the bags have the same number of weights inside them and that the goal is to solve the puzzle: How many weights are in each bag? Soon the students should come to realise that they can remove two weights from each side of the scale, and that they can remove three bags from each side. The scale remains balanced with 2 bags on one side and 7 weights on the other. They can then figure out that each bag must contain half of 7, or 3½ weights. Make sure that all the students really understand each step that was done in order to solve the puzzle. Review it thoroughly the next day, and then show the equivalent puzzle being solved as an equation, like this:

$$\begin{array}{rcl} 3x + 9 & = & 5x + 2 \\ -2 & = & -2 \\ \hline 3x + 7 & = & 5x \\ -3x & & -3x \\ \hline 7 & = & 2x \\ \div 2 & & \div 2 \\ 3\frac{1}{2} & = & x \end{array}$$

Solving by guess and check (trial and error)

The idea with this method is to guess what the solution is and then check to see if it works.

This method is obviously not very efficient, and would almost surely fail if the solution to the equation happened to be a fraction (e.g. $^{13}/_{21}$).

Example: Solve for x: $3x + 8 = 8x - 2$

We simply try plugging in different values for x, and see if it balances the equations. If we put in 5 for x, we get 23 on the left side of the equation, and 38 on the right side. Therefore, 5 is not a solution to the equation. After a while, and with a bit of luck, we finally guess the correct answer, which is $x = 2$. We see that it works, because when we put in 2 for x we get 14 on both sides of the equation.

The golden rule of equations

What is done to one side of the equation must also be done to the other.

It is crucial for the students to understand and remember this.

Solving equations by balancing

Solve simple equations by showing that the same is done to both sides, step-by-step (balancing).

This is the most important concept of the entire main lesson. Every student should come to a thorough understanding of the following example.

Example: Solve for x:
$3x - 23 - 7x = 11 + 8x + 2$

$$
\begin{aligned}
3x - 23 - 7x &= 11 + 8x + 2 \\
-4x - 23 &= 8x + 13 \\
+4x & +4x \\
\hline
-23 &= 12x + 13 \\
-13 & -13 \\
\hline
-36 &= 12x \\
\div 12 & \div 12 \\
\hline
-3 &= x
\end{aligned}
$$

Solve equations that have fractional solutions, such as:

Example: $7x + 4 = 10$ (Answer: $x = {}^6/_7$)

Work up to equations with fractional coefficients and constants. (This can be delayed until Class Eight.)

Example: $\frac{2}{3}x + \frac{7}{8} - x = \frac{3}{4} - \frac{3}{5}x$

$$\frac{2}{3}x + \frac{7}{8} - x = \frac{3}{4} - \frac{3}{5}x$$

$$\frac{2}{3}x + \frac{7}{8} - \frac{3}{3}x = \frac{3}{4} - \frac{3}{5}x$$

$$-\frac{1}{3}x + \frac{7}{8} = \frac{3}{4} - \frac{3}{5}x$$

$$+\frac{3}{5}x +\frac{3}{5}x$$

$$\frac{4}{15}x + \frac{7}{8} = \frac{3}{4}$$

(because $-\frac{1}{3}x + \frac{3}{5}x$ is $\frac{4}{15}x$)

$$-\frac{7}{8} -\frac{7}{8}$$

$$\frac{4}{15}x = -\frac{1}{8}$$

(because $\frac{3}{4} - \frac{7}{8}$ is $-\frac{1}{8}$)

$$\div \frac{4}{15} \div \frac{4}{15}$$

$$1x = -\frac{1}{8} \times \frac{15}{4}$$

Answer: $x = -\frac{15}{32}$

Class Seven Algebra

Algebraic word problems

Key ideas

Word problems are not a major theme of the main lesson. Don't overdo it! The idea is to show the students that algebra is a powerful tool that can be used to solve problems or puzzles. Be careful not to lose any of the students here. It may be fine to do no algebraic word problems during this main lesson block.

With an algebraic word problem, we must translate an English statement into an algebraic equation.

Mathematical thoughts can be expressed more clearly and concisely in algebra than in English.

Example: The English sentence: 'Two less than a number is ten more than two times that number', is translated into the equation: $x - 2 = 2x + 10$.

Algebra is a universal language. No matter where you are in the world, algebra is the language for communicating mathematical ideas.

Perhaps it is best to only do one very clear problem, which is then put into their main lesson book.

Example: 4 less than 5 times a number is 14 more than two times that same number. What is that number?

Remembering that 'is' means '=', we translate this perplexing sentence into the equation: $5x - 4 = 2x + 14$, which we can easily solve to get an answer of $x = 6$.

Class Seven Geometry

Area

Review *Area* from Class Six (p. 72).

Shear and stretch

This is a 'visual proof' of the formula for the area of a parallelogram and of a non-right triangle (see below).

There are three different variations of shear and stretch that Euclid proves as theorems in his book *The Elements*. They are:
- If two parallelograms lie between the same two parallel lines, and their bases have the same length, then their areas are equal (see drawing below).
- If two triangles lie between the same two parallel lines, and their bases have the same length, then their areas are equal (see drawing below).
- If a triangle and a parallelogram lie between the same two parallel lines and have the same length base, then the area of the triangle is half the area of the parallelogram (drawing not shown).

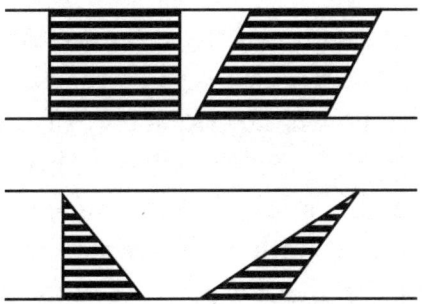

The central idea is to imagine slicing the parallelogram (or triangle) into infinitely many thin strips, and then sliding its top along the upper parallel line, thereby stretching it out. In this way, we can transform any parallelogram into a rectangle of equal area, or transform any non-right triangle into a right triangle.

In order to visualise the height, the students should imagine dropping a ball from the top. The height is how far the ball drops before hitting the ground. In this way, we can see that the heights remain the same. And since the height and base have not changed, the area of the figure does not change either as the figure is stretched.

Show that this also works if the parallel lines run vertically or at a slant (in preparation for Baravalle's proof of the Pythagorean Theorem in Class Eight).

Area of a parallelogram

We only need to know the length of the base and the height.

The area is the *base* times the *height*, which is: $a = b \times h$.

Example: Find the area of the parallelogram below.

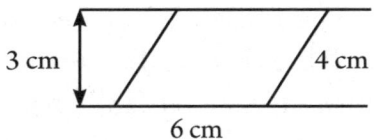

It is best for the students to picture the parallelogram 'righting' itself by having its top sliding over until it becomes a rectangle. We can see that the length of the side (4 cm) doesn't matter. The area is: $3 \times 6 = 18$ cm².

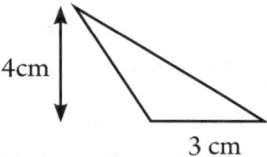

Area of a non-right triangle
We only need to know the length of the base and the height.

The area is half the base times height, which is: $a = \frac{1}{2} b \times h$.

Example: Find the area of the triangle below.

Again, we picture the apex of the triangle sliding parallel to the base until it becomes a right triangle, then we can see that the area is equal to: $\frac{1}{2} \times 3 \times 4 = 6$ cm².

Geometric drawing
Review Class Six, *Geometric drawing* (p. 61).

More than just pretty pictures
In Class Six, the geometry main lesson allows the students to dive into the artistic realm with their geometric drawings. I believe that the emphasis with Class Seven geometry should be less on the artistic and more on accuracy and thought content. The material presented should be a good balance between the thinking realm and the artistic. This main lesson is best done toward the end of the year.

Triangle constructions (optional)
The instructions given here for each drawing are intended for the teacher only. Mostly, the students should learn to do each drawing by watching the teacher do it on the board.

SSS (side-side-side)
Constructing a triangle given three line segments.

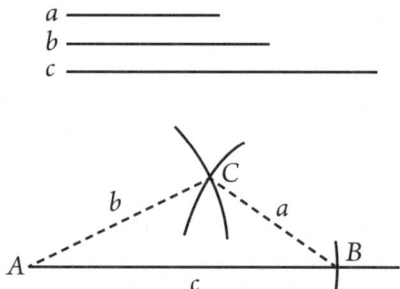

Instructions (for the teacher only): We are given three line segments (a, b, c), and our objective is to construct a triangle that has its sides equal to the length of these three segments. Start by drawing a horizontal line segment that is somewhat longer than segment c. Using a compass, copy the length of c onto this line segment (see Class Six Geometry, *Copying a line segment*, p. 62). This is now the base of our triangle.

Set the width of the compass equal to the length of segment a, and by placing the compass needle on the right end of the base of the triangle (point b), draw a short arc close to where the apex of the triangle will end up. Now set the width of the compass equal to the length of segment b, place the compass needle on the left end of the base of the triangle (point *a*), and draw an arc that passes through the arc previously drawn. These two arcs pass through the third point (the apex, or point *c*) of the triangle. Check, by using your compass, to see if the three sides of the triangle *abc* are indeed equal in length to the original three given line segments.

Note: This construction will not work if the longest given line segment is equal to, or longer than, the sum of the other two given line segments.

SAS (side-angle-side)
Constructing a triangle given two sides and an in-between angle.

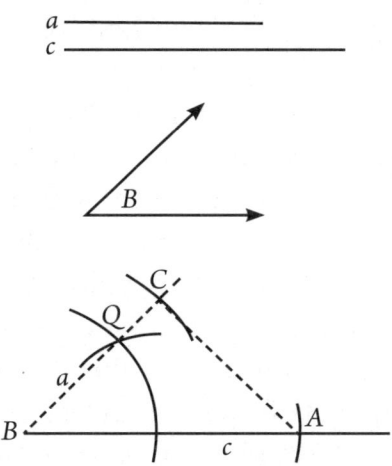

Instructions (*for the teacher only*): We are given two line segments (*a* and *c*) and an angle (*B*), and our objective is to construct a triangle that has two of its sides equal in length to these two given sides, and that has the angle that is in-between these two sides equal to the given angle. Start by drawing a horizontal line segment that is somewhat longer than segment *c*. Using a compass, copy the length of *c* onto this line segment. This is now the base of our triangle.

Now copy angle *B* so that its vertex falls on the left side of the base of the triangle. In the drawing here, this is shown as the two arcs intersecting at point *Q*. (See Class Six Geometry, *Copying an angle*, p. 62.) Draw a line segment from point B through and beyond point *Q*, making sure that it is longer than the line segment *a* (the original given line segment). Now copy line segment *a* onto the line segment *BQ*, so that the length from *B* to *C* is equal to the given line segment *a*. Lastly, draw a line connecting points *A* and *C*. Triangle *ABC* is the desired triangle.

Note: This construction will work for any angle and any two line segments.

ASA (angle-side-angle)
Constructing a triangle given two angles and an in-between side.

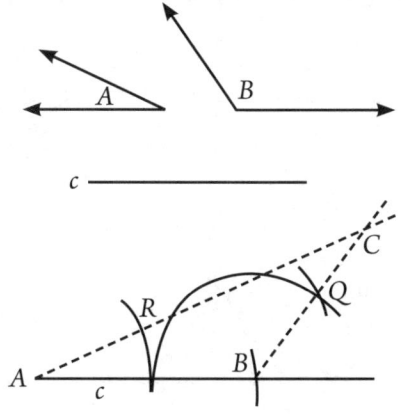

Class Seven Geometry

Instructions (for the teacher only): We are given one line segment (*c*) and two angles (*A* and *B*). Our objective is to construct a triangle that has a side equal in length to the given side (*c*), and that has the two angles that are adjacent to that side and equal to the two given angles (*A* and *B*). This construction is very similar to the *SAS* construction done above. Start by using the same steps given with the *SAS* construction to draw side *c* with angle *A* constructed onto its left end.

Then copy the second angle (*B*) onto the other end of side *c*. The drawing here shows that points *R* and *Q* are used to copy angles *A* and *B* to the triangle. We then extend the lines *AR* and *BQ* until they intersect at point *C*, which is the third point of the triangle. We finish by drawing a line that connects points *A* and *C*, and then a line that connects points *B* and *C*. Triangle *ABC* is the desired triangle.

Note: This drawing will not work if the two angles combine to 180° or more.

SSA (side-side-angle)

Constructing a triangle given two sides and a non-in-between angle.

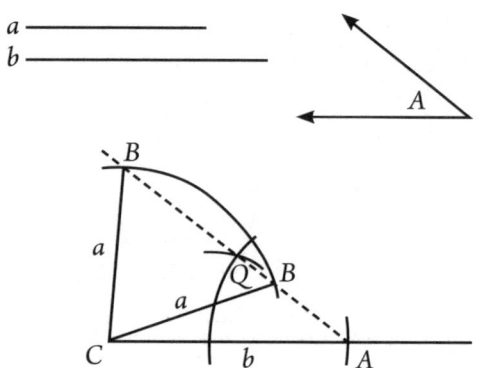

Instructions (for the teacher only): As with the *SAS* construction, we are given two sides and an angle. This drawing is, however, much more complicated. Of the two given line segments, one (*b*) is intended to be adjacent to the triangle's given angle (*A*), and the other line segment (*a*) is then attached to the other end of side *b*. Since the angle in-between these two sides is not given, we can imagine that there is a hinge between sides *a* and *b* that swings open or closed until it finds the proper moment when the desired triangle is found.

The actual construction is not very complicated. As with the *SAS* construction, we simply copy line segment *b* onto the base of the triangle (with endpoints *A* and *C*), and then copy angle *A* (by finding point *Q*) so that angle *A* lies on the right side of side *b*. Now extend *AQ* well beyond *Q*. Then set the compass to the length of given segment *a*, and by placing the compass needle at point *C*, draw an arc. Depending on the sizes of the given angle and sides, this arc may end up crossing the extended line *AQ* in one or two places, or not at all. In the drawing shown, the arc crosses line *AQ* in two places. This means that for this drawing there are two possible shapes for the desired triangle *ABC*, since *B* could be in either of two places (as shown in the drawing).

Note: In general, there are 6 possibilities for this *SSA* construction, depending on the sizes of the two sides and the given angle:

1. The angle is acute, and side *a* (the 'swinging' side) is shorter than side *b* and crosses the line *AQ* in two places. This results in two

possible triangles as the solution. (This case is shown in the above drawing.)

2. The angle is acute, and side *a* is shorter than side *b* but barely reaches the line *AQ*, thereby forming a right angle. The result is one right triangle as a solution.
3. The angle is acute, and side *a* is shorter than side *b*, and is not long enough to reach line *AQ*. The result is an impossible triangle; there is no solution.
4. The angle is acute, and side *a* is longer than side *b*, therefore crossing line *AQ* in just one place, and resulting in one solution.
5. The angle is either right or obtuse, and side *a* is longer than side *b*. This results in exactly one solution.
6. The angle is either right or obtuse, and side *a* is shorter than side *b*. This triangle is impossible because side *a* cannot reach the line *AQ*; there is no solution.

AAS (angle-angle-side) (optional)
A triangle given two angles and a non-in-between side.

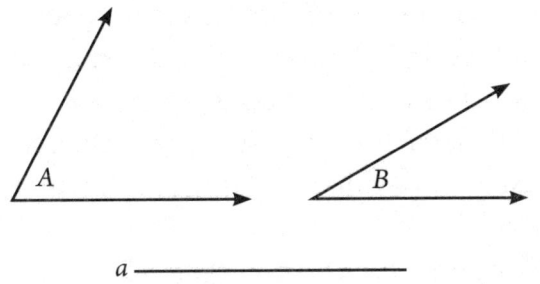

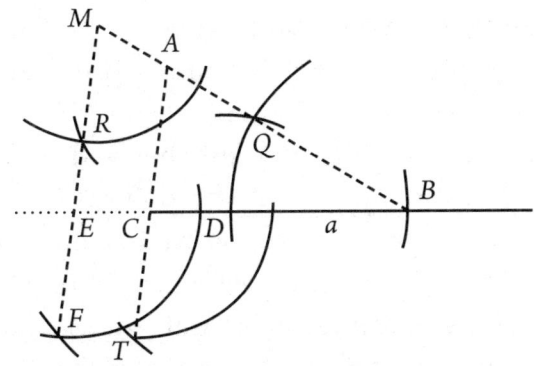

Instructions (for the teacher only): This is the most complicated construction. We are given two of the three angles in a triangle and a side that is not in-between them. We start by copying line segment *a* to the base of the triangle, and angle *B* adjacent to it, as we did with the *SAS* construction. We then label the endpoints of this base as *C* and *B*.

Next, we extend the other side of angle *B* (in the drawing, this is segment *BQ*) well beyond *Q* and label its (arbitrary) endpoint as point *M*. Then, we copy angle *A* to point *M* (by finding point *R*).

We now need to construct the third side of the triangle, which passes through point *C* and is parallel to *MR*. We do this by first extending segments *BC* and *MR* to meet at point *E*. Now, copy angle *CEF* to *DCT*. (We could have instead copied angle *CEM* to angle *BCA*.) We have now located point *A* and have therefore determined the third side (*AC*) of the desired triangle *ABC*.

Euclidean constructions – the Greek 'geometric game' (optional)

The three rules of the game

1. A straightedge can only be used to draw a line through two chosen points.
2. A compass can only be used to draw a circle (or a part of a circle) with a chosen point as its centre and a determined distance (the width of the compass) as its radius.
3. Other than a compass and straightedge, no other tools (e.g. a ruler, a protractor, drawing triangle, etc.) may be used.

Why compass and straightedge only? According to the Greeks, all geometric constructions were to be done using only two tools: a compass and a straightedge (without any marks for the purpose of measurement). Marked rulers, protractors and right-angled drawing triangles were not allowed. For the Greeks, this was a challenging mental game. The objective was to come up with theoretically perfect methods to do certain constructions using only these two tools. Some constructions turn out to be very simple, such as bisecting an angle, or putting a hexagon in a circle. Some constructions were fairly complicated, such as constructing a pentagon, or constructing a square that is equal in area to a given polygon. Some construction puzzles were never solved by the Greeks, such as the construction of a 7-gon, the construction of a 17-gon and the trisection of an angle. Some two thousand years later, a few of the solutions (e.g. the 17-gon) were discovered, but most were proved to be impossible (e.g. the 7-gon, and the trisection of an angle).

Julia Diggins' book, *String, Straightedge and Shadow*, gives a great, readable summary of the history and thinking of Greek geometry.

Various methods for doing constructions (optional)

There are four methods for doing constructions:

1. *Euclidean constructions with compass and straightedge.* These are the theoretically exact, Euclid-approved constructions (i.e. the 'game' described above) that are done in Class Six and Seven. The students should come to an understanding that *in practice* no construction can be absolutely perfect. A perfect square, for instance, has four sides that are *exactly* equal, and its angles are all *exactly* 90°. Nobody can construct a *perfect* square. On the other hand, *in theory*, we can imagine in our minds a construction that is absolutely perfect.

2. *Measurement constructions.* These constructions allow the use of a protractor, a drawing triangle or a ruler (as opposed to just a straightedge), and can be, *in practice*, quite accurate, but because you can never measure anything with *perfect* accuracy, they are not *theoretically perfect*, and therefore would have been frowned upon by Euclid.

    Example: Most people construct a square using a drawing triangle (or protractor) and a ruler.

3. *The guess and check method.* Here we use a compass (or perhaps something else) as a tool for *guessing* how big a length should be,

see how much error results and then adjust the compass and redo the construction. We keep guessing, checking and adjusting until we get satisfactory results. This method is not theoretically perfect (and not Euclid-approved), but can be in practice as close to perfect as we would like. Any regular polygon can be done quite accurately and quickly this way.

Example: To construct a 15-gon inside a circle, we first guess what the length of a side of the 15-gon will be, and set the compass width equal to that. Mark a point on the circle, place the compass needle on that point and then make a cross on the circle. We now have two of the 15 required points on the circle. Using that same compass width, step around the circle marking one point at a time. If the results are good, then the 15th step should come out right at the original point on the circle. If the results aren't satisfactory, then simply adjust the compass slightly and try it again. Usually the third guess produces very accurate results.

4. *Approximate constructions*. These constructions are done mostly for Euclidean impossible constructions, and are useful because they are a specific method that can, in practice, quickly produce very accurate constructions. They are not theoretically perfect, but they have little error.

Example: Many different approximate constructions are known for cases that are impossible by Euclidean means. One such case is the construction of a regular 7-gon inside a given circle, which uses the fact that the length of the side of the 7-gon (*a* in the below left figure) is *almost* equal to the length of the inscribed hexagon's short radius (*b* in the right figure below). This has, in theory, only 0.2% error!

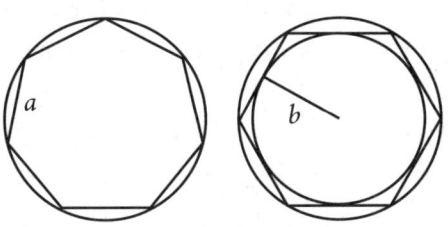

Geometric division

This is a good way to practise some of the skills learned in Class Six, and in the process some very beautiful drawings can be created.

We can best do geometric division with a polygon that has a large number of sides (*n*), where *n* is not a prime number. 12-gons, 15-gons, 20-gons and 24-gons all produce good results.

Geometric division of a 12-gon (dodecagon)
Construction: Start by drawing 6 circles and then mark the 12 points of the 12-gon around each circle (see Class Six Geometry, *Constructing a dodecagon*, p. 67). With the first circle, draw lines that connect consecutive points. This is division by 1, since each step moves one point over. In the next circle (division by 2), draw lines that connect every other point, which produces (look carefully!) two overlapping hexagons.

In the next circle, draw lines that connect every third point. This is division by 3, and it produces three squares. In the next circle (division by 4), we connect every fourth point, which results in four triangles.

In the next circle (division by 5), we get a 12-pointed star. Here, we end up going around the circle completely 5 times before we finally return to the point where we started. To prove this to yourself, place your finger on the topmost point of the star (labelled '÷5'), and then trace with your finger following along the lines until you get back to where you started. Finally, division by 6 produces just six diagonals of the circle. For an added challenge, ask the class what happens if we divide by 7, 8, 9, 10 and 11.

The drawings are the same! Division by 7 is the same as division by 5; division by 8 is the same as division by 4, etc.

Geometric division of a 15-gon
Construction: Start by drawing 6 circles of equal size, and then mark off the 15 points around each circle by using the guess and check method as described above. Then draw the different forms resulting from each division by following the same general procedure as outlined above in *Geometric division of a 12-gon*.

Notice that division by 2, by 4 and by 7 all produce different 15-pointed stars.

The surprise with this construction is that a 15-gon is geometrically divisible by 6 (producing 3 pentagrams), even though the number 15 is not evenly divisible by 6. This is because 6 and 15 have a common factor of 3.

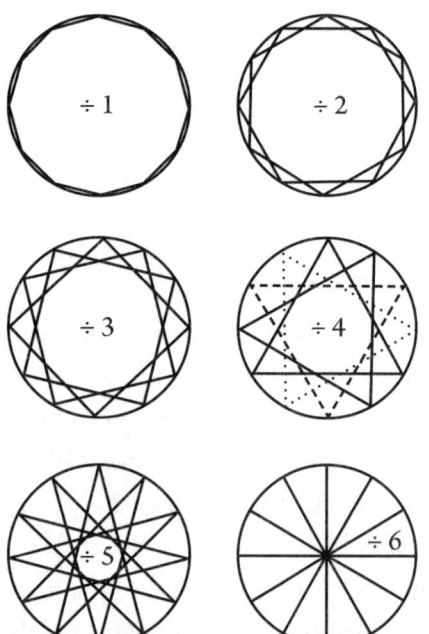

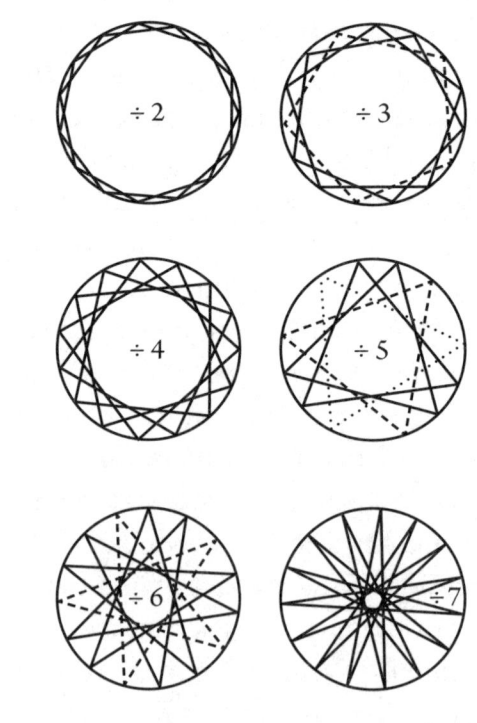

108

A Teacher's Source Book for Mathematics in Classes 6 to 8

Star patterns with geometric division

Looking at the drawings in the Appendix, p. 202, we can see that the top drawing of each column is a certain geometric division of the 12-gon. The three star patterns, which are drawn under each one, result from taking the top drawing and then carefully erasing parts of the lines.

The pentagon and the golden ratio (or golden section)

Constructing the pentagon
(with nested pentagons and pentagrams)

Method 1
Draw a diameter of the circle, and then find the midpoint, Y, of the radius. Draw the perpendicular bisector of the diameter, which intersects the circle at point A. Placing the needle of the compass at Y, draw an arc through A to point Z on the diameter. The distance from A to Z is precisely the length of the sides of the desired pentagon. Place the needle of the compass at A, and draw an arc through Z that intersects the circle at points B and E. Points A, B and E are three of the points of the pentagon. Now, keeping the compass at the same width, place the needle at B and draw an arc that crosses the circle at C. Similarly, place the needle at E, and draw an arc that crosses the circle at D. The desired pentagon has points A, B, C, D, E equally spread out on the circle. Use a compass to check that the five sides have equal length.

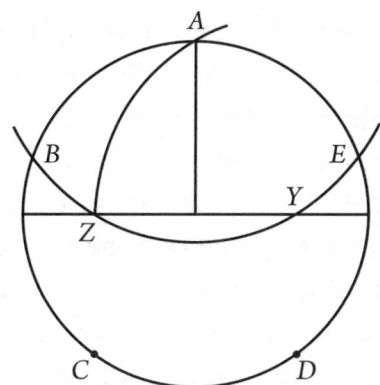

Method 2
Draw horizontal and vertical diametres of the circle. Draw two half-sized circles along the diameter of the original circle. Draw line AX so that it intersects one of the half-sized circles at points B and C. Place the compass needle at point A and draw an arc using AB as the radius, which locates points 3 and 4 on the original circle. Now draw a second arc using AC as the radius (keeping the needle on point A), which locates points 2 and 5 on the original circle. The desired pentagon has points 1, 2, 3, 4, 5 equally spread out on the circle. Use a compass to check that the five sides have equal length.

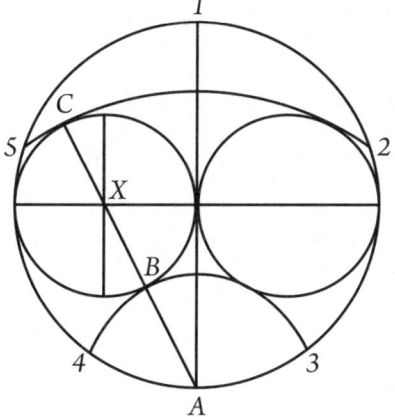

Class Seven Geometry

Places where the pentagon appears

- *A human being.* A person's head, hands and feet form the five points of a pentagon.
- *An apple.* If you cut an apple horizontally such that the knife cuts through the 'equator' of the apple, then the core is seen as a pentagon.
- *Flowers.* Several flowers have five petals.
- *Sea life.* Starfish and sea urchins have five limbs.
- *A paper knot.* If a half-hitch (a simple knot) is tied in a rope, then a pentagon is formed. This can be seen most clearly by taking a strip of ordinary paper (perhaps 2 cm by 22 cm), and carefully tying a simple half hitch in it and flattening it out. A pentagon, with a pentagram inside it, can then be seen if it is held up to a light.

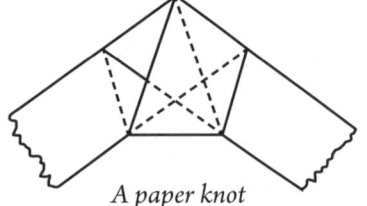
A paper knot

The geometrical properties *of the nested pentagon*

Of all the triangles to be found in this drawing, there are only two shapes. Every triangle is either similar to the tall isosceles triangle, or similar to the wide (obtuse-angled) isosceles triangle.

Point out similar rhombuses, and trapeziums.*

Each angle of the pentagon is trisected (divided into three equal angles) by the pentagram that sits inside it.

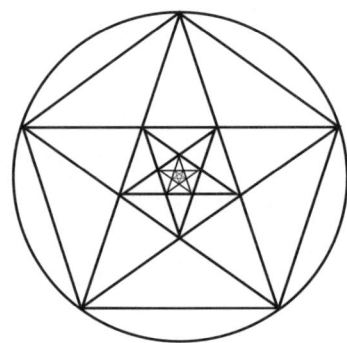

Question: Given that the angle in the pentagon is trisected, what are all the angles inside each of the two types of isosceles triangles?

There are five overlapping tall isosceles triangles inside the largest pentagon. Given that the angle of the pentagon is trisected, we can see that the base angle of one of these triangles is bisected by the apex of another one of these triangles. Therefore the base angle is twice the apex angle. By using the fact that the angles

---

* A rhombus is a diamond – a quadrilateral with four sides of equal length. A trapezium (or trapezoid) is a quadrilateral with at least two parallel sides.

inside a triangle add to 180°, and setting the apex angle to X, and the base angle to $2X$, we get: $X + 2X + 2X = 180$. Solving this gives us $X = 36°$, and that the base angles ($2X$) are 72°. It follows that the wide isosceles triangle has its base angles equal to 36° and its apex angle is 108°. Notice that this also shows that the angle inside a regular pentagon is 108°.

The golden ratio ϕ

Look at the drawing of the nested pentagons and pentagrams above. There are many line segments of differing lengths within this drawing. Carefully copy all line segments of different length so that they lie above one another in order of longest to shortest (see drawing below). There are two amazing properties that can be stated regarding these line segments:

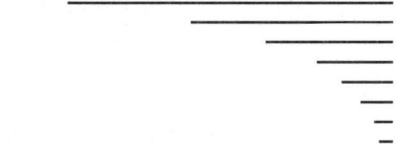

1. The length of any line segment is equal to the sum of the lengths of the previous two shorter segments.
2. Each line segment is approximately 61.8% longer than the previous one. Alternatively, we can say that each line is about 1.618 times as big as the previous one. This number (approximately 1.618) is known as the golden ratio, or ϕ.

Mathematically, we say that the ratio of the lengths of the diagonal to the side of a pentagon is ϕ:1.

ϕ (pronounced 'phi' rhyming with 'my') is, like π, an irrational number. Expressed as a decimal, it never repeats or ends, and is approximately equal to 1.61803398874989485...

Amazingly, if we square this number (with its infinitely many decimal digits) we get the exact same number, but starting instead with a 2 (i.e. **2**.618033...). And if we take the reciprocal (i.e. divide it into 1), then we get the exact same number, but starting with a 0 (i.e. **0**.618033...).

The successive bones in a human hand are approximately in a ratio of ϕ:1.

The Fibonacci sequence

1, 1, 2, 3, 5, 8, 13, 21, 34, 55, 89, 144, 233...

In 1225, Leonardo de Pisa (best known as Fibonacci) came up with his famous sequence.

To get the sequence, you start with two 1's, and then each term is simply the sum of the previous two terms.

There are many amazing properties associated with this sequence. One surprising property is that the further you move along the sequence, the closer the ratio (e.g. in whole number form) gets to ϕ (approximately 1.618033). For example, 233 ÷ 144 ≈ 1.618056. Furthermore, the same thing happens even if you modify the sequence by starting with two different numbers. For example, start with 4 and 7. Once again, the further you go, the closer the ratio gets to ϕ. Try it!

The golden rectangle

One method for constructing a golden rectangle is to use the length of the side of a pentagon as the rectangle's height, and to use the length of that same pentagon's diagonal as the rectangle's base.

With the golden rectangle, the ratio of the length to the width is $\phi:1$ (which is also the ratio of the diagonal to the side of a pentagon).

This is the only shape for a rectangle where you can cut off a square (*ABCD*), and the remaining smaller rectangle (*BEFC*) will be similar to the original rectangle (*AEFD*).

An alternate method is to construct a square. Mark the corners clockwise from top left *A, B, C, D*. Extend lines *AB*, and *DC* to the right. Using a compass, construct the midpoint (*X*) of *AB*, and the midpoint (*Y*) of *DC*. Place the needle at *X*, and draw an arc so that it passes through point *C* and intersects the extended part of the line *AB* to the right of *B* at point *E*. Draw another arc with the needle at y, so that it passes through point *B* and intersects the extended part of the line *DC* to the right of *C* at point *F*. *AEFD* is a golden rectangle, and so is *BEFC*.

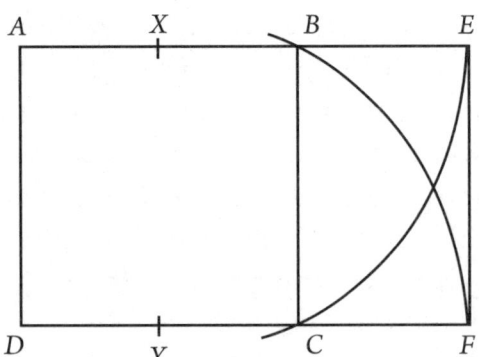

Historical importance

The golden rectangle was considered the most aesthetically pleasing proportions for a rectangle.

The Parthenon was built using golden rectangles.

If we take a golden rectangle, split it along its diagonal and join the two resulting right triangles along their middle-sized sides, then we get the shape of the isosceles triangle that was used to build the Great Pyramid (see drawing below).

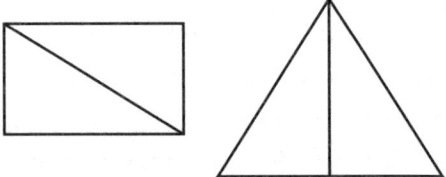

The rectangle of whirling squares (the golden spiral)

Construct a large golden rectangle and then draw a line that divides the rectangle into a square and a smaller golden rectangle. Draw a diagonal across the original (larger) rectangle, and a diagonal across the smaller rectangle, so that they intersect. Draw a line dividing the smaller rectangle into a square and another golden rectangle, and divide that rectangle, and every succeeding one in the same manner, so that the squares spiral in toward the intersection of the two diagonals. The students should draw the spiral freehand.

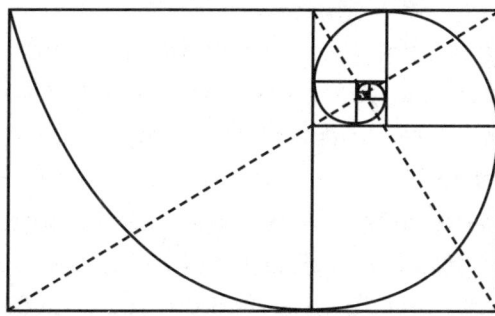

Angle theorems and proofs

Review these three ideas from Class Six (without giving proofs).
- The sum of angles forming a straight line equals 180°.
- The sum of angles forming a full rotation equals 360°.
- Vertical angles are congruent.

The golden triangle and its spiral (optional)
Start with the tall acute triangle that appears in the nested pentagon drawing, as described above. (Alternatively, you can construct the same triangle by using a protractor to make the apex angle equal to 36° and the two base angles equal to 72°.) Draw a line that bisects the base angle on the right side, thereby creating two smaller triangles, one of which is similar to the original. As was done with the *rectangle of whirling squares*, keep dividing the smaller triangle into two triangles, so that the smaller triangles spiral in toward a point.

Theorems arising from two parallel lines cut by a transversal
A *transversal* is a line that crosses two parallel lines.

Corresponding angles are congruent (equal)
Corresponding angles are two angles in similar locations at different intersections, when two parallel lines are cut by a transversal. Angles *A* and *D* are corresponding angles in the drawing below – they are both at the northeast corner of their intersections.

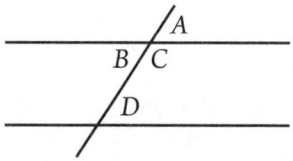

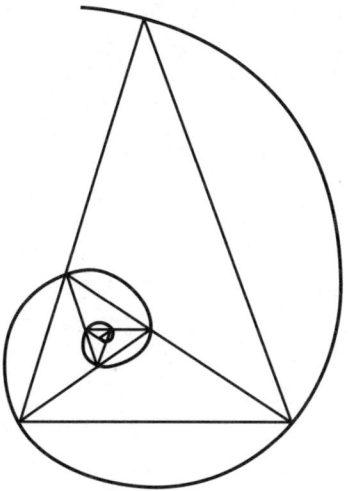

Proof: Of the two parallel lines, imagine that the bottom one moves toward the top one, while keeping the two lines parallel. This pushes angle *D* upward, but does not change it. We keep moving the bottom line upward until it coincides with the top line. At that moment, angle *D* coincides with angle *A*, so we can see that angles *D* and *A* are congruent.

Class Seven Geometry

Alternate interior angles are congruent
B and D are alternate interior angles in the above drawing.

Proof (this should only be given orally to the students): We know that angles A and D are congruent because they are corresponding angles, and we know that angles A and B are congruent because they are vertical angles. And because angles B and D are both congruent to angle A, they must be congruent to each other.

Same-side interior angles add to 180°
C and D are same-side interior angles in the above drawing.

Proof (this should only be given orally to the students): We know that angles A and C are supplementary, because they form a straight line. Angles A and D are corresponding angles and therefore congruent. So instead of saying that A and C are supplementary, we can replace A with D and therefore say that D and C are supplementary.

The angles in a triangle add to 180°
Cutting out angles
Construct any random triangle, and then use a coloured pencil to shade in inside the vertex of each angle. Cut out the three angles with scissors. Place the shaded-in angles point to point in order to see that they form a straight line (180°). While this is not a 'mathematically exact' proof, it is a wonderful way to give the students a sense of truth about the fact that the angles in a triangle add to 180°.

The half-wheel theorem
Imagine that the base of the triangle moves upward. As it moves upward, the two base angles are pushed upward, but remain unchanged in size (degree measure). At the moment that the triangle has become infinitely small, we can see that the three angles of the triangles form a straight line (180°). This sequence can be made clearer by colouring in the angles rather than labelling them as A, B, C. In the above drawing, all the angles labeled A could be green, the B angles could be red and the C angles could be blue.

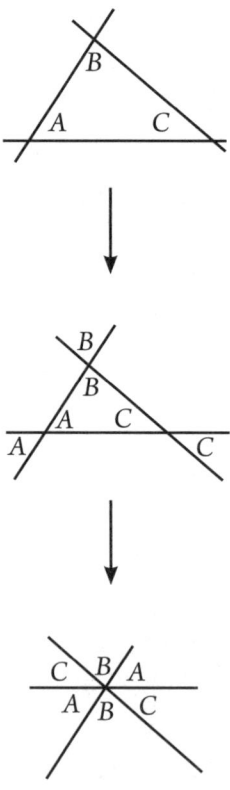

The angles in polygons other than triangles (optional)

The angles in any quadrilateral add to 360°

To prove this, simply demonstrate that any quadrilateral can be divided into two triangles. Since the number of degrees in one triangle is 180°, then a quadrilateral must have 2 × 180°, which is 360°.

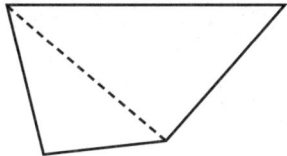

The angles in any pentagon add to 540°

To prove this, simply demonstrate that any pentagon can be divided into three triangles Since the number of degrees in one triangle is 180°, then a pentagon must have 3 × 180°, which is 540°.

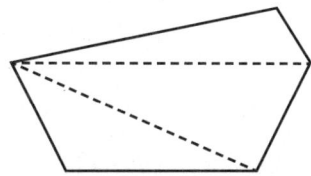

For any polygon

We simply need to figure out how many triangles (n) it can be divided into, and then multiply that number (n) times 180°

Example: Any octagon can be divided into 6 triangles, so the number of degrees in any octagon is: 6 × 180° = 1080°.

Angle puzzles (optional)

There are limitless possibilities for making puzzles with angles. Build up to problems like this (see drawing below):

Example: Fill in all the missing angles, given that the top and bottom lines are parallel, and $X = 60°$ and $Y = 110°$.

We use all that we know about two parallel lines and a transversal, supplementary angles and the fact that the angles in a triangle add to 180°. A key realisation is that Q and X are corresponding angles (and therefore equal), and so are angles Y and F.

$A = B = R = T = 120°$;
$C = Q = S = 60$;
$L = F = D = 110°$;
$E = G = M = P = 70°$;
$J = H = 50°$; $K = I = 130°$

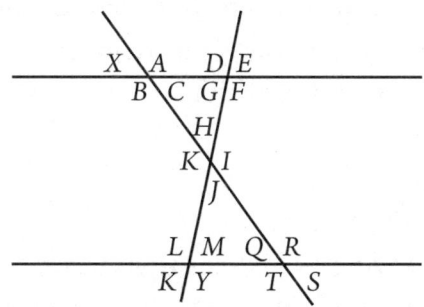

Theorem of Thales

Any triangle (or angle) inscribed in a semi-circle is a right triangle (or right angle).

Theorem of Morley (optional)
The six angle trisectors of any triangle meet to form an equilateral triangle.

(See Appendix, p. 203, for drawing.)

Since there is no general method for trisecting an angle, the students will need to use a protractor in order to do this construction.

This drawing is a wonderful example of how order can emerge from chaos.

Pythagorean Theorem

With any right triangle, the area of the square of the hypotenuse is equal to the sum of the areas of the squares of the other two sides.

Important: the emphasis in Class Seven is on the general concept of the theorem – the relationship between the areas of the squares – rather than using the theorem to find the length of a missing side.

Visual proofs
A cutout puzzle
With any non-isosceles right triangle (perhaps students work in groups, and each group draws a slightly different right triangle), draw a square coming off each of the three sides. Extend two lines from the sides of the largest square so that they cut through the other two squares, in each case dividing the squares into a triangle and a trapezium. Draw a line perpendicular to the line that divided the second largest square, by starting at the intersection point on the edge of that square. The second largest square has now been cut into three pieces: two triangles and a quadrilateral having two right angles. Cut the 5 pieces (see drawing below) out of the two smaller squares. Place these 5 pieces in the large square so that they fit perfectly. This is a great geometric puzzle! Have the class do this *before* saying anything about the theorem, and then ask them what the drawing shows. It shows that the sum of the areas of the two smaller squares equals the area of the largest square.

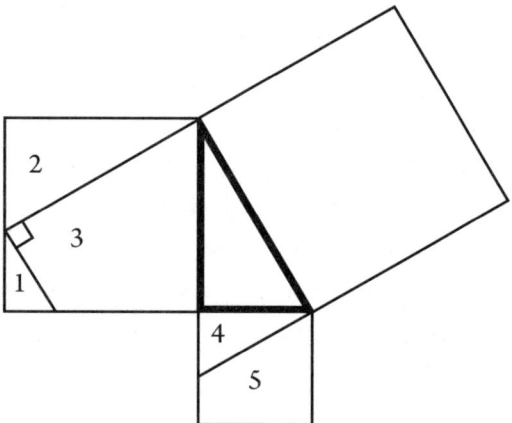

The case of the isosceles right triangle
With an isosceles right triangle, draw squares off each of the triangles. Draw two diagonals across the large square, and one diagonal across each of the smaller squares. We now see that there are nine equal-sized triangles in the drawing, and that the largest square therefore is composed of the same number of triangles (four) as the sum of the number of triangles found in the two smaller squares.

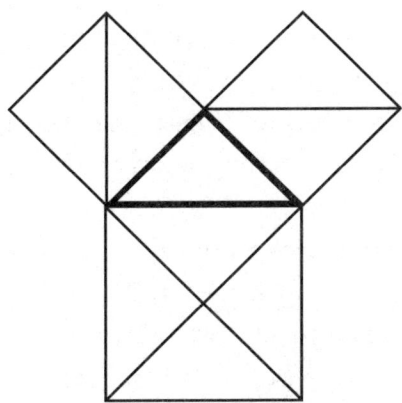

The isosceles right triangle

The case of the 3-4-5 triangle

Draw a 3 by 4 by 5 cm (or inches) right triangle with squares off each of the three sides of the triangle. Divide each square into a grid of one-cm squares The students can now easily count the number of square centimetres found inside each square, and therefore see for themselves that the area of the two smaller squares (9 and 16 square cm) adds up to the area of the largest square (25 square cm).

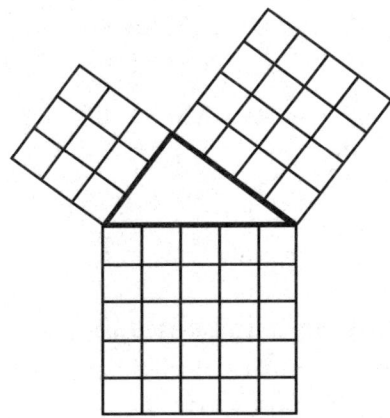

The 3-4-5 right triangle

This construction can be done for any right triangle where the three sides work out to be a Pythagorean triple (e.g. 5-12-13).

Pythagorean triples

This is optional; it can instead be covered in Class Eight).

Pythagorean triples are the three sides of a right triangle, where all three sides work out as whole numbers.

Example: If the two legs are 28 and 96, then we calculate the areas of the squares of these two sides to be 28^2 and 96^2, which is 784 and 9,216. According to the Pythagorean Theorem, the area of the third square (off the side of the hypotenuse), must be the sum of these two squares, 784 + 9,216, which is 10,000. The length the hypotenuse is therefore equal to $\sqrt{10,000}$, which is 100 (a whole number). Therefore, all three sides are whole numbers, and 28, 96 and 100 make a Pythagorean triple. This triple can be reduced (by dividing all three sides by 4) to the primitive triple 7, 24, 25.

Example: If the two legs of a right triangle are 2 and 3, then by using the Pythagorean Theorem, we see that the area of the square attached to the hypotenuse must be $2^2 + 3^2 = 13$. The length of the hypotenuse must therefore be $\sqrt{13}$, which is not a whole number. Therefore the three sides of this right triangle (2, 3, $\sqrt{13}$) do *not* constitute a Pythagorean triple.

Pythagoras' formula for creating Pythagorean triples
$x = 2n + 1$;
$y = 2n^2 + 2n$;
$z = 2n^2 + 2n + 1$

Choose any positive whole number value for n, put it into the above formulas and x, y and z will be a Pythagorean triple.

This formula only produces the triples that have two sides that are one apart (e.g. 5, 12, 13).

Example: Choosing $n = 5$ we get
$x = 2 \times 5 + 1 = 11$;
$y = 2 \times 5^2 + 2 \times 5 = 60$;
and $z = 2 \times 5^2 + 2 \times 5 + 1 = 61$.

Plato's formula for creating Pythagorean triples
$x = 2n$;
$y = n^2 - 1$;
$z = n^2 + 1$ (beginning with $n = 2$)

This formula only produces the triples that have two sides that are two apart (e.g. 8, 15, 17), and some of them are not reduced triples (e.g. 6, 8, 10).

Example: Choosing $n = 5$ we get
$x = 2 \times 5 = 10$;
$y = 5^2 - 1 = 24$;
and $z = 5^2 + 1 = 26$.

The Arabian formula for creating Pythagorean triples
$x = u^2 - v^2$;
$y = 2uv$;
$z = u^2 + v^2$

This is similar to what Euclid did.

This is a more sophisticated formula. By choosing any positive whole numbers for u and v, where u is greater than v, the above formulas will generate a Pythagorean triple. As opposed to the Pythagorean formula and Plato's formula, it generates all the Pythagorean triples.

In order to produce a reduced Pythagorean triple, you must choose u and v so that one is odd and one is even, and so that they are relatively prime (i.e. so that they don't have any common factor).

Example: Choosing $u = 7$, and $v = 4$, we get
$x = 7^2 - 4^2 = 33$;
$y = 2 \times 7 \times 4 = 56$;
and $z = 7^2 + 4^2 = 65$.

If a Pythagorean triple cannot be reduced (e.g. 6,8,10 reduces to 3,4,5) then we refer to it as primitive The following is a list of the primitive Pythagorean triples that have all three numbers less than 100:

3, 4, 5	11, 60, 61
5, 12, 13	16, 63, 65
8, 15, 17	33, 56, 65
7, 24, 25	48, 55, 73
20, 21, 29	13, 84, 85
12, 35, 37	36, 77, 85
9, 40, 41	39, 80, 89
28, 45, 53	65, 72, 97

Calculating missing sides of triangles
Given the lengths of two sides of a right triangle, find the length of the missing side.

Don't introduce the formula $c^2 = a^2 + b^2$ until Class Eight.

Give only a few simple examples. Much practise using the Pythagorean Theorem is done in Class 8.

Example: Find the length of the hypotenuse of a triangle that has legs of length 10 and 24 cm.

Using the Pythagorean Theorem, we can say that the areas of the squares off the two given sides are 100 (which is 10^2) square cm and 576 (which is 24^2) square cm. The Pythagorean Theorem says that the area off the hypotenuse must have an area equal to 100 + 576 = 676 square cm. It follows that the length of the square is $\sqrt{676}$, which we determine either by using the square root algorithm, or a bit of trial and error, giving us an answer of 26 cm.

Other topics

Perspective drawing is often done in the track classes, or as the 'artistic element' of another main lesson. See Baravalle's book: *Perspective Drawing*.

Islamic Art (optional) which often deals with geometric designs and symmetry.

Drawings showing *reflection* (optional).

Drawings showing *reducing/enlarging* (optional). (See Appendix, *Perspective reduction*, p. 204, for drawing.)

Drawings with *shadows* (optional) e.g. a circle often has an elliptical shadow. (See Stockmeyer, p. 63.)

Curves arising out of a network of lines (optional), e.g. string boards. (See Sheen's book, p. 47–51.)

Wilderness *navigating and orienteering* (optional) done on a camping/nature trip, put geometry into practice.

Class Eight Arithmetic

The year before upper school

What is covered in the Class Eight year may vary somewhat depending on whether the students will be attending a Waldorf upper school, or going elsewhere. At my school, we have a upper school and, for the most part, I go on the assumption that the students will be continuing on into our upper school. Most of our students who leave our school after Class Eight and go to another school end up doing fine in maths, even though they have had a different middle school maths curriculum. What about the topics covered in state schools (e.g. probability) that we haven't covered yet? It is my experience that solid basic maths skills, a healthy imagination and enthusiasm for learning more than compensate for this. It is best to avoid the temptation to sacrifice the real goals of a maths program in order to 'prepare' our students for what we think they must have before upper school. Also, avoid the temptation to fall back on what is familiar (e.g. lots of algebra), because it's easier to teach. They will get the algebra they need at whatever school they attend.

The order of topics

The order of the units in the workbook is as follows:
- Number bases
- Pythagorean theorem
- Mensuration
- Percents and growth
- Dimensional analysis and proportions
- Algebra
- Year–end review

Main lessons and priorities

I recommend that two maths main lessons be taught (each one with two independent topics):
- Number bases and loci
- Mensuration and stereometry

If there is only room in the main lesson schedule for one maths main lesson during the year, then number bases and mensuration are topics that could instead be done during the ongoing class, which leaves one maths main lesson consisting of stereometry and loci. This, of course, may result in some topic(s) needing to be left out of Class Eight altogether. If time is running short, and you must decide what to leave out, then it is recommended that it be number bases and/or loci (even though they are two of my most favourite topics). The rest of the units (Pythagorean Theorem, mensuration, percents and growth, dimensional analysis and proportions) are topics that students ought to have some exposure to before entering upper school.

Number bases

This unit gives students insights into our base-ten system while learning other 'counting' systems. The students journey back, in a manner of speaking, to their earlier years of school, and relearn how to count and do basic arithmetic, but in other bases. The real purpose of this unit is to stretch the students' thinking. In the end, they also get a general idea of how a computer stores information in its memory (see Class Eight Computers, p. 148).

This unit works well as half a main lesson block, at the beginning of the year, perhaps with the topic *loci* as the other half.

It is best to cover this unit at the beginning of the year, so that it comes before the computer unit and before the unit on the Pythagorean Theorem, which requires the use of the square root algorithm (which is part of the computer unit).

See Ulin's *Finding the Path* and Baravalle's *The Waldorf Approach to Arithmetic* for a detailed account of number bases.

Briefly cover the Babylonian, Egyptian and Roman number systems thereby giving a picture of the history of numbers. (See Ulin's book for details.)

Only spend a brief amount of time on expanded notation.

Example: $6472 \to 6 \times 10^3 + 4 \times 10^2 + 7 \times 10^1 + 2 \times 10^0$ (where 10^0 is equal to 1)*.

Only spend a brief amount of time on scientific notation.

Example: 2,384,000,000 in scientific notation is 2.384×10^9

Example: 0.0000451 in scientific notation is 4.51×10^{-5}

Note: A full treatment of negative exponents should be handled in Class Nine. Here, we only say that a negative exponent makes the decimal point move to the left, thereby making the number smaller.

Base-eight, octal

A good question to start with is: How would our number system be different if we only had 8 fingers?

What are the digits? A key realisation for the students to come to is that the octal system uses only the digits 0 through 7. The digits 8 and 9 would be completely unrecognisable by anyone familiar with only the octal system. (This is assuming that all the digits used in the octal system (0, 1, 2, 3, 4, 5, 6, 7) are digits used in our base-ten number system.)

---

* This odd fact (that $10^0 = 1$) isn't really explained fully until Class Nine. But in Class Eight, we could say the following: just as there is an invisible 1 in front of the x^2 in the expression $6 + x^2$, there is also an invisible 1 in front of 10^0. Now, the exponent always tells us how many of something we have. For example, 7^3 tells us that there are three 7s being multiplied by one another. Therefore 10^0 really means 1×10^0, and since the exponent says that we have zero 10s, we are left with just the (invisible) 1 in front. This is why 10^0 is 1. Similarly, it follows that anything to the zero is 1 (e.g. $13^0 = 1$).

Class Eight Arithmetic

Have the students count in octal. It is best if they come to the realisation on their own that they shouldn't use the digits 8 or 9.

A key example (it will probably take the class a while to really get this):

Bob (who uses base-ten) and Fred (who uses octal) are looking at a field of sheep. Draw dots on the board to represent the sheep. Then show how Bob counts by grouping in 10s, 100s, and 1,000s, etc., and Fred counts by grouping in 8s, 64s, and 512s, etc. Why 64? Because 64 is eight 8s, just like our 100 place is ten 10s. Similarly, Fred uses 512 because it is eight 64s, just like our 1,000 is ten 100s. A slightly different perspective is that 512 is 8^3, just like our 1,000 is 10^3.

Example: If Bob writes down 35 as the number of sheep, how would Fred write it?

Fred sees 4 groups of eight, and then there are 3 left over. The answer is then: 43.

Example: If Bob writes down 153 as the number of sheep, how would Fred write it?

Fred first sees 2 groups of 64. That leaves 25 sheep ($153 - 2 \times 64$) that are uncounted. From these 25 sheep, Fred sees 3 groups of eight with one left over. So Fred writes it as 231.

Notation. The number base of a given number is indicated with a subscript at the end of the number.

bin = base-two (binary)
oct = base-eight (octal)
five = base-five
dec = base-ten (decimal)
hex = base-sixteen (hexadecimal)

Example: Using the problem given above we can say that $35_{dec} = 43_{oct}$ and $153_{dec} = 231_{oct}$. The first one should be read as, 'Three-five decimal is equal to four-three octal'.

The place values with the octal system (see also Appendix *Place value table*, p. 245)

The right-most place is the 1s place.

The second place (from the right) is the 8s place.

The third place (from the right) is the 64s place (because $8^2 = 64$).

The fourth place (from the right) is the 512s place (because $8^3 = 512$).

The fifth place (from the right) is the 4,096s place (because $8^4 = 4,096$).

The six place (from the right) is the 32,768s place (because $8^5 = 32,768$).

In summary, the place values (from right to left) are: 1, 8, 64, 512, 4 096, 32 768, etc.

Conversion problems with octal

Build up to problems like the following.

Example: What is $26,573_{oct}$ in base-ten?

Be careful that the students don't just memorise some procedure. Before writing anything down for this problem, they should say to themselves, 'This number is three 1s, seven 8s, five 64s, six 512s, and two 4,096s.' Only after they say this to themselves should they write this as:

$2 \times 4096 + 6 \times 512 + 5 \times 64 + 7 \times 8 + 3 \times 1$
$= 11643_{dec}$

Example: What is $1,383_{dec}$ in octal?

Going from base-ten is more difficult. The question that we must ask ourselves is: 'How many of each octal place value can we take out of the given base-ten number (1,383)?' Of course, we are limited to a single digit of each place value. Another way of looking at it is to think that each octal place value is an empty box, and we need to fill in all the boxes with a single octal digit so that all these digits together form an octal number that is equal to the given base-ten number. Here are the empty boxes:

4096s' place	512s' place	64s' place	8s' place	1s' place

We first look to see what the largest octal place value is that goes into $1,383_{dec}$. 4,096 is too big, so it will be left empty. Therefore the 512s' place is the biggest that will fit into 1,383. It goes in 2 times. We therefore put a 2 in the 512s' place, and we get this:

	2			
4096s' place	512s' place	64s' place	8s' place	1s' place

We now have accounted for 2 × 512 = 1,024 out of the original number ($1,383_{dec}$). Subtracting this 1,024 from 1,383 gives us 359 that is still unaccounted for. So we ask, 'How many 64s can we get out of 359?' 64 goes into 359 5 times. So we put a 5 in the 64s' place, giving us, for the moment:

	2	5		
4096s' place	512s' place	64s' place	8s' place	1s' place

These five 64s account for another 320 out of the 359 that was remaining. Subtracting 320 from 359, tells us that we still have 39 that is unaccounted for. We then ask, 'How many 8s can we get out 39?' 8 goes into 39 4 times. So we write 4 into the 8s' place, giving us:

	2	5	4	
4096s' place	512s' place	64s' place	8s' place	1s' place

These four 8s account for another 32 out of the 39 that was left. Subtracting 32 from 39 tells us that we have 7 ones left over. So we write 7 into the 1s' place, and get:

	2	5	4	7
4096s' place	512s' place	64s' place	8s' place	1s' place

Our final answer is, therefore, $2,547_{oct}$, which is indeed equal to $1,383_{dec}$.

Base-five

This can be done in a similar fashion to the octal system, but covered more quickly.

What are the digits? The five digits in a base-five system are 0, 1, 2, 3, 4.

Counting. Have the students count in base-five.

The place values (from right to left) are 5^0, 5^1, 5^2, 5^3, 5^4, 5^5, etc., which is: 1, 5, 25, 125, 625, 3,125, etc.

Conversion problems
Do a few conversion problems with base-five.
Example: What is $2,243_{five}$ in base-ten?
Again, the students first need to say to themselves, 'This number is three 1s, four 5s, two 25s and two 125s'. Then they simply do the calculation: $2 \times 125 + 2 \times 25 + 4 \times 5 + 3 \times 1 = 323_{dec}$.

Example: What is 967_{dec} in base-five?
Again, going from base-ten is more difficult. Carefully look over the above conversion problem that converted $1,383_{dec}$ to octal. The question with this new problem that we must ask ourselves is, 'How many of each base-five place values can we take out of the given base-ten number (967)?' Of course, we are limited to a single digit of each place value. Another way of looking at it is to think that each base-five place value is an empty box, and we need to fill in all the boxes with a single base-five digit so that all these digits together form a base-five number that is equal to the given base-ten number (967). Here are the empty boxes:

3125s' place	625s' place	125s' place	25s' place	5s' place	1s' place

We first look to see what the largest base-five place value is that goes into 967. It is the 625s' place (since 3,125 is too big, its box shall be left empty). It goes in 1 time, so we put a 1 into the 625s' place (box), and then subtract that from 967, resulting in a remainder of 342. 125 goes into 342 2 times, so we put a 2 into the 125s' place, and subtract to get a remainder of 92. 25 goes into 92 3 times (so we put a 3 in the 25s' place) with a remainder of 17. 5 goes into 17 3 times, so a 3 goes into the 5s' place, which leaves us with a remainder of 2 to be put into the 1s' place. In the end we get this:

	1	2	3	3	2
3125s' place	625s' place	125s' place	25s' place	5s' place	1s' place

so our answer is $12,332_{five}$, which equals 967_{dec}.

Base-sixteen, hexadecimal
The hexadecimal number system is used frequently in computers as a shorthand way to represent a binary number (see *Binary numbers*, below).

What are the digits? Here we need a total of 16 digits, so we must add digits to our standard 10 digits. The hexadecimal digits that we will use are 0, 1, 2, 3, 4, 5, 6, 7, 8, 9, A, B, C, D, E, F. These new single digits represent the base-ten equivalents of 10, 11, 12, 13, 14, 15.

The place values (from right to left) for hexadecimal are 16^0, 16^1, 16^2, 16^3, 16^4, etc., which is 1, 16, 256, 4,096, 65,536, etc. (See also Appendix *Place value table*, p. 245.)

Counting. Have the students count in hexadecimal.
Example: What is the hexadecimal number that follows each of these:

9?   (answer: A)
F?   (answer: 10)
3B49?   (answer: 3B4A)
D374F?   (answer: D3750)
69FF?   (answer: 6A00)

Conversion problems

Do many conversion problems with hexadecimal. Build up to problems like the following examples:

Example: What is $3C4D_{hex}$ in base-ten?

Again, the students first need to say to themselves, 'This number is D (thirteen) 1s, four 16s, C (twelve) 256s and three 4,096s'. Therefore, we get $3 \times 4,096 + 12 \times 256 + 4 \times 16 + 13 \times 1 = 15,437_{dec}$.

Example: What is $15,076_{dec}$ in hexadecimal (hexadecimal)?

Again, going from base-ten is more difficult. Carefully look over the above conversion problem that converts $1,383_{dec}$ to octal. The question with this new problem that we must ask ourselves is, 'How many of each hexadecimal place value can we take out of the given base-ten number (15,076)?' Of course, we are limited to a single digit (0, 1, 2, 3 up to F) of each place value. Another way of looking at it is to think that each hexadecimal place value is an empty box, and we need to fill in all the boxes with a single hexadecimal digit so that all these digits together form a hexadecimal number that is equal to the given base-ten number. Here are the empty boxes:

65536s'	4096s'	256s'	16s'	1s'
place	place	place	place	place

We first look to see what the largest hexadecimal place value is that goes into 15,076. It is the 4,096s' place. It goes in 3 times, so we put a 3 into the 4,096s' place. This accounts for 3 × 4,096, which, when subtracted from 15,076, results in a remainder of 2,788. 256 goes into 2,788 ten times (which in hexadecimal is the single digit A). So we put 'A' into the 256s' place. When we subtract these ten 256s from what was the remainder (2,788), we get a new remainder of 228. 16 goes into 228 fourteen times (which is E in hexadecimal). So we put 'E' into the 16s' place. Then we subtract these fourteen 16s from the remainder 228, and get a new remainder of 4, which we put into the 1s' place. In the end our boxes look like this:

	3	A	E	4
65536s'	4096s'	256s'	16s'	1s'
place	place	place	place	place

so our answer is $3AE4_{hex}$, which equals $15,076_{dec}$.

Binary base-two

What are the digits? Here we have only two digits: 0 and 1.

The place values (from right to left) for binary are $2^0, 2^1, 2^2, 2^3, 2^4$, etc., which is: 1, 2, 4, 8, 16, etc.

The connection with computers. Here, with

the binary number base, we see some real practical application of number bases – specifically with computers (see Class Eight Computers, p. 148).

Counting in binary
Example: What is the binary number that comes after:
101?   (answer: 1,110)
101,011? (answer: 101,100)
111?   (answer: 1,000)

Counting race
Be sure to do a row of 5 students counting in binary by raising and lowering their hands. A hand up represents '1' and a hand down is '0'. They then count from zero (all hands down) to 31 (all hands up). See if the students can state a rule about under what conditions someone must raise their arm. The rule is this: the person in the 1s' place simply moves their hand up and down, while all the other people only change their position following the moment that all those before them have their hands up. For an added challenge, you can have three people using both of their hands (6 digits therefore) and counting from 0 to 63 as fast as possible.

Conversions problems
Do many conversion problems with binary, such as the following:
  Example: What is $10,011_{bin}$ in base-ten?
  Converting from binary is much easier than converting from other bases, because there is no need to multiply. It's never a question of how many of a certain place value you have – it's either there (a '1') or it's not there (a '0'). Therefore, in the case of $10,011_{bin}$, we can say, 'This number has a 1, a 2 and a 16', because those are the places that have a '1' in them. (The two zeros in 10011 signify that there is no 4 and no 8.) Therefore our answer is: $1 + 2 + 16 = 19_{dec}$.

  Example: What is 38_{dec} in binary (base-two)?
  Again, going from base-ten is more difficult. Carefully look over the above conversion problem that converted $1,383_{dec}$ to octal. We can create the empty boxes:

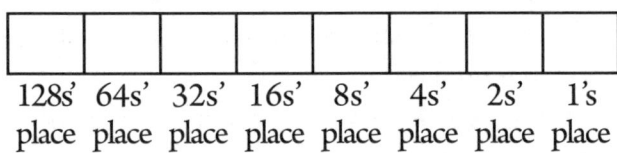

128s' 64s' 32s' 16s' 8s' 4s' 2s' 1's
place place place place place place place place

We first look to see what the largest binary place value is that goes into 38_{dec}. The 64s' place and the 128s' place are both too big, so we'll leave them empty. The first place we can use is the 32s' place. Recall, that we don't have to ask 'how many times does 32 go into 38?', because it can't be more than 1. It either goes in once or not at all (recall that '2' is not a legal digit in binary). So we put a 1 in the 32s' place, and then subtract 32 from 38 to get a remainder of 6. We can't get a 16 or an 8 out of this remainder, so we put a 0 in the 16s' place and a 0 in the 8s' place. But we can get a 4 out of our remainder of 6, so we put a 1 in the 4s' place, and, after we subtract this 4 from the 6, we are left with a new remainder of 2. Now, we put a 1 in the 2s' place, and since there's no remainder left, we finish by putting a 0 in the 1s' place. In the end, our boxes look like this:

		1	0	0	1	1	0
128s' place	64s' place	32s' place	16s' place	8s' place	4s' place	2s' place	1's place

so our answer is $100{,}110_{bin}$, which equals 38_{dec}.

Arithmetic in various bases

When doing an arithmetic problem in a certain base, be sure to do all work in that base. You shouldn't convert into base-ten in order to do the calculation, and then convert back – that would take too long, and it misses the point.

Example: $6_{oct} + 5_{oct}$ should not be thought of as: '6 plus 5 is normally 11, and that is 13_{oct}'; but rather: 'if we take 2 from the 5, then it can be combined with the 6 to make one 8 with a 3 left over, giving us a base eight answer of 13_{oct}.'

Example: With $34_{five} + 23_{five}$ we add the 4 and 3 in the right column and think that it is two beyond 5, so 4 + 3 is 12. We write down the 2 and carry the 1. Now with the left column, 3 + 2 is just 5, plus the 1 that we carried gives us 11, so we write that down, which gives us a final answer of 112_{five}.

Multiplication tables

Students should make the multiplication tables for the various bases. They should look for patterns. Perhaps the hexadecimal multiplication table should be a challenge problem. They can then use these multiplication tables in order to do multiplication and division problems in different bases. The students become appreciative of the fact that people don't have 16 fingers – the hexadecimal table would have been very difficult to memorise! They may well wish that we had always operated with the binary (base-two) system – its table would have been a piece of cake!

The climax of the unit

See Appendix, *Multiplication tables for number bases*, p. 244, for the octal, base-five, binary and hexadecimal multiplication tables. These tables will be needed for multiplication and division problems. Do many arithmetic problems, such as:

Example: $110_{bin} + 11_{bin} + 101_{bin}$

Starting with the right-most column, 0 + 1 + 1 is 10, so we write down 0 and carry the 1. With the next column, we have 1 (the carry) + 1 + 1 + 0, which is 11, so we write down 1 and carry 1. The last column is the 1 (the carry) + 1 + 1, which is 11. So our answer is $1{,}110_{bin}$.

```
    110bin
     11bin
 + 101bin
 ─────────
   1110bin
```

Example: $132_{five} - 34_{five}$

Borrowing from the 3 in the middle column gives us 12 – 4 in the right-most column, which is 3 (12 is 3 numbers up from 4). We write down the 3 and then do the next column 12 − 3, which is 4. Our answer is 43_{five}.

$$\begin{array}{r} \overset{12\ 1}{13}2_{five} \\ -\ 34_{five} \\ \hline 43_{five} \end{array}$$

Example: $64_{oct} \times 26_{oct}$

Using the octal times table, we first do $6 \times 4 = 30$, so we write down the 0 and carry the 3. Then, $6 \times 6 = 44$, plus the 3 that was carried is 47. The rest of the problem is shown below. The answer is $2{,}170_{oct}$.

$$\begin{array}{r} 64_{oct} \\ \times\ 26_{oct} \\ \hline 470 \\ 150 \\ \hline 2170_{oct} \end{array}$$

Example: $BC8_{hex} + 9A5_{hex}$

The solution is $156D_{hex}$, and is shown below.

$$\begin{array}{r} BC8_{hex} \\ +\ 9A5_{hex} \\ \hline 156D_{hex} \end{array}$$

Example: $9C_{hex} \times B5_{hex}$

The hexadecimal times table is needed. The solution is $6E4C_{hex}$, and is shown below.

$$\begin{array}{r} 9C_{hex} \\ \times\ B5_{hex} \\ \hline 30C \\ 6B4 \\ \hline 6E4C_{hex} \end{array}$$

Example: $2AF8_{hex} \div C8_{hex}$

The hexadecimal times table is needed. The solution is 37_{hex}, and is shown below.

$$\begin{array}{r} 37 \\ C8\overline{\smash{)}2AF8} \\ -\ 258 \\ \hline 578 \\ -\ 578 \\ \hline 0 \end{array}$$

Multiplication with zeros

We know that in base-ten we can multiply $3{,}496 \times 100$ and quickly get $349{,}600$. We can do the same in other bases.

Example: in binary $11{,}011 \times 100 = 1{,}101{,}100$ (This is $27 \times 4 = 108$ in base-ten.)

Example: In hexadecimal $E8F \times 1{,}000 = E8F \times 1{,}000$. (This is $3{,}727 \times 4{,}096 = 15{,}265{,}792$ in base-ten.)

Converting between binary and hexadecimal (optional)

Decimal	Binary	Hexadecimal
0	0000	0
1	0001	1
2	0010	2
3	0011	3
4	0100	4
5	0101	5
6	0110	6
7	0111	7
8	1000	8
9	1001	9
10	1010	A
11	1011	B
12	1100	C
13	1101	D
14	1110	E
15	1111	F

Notice that the 'Decimal' column in the above table is only for reference, and is not actually used when doing a conversion straight from hexadecimal to binary, or back.

It is much easier to convert straight from binary to hexadecimal (or straight from hexadecimal to binary) rather than to convert first into decimal and then from decimal into the desired base.

Example: What is $3A8_{hex}$ in binary?

We simply look up each hexadecimal digit on the table to see what its equivalent four digits are in binary. We see that 3 is 0011, A is 1010 and 8 is 1000. This gives us $(00)11\ 1010\ 1000_{bin}$.

Example: What is 1001111110_{bin} in hexadecimal?

Starting from the right, we separate the digits into groups of four. The right-most group is 1110, which we look up on the table and get 'E' in hexadecimal. The next group, 0111 in binary, is 7 in hexadecimal. The last group is 10, so we add two zeros on the front, and look up 0010 on the table resulting in a 2 in hexadecimal. Putting these hexadecimal digits together we get $27E_{hex}$.

The world of numbers

The square root algorithm (without zeros)

The square root algorithm – without zeros should be taught in Class Eight if it wasn't taught in Class Seven.

The square root algorithm, if done in Class Seven as outlined in Appendix, p. 206, is very challenging, because it focuses on getting the students to understand *why* it works. In Class Eight, the task is much easier – the students simply memorise a step-by-step procedure (called an *algorithm*), which allows them to calculate square roots by hand.

The square root algorithm (without zeros) as taught here in Class Eight, is a slight variation of *The square root algorithm (with zeros)* as taught in Class Seven. Specifically, in the Class Eight version:

- Extra zeros are not written down.

- We bring down only two digits at a time, similar to what happens in long division.
- We can more easily calculate decimal approximations for uneven square roots (e.g. $\sqrt{30}$).

The unit on computers (p. 148) should be done just before this unit on the square root algorithm since it culminates nicely with the square root algorithm.

Have students calculate the square roots of 2 through 10 to three decimal places by using the square root algorithm (p. 206 and then memorise these approximations as shown below.

$\sqrt{2} \approx 1.414$ $\sqrt{7} \approx 2.65$
$\sqrt{3} \approx 1.73$ $\sqrt{8} \approx 2.83$
$\sqrt{4} = 2$ $\sqrt{9} = 3$
$\sqrt{5} \approx 2.24$ $\sqrt{10} \approx 3.16$
$\sqrt{6} \approx 2.45$

Simplifying square roots is saved for Class Nine (e.g. $\sqrt{75}$ simplifies to $5\sqrt{3}$).

The Pythagorean Theorem

With any right triangle, (the area of) the square of the hypotenuse is equal to the sum (of the areas) of the squares of the other two sides.

In Class Seven, the Pythagorean Theorem talked only about the *area* of the squares. Now, in Class Eight, we will use the Pythagorean Theorem as a tool for finding the length of the missing side of right triangles. We therefore don't need to visualise the squares each time, but can do things more mechanically. To make this transition, we can take the above statement and, surprisingly, drop the words in the parentheses, and then it becomes clear that the word 'square' has two meanings – a geometrical figure, and an exponent of two. Through this, we introduce these two formulas (in each case *a* and *b* are the lengths of the two legs and c is the length of the hypotenuse):

The hypotenuse formula
$$c^2 = a^2 + b^2$$
which is used to find the length of the hypotenuse.

The leg formula
$$a^2 = c^2 - b^2$$
which is used to find the length of one of the legs.

See Class Eight Geometry, *Mensuration*, p. 151, for Baravalle's proof of the Pythagorean Theorem, which should be done during the mensuration unit.

Do many problems that find the missing sides of right triangles including answers that are *not* whole numbers. This is a good opportunity to practise the square root algorithm.

Example (using ratios): What is the length of the hypotenuse of a right triangle if the two legs are 36 cm and 105 cm long?

With this problem we can work out the answer by simply using ratios, without using a formula. The ratio 36 : 105 reduces (÷ 3) to 12 : 35. The primitive Pythagorean triple (see pp. 117f) is 12, 35, 37. Therefore the answer is: $37 \times 3 = 111$.

Example (using algebra and the square root algorithm): If the length of the hypotenuse of a right triangle is 9 cm and one leg is 5 cm long, then what is the length of the other leg?

Using the *hypotenuse formula*, we first need to know that c is always the hypotenuse ('9' in this case). The '5' can be either a or b. Using this formula and solving, we get:

$$c^2 = a^2 + b^2$$
$$9^2 = a^2 + 5^2$$
$$81 = a^2 + 25$$
$$81 - 25 = a^2$$
$$a^2 = 56$$
$$a = \sqrt{56}$$

Using the square root algorithm, we get $a \approx 7.48$.

Alternatively, most students usually prefer to use the leg formula, $a^2 = c^2 - b^2$, for this type of problem where we need to find a leg. We simply do:

$$a^2 = 9^2 - 5^2$$
$$a^2 = 81 - 25$$
$$a^2 = 56$$
$$a = \sqrt{56}$$
$$a \approx 7.48.$$

Percents and growth

Review percents from Classes Six and Seven very thoroughly.

Calculators
The teacher needs to decide whether or not it is appropriate for the students to use calculators for this unit.

Four ways to find the base
Review Class Seven, *Finding the base* (see Class Seven *Percents*, p. 76).

An easy problem
Joe has 20% as much money as Kate. How much does Kate have if Joe has £12?

The even multiple method: (This method is only possible for 'easy' problems where the given percentage translates quickly to a fraction with a '1' in the numerator, such as 10%, 20%, 25%, etc.). With the above problem, 20% translates into $\frac{1}{5}$ as a fraction. Therefore, since Joe has $\frac{1}{5}$ as much as Kate, we can say that Kate has 5 times as much as Joe. Our answer is that Kate has $5 \times 12 = £60$.

Class Eight Arithmetic

A harder problem
Joe has 37.5% as much money as Kate. How much does Kate have if Joe has £12?

The decimal method: Thinking of 37.5% as a decimal, we can say that Joe has 0.375 times as much as Kate. We can then see that the opposite is also true: Kate has Joe's amount divided by 0.375. So our answer is 12 ÷ 0.375 = £32.

The fraction method: Thinking of 37.5% as a fraction, we can say that Joe has $3/8$ as much as Kate. So we know that the opposite is also true: Kate has $8/3$ as much as Joe. So our answer is: $12 \times 8/3$ = £32.

The algebra method: (Use this method only in Class Eight, and only if you're really stuck.) We use the formula $n = p \times b$, which says that a *number* (n) is a certain *percentage* (p) of a *base* (b). For this problem, n is 12, and p is $37.5/100$, which is more easily expressed as $3/8$ or as 0.375. This gives the equation: $12 = 3/8 \times b$ or $12 = 0.375 \times b$. Solving either equation gives us b = £32.

Example: Jill is 86% as tall as Fred. If Fred is 172 cm tall, then how tall is Jill (to the nearest cm)?

This is a 'normal' percent problem; we are finding the smaller number. The easiest way is to multiply 172 times 0.86, which is 147.92. Our rounded answer is 148 cm.

Example: Jill is 86% as tall as Fred. If Jill is 162 cm tall, then how tall is Fred (to the nearest cm)?

Here we are finding the larger number. We can use the decimal method (162 ÷ 0.86), the fraction method ($162 \times \frac{100}{86}$) or the algebra method ($162 = 0.86 \times b$). The answer (rounded) is 188 cm.

Increase/decrease problems

Rewording a percent increase problem

'My rent has increased by 50%', is the same as saying, 'My rent is 150% of what it was'.

'My rent has increased by 150%', is the same as saying, 'My rent is 250% of what it was'.

Increasing a number by 100% is the same as taking 200% of that number, or multiplying by two.

Increasing a number by 20% is the same as taking 120% of that number, or multiplying by 1.2.

Example: What is 48 increased by 7%?

We simply change the wording to: 'What is 107% of 48?' which gives us $1.07 \times 48 \to 51.36$.

Rewording a percent decrease problem

Decreasing a number by 20% is the same as 80% (which is 100% − 0%) of that number, or multiplying that number by 0.8.

Example: What is 32 decreased by 20%?

We change the wording to: 'What is 80% of 32?' which gives us $0.8 \times 32 \to 25.6$.

Example: What is 510 decreased by 15%?

The wording is changed to: 'What is 85% of 510?' which gives us $0.85 \times 510 \to 433.5$.

Calculating the percentage of increase or decrease

Review Class Seven, *Calculating the percentage of increase or decrease,* (p. 78) especially the formulas:

$$\% \text{ increase} = \frac{\text{amount of increase}}{\text{starting point}}$$

$$\% \text{ decrease} = \frac{\text{amount of decrease}}{\text{starting point}}$$

In Class Eight, we can do the calculation more directly, by dividing the ending point by the starting point. How far this answer is from 100% tells us the percentage of increase or decrease.

Example: Going from 120 to 162 is what percent increase?

We simply divide 162 by 120 (the starting point), which gives us 1.35. This tells us that 162 is 135% of 120, and therefore we can say that it is a 35% increase.

Example: Going from 75 to 63 is what percent decrease?

We divide 63 by 75 (the starting point), which gives us 0.84. This tells us that 63 is 84% of 75, and therefore we can say that it is a 16% decrease (100% − 84% = 16%).

Example: If Jill is 1.81 m tall and Fred is 1.45 m tall, then (A) Jill is what percent of Fred's height? (B) Jill is what percent taller than Fred?

(A) We do 1.81 ÷ 1.45 ≈ 1.248, so Jill is 124.8% of Fred's height.

(B) Looking at the solution from part A, we can see that Jill is 24.8% taller. Alternatively, we can use the method introduced in Class Seven. We determine the amount of increase and then divide by the starting point. So we do 0.36 ÷ 1.45, which is 0.248, or 24.8%.

Calculating the starting point

These are the trickiest problems. They can be done using algebra, but I would recommend the following: First, reword (see above) the problem, and then solve it using one of the methods described above in *Four ways to find the base* (p. 131). The following examples should help clarify things:

Example: In a game of cricket, Fullerton School scored 12.5% more than St Peter's. If Fullerton scored 99 runs, how many runs did St Peter's score?

The problem is first reworded as: The Fullerton score (99) is 112.5% of the St Peter's score. This can then be further simplified to: 99 is 112.5% of what number? Now, we can use any of the last three methods described under *Four ways to find the base*:

The decimal method: 112.5% is written as 1.125, and then we do 99 ÷ 1.125.

The fraction method: 112.5% is written as 9/8, and then we do 99 × 8/9.

The algebra method: we solve the equation $99 = 1.125 \times b$ or $99 = 9/8 \times b$.

Using any of these methods, we get $b = 88$.

Example: Larry sold a car for £22,400. If this is a 36% loss from the price that he originally paid, then what was that original price?

Knowing that 36% less than 100% is 64%, we reword the problem as: 'Larry sold the car (£22,400) for 64% of what he paid'. This can then become further simplified to: £22,400 is 64% of what number? Here, we can use the decimal method, and do 22,400 ÷ 0.64 to get an answer of £35,000.

Class Eight Arithmetic

Exponential growth

The difference between linear growth and exponential growth (constant percentage growth) can be nicely shown by using the example of a town that starts with a population of 5,000:

Linear growth is when the population increases by the same amount every year. If the town grows by 550 people per year, then it goes from 5,000 to 5,550 to 6,100 to 6,650 to 7,200, etc.

Exponential growth is when the population increases by the same percentage every year. For 10% annual growth, the population goes from 5,000 to 5,500 to 6,050 to 6,655 to 7,320.5, etc.

Exponential growth is exemplified by population growth, bank accounts (compound interest), inflation and with many things in nature. Linear growth is exemplified by rates (e.g. speed, rate of pay).

In the long run, exponential growth always outstrips linear growth – it's just a matter of time before it catches up.

The exponential growth formula
$$P = P_0(1 + r)^t$$
where P_0 ('P zero') is the initial amount, r is the percentage growth rate as a decimal, t is the time (i.e. number of years) and P is the end amount after t years.

This formula is used for compound interest or population growth P can stand for principle or population.

Review Class Seven, *Compound interest*, (p. 78).

Understanding why the formula works is important. For example, 5% interest compounded annually means that we calculate a particular year's balance by taking 105% (which means multiplying by 1.05) of the previous year's balance. If the account starts at £2,000, then the balance at the end of the first year is 105% of 2,000, which is 1.05 × 2,000, or £2,100. To get the next year, we multiply by 1.05 again. And to get the balance after the third year, we multiply once again by 1.05.

So, if the question is to find the balance after three years at 5% interest of an account that starts at £2,000, then what we must do is multiply £2,000 by 1.05, and that result by 1.05, and then that result again by 1.05. This can be written as 2,000 × 1.05 × 1.05 × 1.05, or more succinctly as $2,000 \times 1.05^3$, which is exactly what the formula $P = P_0(1 + r)^t$ says that you must do, using $P_0 = 2,000$, $r = 0.05$, $t = 3$. (Recall that you must cube 1.05 before multiplying by 2,000.) The final answer is: $2,000 \times 1.05^3$ → $2,000 \times 1.157625$, which is £2,315.25.

The growth rate table
This table compares different growth rates over a 200-year period (see Appendix, p. 251).

The table gives values for $(1 + r)^t$ given various values of t and r.

Each column uses a different rate $(1+r)$. Each row shows a different period of time (t). The calculated value of $(1 + r)^t$ appears in the box.

This table can be used in various ways. For one, we can determine how much percent increase we get with given values for r and t. For example, with 5% annual growth over a 20-year period, the table shows 2.6533, which tells us that the initial value is now about 265% as much as when it started. This is about a 165% increase.

Also, we can solve specific problems.

Example: What is the balance in a savings account after 20 years at 5% interest if the initial deposit was £300?

Here, we use the formula $P = P_0(1 + r)^t$. Now, using 20 for the value t, and 1.05 for the value for $(1+r)$, and see that the table tells us that $(1 + r)^t$ is 2.6533. Then we get the final balance by multiplying that number by the value of P_0, which is 300. This gives us an answer of £795.99.

Doubling times. The table shows that at 10% it takes a little more than 7 years for the initial investment to double.

Have the students do many calculations that use the formula $P = P_0(1 + r)^t$. Do some dramatic examples, such as:

Example: If £50 is invested and earns a return of 15% annually, how much money will be in the account after (a) 3 years (b) 20 years (c) 100 years?

   (a) £76.04
   (b) £818.33
   (c) £58,715,650 using table, or
      £58,715,672.53 using calculator.

Example: If a town starts with a population of 700 residents and then grows at an rate of 8% annually, what will its population be (to the nearest whole person) after (a) 10 years (b) 50 years (c) 200 years?

   (a) 1,511
   (b) 32,831
   (c) 3,387,265,000 (from table), or
      3,387,264,709 (calculator). This is about half the current population of the planet!

Depreciation (optional)

Depreciation is when the value of something drops, usually at a fairly steady annual percentage rate. For example, the depreciation of a car is typically 30% in the first year.

The formula for depreciation is a slight variation of the *exponential growth formula*; we simply change the plus to a minus to get: $P = P_0(1 - r)^t$.

Example: If Betty buys a used car for £14,000 and it depreciates at a rate of 12% annually, then how much will it be worth after eight years?

The depreciation formula gives us: $P = 14000(0.88)^8$, which, after plugging into a calculator, gives us an answer of £5,034.88.

The rule of 72

This is a trick that allows us to quickly estimate the number of years required for an amount to double given an annual growth rate, or to estimate the growth rate given the number of years for the amount to double. The rule is:

$$R \times t \approx 72$$

Class Eight Arithmetic

Where *R* is the annual growth rate (in percentage points), and *t* is the number years it takes to double. In some cases, we choose 70 instead of 72, depending on which one makes the division problem easier.

Example: How long does it take a city's population to double if its current annual growth rate is 6%?

We simply divide 6 into 72 for a result of 12. We can therefore conclude that the population is doubling about every 12 years. (The exact answer is 11.90 years.)

Example: If somebody's investment is doubling every 5 years, then what approximately is the annual rate of return?

Here we choose 70 instead of 72, because it is easier. We simply divide 5 into 70 for a result of 14. We can therefore estimate that the annual rate of return (annual profit) is about 14%. (The exact answer is 14.87%.)

Dimensional analysis

Dimensional analysis is the study of units of measurement. Often, it focuses on changing a quantity from one unit base to another (e.g. from miles per hour to metres per second).

This unit is important in order for the students to be adequately prepared for upper school science.

This unit should be done after mensuration, and after the physics main lesson block. I usually do it towards the end of the year.

Calculators

For this whole unit, it is best to allow the students to use a calculator, so they don't get bogged down in tedious calculations.

Conversion table

See p. 252, for a table listing useful conversion factors. Keep in mind that most of these are approximations. The students should memorise the ones indicated.

Accuracy

Since the conversion factors are approximations, it is likely that students will get answers that are slightly different, especially if they do the problems differently. I generally tell them to go to three significant digits. The third digit may be slightly off.

Showing work

The students need to be sure that they show their work, and write down the numbers that they put into the calculator, so they can find any mistakes that they make.

Two methods for doing unit conversion problems

Example: how many stone are in 15.2 kg?

The intuitive approach: Since there is nothing on the *Conversion table* (p. 252) that tells us how to go directly from stones to kg, we must do the problem in two steps. One possibility is to ask how many pounds are in 15.2 kg, and then convert the pounds to stone. In converting from lb to kg, we know that one kg is about 2.2 lb. We then ask ourselves whether we should multiply 15.2 by 2.2, or divide 15.2 by 2.2. Since pounds are smaller than kg, we need more, so we multiply. Therefore $15.2 \times 2.2 = 33.44$ lb.

Now, in converting to stone, we know that one stone is 14 lb. We ask ourselves whether to multiply 33.44 by 14 or divide 33.44 by 14. Only dividing gives a reasonable answer. Therefore, our final answer is: $33.44 \div 14 \approx 2.39$ stone.

The chain method focuses on the idea of getting units to cancel until only the desired unit is left. Mathematically speaking, we are multiplying our original amount by fractions that are equal to one – in other words, where their numerators and denominators are equal. The work looks like this:

$$\frac{15.2 \text{ kg}}{1} \times \frac{2.2 \text{ lb}}{1 \text{ kg}} \times \frac{1 \text{ stone}}{14 \text{ lb}}$$

Notice that all the units cross cancel, except for 'stone', and the arithmetic amounts to $15.2 \times 2.2 \div 14$, which gives our answer of 2.39 stone.

Converting between the imperial and metric system

Example: 350 yards is how many metres?

The intuitive approach: $350 \text{ yd} \times 3 \to 1050 \text{ ft}$
$1050 \text{ ft} \div 3.28 \to 320.12 \text{ m}$

The chain method: $\frac{350 \text{ yd}}{1} \times \frac{3 \text{ ft}}{1 \text{ yd}} \times \frac{1 \text{ m}}{3.28 \text{ ft}}$
$\to 320.12$ m.

Example: Mount Everest has a height of 29,028 ft. How many kilometres is this?

The intuitive approach: $29,028 \text{ ft} \div 3.28 \to 8850 \text{ m} \to 8.85$ km.

The chain method: $\frac{29,028 \text{ ft}}{1} \times \frac{1}{3.28 \text{ ft}} \times \frac{1 \text{ km}}{1000 \text{ m}}$
$\to 8.85$ km.

Converting units for speed

Review Class Seven *Average speed*, p. 91.

Example: If a train is traveling 38 m/s (metres per second), how fast is this in mph (mi/hr)?

The intuitive approach: (Note: 'm' means metres, and 'mi' means miles):

$38 \frac{\text{m}}{\text{s}} \times 3600 \to 136{,}800 \frac{\text{m}}{\text{hr}}$

(because 1 hr = 3600 sec)

$136{,}800 \frac{\text{m}}{\text{hr}} \div 1000 \to 136.8 \frac{\text{km}}{\text{hr}}$

(because 1 km = 1000 m)

$136.8 \frac{\text{km}}{\text{hr}} \div 1.61 \to 84.97 \frac{\text{mi}}{\text{hr}}$

(because 1 mi ≈ 1.61 km)

The chain method:

$\frac{38 \text{ m}}{\text{s}} \times \frac{3600 \text{ sec}}{\text{hr}} \times \frac{1 \text{ km}}{1000 \text{ m}} \times \frac{1 \text{ mi}}{1.61 \text{ km}} \to$
84.97 mph

The students should be able to picture the train traveling 84.97 miles every hour, and imagine that this is the equivalent of traveling 38 metres every second (or 136.8 km/h).

Converting unit cost

Example: In 2002 the cost of petrol at a station in the U.S. was $1.59 per U.S. gallon, and at a station in Holland it was €1.21 per litre. If the exchange rate for buying euros is 85¢ per euro, then how much more expensive (as a percentage) is petrol in Holland than in the U.S.? (Note: a U.S. gallon is smaller than an imperial gallon!)

The intuitive approach: Given 1 U.S. gallon ≈ 3.785 litres, we convert the price at the station in Holland into dollars per U.S. gallon:

$$1.21 \frac{\text{euros}}{\text{litre}} \times 3.785 \to 4.580 \frac{\text{euros}}{\text{U.S. gal}}$$

$$4.580 \frac{\text{euros}}{\text{U.S. gal}} \times 0.85 \to \$3.89/\text{U.S. gal}$$

To find out how much more expensive, as a percentage, $3.89 is than $1.59, we divide 1.59 into 3.89 which is 2.45, which means that $3.89 is 245% of $1.59. Therefore, we can say that petrol is 145% more expensive in Holland than in the U.S.

The chain method: $\frac{1.21 \text{ euros}}{\text{litre}} \times \frac{3.785 \text{ litres}}{\text{U.S. gal}} \times \frac{\$0.85}{\text{euro}} \to \$3.89/\text{U.S. gal}$, which is 145% more expensive than $1.59.

Inverse ratios and reciprocals

Example: Given that 1 metre is about 3.28 feet, how many metres is 1 foot?

We want to know how many metres per feet ($^m/_{ft}$) there are, and we are given 3.28 feet per metre ($^{ft}/_m$). Since $^m/_{ft}$ and $^{ft}/_m$ are reciprocals of each other, it seems reasonable that we simply need to take the reciprocal of 3.28, which is $\frac{1}{3.28}$.

Dividing 3.28 into 1 gives us: 1ft ≈ 0.305 m. The important thing to realise is that we got our answer by taking the reciprocal of 3.28.

Example: Given that 1 mile is about 1.61 kilometres, how many miles is 1 kilometre?

We simply take the reciprocal (see above solution) of 1.61. So we divide 1.61 into 1 to get 1km ≈ 0.621 mi.

Fuel consumption

On the Continent of Europe and in the Republic of Ireland fuel consumption is given as litres/100 km – in other words, how much fuel you need for a given distance. In the UK (despite fuel being sold in litres) consumption is given as miles per (imperial) gallon (mpg) – in other words the distance that can be covered with a given amount of fuel. The units are in reciprocal relation: the most economic cars have a *low* ℓ/100 km and a *high* mpg.

Example: What is $\frac{6.8 \, \ell}{100 \text{ km}}$ in mpg?

We can either first convert litres to gallons, or start with converting km to miles.

$$\frac{6.8 \, \ell}{100 \text{ km}} \to \frac{(6.8 \div 4.55)}{100 \text{ km}} \to \frac{1.49 \text{ gal}}{100 \text{ km}}.$$ So with 1.49 gal we can drive 100 km. As 1 km ≈ 0.62 miles, we can say we use $\frac{1.49 \text{ gal}}{62 \text{ miles}}$. To find how many miles are we can go with 1 gal, we divide 62 by 1.49 to get 41.6 mpg.

Alternatively, starting by converting 100 km to miles (1 km ≈ 0.62) we get 62 miles. We can now say we go 62 miles per 6.8 ℓ. Converting the litres to gallons, we do 6.8 ÷ 4.55 to get 1.49 gal. So we get 62 miles per 1.49 gallons. Dividing by 1.49 we get 41.6 mpg.

Converting areas and volumes
Try to have the students derive the following relationships, and give them problems that practise them:

$$1 \text{ m}^2 = 10{,}000 \text{ cm}^2$$
$$1 \text{ km}^2 = 1{,}000{,}000 \text{ m}^2$$
$$1 \text{ ft}^2 = 144 \text{ in}^2 \text{ (which is } 12 \text{ in} \times 12 \text{ in)}$$
$$1 \text{ yd}^2 = 9 \text{ ft}^2$$
$$1 \text{ in}^2 \approx 6.45 \text{ cm}^2 \text{ (which is } 2.54^2)$$
$$1 \text{ m}^2 \approx 10.76 \text{ ft}^2$$
$$1 \text{ m}^3 = 1{,}000{,}000 \text{ cm}^3$$
$$1 \text{ km}^3 = 1{,}000{,}000{,}000 \text{ m}^3$$
$$1 \text{ ft}^3 = 1728 \text{ in}^3 \text{ (which is } 12 \text{ in} \times 12 \text{ in} \times 12 \text{ in)}$$
$$1 \text{ in}^3 \approx 16.39 \text{ cm}^3 \text{ (which is } 2.54^3)$$
$$1 \text{ m}^3 \approx 35.31 \text{ ft}^3$$

Example: 4 cubic yards is equal to how many cubic metres?

The intuitive approach: 4 yd³ × 27 → 108 ft³
108 ft³ ÷ 35.31 → 3.06 m³.

The chain method: $\frac{4 \text{ yd}^3}{1} \times \frac{27 \text{ ft}^3}{1 \text{ yd}^3} \times \frac{1 \text{ m}^3}{35.31 \text{ ft}^3}$.
The answer is 3.06 m³.

Grains of rice problem
This is a great problem to do in order to understand doubling, and at the same time to practise volumes and dimensional analysis.

Question: A wise man is granted a request. He requests that a single grain of rice be placed on the first square of a chess board, 2 grains on the second square, 4 grains on the third, 8 grains on the fourth, and so on, doubling with every square up until the last square – the 64th square. How many grains of rice is that, and what is the total volume of that much rice?

The answer is 164 km³ (Yes, cubic km!) For the detailed story and solution see our book, *Fun with Puzzles*.

Density
The key idea is that density is weight per volume. For example, the density of gold is 1,205 lb/ft³, which tells us that a cubic foot of gold weighs 1,205 pounds. The density of gold can also be given as 19.3 g/cm³, which says that a cubic centimetre weighs 19.3 grams.

Density can be expressed in many different ways, such as grams per cubic centimetre (g/cm³), pounds per cubic foot (lb/ft³) or ounces per cubic inch (oz/in³). We can go between these different units of density by using these conversion facts:

$$1 \frac{\text{g}}{\text{cm}^3} \approx 62.43 \frac{\text{lb}}{\text{ft}^3} \approx 0.578 \frac{\text{oz}}{\text{in}^3}$$
$$1 \frac{\text{oz}}{\text{in}^3} \approx 1.73 \frac{\text{g}}{\text{cm}^3}$$

Class Eight Arithmetic

Notice that water is used as a standard – it has a density of 1 g/cm³ in both the metric and 1 fl oz/in³ in the imperial systems.

1 ml (i.e. 1 cm³) of water (at 4°C) weighs exactly 1 gram*.

1 litre of water (at 4°C) weighs exactly 1 kilogram.

1 cubic metre of water (at 4°C) weighs exactly 1 metric ton (1,000 kg).

1 fl. oz. of water weighs 1 ounce†.

When a density is given in terms of g/cm³ we can easily compare it to water, which has a density (at 4°C) of exactly 1 g/cm³ (1 cm³ of water weighs 1 gram). For example, with gold's density of 19.3 g/cm³, we can say that gold is 19.3 times heavier than water.

For densities of various materials see Appendix, *Conversion table*, p. 252.

In order to calculate density, we divide weight by volume.

Example: What is the density (in g/cm³) of a rock that has a weight of 2.41 kg and a volume of 502 cm³?

2.41 kg is 2,410 g. So we divide 2,410 g by 502 cm³ to get an answer of 4.80 g/cm³.

Do several density word problems building up to ones like these:

Example: How much does a block of gold weigh that is 10 cm × 12 cm × 24 cm (the size of a tissue box)?

---

* This is the temperature where water has maximum density.
† There is a small difference (about 4%) between the imperial (British) fluid ounce and the U.S. fluid ounce. Neither is the exact weight of 1 ounce.

We calculate the volume as 10 cm × 12 cm × 24 cm, which is 2880 cm³. Looking on the conversion table, we see that the density of gold is 19.3 g/cm³, we then calculate:

$$\frac{2880 \text{ cm}^3}{1} \times \frac{19.3 \text{g}}{\text{cm}^3} \times \frac{1 \text{kg}}{1000 \text{g}} \approx 55.58 \text{ kg}$$

Example: How much does a cube of iron weigh that measures 8 inches on a side?

Given that the density of iron is 443 lb per ft³, we can do the problem in two possible ways:

The intuitive approach: 8 inches is ⅔ of a foot, thereby giving the cube a volume of (⅔)³ or ⁸⁄₂₇ of a cubic foot. Our answer is thus: ⁸⁄₂₇ × 443, which is about 131.3 lb (about 60kg).

The chain method: The volume is 8³ or 512 in³. We do $\frac{512 \text{ in}^3}{1} \times \frac{1 \text{ ft}^3}{1728 \text{ in}^3} \times \frac{443 \text{ lb}}{1 \text{ ft}^3}$ which is 131.3 lb.

Example: A small stone pyramid weighs 5.52 kg, has a square base with a length 20 cm, and is 12 cm high. (a) What is its density? (b) What is its weight in water?

(a) In order to calculate the density in terms of grams per cubic centimetre, we first convert the weight to 5,520 grams. Next, to find the volume of the pyramid, we use the formula $V = ⅓ A_{\text{base}} \times H$ (see Class Eight, *Mensuration*, p. 151), which results in ⅓(20)² × 12, which is 1,600 cm³. We get the density by dividing 5,520 by 1,600, which results in 3.45 g/cm³.

(b) To find its weight in water, the class must be familiar with Archimedes' Principle from the Class Eight Physics (hydraulics) main lesson block. Archimedes said that an object that sinks becomes lighter by the weight of the water that it displaces. Since it displaces 1,600 cm³ of water, and that amount of water weighs 1,600 grams (assuming water temperature of 4°C), then we can say that, once the pyramid is submerged in water, it weighs 5,520 − 1,600 = 3,920 grams, or 3.92 kg.

Example: Does a plastic ball float, given that it weighs exactly 200 g and is 8 cm in diameter?

We need to calculate its density. First, we find the volume by using the formula $V = \frac{4}{3}\pi r^3$, and since the radius of the ball is 4, we get:

$V = \frac{4}{3}\pi 4^3 \to V = \frac{4}{3} \times (3.14) \times 64$ (because 4³ is 64), which works out to 267.9 cm³.

In order to get g/cm³ we divide its weight (200) by its volume (267.9), for a result of 0.747 g/cm³. Since this density is less than that of water, which has a density of 1.0 g/cm³, we can say that it *floats*.

Example: A cylindrical bucket is 10 cm in both diameter and height.

(a) What is the volume of the bucket, both in cubic cm and in litres?

(b) How much do the contents of the bucket weigh if it is filled with water?

(c) How much do the contents of the bucket weigh if it is filled with mercury?

(a) We get the area of the base by using the formula for the area of a circle, $A = \pi \times r^2$, which gives us an area of $\pi \times 5^2 = 25\pi$. The volume equals the area of the base times the height, giving us 250π or 785 cm³. Given that there are 231 in³ in a gallon, we divide 785 by 231 to get an answer of approximately 3.40 gallons.

(b) Given that a litre of water weighs 1 kg, the weight of water is 0.785 kg (or 785g).

(c) *The intuitive method*: Given that mercury is 13.5 times denser than water, we simply multiply the weight of the water in the bucket (0.785 kg) by 13.5 to get 10.60 kg.

Proportions

Review Class Seven *Ratios*, p. 80.

When two ratios are equal to each other, we can use an equation to set the two ratios (as fractions) equal. This kind of equation is called a *proportion* (e.g. $\frac{3}{4} = \frac{x}{8}$). A proportion is an equation with a ratio or fraction on each side, such as: $6 : x = 4 : 7$, which is the same as $\frac{6}{x} = \frac{4}{7}$. (See example below for solution.)

Shortcuts for solving proportions
Moving along diagonals
Explanation: Starting with $\frac{3}{4} = \frac{6}{8}$ we notice that any of the four terms can be moved diagonally across the equal sign to produce a number of variations (each one still being a true statement), such as:

$\frac{3 \times 8}{4} = \frac{6}{1}$ or $\frac{3}{1} = \frac{4 \times 6}{8}$ or $\frac{3}{6} = \frac{4}{8}$ or $\frac{3}{4 \times 6} = \frac{1}{8}$ or $3 \times 8 = 4 \times 6$. (There are more possibilities.)

The idea is that as long as we start with a proportion (equation) that is in balance (equal), then we can move any of the four terms along a diagonal, and the equation will still be valid.

Class Eight Arithmetic

Example: Solve: $\frac{6}{x} = \frac{4}{7}$

Our objective is to get x on the top of a fraction, and then to get it alone on one side of the equation, with all the constants on the other side. We do this by taking the original equation and first moving the x up to the right, giving us for the moment:
$$\frac{6}{1} = \frac{4x}{7}.$$

We can now move the 4 and 7 along diagonals to the other side, allowing us to finally reach our goal, where x is alone on one side: $\frac{6 \times 7}{4} = x$, which becomes $x = 10\frac{1}{2}$. With practise, this can be done very quickly.

Cross multiplying

Cross multiplying is a variation of the theme *moving along diagonals*, but a popular way of eliminating fractions. The idea is simply to move both of the denominators up along diagonals to the other side of the equation

Example: Using the same example as above: $\frac{6}{x} = \frac{4}{7}$

Cross multiplying means to move both denominators up along the diagonals to get: $6 \times 7 = 4 \times x$. Dividing both sides by 4 then gives an answer of $x = 10\frac{1}{2}$.

See cross multiplying in the Class Eight Algebra (p.146) for a more complicated example.

Caution! Both moving along diagonals and cross multiplication can only be used for 'true' proportions, namely only if the equation is such that one fraction is equal to one fraction. It cannot be immediately used for equations such as: $3 + \frac{2}{x} = \frac{5}{7}$ (the left side is not a single fraction). This is solved in upper school.

Word problems that use proportions

This unit can be done simultaneously with dimensional analysis. Review Class Seven similar triangles.

Recipe problems

Example: If a recipe calls for 600 ml of flour and 400 ml of water, then how much water is needed if the recipe is expanded and 1,000 ml of flour are used?

We set up a proportion in terms of flour : water = flour : water
$$600 : 400 = 1000 : x \rightarrow \frac{600}{400} = \frac{1000}{x}$$

By moving along diagonals we get: $x = \frac{1000 \times 400}{600}$ which results in an answer of $666\frac{2}{3}$ ml of water.

Map scale problems

Maps can have two possible types of scales:

Fractional scale. This is given usually as a ratio. For example, a scale of 1 : 24,000 means that real distances are 24,000 times greater than the distances between points on the map.

Verbal scale. This kind of scale, which is common for road atlases, states how many miles (or km) in the real world are represented by one inch (or cm) on the map. For example, a scale of 1 inch = 60 miles means that every inch on the map represents 60 miles in reality.

Example: A verbal scale of 1 inch = 5 miles, is the equivalent of what fractional scale?

Multiplying 5 by 5,280 and 12, we see that 5

miles is equal to 316,800 inches. We can then say that 1 inch on the map represents 316,800 inches in the real world, and therefore the fractional scale is 1 : 316,800.

Example: If Greenville and Browntown are 3¾ inches apart on a map, and the scale is 1 inch = 4 miles, then how far apart are they in reality?

We set up a proportion in terms of inches : miles = inches : miles, which gives us: 1:4 = 3.75 : x. This leads to $x = 4 \times 3¾$, which gives an answer of 15 miles.

Example: A map of China has a scale of 1 : 6,000,000. If Wuhan and Shanghai are 11.4 cm apart on the map, then how far apart (in kilometres) are they in reality?

We can set up a proportion in terms of centimetres : kilometres = centimetres : kilometres, or we can simply realise that the distance in reality is 6 million times further than the distance on the map, so we multiply 11.4 times 6 million, which gives the result that the two cities are 68,400,000 cm apart. Since there are 100,000 cm in a kilometre, we move the decimal point 5 places to get 684 km.

Other problems
Review Class Seven speed problems (p.90). Also include speed problems from *Dimensional analysis*, p.136.

Do new problems, such as the following:
Example: Which of the following is a better buy: A 12-ounce block of cheese for £3.32, or a kilogram of cheese for £10.12?

One way to solve this problem is to convert both prices to £ per kg. The 12 ounce block weighs 12 × 28.35 grams = 340 g, or 0.340 kg. It cost £3.32. Dividing by the weight we get 3.32 ÷ 0.340 = £9.76/kg. The 1 kg block cost £10.12, therefore, the 12-ounce block is a better buy.

Example: At Bill's Bikes, Tina can assemble 4 bikes in 7 hours.

(a) How many bikes can she assemble in 20 hours?

(b) How long does it take her to assemble 13 bikes?

(a) Since she can assemble 4 bikes in 7 hours, she can do $\frac{1}{7}$ as much in one hour, which is $\frac{4}{7}$ of a bike. In other words, her rate of work is $\frac{4}{7}$ of a bike per hour. Therefore, in 20 hours she can assemble $20 \times \frac{4}{7}$, which is $\frac{80}{7}$ or 11$\frac{3}{7}$ bikes.

Alternatively, we can do the problem by setting up a proportion of bikes : hours = bikes : hours, which gives us the equation 4 : 7 = x : 20. This becomes $\frac{4}{7} = \frac{x}{20}$, and moving along diagonals gives us $x = \frac{80}{7}$, which gives us an answer of 11$\frac{3}{7}$ bikes.

(b) Since she does 4 bikes in 7 hours, it takes ¼ as long to do one bike, which is $\frac{7}{4}$, or 1¾ of an hour 13 bikes then take $13 \times \frac{7}{4}$ or 22¾ hours.

Alternatively, we can do the problem by setting up a proportion of bikes : hours = bikes : hours, which gives us the equation 4 : 7 = 13 : x. This becomes $\frac{4}{7} = \frac{13}{x}$, and moving along diagonals gives us $x = \frac{91}{4}$, which gives us an answer of 22¾ hours.

Class Eight Arithmetic

Class Eight Algebra

For some general thoughts on teaching algebra, see Introduction, *How much algebra?*, p. 21.

A reminder: don't do too much algebra for the sake of (perhaps unconsciously) showing people that the class is advanced in mathematics, or because it is what you are most familiar with. The only algebra topics that are absolutely necessary in Class Eight are a review of the Class Seven main lesson block, and proportions.

Any upper school algebra course begins with a review of the basic algebra concepts we cover in our Class Seven algebra main lesson. If you don't get to a topic that is listed here under Class Eight algebra, then you can be assured that the students will have it in upper school. On the other hand, many of the non-algebra Class Eight maths topics listed here (e.g. number bases, Platonic solids, loci, etc.) are not covered in upper school.

Review Class Seven algebra very thoroughly. This is very important!

Expressions

Order of operations
The order is: (**P**lease **E**xcuse **M**y **D**ear **A**unt **S**ally).
1. Simplify inside **p**arentheses
2. **E**xponents
3. **M**ultiplication or **d**ivision (left to right)
4. **A**ddition or **s**ubtraction (left to right)

Give several problems so that the students can practise the order of operations.

Example: Simplify $25 - 5 \times 3$

Before we do the subtraction, we must first multiply 5 times 3. We take that result (15), and subtract it from 25 to get a final answer of 10.

Example: Simplify $16 - 5 \times 3^2 - 20 + 5 - (10-8)^3$

First, we do inside the parentheses, which is 2, and then becomes 8 when cubed. Next, we simplify the 5×3^2 by first squaring the 3 to get 9, and then we multiply that by 5, which gives us 45. At this point, the original problem has become $16 - 45 - 20 + 5 - 8$, which can be rearranged to $16 + 5 - 45 - 20 - 8$, which leads to our final answer of -52. The work should be written down somewhat like this:

$16 - 5 \times 3^2 - 20 + 5 - (10-8)^3$
$16 - 5 \times 9 - 20 + 5 - (2)^3$
$16 - 45 - 20 + 5 - 8$
$16 + 5 - 45 - 20 - 8$
$21 - 73$
-52

Evaluating expressions
Evaluate expressions by plugging in values.

Example: Evaluate $x^2 + 4y - xy$ given $x = -3$; $y = -2$

Everywhere we see an x, we put in -3, and for each y we put in -2. The problem now becomes $(-3)^2 + 4(-2) - (-3)(-2)$. Order of operations says we must first do $(-3)^2$, which is 9. Then we do each of the multiplications where $4(-2)$ is -8, and $(-3)(-2)$ is $+6$. At this point we have $9 + (-8) - (+6)$, which is just $9 - 8 - 6$. Here we can combine the -8 and -6 to get -14. The final answer is $9 - 14$, which is -5. The work should be written down somewhat like this:

$x^2 + 4y - xy$
(given $x = -3$; $y = -2$)
$(-3)^2 + 4(-2) - (-3)(-2)$
$9 + -8 - +6$
$9 - 8 - 6$
$9 - 14$
-5

The laws of exponents

These rules should be covered fairly briefly. They receive much attention in Class Nine.

Don't give the general formulas (e.g. $x^n \times x^m = x^{(n+m)}$). This is too abstract for Class Eight.

Add exponents when multiplying terms with the same base.
  Example: $2^5 \times 2^3 \to 2^8$
  Example: $x^4 \times x^3 \to x^7$

Multiply exponents if one exponent is raised to another.
  Example: $(3^4)^2 \to 3^8$
  Example: $(x^4)^3 \to x^{12}$
  Example: $(3y^2)^3 \to 27y^6$

When adding like terms with exponents, the exponents don't change.
  Example: $3x^5 + 4x^5 \to 7x^5$
  Example: $3x^2 + 4x^3$ can't be simplified

Square rooting a term with an exponent (optional).
  Example: $\sqrt{5^6} \to 5^3$
  Example: $\sqrt{x^{16}} \to x^8$

Fractions and negatives

It doesn't matter where the negative sign goes in a fraction.
  Example: $\frac{3}{-4}$ is the same as $\frac{-3}{4}$ and the same as $\frac{-3}{4}$

Equations

Use of equal sign (for the teacher only)

There are three different ways to show work when simplifying or evaluating expressions:
1. Use an arrow ($\to$) to show going from one step to the next.
2. Use an equivalence sign ($\equiv$) to show going from one step to the next.
3. Show the steps under one another.

Use equal signs ($=$) only for equations, otherwise some students will incorrectly think that they have an equation that needs to be solved.

  Example: Simplify $6x - 5 + 4x + 11$

There are three possibilities to show the work:
1. $6x - 5 + 4x + 11 \to 10x + 6$
2. $6x - 5 + 4x + 11 \equiv 10x + 6$
3. $6x - 5 + 4x + 11$
   $10x + 6$

The work should not be shown like this: $6x - 5 + 4x + 11 = 10x + 6$ because now it looks like an equation and some students will try to 'solve' it.

Distributive property

Do lots of practice, especially when the distributive property (a number or term multiplying several others which follow in parentheses) is used in equations, such as:

Example: Solve: $5 - 3(2x - 3) - x = 7x - 2 + 4(x + 3)$

Start by simplifying both sides.

$$5 - 3(2x - 3) - x = 7x - 2 + 4(x+3)$$
$$5 - 6x + 9 - x = 7x - 2 + 4x + 12$$
$$-7x + 14 = 11x + 10$$
$$+7x - 10 \quad +7x - 10$$
$$4 = 18x$$
$$\div 18 \quad \div 18$$
$$\tfrac{4}{18} = x \rightarrow \text{Answer is } x = \tfrac{2}{9}$$

Equations with fractions

This is a great way to integrate fraction review.

Show that fractional answers can be plugged in and will work.

Example: The answer for the previous problem was $\tfrac{2}{9}$. Check to see that it is correct.

We simply put $\tfrac{2}{9}$ in the original equation to see if it really balances.

$$5 - 3(2x - 3) - x = 7x - 2 + 4(x + 3)$$
$$5 - 3(2 \times \tfrac{2}{9} - 3) - \tfrac{2}{9} = 7 \times \tfrac{2}{9} - 2 + 4(\tfrac{2}{9} + 3)$$
$$5 - 3(\tfrac{4}{9} - 3) - \tfrac{2}{9} = \tfrac{14}{9} - 2 + 4(3\tfrac{2}{9})$$
$$5 - 3(\tfrac{4}{9} - \tfrac{27}{9}) - \tfrac{2}{9} = \tfrac{14}{9} - 2 + 4(\tfrac{29}{9})$$
$$5 - 3(-\tfrac{23}{9}) - \tfrac{2}{9} = \tfrac{14}{9} - 2 + \tfrac{116}{9}$$
$$\tfrac{45}{9} + \tfrac{69}{9} - \tfrac{2}{9} = \tfrac{14}{9} - \tfrac{18}{9} + \tfrac{116}{9}$$
$$\tfrac{112}{9} = \tfrac{112}{9}$$

Both sides are equal, so $x = \tfrac{2}{9}$ works!

Equations with fractional constants and coefficients

Example: $\tfrac{2}{3}x - \tfrac{3}{4} = \tfrac{1}{5}x + \tfrac{2}{5}$

$$\tfrac{2}{3}x - \tfrac{3}{4} = \tfrac{1}{5}x + \tfrac{2}{5}$$
$$-\tfrac{1}{5}x + \tfrac{3}{4} \quad -\tfrac{1}{5}x + \tfrac{3}{4}$$

$(\tfrac{2}{3} - \tfrac{1}{5} \rightarrow \tfrac{7}{15}$ and $\tfrac{2}{5} + \tfrac{3}{4} \rightarrow \tfrac{23}{20})$

$$\tfrac{7}{15}x = \tfrac{23}{20}$$
$$\div \tfrac{7}{15} \quad \div \tfrac{7}{15}$$

$$x = \tfrac{23}{20} \times \tfrac{15}{7}$$

cross cancelling $\rightarrow x = \tfrac{23}{4} \times \tfrac{3}{7} \rightarrow x = \tfrac{69}{28}$ or $2\tfrac{13}{28}$

Cross multiplying

See *Moving along diagonals and cross multiplying* in the Class Eight *Proportions* unit, above, p. 142.

In the algebra unit, cross multiplying is taken a step further to include problems where the x appears on both sides of the equation.

Example: $\tfrac{x+3}{2} = \tfrac{2x-4}{3}$

We simply cross multiply to get $3(x + 3) = 2(2x - 4)$. Solving gives an answer of $x = 17$.

Strange solutions (optional)

These are best introduced once the class is fairly confident with solving basic equations. There are three types of situations to discuss here:

Equations with a solution of x = 0
There is one solution.
   Example: $8x + 5 = 3x + 5$
There is only one solution, and that solution happens to be $x = 0$.

Equations where any value for x will work
There are infinitely many solutions.
   Example: $8x + 7 = 4 + 8x + 3$
When we start to solve this, we get $8x + 7 = 8x + 7$, and notice that both sides of the equation are identical. If we continued solving this equation (which would be unnecessary), then x would disappear and we would end up with just $0 = 0$, which is always true.
   No matter what we put in for x in the original equation, the equation will balance Try it!

Untrue equations
Example: $8x + 3 = 8x - 7$
   This occurs when we notice that x disappears, leaving us with zero on one side of the equation, and some constant on the other side. In the above example, we end up with $0 = -10$, which is never true. No matter what we put into x, the equation cannot balance.

Converting repeating decimals into fractions (optional)

Review the Class Six method for converting repeating decimals into fractions. (See Class Six, *Converting repeating decimals to fractions*, p. 46.)
   Introduce the following new method that uses algebra.

Example: What is $0.3\overline{42}$ as a fraction?
   Let $x = 0.3\overline{42}$. Therefore $100x = 34.2\overline{42}$. We chose 100 because there are two digits under the repeat bar. Subtracting the former equation from the latter, we get:

$$\begin{aligned} 100x &= 34.2\overline{42} \\ -1x &= -0.3\overline{42} \\ \hline 99x &= 33.9, \end{aligned}$$

(Notice how the repeating parts line up and cancel!)

which leads to $x = \frac{33.9}{99}$ which is $\frac{339}{990}$ and this reduces to a final answer of $\frac{113}{330}$.

Example: What is $0.12\overline{037}$ as a fraction?
   Let $x = 0.12\overline{037}$ Therefore $1000x = 120.37\overline{037}$. We chose 1,000 because there are three digits under the repeat bar. Subtracting the former equation from the latter, we get:

$$\begin{aligned} 1000x &= 120.37\overline{037} \\ -1x &= -0.12\overline{037} \\ \hline 999x &= 120.25 \end{aligned}$$

which leads to $x = \frac{120.25}{999}$ which is $\frac{12025}{99900}$ reducing to a final answer of $\frac{13}{108}$.

Class Eight Algebra

Class Eight Computers

I do a brief unit on computers in an effort to meet the needs of Class Eight students who have a hunger for knowledge of the modern world as they prepare to enter the upper school. I believe that actual work with computers should be delayed until the upper school. In order to begin to understand about how computers store information, I do a unit on *number bases* and *ASCII code,* which gives a basic picture of how computer memory works.

One aspect of what I am proposing here – teaching about computer programming – is quite different from what is done in a typical Waldorf school. I call this unit *algorithms;* it is the 'thinking' behind the computer.

I have the students experience the thought process of computer programming without getting on a computer. Essentially, the students get to see algorithms, written in English, which are similar to computer programs.

Computer memory and ASCII code

This should be done after the unit on number bases (see *Number bases,* p 121.)

ASCII stands for **A**merican **S**tandard **C**ode for **I**nformation **I**nterchange.

Binary codes using flags
Try introducing this by imagining that you are sending codes from one tower to another with a line of flags, where each flag can be one of two possible colours. How many codes are possible with a row of 4 flags? (Answer: $2^4 = 16$.) How many codes are possible with 8 flags? (Answer: $2^8 = 256$.) Computers do basically the same thing, but use bits instead of flags.

A computer bit as a switch
Computers use the ASCII coding system, which is based on binary digits. A bit is a very small circuit in the computer that can be thought of as a switch; it is either 'on' or 'off'. At any given moment, an electrical current is either passing through it or not. We represent these two possibilities in binary either as '1' (for 'on') or '0' (for 'off'). This is why people say that the memory of a computer is just a bunch of zeros and ones – it really means that it's a bunch of switches, with each one either 'on' or 'off'. The students need to understand that when any key on the computer keyboard is hit, that its ASCII code is 'written' into the computer memory as a string of binary digits – switches that are either on or off.

One byte of memory
One byte consists (usually) of 8 bits. A single keyboard character has a binary code that is one byte (8 bits) long. One 8-bit byte has 256 possible codes, just like our 8 flags on the tower had 256 possible codes.

Example: How is the character 'L' represented in the computer's memory?

In the ASCII code table (see Appendix, p. 246), we see that the hex code for 'L' is 4C. Since 4 in hexadecimal is equal to 0100 in binary, and C in hexadecimal is equal to 1100 in binary, we can say that 'L' is represented in binary ASCII code as 01001100.

Decoding strings of binary code
See the ASCII code table, p. 246.

Have the students decode one byte at a time from binary to hexadecimal, then look up the code in the ASCII code table.

Example: Decode this string: 01101000, 01101111, 01110010, 01110011, 01100101

These five bytes are written as 68, 6F, 72, 73, 65 in hexadecimal, which is then converted (by looking on the ASCII code table) into the five characters, 'horse'.

Example: The following string of binary code is actually a riddle. Decode it and answer the riddle.

01010111, 01101000, 01100001, 01110100,
00100000, 01100010, 01100001, 01110011,
01100101, 00100000, 01101001, 01110011,
00100000, 01110100, 01101000, 01101001,
01110011, 00111010, 00100000, 00110011,
00110100, 00101011, 00110100, 00110100,
00111101, 00110001, 00110000, 00110000,
00111111

The binary bytes are first converted into the following in hexadecimal (in the same order):

57	68	61	74
20	62	61	73
65	20	69	73
20	74	68	69
73	3A	20	33
34	2B	34	34
3D	31	30	30
3F			

Using the ASCII code table in Appendix D, we decode these bytes to (in the same order):

W	h	a	t
space	b	a	s
e	space	i	s
space	t	h	i
s	:	space	3
4	+	4	4
=	1	0	0
?			

which is the string: 'What base is this: 34 + 44 = 100?' The answer to this riddle is that it is octal, since 34 + 44 is equal to 100 in octal (see *Number bases*, p. 121).

Computer algorithms

This unit deals with how computers manipulate information through computer programming.

Only spend a couple of days on this unit. Even a brief amount of time gives the students a glimpse into the basic idea of a computer program.

The term *algorithm* (coming from al-Khwarizmi's name) existed in mathematics long before computers, and has become popularised with their development. An algorithm is a procedure that is described in a detailed, step-by-step manner.

Computers don't think. The computer programmer does the thinking. The computer simply follows the step-by-step instructions as given in the computer program.

Some key words that an algorithm (or program) may use are: If ... then ... else, Until, Goto, Input, Print.

Students should not be expected to write algorithms on their own. For the most part, that kind of thinking is for Classes Ten and Eleven. The idea here is simply to give them an idea of how computers work, and to be able to follow the steps of these algorithms thereby gaining a basic understanding of what a computer does when a program is being executed.

Writing familiar algorithms

Take a familiar procedure (e.g. addition, long division) and describe it thoroughly in words. Then write it down as an algorithm. The language is English, but careful thought must be given when choosing the wording.

An algorithm for addition

See Appendix for the *Algorithm for addition* (p. 247) written out in the style of a computer program, but in English.

The class should try to create it together on the board, so that everyone sees it evolve.

An algorithm for long division (optional)

See Appendix for the *Algorithm for long division*, p. 247) written out in the style of a computer program, but in English.

Students wanting an extra challenge may attempt to write this on their own. They should imagine that they have a friend who knows how to add, subtract and multiply, but does not know how to do long division. They have to write a letter to this friend and explain how to do long division, step-by-step, and without referring to a specific example.

Emphasise to the students that there are many possible answers for writing down this algorithm.

Examples of new algorithms

Below are a couple of new algorithms for the students to try to follow. The students should simply follow the step-by-step instructions stated in the program, thereby imitating what a computer does when it executes a program.

The prime number algorithm

This is similar to the Sieve of Eratosthenes, see Appendix for the *Algorithm for prime numbers* (p. 248) written out in the style of a computer program, but in English.

Don't explain any of the steps to the students. The main purpose is for the students to experience how a computer operates – it simply follows instructions. They should do the same!

The square root algorithm – without zeros

See Appendix for the *Square root algorithm – without zeros* (p. 213) written out in the style of a computer program, but in English.

Read my notes given in Class Seven Arithmetic (p. 89) for the importance of teaching the square root algorithm so that students can calculate square roots by hand.

Class Eight Geometry

Mensuration (areas and volumes)
Beware of formulas
A common approach to teaching areas and volumes is to have the students use, and therefore memorise, a lot of formulas. This approach reduces maths to blindly sticking numbers into formulas, often without the students having a clue about what they are really doing. I do the opposite – I try to use as few formulas as possible. Almost always, I show the students where a formula comes from, and most of my formulas are quite general (e.g. one of my formulas can be used for either a cone or a pyramid). I encourage the students to think their way through every problem.

Area
Review
Review Class Seven, *Area* (p. 101).
Review one, two and three dimensions from Class Six (p. 60).
Emphasise that *length* is measured using lines (e.g. metre, foot, etc.); *area* is measured using squares (e.g. m², cm², in², etc.) and *volume* is measured using cubes (e.g., m³, cm³, in³, etc.).

The Pythagorean Theorem
Review *shear and stretch* from Class Seven (p. 101).
Give Baravalle's proof using sheer and stretch, as shown below. (Hermann von Baravalle was a maths teacher in the first Waldorf School.)

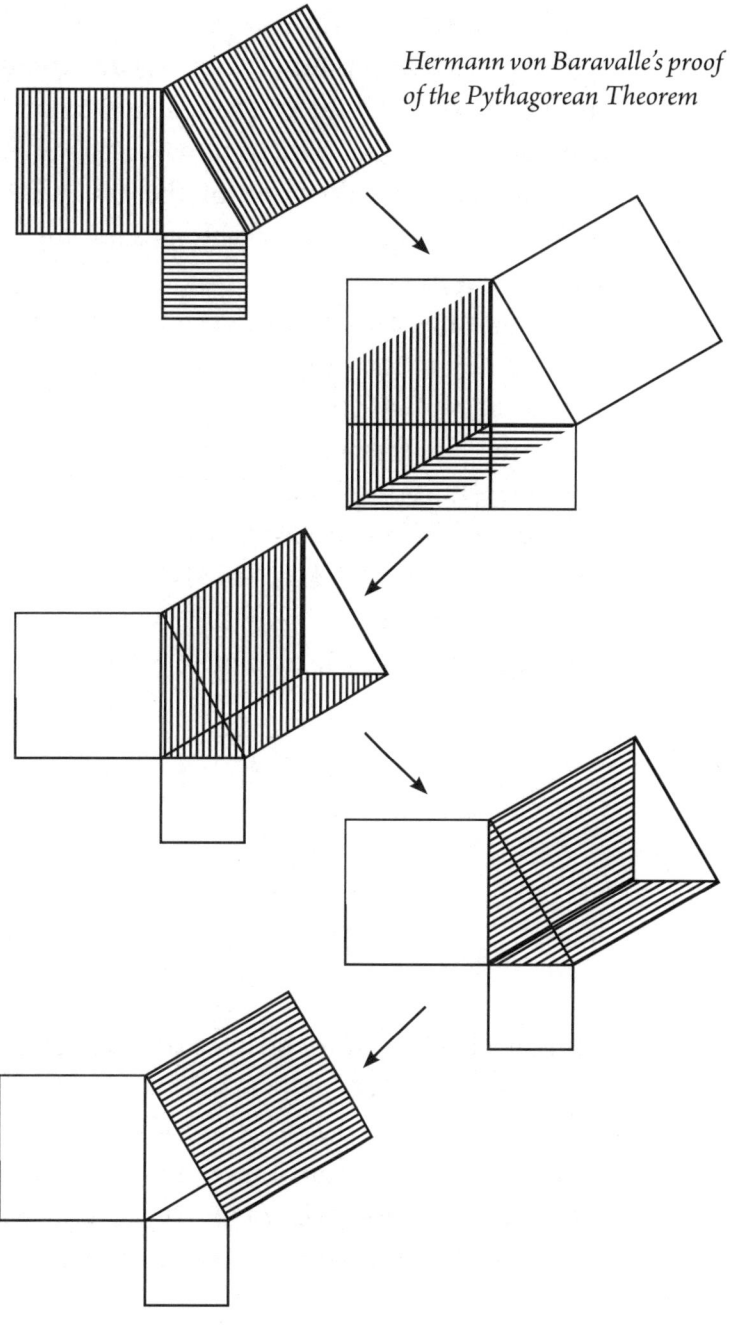

Hermann von Baravalle's proof of the Pythagorean Theorem

Area of a trapezium

The formula for calculating the area of a trapezium $A = \frac{1}{2}h(b_1 + b_2)$ is given in maths textbooks, but I don't give it to the students. As a challenge problem, I often ask a student to come up with the formula.

Have the students find the area of any trapezium by dividing it into a triangle and a parallelogram (or a rectangle), or into two triangles.

Example: Find the area of the trapezium shown on the right. Assume all measurements are given in metres.

We first divide the trapezium by drawing a line parallel to one side from one of the obtuse angles, as shown in the drawing below. We then calculate the area of the parallelogram as its base (9) times its height, which is 4 (not 5), resulting in an area of 36 m². The triangle also has a height of 4, and its base is 8, so its area is ½(8)(4), which is 16 m². The whole trapezium, therefore, has an area of 36 + 16 = 52 m².

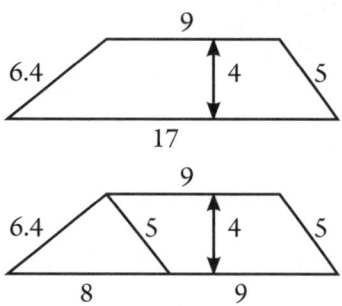

Heron's formula for the area of a triangle

Area = $\sqrt{s \times (s-a) \times (s-b) \times (s-c)}$

where $s = \frac{1}{2}(a+b+c)$ is the semi-perimeter.

This formula is attributed to the Greek, Heron of Alexandria (c. AD 10–20), but it may have been Archimedes that came up with it first.

Heron's amazing proof of this formula is, for me, the climax of the study of geometry in Class Ten.

Before seeing this formula, the students should first be able to calculate the areas of non-right triangles where the base and height are given. (See Class Seven Geometry, *Area*, p. 102).

The beauty of this little-known formula is that you don't need to know the height of the triangle. Without this formula, you would have to use trigonometry (studied in upper school) to calculate the height, and it would be more complicated.

Example: Find the area of the triangle that has sides of length 5 m, 6 m and 7 m.

The perimeter is 18 m, so the semi-perimeter is 9 m. Putting all the numbers into the formula, we get: Area = $\sqrt{9(9-5)(9-6)(9-7)}$, which is $\sqrt{9 \times 4 \times 3 \times 2}$, and becomes $\sqrt{216}$. Using the square root algorithm, we get an area of 14.70 m² (rounded).

Calculating the area of four types of triangles

A right triangle

We are given the base and the height, so finding the area is easy.

Example: With the triangle here, the area is:
$A = \frac{1}{2} \times b \times h \rightarrow A = \frac{1}{2} \times 20 \times 21 \rightarrow A = 210$ m²

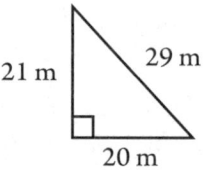

An isosceles triangle
Here, we can use the Pythagorean Theorem in order to calculate the height. We then use this height in order to calculate the area.

Example: We start with a triangle with one side 20 m long and two sides 26 m long. To find the height, we cut the triangle in half, which makes a right triangle with sides 26 m, 10 m and h, which is the height of the original triangle. Using the leg formula we get: $h^2 = 26^2 - 10^2 \rightarrow h^2 = 676 - 100 \rightarrow h^2 = 576 \rightarrow h = 24$

(We also could have determined h more quickly by using Pythagorean triples.)

Now we know that the height of the original triangle is 24. So the area is:
$A = ½ \times b \times h \rightarrow A = ½ \times 20 \times 24 \rightarrow A = 240$ m²

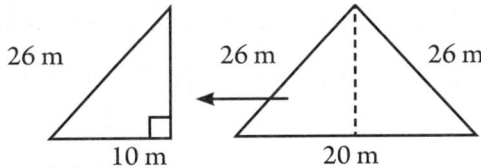

An equilateral triangle
In this case, we could use the same method as described above for the isosceles triangle, but Heron's formula is generally easier.

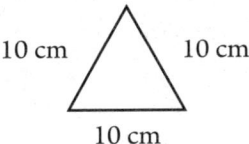

Example: With an equilateral triangle that has all sides equal to 10 cm, the perimeter is 30 cm, so the semi-perimeter (s) is 15. The area of the triangle is then:
$A = \sqrt{15 \times (15 - 10) \times (15 - 10) \times (15 - 10)}$ $\rightarrow \sqrt{15 \times 5 \times 5 \times 5} \rightarrow \sqrt{3 \times 5^2 \times 5^2} \rightarrow 5 \times 5 \times \sqrt{3} \rightarrow 25 \times (1.73) \approx 43.25$ cm²

A scalene triangle (each side is different)
In this case, we must use Heron's formula.

Example: Using Heron's formula with the triangle here, the perimeter is 72 cm, so the semi-perimeter (s) is half of 72, which is 36. The area of the triangle is then:
$A = \sqrt{36 \times (36 - 28) \times (36 - 24) \times (36 - 20)}$ $\rightarrow \sqrt{36 \times 8 \times 12 \times 16} \rightarrow \sqrt{55296} \approx 235.1$ cm²

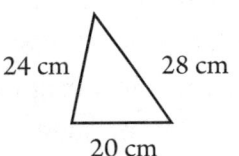

Area of a circle
$$A = \pi r^2$$
Proof: Have students (perhaps in groups) derive the formula by following this procedure:

Cut three congruent circles, each with a radius of 5 cm, into 4, 8 and 16 pie pieces.

From each circle, take the pie pieces and put them side-by-side, alternating top up and top down, so that a kind of parallelogram is formed that has a wavy top and bottom. (Only the case of 16 pieces is shown below.)

 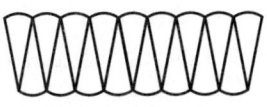

Class Eight Geometry

Compare the three cases. Ask the class the following questions:

What happens as the circle is cut into more and more pie pieces?

The pie pieces become thinner and thinner, and the wavy parallelogram gets closer and closer to becoming a rectangle. *It becomes a rectangle once the circle is cut into infinitely many pieces.*

What is the area of this rectangle, and of the circle?

The area of the rectangle is the same as the area of the circle, because the rectangle was made from the pieces of the circle. The height of the rectangle is 5 cm (the radius of the circle). The base of the rectangle is half the circle's circumference (which is 2π), since half the circumference is on the top of the rectangle and half is on the bottom. Therefore, the area of the rectangle, and also the area of the circle, is $5(5\pi) = 25\pi \approx 78.54$ cm².

What is the formula for the area of a circle?

To determine the formula, we do the same process as just done above, except we use r for the radius instead of 5 cm. The height of the rectangle is r, and the base is $r \times \pi$. So the area of the rectangle, and also the area of the circle, is $(\pi \times r) \times r$, or Area $= \pi \times r^2$.

Archimedes' version of the area of a circle

Archimedes saw the area of a circle as being equal to the area of the right triangle that has a base equal to the circumference of the circle, and a height equal to the circle's radius. This triangle is twice as long as the above rectangle.

And since the triangle's area is ½ × base × height, we calculate the area of this triangle, and also the circle, to be: ½ × $2\pi r$ × $r = \pi \times r^2$.

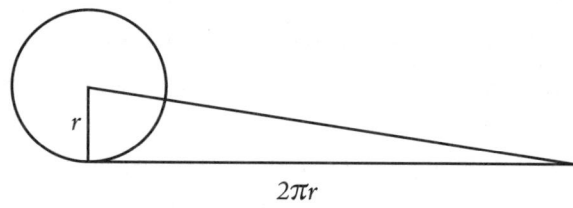

Portions of circles
Finding the length of an arc
An arc is part of the circumference of a circle.

Example: What is the length of an 80° arc of a circle that has a diameter of 20 m?

The circumference of the whole circle (using $C = \pi \times d$) is 20π. Since the whole circle consists of 360°, the arc is $\frac{2}{9}$ (reducing $\frac{80}{360}$) as long as the circumference of the whole circle. So the length of the arc is: $\frac{2}{9} \times 20\pi \rightarrow \frac{40\pi}{9} \rightarrow \frac{40 \times 3.14}{9} \approx$ 13.96 m.

Finding the area of a segment of a circle.
Example: Find the area of a circle with a radius of 5 cm that has a 60° segment (pie piece) missing.

The circle is 300° out of 360°, or ⅚ complete. The area of the segment is therefore ⅚ of the area of the whole circle ($A = \pi \times r^2$). The segment's area is then: $\frac{5}{6} \times \pi (5)^2 \rightarrow \frac{125\pi}{6} \approx 65.42$ cm².

Volumes of solids

Cubic measurement

Introduce the concept of volume with models of various cubes (cubic m, cubic cm, etc.), and talk about how each one of these cubes can be used to measure volume.

Notation

Be sure when using the abbreviated form that you are careful to say 'cubic centimetres' and not 'centimetres cubed'.

Be aware that some students may look at 8 cm^3 and think that we should calculate 8^3.

Don't give many formulas

Don't give the students separate formulas for each specific solid (e.g. cylinder, pyramid, cone, prism, etc.). (See *Beware of formulas*, p. 151, for more details.) Instead, I mostly use two general formulas, both of which the students (ideally) derive for themselves.

Volumes of prisms and cylinders

The transition from area to volume

Imagine a rectangular room, 6 m by 4 m, which is filling with water. We should lead the students through the following sequence of questions:

How much water is there in the room when the water is 1 metre deep?

Here we should be able to picture *one* layer of boxes placed next to one another on the floor, where each box is one cubic metre and filled with water. The total number of cubic metres is then 6 × 4 = 24 cubic metres.

How much water is there if the water is 2 metres deep?

The picture is basically the same, except now there are two layers, each layer having 24 cubic metres. Therefore, our answer is 2 × 24 = 48 cubic metres.

How much water is there if the water reaches the ceiling (3 metres high)?

Now there are 3 layers of boxes, where each layer has 24 boxes. Our answer is 3 × 24 = 72 m^3.

The students should now be able to derive the general formula for this situation, which is our first volume formula:

$$V = A_{\text{Base}} \times h$$

Where A_{Base} is the area of the base, and h is the height.

This formula is used for solids where the top and bottom are flat and identical (e.g. prisms, cylinders, etc.).

3D shear and stretch for finding volumes

Use a deck of cards (or a stack of books). The volume of a deck of cards is the same whether the deck is straight up, or knocked over slightly and rising up at an angle.

Imagination exercise. In the corner of the room there is a prism (box), such that the base of the prism, placed on the floor, is a square, 50 cm on each side, and the top of the prism (square of the same size) is positioned directly above the base and sits on the ceiling. The four sides of the prism are rectangles and are made of a thin stretchable substance. If the height of the prism is 3 metres, then the volume is 0.5 × 0.5 × 3 or 0.75 m^3.

Now, imagine that the top of the prism is allowed to slide anywhere along the ceiling of the room while the bottom remains fixed in the corner of the room. The four sides of the prism then become stretched out to form parallelograms. As the top moves further away from the bottom, the prism becomes longer and thinner. We can imagine this to be the same scenario as the deck of cards; the prism is just a stack of squares, no matter where the top of the prism is on the ceiling, and therefore we can see that the volume of the prism always remains 0.75 m³.

The volume of a prism, whether 'tilted' or perfectly vertical, depends only on the area of its base and on its height above the ground, and thus the formula given above ($V = A_{\text{Base}} \times h$) is valid for this case as well.

A surprising variation

If we take any 4 points in space (not all points on the same plane), then we have a tetrahedron (probably irregular). The volume of the tetrahedron will remain the same if we slide two of the points anywhere along the line that they lie on. This can be explained by thinking of the tetrahedron as lying on a table. The volume of this tetrahedron is ⅓ the area of the base times the tetrahedron's height (see volume formulas, below). If we slide two of the three points of the triangular base along the line that they share, then the area of this triangular base does not change (see Class Seven Geometry, *Shear and Stretch*, p. 101); nor is the height of the whole tetrahedron altered. Since area of the base and the height are unchanged, then we can say that the volume is also unchanged.

Volumes of pyramids and cones

Three pyramids in a cube

Demonstration (Must do!): We start with a normal, Egyptian-style, pyramid, but it is made so that the height is equal to the length of its square base. This allows the pyramid to fit perfectly into a cube (with an open top) that has the same size square base as the pyramid. Both the cube and the pyramid also have the same height. We now construct three 'tilting pyramids'. Each one is identical, with the same square base and the same height as the original pyramid. However, with each tilting pyramid, its *apex* is located *directly above* one of the corners of the square base.

Now we have a puzzle. The objective is to fit the three tilting pyramids perfectly together inside the cube. (It really works!) This shows that the volume of one tilting pyramid is ⅓ the volume of the cube. And since the shear and stretch principle says that the original pyramid has the same volume as one of the tilting pyramids, we can say that the original pyramid has a volume equal to ⅓ of the volume of the cube. The net opposite (try enlarging it in a photocopier) folds up into a tilting pyramid.

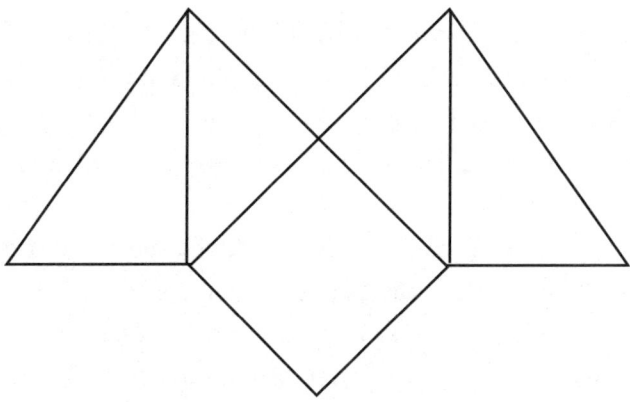
A net for constructing a tilting pyramid

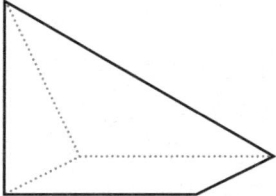
A tilting pyramid

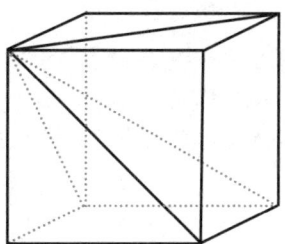
3 tilting pyramids in a cube

The students should now be able to derive the formula for a pyramid, which is:
$$V = \frac{1}{3} A_{\text{Base}} \times h$$
Where A_{Base} is the area of the base, and h is the height.

This formula can be used when the bottom of a solid is flat and the top is a point (e.g. pyramid, cone).

It was discovered by Democritus, *ca.* 430 BC.

Archimedes' ratio

Imagine that a sphere fits perfectly into a cylinder such that the diameter of the sphere is equal to both the height and the base diameter of the cylinder. Imagine a cone, which also fits perfectly into the cylinder, since its height and base diameter are the same as the cylinder's.

Archimedes discovered that the ratio of the volume of the cone to the sphere to the cylinder is:

Cone : Sphere : Cylinder = 1 : 2 : 3

This means that the cone's volume is ⅓ of the volume of the cylinder (which the formula $V = \frac{1}{3} A_{\text{Base}} \times h$ tells us), and that the sphere's volume is twice the volume of the cone, and ⅔ the volume of the cylinder.

We can also say that the volume of the cylinder is equal to the sum of the volumes of the cone and the sphere. The following demonstration can be done if you have a cone, ball and cylinder (with an open top) all with the same height, or alternatively, you can lead the students through it imaginatively:

Fill the cone completely with water and pour the water into the cylinder. The cylinder is now ⅓ full with water. Slowly push the ball (sphere) into the cylinder. The water should rise exactly to the top of the cylinder, without spilling, thereby showing that the volume of the cylinder is equal to the sum of the volumes of the cone and the sphere.

The proof of Archimedes' ratio is done in Class Ten.

The volume of a sphere
$$V = \frac{4}{3}\pi r^3$$
where r is the radius of the sphere.

Derivation of this formula (given Archimedes' ratio): a cylinder with a height equal to its base diameter has a volume equal to the area of its base times its height, which is $\pi r^2 \times 2r$, or $2\pi r^3$. Archimedes' ratio says that the volume of the sphere is ⅔ the volume of this cylinder. Therefore:
$$V = \frac{2}{3}(2\pi r^3) = \frac{4}{3}\pi r^3$$

Surface area

Surface area can be covered fairly briefly.

Example: What is the surface area of a cube that has an edge of length 10 cm?

We add up six squares, each with an area of 100 cm², and get 600 cm².

Example: What is the surface area of a box that is 2 m by 3 m by 4 m?

We have two rectangles that are 2 by 3, two that are 3 by 4, and two that are 2 by 4. The total surface area is therefore: $2(2 \times 3) + 2(3 \times 4) + 2(2 \times 4) \rightarrow 52$ m².

Example: What is the surface area of a cylinder that is 3 cm tall and has a base diameter of 10 cm?

We can see that the cylinder has three parts. First, we imagine removing the top and bottom, and then cutting the side (tube) of the cylinder vertically, so that it rolls out flat into a rectangle. This rectangle has a height of 3 cm and a length equal to the cylinder's circumference (10π cm), which results in the rectangle's area being $3 \times 10\pi = 30\pi$ cm². The top and bottom of the cylinder each have an area of $\pi(5)^2$, which is 25π cm². The total surface area is the sum of these three parts:

$30\pi + 25\pi + 25\pi$, which is 80π or ≈ 251.2 cm².

Example: What is the surface area of an icosahedron that has edges 10 cm long?

Each of the twenty triangular faces has a height of $\sqrt{75}$ cm and an area of 43.3 cm². Since there are 20 triangles on an icosahedron, the total area is: $20 \times 43.3 \rightarrow \approx 866$ cm².

Surface area of a sphere
$$S = 4\pi r^2$$

This formula tells us that the area of the hemisphere (half the sphere) is twice the area of the circle on which it sits, or that the whole sphere's surface area is 4 times the area of the greatest circle inside it.

Example: What is the surface area of a sphere that has a radius of 5 cm?

The answer is $4\pi(5)^2$, which is 100π cm² ≈ 314 cm².

Surface area of a cone (optional)
$$S = \pi k r$$

r is the radius of the base of the cone, and k is the distance along the edge of the cone.

This formula does not include the area of the circular base.

Example: What is the surface area of a cone (without its base), with a 10 cm diameter and a 12 cm height?

We must find the length of the cone's edge. Here we need to imagine the right triangle that goes from the vertex of the cone, straight down along the central axis of the cone to the centre of the circular base, then out to the edge of the base, and finally, from there, up along the edge of the cone, returning to the vertex. The two legs of this triangle have been given as 5 cm and 12 cm, and by using the hypotenuse formula we find the length of the hypotenuse of the triangle (which is the same as the edge of the cone) to be 13 cm. Putting $k = 13$ and $r = 5$ into our formula, we find that the surface area of the cone is $\pi \times 13 \times 5$, which is 65π, or ≈ 204.1 cm².

Proof of the formula $S = \pi\,k\,r$
We can cut any cone (with edge length k and base radius r) straight down the edge, and then press it flat onto a table. We now have a segment of a circle ('a portion of a pie'), which has a radius equal to k. We can imagine that if the cone is tall and narrow, that it will produce a circle segment that is only a small portion of the pie. Likewise, if the cone is short and wide, then it will produce a circle segment that, when flattened out, is nearly a whole pie (only a narrow sliver is missing).

With a given cone, how can we know exactly what portion of the pie we have? The answer is that the cone, once it is flattened, is r/k of the pie. This means that if k is 6 and r is 3, then the circle segment that results from flattening the cone is 3/6 or ½ of the pie (a semi-circle). If k is 8 and r is 6, then the cone, which is fairly short and wide, will be flattened into a circle segment that is 6/8, or ¾ of the

whole pie*. Now we can say that the area of the circle segment (which is equal to the cone's surface area) is r/k of the area of the whole pie (πk^2).

Therefore: $S = (r/k) \times \pi k^2 = \pi k r$

Mensuration practice problems
Example: What is the volume of a cylindrical can with a height of 8 cm and a base diameter of 6 cm?

The radius of the base is 3 cm, so the area of the base is $\pi \times 3^2$, which is 9π. The volume is simply equal to the area of the base times the height (8), which gives an answer of:

$8 \times 9\pi \rightarrow 72\pi$ cm³ ≈ 226.08 cm³.

Example: What is the volume of a box that is 1.5 m by 3 m by 4 m?

We can say that the base is 3 by 4, which has an area of 12 m². Multiplying this area by 1½ (the height) gives a volume of 18 m³.

Example: What is the volume of a sphere that has a radius of 5 cm?

Using the formula $V = 4/3 \pi r^3$, we simply put 5 into r, which gives $V = 4/3 \pi\, 5^3$. Remembering to first cube the 5 (which is 125), we get:

$V = 4/3 \pi 5^3 \rightarrow \dfrac{4 \times 125}{3} \times \pi \rightarrow \dfrac{500}{3} \times \pi \rightarrow \dfrac{500 \times 3.14}{3} \approx 523$ cm³.

* The reason for this ratio (r/k) is that the circumference of the whole piece is $2\pi k$, and the distance along the pie's circumference of just the circle segment is equal to the circumference of the base of the cone, which is $2\pi r$. The ratio of these two circumferences is $2\pi r : 2\pi k$, which is $r : k$. This ratio ($r : k$) is therefore also the ratio of the area of the cone to the area of the 'full' circle (which has a radius of k).

Class Eight Geometry

Example: What is the volume of the cone shown below?

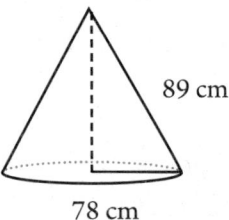

We first need to calculate the height of the cone. So we draw a right triangle inside the cone that goes from the top of the cone down to the middle of the base (this is the height, h), then out to the edge of the base (a distance of 39 cm, which is the radius of the circular base), and then up along the outside of the cone back to the top (a distance of 89 cm). We use the leg formula to find h: $h^2 = 89^2 - 39^2 \to h^2 = 7{,}921 - 1{,}521 \to h^2 = 6{,}400 \to h = 80$.

Now that we have determined the height, we can easily find the volume: $V = \frac{1}{3} A_{Base} \times h \to V = \frac{1}{3}(\pi \times 39^2) \times 80$, which gives an answer of $\approx 127{,}358.4$ cm^3.

Example: What is the volume of a triangular prism where the edges of the triangles are all 10 cm, and the length of the rectangular sides is 15 cm?

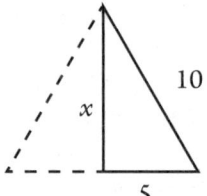 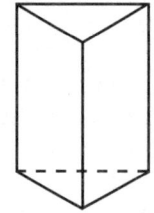

It is easiest if we view the prism as standing on one of its triangular ends, so that the rectangular sides are standing vertically. The volume can then be seen to be equal to the area of the triangular base times the height (which is the length of any of the rectangles). We can find the area of the triangular base either by splitting the triangle in half (as shown on the right) and using the leg formula to find the height: $h^2 = 10^2 - 5^2$, leading to $h = \sqrt{75} \approx 8.66$, and then the area of the triangular base is: $A_{Base} \approx \frac{1}{2} \times 10 \times \sqrt{75} \to 5\sqrt{75} \to 43.3$ cm^2. Alternatively, we could have more easily used Heron's formula, as was done above for the same triangle (see above, p. 153). Either way, once we have the area of the triangular base, we can then calculate the volume of the whole prism: $V = A_{Base} \times h \to 43.3 \times 15 \to 649.5$ cm^3.

Example: Given the pyramid shown below,
(a) Calculate the volume
(b) Calculate the surface area

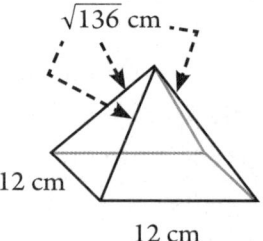

(a): This is one of the most difficult problems in this unit, because we are not given the height of the pyramid, and calculating this height is fairly difficult. The height (shown as 'h' in the drawing on the right) can be imagined as the distance that a ball would fall if it were dropped from the top of the hollow pyramid onto the middle of the floor, which is a square.

We can then draw a triangle that has h as one of its sides. (It stands inside the pyramid, and is shown below with dotted lines.) We could find h fairly quickly if we knew the other two sides of this dotted triangle, but unfortunately, we only know the length of one of the sides. So we draw a second triangle, which is half of one of the sides of the pyramid (shaded in the drawing). The advantage of the shaded triangle is that we know two of its sides and it shares a side with the dotted triangle. Using the leg formula with the shaded triangle, we get: $x^2 = (\sqrt{136})^2 - 6^2 \to x^2 = 136 - 36 \to x^2 = 100 \to x = 10$.

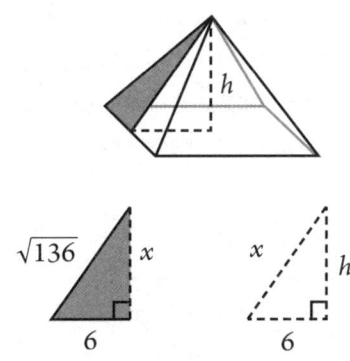

Finding x is a major step, because now we have the length for a second side of the dotted triangle. Now, using the leg formula with the dotted triangle, we get:

$h^2 = x^2 - 6^2 \to h^2 = 10^2 - 6^2 \to h^2 = 100 - 36 \to h^2 = 64 \to h = 8$

Now that we have found the height of the entire pyramid (h), finding the volume is easy:

$V = \frac{1}{3}(A_{\text{base}}) \times h \to V = \frac{1}{3}(144) \times 8 \to V = 384 \text{ cm}^3$

(b): To find the surface area, we simply add up the area of the five faces of the pyramid (four triangles and a square). Each triangle has a base of 12 cm, and a height of 10 cm. (Notice that this height is given as x, and was calculated in the solution for part (a). Also, note that x is the height of a triangle, and h is the height of the whole pyramid.) Each triangle, therefore, has an area of $A = \frac{1}{2}(12)(10) \to 60 \text{ cm}^2$. The whole pyramid then has a surface area equal to the area of the four triangles plus the area of the square, which is

$4 \times 60 + 144 \to S = 384 \text{ cm}^2$.

(It is coincidental that 384 also appeared in the answer for the volume. It is, of course, not correct to say that the volume is equal to the surface area, since cm^2 and cm^3 are completely different units. If we had instead measured in inches, or in metres, then the volume and surface area would have produced completely different numbers.)

Example: A conical drinking glass is 12 cm deep and 10 cm across at the top.

(a) What is its volume in cm^3?

(b) What is its volume in mℓ?

(c) If it is filled halfway to the top with water, then how much water is that (in mℓ)?

Class Eight Geometry

Solution: (a) Using the formula $V = \frac{1}{3} \times A_{Base} \times h$, we get $\frac{1}{3} \times (\pi \times 5^2) \times (12) \approx 314$ cm^3

(b) Since 1 cm^3 equals one millilitre, the volume of the glass is 314 mℓ.

(c) This is deceptive! Filling it halfway up means that both the diameter and the height are cut in half. Using then a depth of 6 cm, and a diameter of 5 cm, we get:

$V = \frac{1}{3} \times A_{Base} \times h \rightarrow V = \frac{1}{3}(\pi \times 2.5^2) \times 6 \approx 39.25$ cm^3, which is 39.25 mℓ. Now, dividing 39.25 (the volume of the glass filled halfway to the top) by 314 (the volume of the glass filled), we get 0.125, which is equal to $\frac{1}{8}$. Surprisingly, the glass has only been filled to $\frac{1}{8}$ of its full volume!

The volume of an octahedron and tetrahedron
See Appendix, p. 215, for details.

These are great problems for those students needing an extra challenge.

'Tricks' with dimensions
A volume of a given shape can be 'made' into a one-dimensional straight line.

Example: There is a room that has a floor measuring 10 metres by 7 metres and is 3 metres high. The volume of the room is therefore $10 \times 7 \times 3 = 210$ cubic metres. We can picture that 210 boxes, each one exactly one cubic metre in size, could be neatly stacked into this room.

Alternatively, we can imagine taking all the boxes out of the room, and putting them side by side into a straight line. This line of boxes would be 210 metres long.

More dramatically, we can imagine filling the same room with very small boxes that are only one cubic cm in size. The room has a volume of $1,000 \times 700 \times 300 = 210,000,000$ cubic cm. If these boxes were put into a straight line, then the line would be 210,000,000 cm long, or 2,100 km long! Note that the room and both of the above mentioned lines of boxes all have the same volume.

Often, people try to make sense of large numbers by translating them into something visual. The results are often intentionally distorted.

Are there too many people on the earth? (Assume 7 billion people.)

Answer 1 (One-dimensional): Yes, far too many people! If all the people in the world were to join hands, the line would be about 26 times longer than the distance to the moon, or about 253 times around the equator. (This assumes that an average person's arm span is 145 cm.)

Answer 2 (Three-dimensional): No, there are not so many people at all! We could take all the people in the world, put each one in a box that has a floor area of 200 square metres with 2.5 m high ceilings, and adding all these boxes together gives a total volume of about 3,500 cubic km, which is considerably less than the volume of the Grand Canyon, which is estimated to be very close to 4,000 cubic km.

Answer 3 (Two-dimensional): There is enough room, for now! If we spread everyone out evenly around the world, there would be one person per 2.1 hectare. (This is based on a total land area on the earth of 149,000,000 km².) If we use the fact that an estimated 32% of the earth's land is 'wasteland' (i.e. too rocky, dry, cold or barren to grow anything), then that would amount to 5.7 hectares of 'fertile land' (i.e. farmland, pasture, forest) per household, assuming that everyone is in a 4-person household

Note that this is the most relevant of the three solutions because it is dealing with the real issue: the amount of land per person.

Stereometry

(Stereometry is the study of 3-D forms including the Platonic and Archimedean solids)

I highly encourage anyone planning to teach Platonic and/or Archimedean solids to read Daud Sutton's book titled *Platonic & Archimedean Solids*.

Vocabulary

The following definitions are intended for the teacher only. The students should come to a familiarity with each of these terms through talking about them and experiencing them, not through definitions.

Polyhedron: a 3-D solid with flat polygons for faces.

Edge: a line along which two faces of a polyhedron meet. (A cube has 12 edges.)

Vertex: a corner, or point, of a polyhedron. (A cube has eight vertices.)

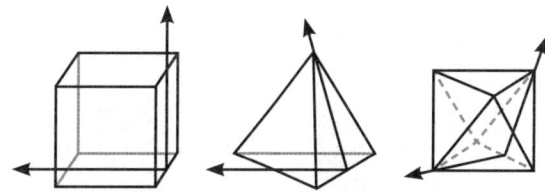

Dihedral angles of a cube, tetrahedron and octahedron

Dihedral angle: the angle at which two planes meet along an edge. Specifically, it is measured as the angle formed by two lines (one lying on each plane) drawn perpendicularly from a point on that edge. More simply, we can think of the dihedral angle by placing the polyhedron on a table, and measuring the angle at which a face meets the table. Looking in this way, we can understand better that the dihedral angle of a cube is 90°; the dihedral angle of a tetrahedron is approximately 70½° – it's less than vertical and the dihedral angle of an octahedron is approximately 109½° – it's more than vertical. Furthermore, a dodecahedron has a dihedral angle equal to approximately 116½°, and an icosahedron has a dihedral angle of about 138°. (Again, this explanation is for the teacher. Try not to show the tetrahedron, octahedron, dodecahedron or icosahedron yet. Let the students discover these for themselves, as described below in *Transformations of the cube*.)

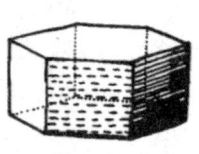 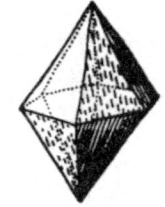

Hexagonal Prism *Hexagonal Bipyramid*

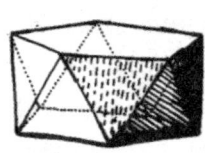 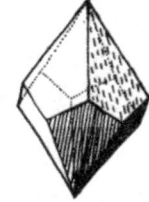

Pentagonal Anti-prism *Pentagonal Trapezohedron*

Types of polyhedra
The following definitions are intended for the teacher only. The students need to become familiar with these terms, but they shouldn't be given these definitions. Instead, they should learn about these forms through experience and observation.

A *Platonic solid* is a regular polyhedron (see *Platonic Solids* below for details).

An *Archimedean solid* or an *Archimedean dual* is a semi-regular polyhedra (see *Archimedean solids* below).

A *pyramid* has a polygon as a base, a point as a top and triangular faces for its sides. The pyramids of Egypt are called square pyramids because they have a square base. A tetrahedron is a pyramid with a triangular base. A pyramid can be created with any polygon as its base.

A *prism* is a polyhedron that has its top and bottom faces both congruent and parallel, and the faces on its sides are all parallelograms. A right prism has rectangles for side faces. A cube is a right square prism.

A *bipyramid* consists of two congruent (or mirror-reflected) pyramids that are combined to form one solid by joining their bases together. An octahedron is a special case of a bipyramid; it is a square bipyramid with congruent faces.

An *anti-prism* has its top and bottom faces both congruent and parallel, but in a different orientation. It has triangular side faces. An octahedron (surprisingly) is a special case of an anti-prism, and can be seen as such when sitting on a flat surface; it has a triangular top and bottom (in different orientations), and it has six triangular side faces.

A *trapezohedron* looks like a 'twisted' bipyramid. It has a zigzag ring of edges going around its mid-section and its faces are all kites. Surprisingly, a cube is a special case of a trapezohedron, where the kites have all become squares. If we balance a cube on its point, and then we can see a zigzag ring consisting of six edges.

The Platonic solids
The four properties
A Platonic solid is a perfectly symmetrical polyhedron having four properties. Try to get the students to arrive at these properties by observing the Platonic solids, rather than listing the properties immediately on the board. They will likely come up with other additional

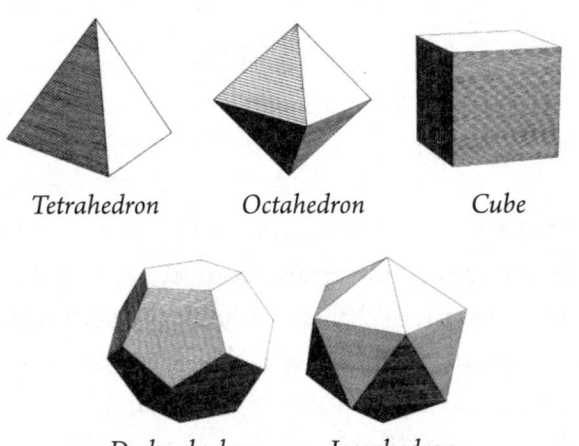

Tetrahedron *Octahedron* *Cube*

Dodecahedron *Icosahedron*

properties on their own. The four properties are*:
- Every face is regular (i.e. an equilateral triangle, square, regular pentagon, etc.).
- Every vertex is identical (i.e. every point is surrounded by the same kind of faces).
- Every face is identical.
- Every dihedral angle is identical.

There exist only five Platonic solids
- The tetrahedron, which has four triangular faces.
- The cube (hexahedron), which has six square faces.
- The octahedron, which has eight triangular faces.
- The dodecahedron, which has twelve pentagonal faces.
- The icosahedron, which has twenty triangular faces.

* It is taken for granted that the solid is required to be *convex*, meaning that it cannot be 'indented' anywhere. This eliminates the stellated solids (see Sutton's book, pages 26-31) as possible Platonic solids.

Give the proof that there exist only five Platonic solids (see Appendix, p. 216.)

Plato's Academy
Plato's study of mathematics included four subjects: Arithmetic, Geometry, Astronomy and Stereometry. Stereometry means 'the putting together of the cosmic figures.' The Greeks considered the Platonic solids to be the most perfect forms (along with the sphere). Plato did not discover these solids, but he studied them in depth, and wrote about them in his book *Timaeus*. Above the door of the Academy was written, 'Let no one unversed in geometry enter here'.

Plato said that when God created the universe, he first created the element of fire, for which he used the tetrahedron. Then he created the element air, for which he used the octahedron. He then created water using the icosahedron, and then used the hexahedron (cube) to create the earth element. Lastly, he used the dodecahedron to create the life element, or quintessence.

Kepler's universe
During Johannes Kepler's quest to discover how it was that the planets revolve around the sun, he was, for a while, convinced that the five Platonic solids were the key. In 1596, he published the book *Mysterium Cosmographicum*, in which he stated his hypothesis on the movement of the planets. It was based on careful astronomical observations, and central to his theory was a way that the Platonic solids could

be nested inside one another. Starting with Mercury moving along the surface of a sphere (with the sun at the centre), an octahedron was then circumscribed about that sphere*. Venus was then said to travel along the surface of a second (and larger) sphere that was circumscribed about the octahedron. (The octahedron now sits in the space between the two spheres.)

This pattern of alternating Platonic solids and spheres, each nested inside the other, continued all the way up to Saturn. In short, the order was: sphere (Mercury), octahedron, sphere (Venus), icosahedron, sphere (Earth), dodecahedron, sphere (Mars), tetrahedron, sphere (Jupiter), cube, sphere (Saturn). The astonishing thing is that the spacing created by such an arrangement of the Platonic solids is very close to the actual spacing between the orbits of the planets.

Shortly after the publication of this book, Kepler received more accurate astronomical data, which indicated that his hypothesis was wrong. In 1609, Kepler published his remarkable (and correct) laws of planetary motion, which included the fact that the planets travel along elliptical paths around the sun. Yet, it remained a mystery to Kepler what kept the planets in orbit; unto his death, he believed the planets were pushed along their orbits by angels.

* *Circumscribed* means 'encircling' or 'wrapped around'. Since the octahedron is circumscribed about the sphere, we can say that the sphere sits inside the octahedron, and the sphere barely touches the centre of each face of the octahedron.

The transformation of solids

Do each transformation mentally first, and then in clay.

The transformation of solids in the mind

The process of transformation is first attempted mentally as a quiet, meditative exercise with the class as a whole. The students concentrate on picturing the specific solid in their mind as the teacher guides the children slowly through, describing in as much detail as possible how the form is changing from one step to the next. If successful, the students can experience each transformation clearly in their mind. It is a powerful experience for them to 'see' a new shape for the very first time by picturing it exactly in their mind. This mental process is then replicated with clay (usually the next day).

The transformation of solids using clay

As the students are working on a transformation with clay, they can recall how far they were able to go in their mind the previous day. When working with the clay, the students should be careful that even if they can quickly see the whole transformation process happening, they should not rush the process – they should slowly live into it. Also, they should be careful not to make one portion of the clay too perfect before moving on to another portion of the solid. Ideally, the whole piece of clay is transformed at the same time (e.g. each face changes at the same time). Practically speaking, this is impossible. So we strive toward this ideal by working on a small area of clay, making a slight improvement, and then quickly, and randomly, rotating it in order to work on another section. Also, when doing a transformation in clay, make sure the edges and points are not too sharply defined, otherwise the transformation becomes too difficult.

The evolution of solids

The sphere is the perfect solid. In the end, the students should come to realise that any solid could evolve from the transformation of the sphere. However, I find it to be a better imaginative exercise to first arrive at a new solid through the transformation of another familiar solid (e.g. the cube). For example, we can arrive at a dodecahedron in two ways. First, the transformation of the sphere by starting with 12 equally-spaced points on a sphere and then pushing in on these points until the twelve pentagons emerge. Or secondly, the transformation of the cube by growing roofs off a cube (see detailed description, below). With any new solid, it is good to first arrive at it by transforming the cube, and then, perhaps later, to try to arrive at it through the transformation of the sphere.

Transforming a cube into an octahedron

This is, I feel, the most basic and important of the transformations. It needs to be done thoroughly (perhaps repeated in some way three days in a row) so that all the students really 'get it.'

The procedure starts with the cube, and then we (slowly!) push in all the points, thereby creating eight small triangles. These triangles slowly grow until the moment comes that they are touching one another point-to-point. The most difficult part comes now as these triangles continue to grow. Their points push against each other causing new edges to arise, thereby transforming the triangles into hexagons. Next, these hexagons continue to grow and they get transformed into large triangles that take over the whole solid. This final form is the octahedron, which consists of eight triangles.

 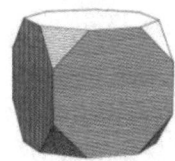

Cube *Truncated Cube*
6 squares, 8 pts *6 octagons, 8 triangles*

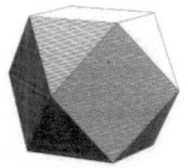 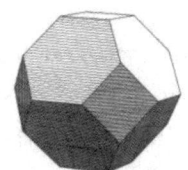

Cuboctahedron *Truncated Octahedron*
6 squares, 8 triangles *6 squares, 8 hexagons*

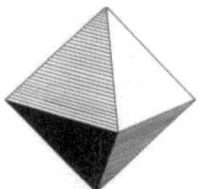

Octahedron
6 points, 8 triangles

Class Eight Geometry

Returning back to the start with the cube, we shall now turn our attention to the faces of the cube. We picture that while the eight points of the cube become the eight triangles of the octahedron, the six faces of the cube transform themselves, shrink down and eventually become the six points of the octahedron.

The challenge with doing this transformation in the mind, is to picture the whole solid fluidly transforming itself – points into faces, and faces into points – all simultaneously.

When working 'meditatively' with the students to get them to visualise this process, it is best to have them visualise colours, for example a cube with yellow faces and red points. We then visualise the red points turning into red triangles, and then the red areas get larger and larger, while at the same time, the yellow areas get smaller and smaller, until, in the end, the result is an octahedron with red faces and yellow points.

Transforming a cube into a tetrahedron
One way is to push in on four oppositely oriented points of the cube (see drawing below). These four points become four triangles which grow bigger and bigger until they all come together to become a tetrahedron.

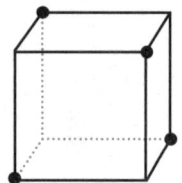

Alternatively, we can use a knife and deeply cut off the four corners of the cube in order to expose the tetrahedron hiding inside the cube.

Transforming a cube into a dodecahedron
This is an interesting, and surprising, way of creating a dodecahedron.

This process grows roofs off each of the faces of the cube. Each roof is designed like the drawing on the left, but any two neighbouring roofs have to be oppositely oriented (i.e. the top lines of neighbouring roofs are perpendicular to one another). After the roofs grow higher off the faces of the cube, sections of neighbouring roofs merge together to form pentagons. In the drawing on the right, the cube is shown with dotted lines, and the top lines of the roofs are shown with heavy lines. When working with clay, it makes it considerably easier to start with a small cube and *add* small bits of clay, thereby slowly building roofs off each face of the cube.

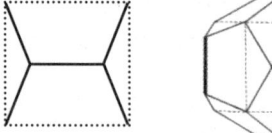

After doing this process, we can ask, 'How is it that a cube can sit inside a dodecahedron?' We can then have the students take a dodecahedron, and make six cuts with a knife thereby cutting off six roofs of the dodecahedron in order to expose the cube hiding inside the dodecahedron.

Transforming a cube into a rhombic dodecahedron

Similar to transforming a cube into a dodecahedron, here we grow pyramids off each of the faces of a cube. Once again, it is easiest to do this in clay by starting with a small cube, and then adding clay, bit-by-bit, onto each face of the cube, thereby allowing the pyramids to grow taller and taller until triangles from the pyramids merge together in pairs to form rhombuses (diamonds). The end result is a solid with 12 rhombic faces, called the rhombic dodecahedron.

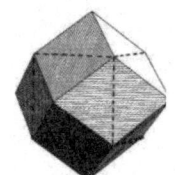

Rhombic dodecahedron

Demonstration: Construct a rhombic dodecahedron from paper. All four sides of the rhombus are congruent, and the angles in the rhombus are 109½° and 70½°. (The exact shape of this rhombus is found in Appendix *Patterns for the Archimedean solids and their duals*, pp. 240f.) Then draw red lines along the long diagonals of all the rhombuses, and green lines along all the short diagonals. Surprisingly, the red lines form an octahedron, and the green lines form a cube!

The ratio of the lengths of the two diagonals of the rhombic face is $\sqrt{2} : 1$, which is also the ratio of a square's diagonal to its side.

The volume of the rhombic dodecahedron is exactly twice the volume of the cube (formed by the dotted lines) that sits inside the rhombic dodecahedron. This is due to the fact that the rhombic dodecahedron can be generated by growing pyramids onto the faces of a cube. If you imagine that a second equal-sized set of pyramids grew from the cube's faces inward toward the cube's centre, then these six pyramids have their apexes meet at the centre. Therefore, the volume of the cube (or the six inner pyramids) equals the volume of the outer pyramids, and the volume of the rhombic dodecahedron is twice that of the cube.

Transforming a dodecahedron into an icosahedron

This is basically the same transformation that led us from the cube to the octahedron (see above). We push in on the points, and continue until the points become faces and the faces become points.

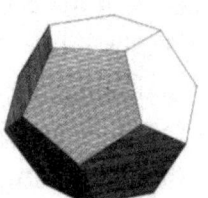 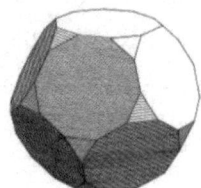

Dodecahedron *Truncated dodecahedron*
12 pentagons, 20 pts *12 decagons, 20 triangles*

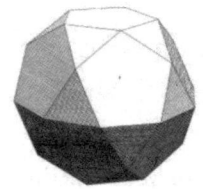 

Icosidodecahedron
12 pentagons, 20 triangles

Truncated icosahedron
12 pent., 20 hexagons

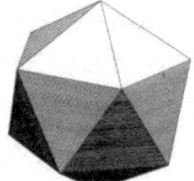

Icosahedron
12 points, 20 triangles

This is very difficult in clay! For most students, it is much easier to get an icosahedron by first clearly marking 12 equally-spaced points on the surface of a sphere, and then pushing in on the space in-between the points, thereby producing the icosahedron's 20 triangles.

Pushing in the points of a tetrahedron

The biggest surprise here is that we don't end up with a new solid. The end result is another tetrahedron, where the first and last stages are 'turned inside-out' from one another.

When doing the meditative imagination of this, it is again best to imagine it in colour. For example, the original tetrahedron has four red faces and four green points, then the next stage has four red hexagons and four green triangles, and the octahedron has four red triangles and four green triangles, then four red triangles and four green hexagons and finally four red points and four green points.

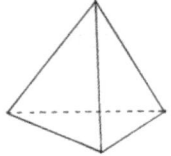 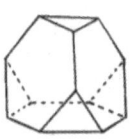

Tetrahedron
4 triangles, 4 points

Truncated Tetrahedron
4 hexagons, 4 triangles

 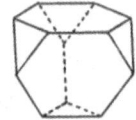

Octahedron
8 triangles

Truncated Tetrahedron
4 triangles, 4 hexagons

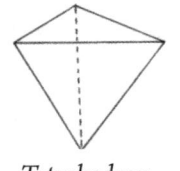

Tetrahedron
4 points, 4 triangles

Orthogonal views

An orthogonal view (or projection) of a solid is the outline that is seen when looking at the solid in a certain orientation. Essentially, it is a 2-D drawing of a 3-D object. Often 'special' orientations are chosen in order to clearly see the symmetry of the solid.

It is interesting to see the similarity of the orthogonal views of the tetrahedron, cube, octahedron and rhombic dodecahedron. Here are two orthogonal views for each of these four solids:

Tetrahedron   *Octahedron*

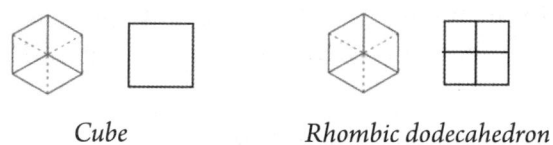

Cube   Rhombic dodecahedron

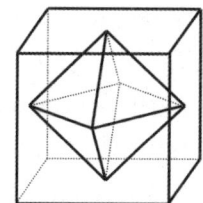

Because the rhombic dodecahedron and the cube have one orthogonal view that is identical (a hexagon), it is actually possible to show someone a rhombic dodecahedron (in that perspective, and at a fair distance) and they will be tricked into seeing a cube!

Duality

In *Transforming a cube into an octahedron* (see above), we saw a step-by-step description of how to make the dual form of a polyhedron. The dual of a cube is an octahedron, and the dual of an octahedron is a cube. In making the dual in this way, we see that *the points become faces, and the faces become points.*

Another way to envision the dual of a solid is to imagine that the dual sits inside the solid. For example, we can picture that the octahedron sits inside the cube such that its six vertices lie on the six centre points of the faces of the cube, and that each of the eight faces of the octahedron lie directly under each of the eight vertices of the cube. In the same way, we can picture that inside the octahedron sits its dual – another cube.

Notice that if a face of a solid is a square (i.e. it is bounded by four edges), then the vertex of the dual under that square face will have four edges coming to it. Using another example, since a dodecahedron has pentagonal faces (faces that are bounded by five edges around them), its dual (an icosahedron) has five edges coming together at each of its vertices.

Examples of dual solids
- The *cube* and the *octahedron* are duals of one another.
- The *dodecahedron* and *icosahedron* are duals of one another.
- The *tetrahedron* is self-dual. (In other words, the dual of a tetrahedron is another tetrahedron.)
- The dual of a *rhombic dodecahedron* is a *cuboctahedron*, which is halfway between a cube and an octahedron.
- The dual of a *hexagonal prism* is a *hexagonal bipyramid*. (See p. 164, for the drawing.)
- The dual of a *pentagonal anti-prism* is a *pentagonal trapezohedron*. (See p. 164, for the drawing.)

The Archimedean solids

(See Appendix, *The Archimedean solids and their duals*, pp. 240f, for drawings.)

There are 13 Archimedean solids.

These solids all satisfy the first two of the *four properties* of the Platonic solids (see above). Namely, Archimedean solids have (1) identical vertices, and (2) regular, non-identical faces*.

Seven out of the 13 Archimedean solids have already been mentioned as intermediate stages that are reached when transforming a Platonic solid into its dual (see above). These seven are:

Truncated tetrahedron	4 triangles and 4 hexagons
Truncated cube	6 octagons and 8 triangles
Cuboctahedron	6 squares and 8 triangles
Truncated octahedron	6 squares and 8 hexagons
Truncated dodecahedron	12 decagons and 20 triangles
Icosidodecahedron	12 pentagons and 20 triangles
Truncated icosahedron (soccer ball)	12 pentagons and 20 hexagons

---

* Prisms and anti-prisms also have these two properties, but, as opposed to the Archimedian solids, the don't have genuine three-dimensional symmetry – i.e. they have two faces that can be said to be a top and bottom.

The other six Archimedean solids result from 'stretching' solids in the ways shown below.

The stretching process

(See Appendix, *The Archimedean solids and their duals*, pp. 240f, for drawings.)

These are great imaginative exercises for the students to try to visualise in their head. It is probably necessary for most students to actually look at a model of the form that they are attempting to 'stretch'. However, some students may be able to do the whole process in their head, with their eyes closed.

The *small rhombicuboctahedron*. To create this, we start with a cube and imagine that it is bright yellow and is wrapped loosely in a translucent, stretchable covering. We then picture all the faces of the cube becoming disconnected and all moving slowly, and perpendicularly, away from the centre of the cube. Imagine that a red light streams out from the centre of the figure so that the spaces between the six square faces of the original cube are all glowing in red. At first, we see 12 red rectangles appear where each edge of the cube once was, and eight small red triangles appear at the vertices of the cube. The faces of the cube continue to move further apart, until, at a given moment, the 12 rectangles have become red squares, equal in size to the original six faces of the cube. This form is our new Archimedean solid. It has 18 squares (6 of which are from the original cube) and eight triangles for faces.

The *small rhombicosidodecahedron*. We reach this form by doing the same 'stretching' process, as described above, but we start with the dodecahedron. The resulting solid has 12 pentagons, 30 squares and 20 triangles.

The *great rhombicuboctahedron*. We reach this by starting with a truncated cube and imagining that the triangular faces are 'holes' defined by the translucent covering that goes over them. The six octagonal faces move away from the centre resulting in squares appearing at the edges between the octagons, and the triangles becoming transformed into hexagons. The end result is a solid with six octagons, 12 squares and eight hexagons.

The *great rhombicosidodecahedron*. We reach this by starting with a truncated dodecahedron and imagining that the triangular faces are 'holes' defined by the translucent covering that goes over them. The 12 decagonal (10-sided) faces move away from the centre resulting in squares appearing at the edges between the decagons, and the triangles becoming transformed into hexagons. The end result is a solid with 12 decagons, 30 squares and 20 hexagons.

The *snub cube*. Here we do the same transformation that led us to the small rhombicuboctahedron, but we take the process one step further. From the small rhombicuboctahedron, we take the original six yellow squares and rotate each one of them a bit clockwise (22.5°). This transforms each of the 12 squares defined by the translucent covering into two triangles.* The result is a form with six squares and 32 triangles. This form is unique in that its mirror image is not identical to itself. It has a 'left-hand' and 'right-hand' version, depending on whether the yellow square faces were rotated clockwise or counter-clockwise.

The *snub dodecahedron*. Here, we do the same as we did to get the snub cube, but we start with a dodecahedron, transform it into a small rhombicosidodecahedron and then we rotate the 12 pentagons slightly clockwise (or counter-clockwise). The result is 12 pentagons and 80 triangles.

Stretching other solids

Other solids can also be stretched in a similar manner, but the results, in each of the cases below, will be something that we have already seen, such as:

An octahedron becomes a small rhombicuboctahedron when stretched.

An icosahedron becomes a small rhombicosidodecahedron when stretched.

A truncated octahedron (with small square holes) becomes a great rhombicuboctahedron when stretched.

---

* It is not the intention that the squares being transformed have their edges locked into place as the transformation occurs. If this was taken literally, then each of these squares would become a 'twisted' parallelogram with a curved surface. Instead, the translucent covering shifts slightly, thereby allowing the squares to become transformed into two triangles.

- A truncated icosahedron (with small pentagonal holes) becomes a great rhombicosidodecahedron when stretched.
- A cuboctahedron with holes at its triangular faces becomes a truncated octahedron when stretched.
- A cuboctahedron with holes at its square faces becomes a truncated cube when stretched.
- An icosidodecahedron with holes at its triangular faces becomes a truncated icosahedron when stretched.
- An icosidodecahedron with holes at its pentagonal faces becomes a truncated dodecahedron when stretched.
- A truncated tetrahedron (with small triangular holes) becomes a truncated octahedron when stretched.

The Archimedean duals
(See Appendix, *The Archimedean solids and their duals*, pp. 240f, and see *duality* (above) for an explanation of duality and its characteristics.)

We have seen that the dual of any Platonic solid is another Platonic solid. In contrast, the dual of an Archimedean solid is not an Archimedean solid. While Archimedean solids have the first two properties of the Platonic solids, all the Archimedean duals have the third and fourth properties of the Platonic solids – namely, all their faces are identical, and all their dihedral angles are identical.

There are 13 Archimedean duals.

Faces and points
A solid and its dual have inverse numbers of faces and points. For example, a dodecahedron has 12 faces and 20 points, and its dual (an icosahedron) has 20 faces and 12 points. Furthermore, we can predict the kind of faces that a dual will have. The cuboctahedron has *four* edges coming to each point, so its dual (the rhombic dodecahedron) has *quadrilateral* faces. Since the snub cube and the snub dodecahedron have *five* edges coming to each of their points, their duals have *pentagonal* faces. Seven of the Archimedean solids have *three* edges coming to each point, which corresponds to the fact that seven of the Archimedean duals have *triangular* faces. Likewise, the number of edges coming to a given point of an Archimedean dual, corresponds to the type of polygon that its dual (an Archimedean solid) sits under.

Constructing paper models

After the students have become quite familiar with certain polyhedrons – through the mental imaginative exercises and through working with clay – they should construct some from paper. Over the course of the main lesson, I have them construct paper models of the five Platonic solids, and then they choose one of the Archimedean solids, or an Archimedean dual, as a final project.

In order to construct a polyhedron, the students should try to figure out the *net* for themselves. (A *net* is the two-dimensional pattern that folds up into a three-dimensional shape.) Don't immediately give the students a photocopied net for them to cut out – this misses the pedagogical value of doing these constructions (See Appendix, *Polyhedron nets*, p. 242. Larger-scale nets are in Allen's *Making Geometry*.)

The number of possible nets
Ask the students how many different nets there are for the tetrahedron, for the cube and for the octahedron. The students enjoy writing all their nets on the board, and trying to see which ones are equivalent (e.g. through a rotation, or a reflection), and which are truly unique.

There are only two possible nets for the tetrahedron.

There are 11 possible nets for both the cube and the octahedron.

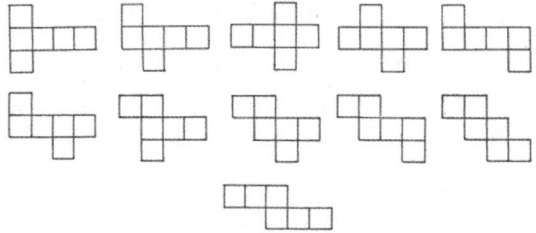

The 11 nets for the cube

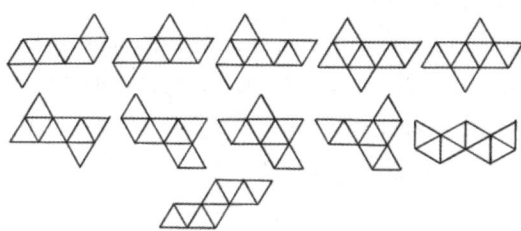

The 11 nets for the octahedron

There are 43,380 possible nets for the dodecahedron, the same number as for the icosahedron.

Tips for constructing paper models
Constructing these models out of paper is a real exercise in accuracy and careful work. Careless work results in a form that can't come together properly.

It is important to use good paper. If the paper is too thin, then it won't hold its form; if it's too thick, then it won't fold nicely. The best paper that I have found is 220 gsm thin card. Alternatively, I find that standard file folders work fairly well.

Use a very sharp pencil when drawing the net.

It is best for the students to do any art work on the paper after it has been cut out, and after the folds have been made, but before it has been glued together.

Drawing the net
Each polyhedron has faces with specific polygonal shapes I give the students photocopies of the specific polygons that are needed to make the net of any solid (See Appendix, *Patterns for the Archimedean solids and their duals* for drawings of these polygons, pp. 240f.) These premade polygons are especially necessary for the construction of an Archimedean dual, because for these solids, the faces (polygons) have to be made with specific angle measures in order for the form to come together properly.

The students first need to make a nearly

perfect *form* of their chosen polygon. This polygon form is then traced out carefully, and multiple times, in order to create a workable *net*. Since the polygon form on the photocopied paper is not stiff enough to use for tracing, they must make a duplicate of it on thick construction paper. To do this, put the photocopy of the desired polygon form on top of the sheet of construction paper. Then, using a pin, push through all the vertices of the photocopied polygon form thereby making tiny holes on the construction paper underneath. Put the photocopied piece of paper aside, and with a ruler carefully draw the polygon form on the construction paper by connecting the holes that were just made. Carefully cut out this polygon. In the case of making an Archimedean solid, more than one polygon form will need to be made.

Think carefully about how the net can be laid out so that it can be cut out and folded up into the desired polyhedron. For example, in order to make a cube, six square forms will have to be traced out in order to create the full net. As stated above, it is important that the students try to come up with the net on their own. (See Appendix, *Polyhedron nets*, p. 242 for the nets of some of the more difficult solids.)

Using the polygon form that has just been cut out, create the net by tracing adjacent polygons on the sheet of construction paper. For best results, leave a pencil's width (0.2 mm) of space along the edge between adjacent polygons, in order to account for the fold that will occur along this edge.

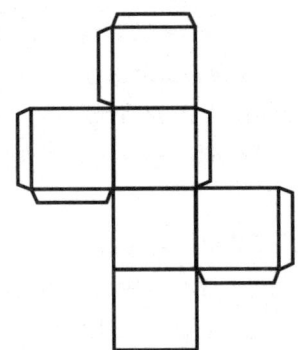

A cube net with tabs

Once the net has been made, placement of the tabs needs to be determined. A tab is a bit of extra paper (past the edge of a face) that is used to glue an edge together once the final polyhedron folds up into its proper shape. The tabs don't need to be drawn or cut out very neatly, since they won't be seen, but they need to run the length of the whole edge. It is important that no edges are left without a tab, and that no edge has two tabs joining it. Considering all this, draw all the tabs in the proper places. One possible net (with tabs) for constructing a cube is shown at the right. Can you see how this pattern will fold together, and how all the tabs will connect?

If making the net is too challenging for students (or teacher) there are large nets for Platonic and Archimedean solids in Jon Allen's book *Making Geometry*.

Putting it together
After the net is cut out, folds need to be made along certain edges by placing a ruler along the edge, folding the paper up and then going over

the fold a couple of times with your finger nail.

The last part of the construction is gluing it together. This is a slow process, since after gluing a few tabs, it must be allowed to dry somewhat before gluing more tabs. It is best if the tabs were strategically placed in the net in such a way that the last face that gets glued has no tabs on it (this is the bottom square in the above drawing). This allows the last face to be gently pressed into place onto tabs (with glue on them) that are connected to other faces.

Close-packing

A polyhedron is said to *close-pack* when an indefinite amount of that exact same polyhedron can be packed together without there being any empty space between them. Spheres cannot be close-packed, because there is space between them.

What can be close-packed? Any box (right-rectangular prism) obviously close-packs. Of all the Platonic solids, Archimedean solids and Archimedean duals (a total of 31 solids), there is only one solid from each group that close-packs. These special solids are the cube, the truncated octahedron and the rhombic dodecahedron.

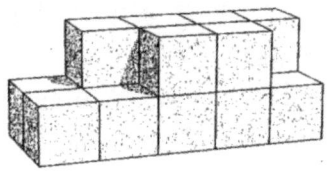

cubes

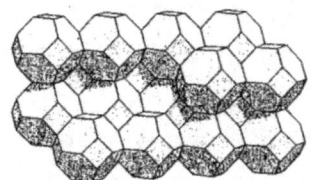

truncated octahedra

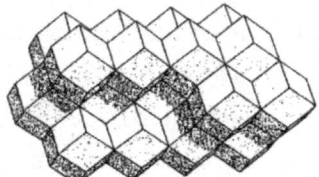

rhombic dodecahedra

Euler's formula

edges = faces + points – 2

This formula relates the number of edges, faces and points in any polyhedron.

Descartes actually knew about this formula before Euler. The Greeks possibly knew about it as well.

Allow the students to discover it. Perhaps it is best to make a table on the board where the columns are labeled: 'solid', 'number of faces', 'number of points' and 'number of edges'. The solid can be any polyhedron – any of the Platonic or Archimedean solids, a triangular prism, a square pyramid, etc. The students carefully count the number of faces, points and edges on each solid and enter the information in the table. Finally, they try to come up with Euler's formula by asking, 'How can we think of a formula that calculates the number of edges in any solid, based upon the number of faces and points?'

Class Eight Geometry

Additional imagination 3-D transformation exercises (optional)

The inner tube problem

This problem requires great concentration, but if done properly, the final result can be clearly 'seen'. Avoid the temptation to actually get a bicycle inner tube and do it. This is a great test of a person's power of 'exact imagination'.

If you cut a hole (about the size of a coin) out of a bicycle inner tube, reach through the hole with your fingers and pull the entire inner tube through that hole, then what shape do you get? Picture this process exactly in your mind.

It's not the same shape as the original inner tube. It is easily described, but probably not a shape that you've ever seen before (I will not give the answer here!)

Reducing solids to tetrahedrons

Describe how it is possible to slice each one of the following solids into the least number of irregular tetrahedrons possible. It is best if the students first try to do it completely in their head, and then later try it with the aid of a paper model, or with clay.

How many tetrahedrons do you get by slicing a triangular prism?

Start by placing the knife along an edge of one of the triangles, and then cut through the solid so that the cutting plane passes through the point that is opposite from the edge where you started to cut. This leaves us with two solids. One is an irregular tetrahedron (four triangular faces), and the other is a rectangular pyramid (a rectangle and four triangular faces). Cut the pyramid along the diagonal of the rectangle, toward and through the vertex where the four triangles meet. This divides the pyramid into two irregular tetrahedrons. Thus, the original triangular prism has been divided into three tetrahedrons.

How many tetrahedrons do you get by slicing a cube?

Cut off four 'opposite' corners, thereby exposing the tetrahedron that is enclosed in the cube. This creates five tetrahedrons.

How many tetrahedrons do you get by slicing an octahedron?

An octahedron can be sliced along any one of three planes in order to divide the octahedron into two square (Egyptian) pyramids. Simply cut along two of these planes in order to produce four tetrahedrons.

Loci

Key ideas

What is loci?

In essence, loci is the study of curves. Loci (pronounced like 'low sigh') is the plural of *locus* (pronounced 'low kus'). A locus of points is defined as a collection of points, all of which satisfy some specific condition. In every case that is considered in this unit, the condition has to do with distances to lines, points or circles. The locus of points, which satisfies the given condition, forms a particular curve. We construct this curve by locating a few of the points that satisfy the condition, and then we connect the dots to draw the curve.

Why do we teach it?
The real purpose of teaching loci is that it works with the students' imagination through seeing curves in movement. Unfortunately, most students in mainstream education graduate from upper school without studying any loci.

Loci as a main lesson
Loci is best covered during a main lesson, but the amount of material is not enough to fill an entire three-week main lesson. I recommend that loci and number bases share a main lesson together; in some ways these two topics complement each other. Or, if there is only room for one maths main lesson in the Class Eight, then loci can share a main lesson with stereometry.

Requirements?
The drawings done in this unit require great care and precision. High quality compasses (a few for drawing extra-large circles), and sharp pencils are essential. Shading in should be simple.

The treasure hunt
The language used for the subject of loci can seem awkward for the Class Eight students. For this reason, it is good to use an analogy that demystifies the language. I use the idea of a treasure hunt. In this way we translate the standard mathematical loci definitions of curves into 'treasure hunt' definitions.

The process is important
Each definition given below is the end result. The students should be presented with each one as a puzzle that they need to figure out.

Curves generated from loci problems
A circle
As a treasure problem: If a treasure is buried 100 metres from a tree in a field, then it could be found anywhere along the circle that has the tree at the centre, and a radius equal to 100 m.

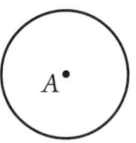

The locus of points a set distance from a point

As a loci problem: The locus of points that are a set distance from a given point (A) is a circle.

Construction: The students can do this drawing on their own.

Two parallel lines
As a treasure problem: If a treasure is buried 100 feet from a straight fence in a field, then it could be found anywhere along the two lines that are 100 feet from either side of the fence.

The locus of points a set distance from a line

As a loci problem: The locus of points that are a set distance from a given line (*a*) is two lines, one on each side of the given line

Construction: The students can do this drawing on their own.

Two concentric circles

As a treasure problem: If a treasure is buried 100 metres from a circular fence (500 metres in diameter), then it could be found anywhere along the two circles that are 100 metres from either side of that fence.

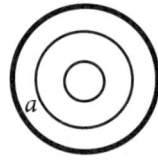

The locus of points a set distance from a circle

As a loci problem: The locus of points that are a set distance from a given circle (*A*) is two circles, one on each side of the given circle.

Construction: The students can do this drawing on their own.

A perpendicular bisector

As a treasure problem: If a treasure is buried such that it is an equal distance from two trees in a field, then it could be found anywhere along the line that cuts perpendicularly between the two trees.

As a loci problem: The locus of points equidistant from two points (*A* and *B*) is the per-

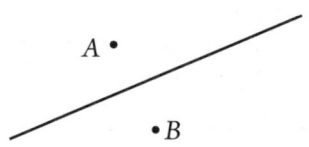

The locus of points equidistant from two points

pendicular bisector of the line segment that joins the two given points.

Construction: Review the Class Six perpendicular bisector construction (p. 62).

Two angle bisectors

As a treasure problem: If a treasure is buried such that it is an equal distance from two straight fences (lines *a* and *b*) that intersect (at a random angle) in a field, then it could be found anywhere along the two lines that are angle bisectors of the two fences.

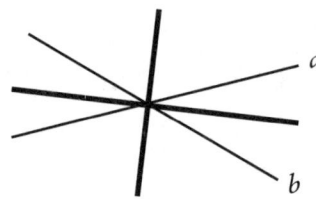

The locus of points equidistant from two intersecting lines

As a loci problem: The locus of points equidistant from two intersecting lines (*a* and *b*) is the two angle bisectors of the given lines.

Construction: Review the Class Six angle bisector construction (p. 63).

A parabola

The drawing below has been slightly reduced in size.

As a treasure problem: If a treasure is buried an equal distance from a tree and a straight fence (where the tree is not on that fence), then it could be found anywhere along a curve known as a parabola.

As a loci problem: The locus of points equidistant from a line and a point (not on that line) is a parabola. (The distance to a line is defined as the shortest distance, namely, approaching the line at 90°.)

The point is called the focus, and the line is called the directrix. The vertex of the parabola is the lowest point and is exactly halfway between the focus and the directrix.

In nature, a parabola is the path followed by a rock thrown in the air, or the water shot from a fountain. The vertex is the highest point that it reaches.

Construction

The paper should be set up with the long side running vertically. Space should be left at the top for a title. Draw a dark line (the directrix) 5 cm from the bottom of the page. Carefully, and lightly, draw lines parallel to this directrix at intervals of one centimetre all the way up and down the page.

A focal point (the focus) is now to be chosen at a specific *set distance* away from the directrix line. This set distance should be 2, 4, 6 or 8 cm. Have a quarter of the class do each distance, so that the results of varying this distance can be observed by the class. (The drawing, which has been reduced in size, used a set distance of 4 cm.) Lightly draw circles, each one having the focus as its centre, that have radii starting at 1 cm and increasing by intervals of 1cm. (These circles, with a common centre, are called concentric.)

Now the students should try to answer the following question on their own, '*Where are the points that are equidistant from the focus and the directrix?*'

The most obvious point that satisfies this condition is the *vertex*, which always is the point halfway between the directrix and the

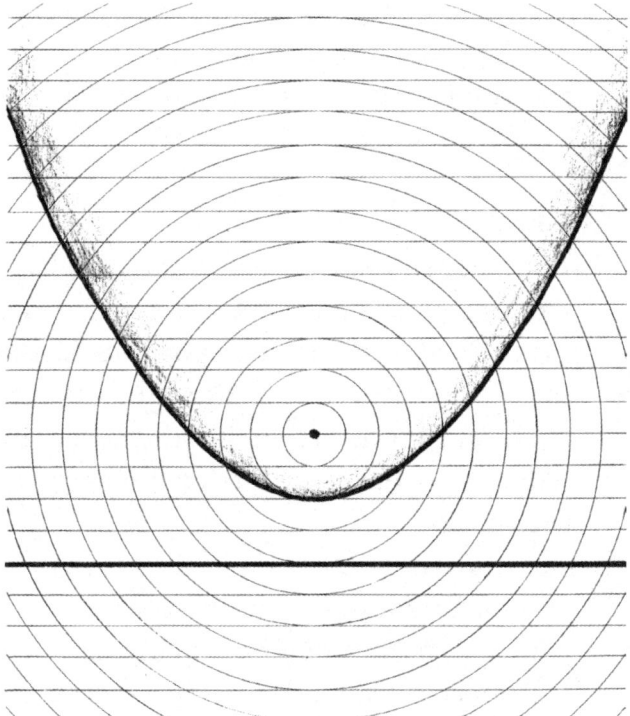

The parabola: the locus of points equidistant from a point and a line

Class Eight Geometry

focus. Referring to the drawing, two more points that satisfy the condition can be found by considering the circle that is 3 cm away from the focus, and the line that is 3 cm away from the directrix. Every point on this circle is 3 cm away from the focus, and every point on the line is 3 cm away from the directrix. Therefore, we know that the two points of intersection of the circle and the line are *both* 3 cm from the focus and 3 cm from the directrix; so these two points also satisfy the condition. Now we have three points that satisfy the condition.

The next two points that satisfy the condition are the two points of intersection between the next largest circle and the next further line – they are 4 cm away from both the focus and the directrix. Simply follow this pattern repeatedly, thereby finding points of intersection between larger circles and further-away lines until it runs off the page.

Draw the parabola by carefully connecting all the solution points with a coloured pencil. All the points on this curve satisfy the condition of being equidistant from the focus and the directrix.

A parabola in movement
How does the shape of the parabola vary as the focal point moves toward the directrix? The students answer this question by observing the differences in the parabolas that their classmates made (the distances from the focus to the directrix are varied from 2 cm to 8 cm). Then, without having a drawing to look at, the students should imagine the parabola changing shape (becoming narrower or wider) as the focus moves toward, or away from, the directrix.

An ellipse
The drawing opposite has been reduced in size.

As a treasure problem: If a treasure is buried an equal distance from a circular fence and a tree inside that fence, then it could be found anywhere along a curve known as an ellipse.

As a loci problem: The locus of points equidistant from a circle and a point inside that circle is an ellipse. (The distance from a point to a circle is defined as the shortest distance, namely, approaching the circle at 90°.)

The point is called the focus and the circle is called the directrix.

Construction
Start by drawing a directrix circle that has a radius measuring an even number of centimetres, and is as large as possible. Lightly draw concentric circles from the directrix circle all the way in to the centre having the radius get smaller by one centimetre with each circle.

A focus is now to be chosen. Pick the focus by selecting a point on one of the circles, which is an even number of circles in from the directrix. Mark this point clearly as the focus. Have students choose different locations for their focus so that the class can see how this affects the curve.

Using the focus as the centre, draw concentric circles out from the focus, allowing the radii to grow by cm with each circle.

Now the students should try to answer the following question on their own, '*Where are the points that are equidistant from the focus and the directrix?*'

In order to find the points that are solutions to the above question, use a similar method to what was used with the parabola. The difference is that here we are finding points of intersection between two sets of circles, rather than the intersection of lines and circles, as was done in constructing the parabola. Now connect the solution points. The resulting curve is an ellipse, which falls within the directrix circle. Notice that the centre of the directrix circle falls within the ellipse and is symmetrically opposite the focus.

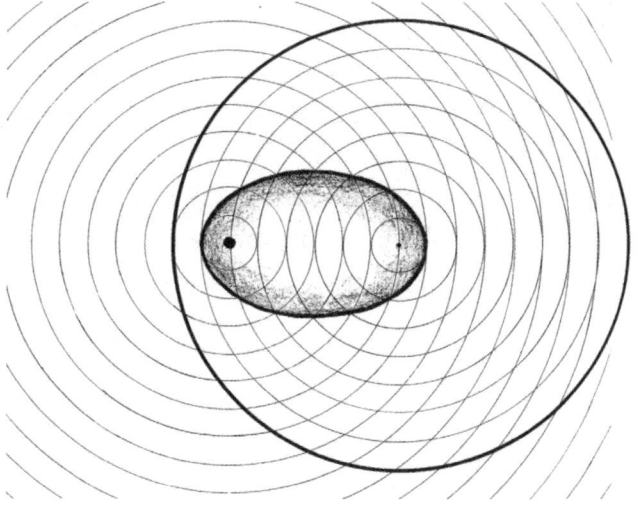

An ellipse in movement

How does the shape of the ellipse change as the focus moves toward the centre of the directrix circle? Have the students observe the differences in the ellipses their classmates made Now, without having a drawing to look at, the students should imagine the ellipse changing shape as the focus moves from the directrix circle toward the centre of the directrix, or back in the other direction.

A hyperbola

The drawing overleaf has been reduced in size.

As a treasure problem: If a treasure is buried an equal distance from a circular fence and a tree outside that fence, then it could be found anywhere along a curve known as a hyperbola.

As a loci problem: The locus of points equidistant from a circle and a point outside that circle is a hyperbola. (The distance from a point to a circle is defined as the shortest distance, namely, approaching the circle at 90°.)

The point is called the focus and the circle is called the directrix.

Construction

A compass that can draw large circles will be necessary for this construction.

Start by drawing a directrix circle that has a diameter that is about one-third the length of the page, and position it to one side of the page. Lightly draw concentric circles from this directrix circle outward such that the radii get larger by one centimetre with each circle, until the page is filled.

A focus is now to be chosen. Pick the focus by selecting a point that is on one of circles and is centred on the opposite side of the page from the directrix circle. It is best if the circle chosen is an even number of centimetres beyond the directrix circle. Let students choose different foci so that their drawings can be compared later.

Using the focus as the centre, draw concentric circles out from the focus, allowing the radii to grow by one centimetre with each circle.

Now the students should try to answer the following question on their own, 'Where are the points that are equidistant from the focus and the directrix?'

The solution is found in the same manner as with the ellipse.

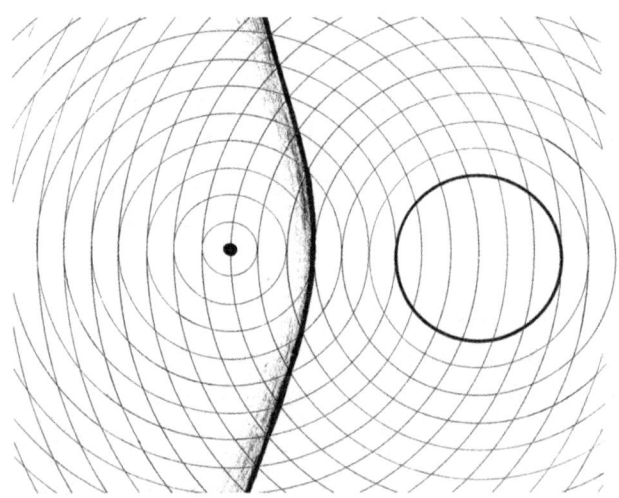

Connect the solution points, and the form of the hyperbola will emerge. It is similar to a parabola, but its sides tend to go outward as nearly straight lines as opposed to the parabola, which tends to have both of its sides get closer and closer to becoming parallel to each other.

A hyperbola in movement

How does the shape of the hyperbola change as the focus moves toward the directrix circle? Have the students observe the differences in the hyperbolas that their classmates made. Now, without having a drawing to look at, the students should imagine the hyperbola changing shape (becoming narrower or wider) as the focus moves toward, or away from, the directrix.

The two branches of a hyperbola

It should be noted that a 'real' hyperbola has two branches, which are mirror reflections of each other. Both branches get closer and closer to two intersecting lines, called *asymptotes*. Sometimes (e.g. with the loci drawing on the left) we only see one branch. We get the other branch when the positions of the focus and the

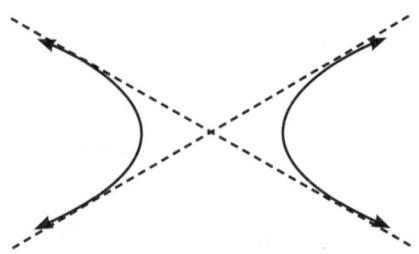

centre of the directrix circle are switched. Even though there are two branches to a hyperbola, it is considered to be one continuous curve. Explaining this strange notion is left until Class Eleven.

Alternative definitions (optional)
The ellipse
Above, the loci definition of an ellipse was given as 'the locus of points equidistant from a directrix circle and a focus inside that circle'. Alternatively, we can consider that the ellipse has two foci – the other one being the centre of the directrix circle. The new definition is:

An ellipse is the locus of points such that the sum of the distances to the two focal points is constant.

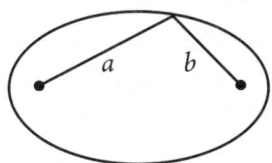

a *plus* b *is always the same number*

The truth of the above definition can be demonstrated by using two pushpins for the foci, and pushing them partway through a piece of cardboard. Next, a piece of string is tied end-to-end in order to form a loop and placed loosely around the two pushpins. A pencil is then placed inside the loop of string and pulled outward to make the string taut. The ellipse can now be drawn by moving the pencil around the pushpins while keeping the string taut.

Proof that the two definitions of the ellipse are equivalent (optional):

According to the loci definition of an ellipse, from any point, X, on the ellipse, the distance to the circle (AX) is equal to the distance to the focus (XF). As an equation, this is $XF = AX$.

XC can be added to both sides of the above equation to get $XF + XC = AX + XC$.

The right side of the equation ($AX + XC$) is just equal to AC, which is the radius of the circle (r), giving us: $XF + XC = r$

Imagine that point A is moving around the circle while point X is tracing the form of the ellipse. As this movement is happening, the lengths of AX, XF and XC are continually changing, but what the above equation says is that the sum of XF plus XC always remains constant (equal to r).

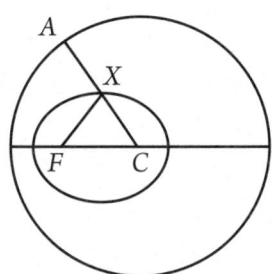

The hyperbola
In light of the new definition of the ellipse, it may come as no surprise that the hyperbola can now be defined as:

A hyperbola is the locus of points such that the difference of the distance to the two focal points is constant.

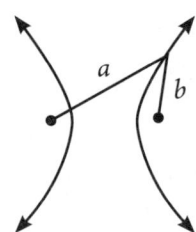

a *minus* b *(or* b *minus* a*) is always the same number*

Here, as with the above ellipse, we have a second focal point rather than a directrix circle.

This definition readily shows both branches of the hyperbola. One branch is closer to one focus and the other branch is closer to the other focus. From any point on the curve (with both branches) the difference of the distances to the two foci is always the same.

Sections

What is a section? A section of a three-dimensional solid is the two-dimensional 'outline' that results from slicing straight through that solid.

Examples:
- What are the possible sections of a *sphere*? Only circles are possible.
- What are the possible sections of a *tetrahedron*? Triangular sections are the most obvious, but a quadrilateral (or even a square) section is possible if the tetrahedron is sliced through all four faces.
- What are the possible sections of a *cube*? By cutting parallel to the cube's face, we get a square section, and by cutting off a corner, we get a triangular section. But we can also get a hexagonal section if we balance the cube on a point, and then cut along a horizontal plane through the centre of the cube. Pentagonal sections are also possible.

Conic sections

A (double) cone is a single solid that resembles two 'ice cream cones' joined at their points. It extends infinitely far in both directions.

The sections of a cone. Guide the students in seeing what curves arise from sectioning a cone. A (single) cone made of clay can be sectioned to show each possibility.

The five conic sections in movement. T is a point located inside the cone. Notice that what appear to be lines going through point T are really planes rising perpendicularly out of the page and slicing through the cone. We begin with plane *d*, which cuts horizontally through the upper half of the cone. We then allow the cutting plane to rotate about point T, from plane *d* to plane *e*, then to plane *f* and finally to plane *g*, which cuts through both the top and the bottom half of the double cone. If we imagine this to be a continuous movement, then we can see that the drawing here shows just four snap-shots of this sequence.

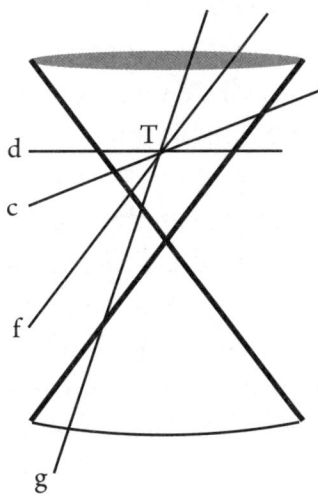

We can say the following regarding this sequence:

- There is exactly one plane (*d*) that produces a *circle* as a section. This occurs only when the plane is perfectly horizontal. This circle is a special case of an ellipse.

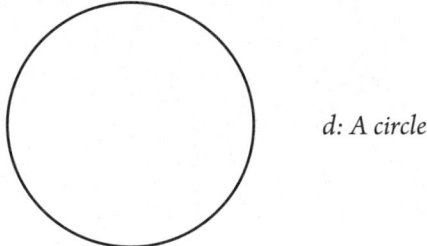

d: A circle

- There are infinitely many planes between plane *d* and plane *f* (plane *e* is only one of them). These planes cut through only the top half of the cone, and produce an *ellipse* as a section.

e: An eclipse

- The section produced by plane *f* is the *critical instant* when the plane is parallel to the edge of the cone. An instant earlier, the section was an ellipse. But at this instant, the ellipse has been infinitely stretched out; its 'end' is no longer connected together. If we advance an instant into the future from this stage, then we will have a hyperbola, which cuts through both halves of the cone. But at the present instant, the second branch of this soon-to-be hyperbola is hidden infinitely far away.

The section produced at this critical instant (by plane *f*) is a *parabola*. *A parabola is the critical instant between an ellipse and a hyperbola.*

f: A parabola

- There are infinitely many planes that are rotated beyond plane *f* (plane *g* is only one of them). They each cut through both the top and bottom half of the cone, and produce a *hyperbola* as a section.

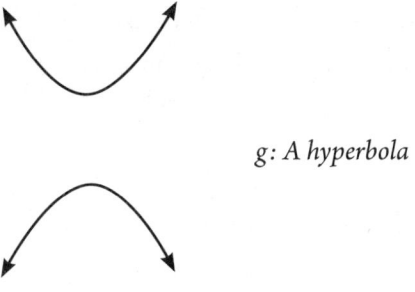

g: A hyperbola

Class Eight Geometry

Conic sections from cones of light

It is best to make your own double cone of light, as described below, so that both branches of the hyperbola can be seen. A flashlight produces only one branch of the hyperbola.

Take a poster board and roll it into a cylinder by joining the two shorter sides. Cut a hole in the middle of the cylinder's side that is just big enough to insert the narrow end of a light bulb. The cylinder now acts as a lampshade that produces a double cone of light. (The light bulb is screwed in through the hole in the cylinder and sits inside the cylinder.) Make sure the students understand that although the lampshade is cylindrical, the light that comes out forms a double cone.

Demonstration

The chalkboard serves as the cutting plane for this double cone of light. After showing each stage separately, try several times to show the sequence in fluid movement.

A *circle* is seen when the light is directed straight at the board.

An *ellipse* is seen when the light is directed at the board at a slight angle.

A *parabola* is seen at the *critical instant* when the edge of the cone is parallel to the board.

A *hyperbola* is seen whenever the board cuts through both halves of the double cone of light. We can then see both branches of the hyperbola quite nicely.

Curves in movement

A family of hyperbolas and ellipses

See drawing, where the students can see both branches of the hyperbolas.

This drawing nicely shows the movement of ellipses and hyperbolas due to the shrinking and expansion of the directrix circle.

Make sure that it is clear to the students where the directrix circle and focus is for each hyperbola, and for each ellipse (there are two possibilities for each ellipse). They should be able to picture the directrix circle growing and shrinking and the movement of the resulting curves.

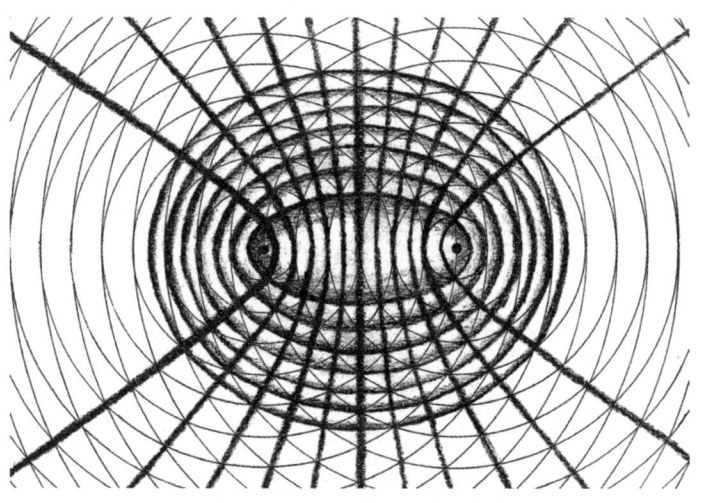

The movement of the focus to the outside of the directrix circle

This sequence doesn't include a parabola. Instead, the ellipse is transformed by flattening out into a ray, and then it emerges as one branch of a hyperbola. Remember that at any given moment the curve represents the locus of points equidistant from the directrix circle and the focus.

The drawings below have been done as a sequence of five snapshots of the transformation of the curve as the focus moves from inside the directrix circle to outside the circle. The students should try to visualise the whole sequence in their heads as a continuous flowing movement. The five steps, as shown in the drawings from top to bottom, are as follows:

The focus is well inside the circle, resulting in a fairly round ellipse.

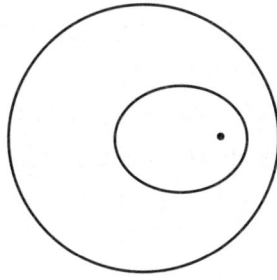

The focus has moved toward the edge of the directrix circle, resulting in a fairly thin ellipse.

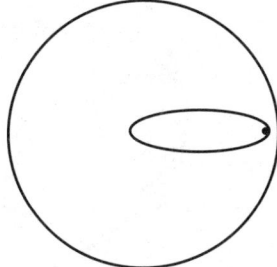

The focus is on the edge of the directrix circle resulting in a ray that starts from the centre of the circle, and then passes through the focus, and then infinitely far beyond the circle. Notice that this ray is a combination of a flattened ellipse and a flattened hyperbola.

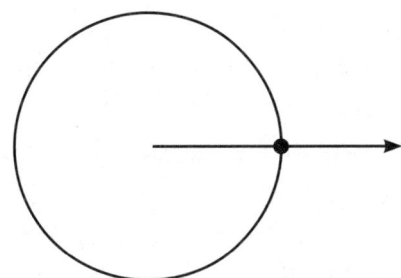

The focus is now outside the directrix circle, but close to its edge, resulting in a fairly narrow hyperbola.

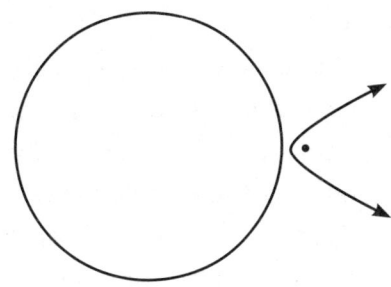

The focus is well outside the directrix circle, resulting in a fairly wide hyperbola.

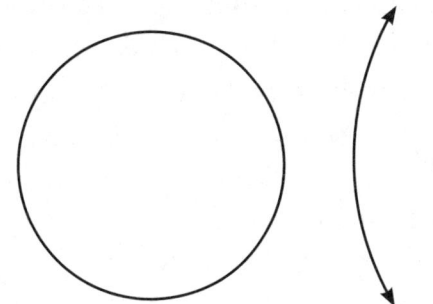

Class Eight Geometry

Turning the directrix circle inside-out

This sequence nicely shows one branch of a hyperbola transforming into a parabola, and then into an ellipse. This happens by having the directrix circle growing and then shrinking while the focus remains fixed. The students should try to visualise the whole sequence in their heads as a continuous flowing movement. With the drawing below, notice that the focus is the same for each curve, and is the dot in the centre of the drawing. The four steps are as follows:

The *hyperbola*. The directrix circle is the circle furthest to the left. The resulting locus of points is the hyperbola (the shaded curve furthest to the left). We can imagine that this directrix circle is growing, and, *as it grows, its right-most point is fixed*, resulting in the directrix circle expanding to the left, while its centre is moving to the left and off the page. As the directrix circle is growing, we visualise that the ends of the hyperbola are being pushed together. The bigger the directrix circle becomes, the more the hyperbola looks like a parabola.

The *parabola*. The directrix circle is now infinitely large – so large that it appears as a vertical line in the drawing. This is the critical instant when the curve becomes a parabola – the instant between a hyperbola and an ellipse.

The *ellipse*. The directrix circle (shown as a large, incomplete circle) has now turned inside out. Its centre, which was initially to the left of the focus, is now to the right of the focus. In the process of encircling the focus, the directrix circle gathers in, and joins together what had been the ends of the hyperbola in order to form an ellipse. We can imagine that the directrix circle now begins to shrink, and, as it shrinks, the ellipse goes from becoming infinitely stretched out (a parabola), to becoming smaller and rounder. At this stage, the directrix circle and the ellipse are like a womb and its egg.

The *circle*. The directrix circle (shown as a small, thin circle to the right of the vertical line) continues to shrink until the instant occurs that the centre of the directrix circle coincides with the focus. At this point, the ellipse has become a perfect circle (shown as a small, shaded circle) that has a radius equal to half the radius of the directrix circle.

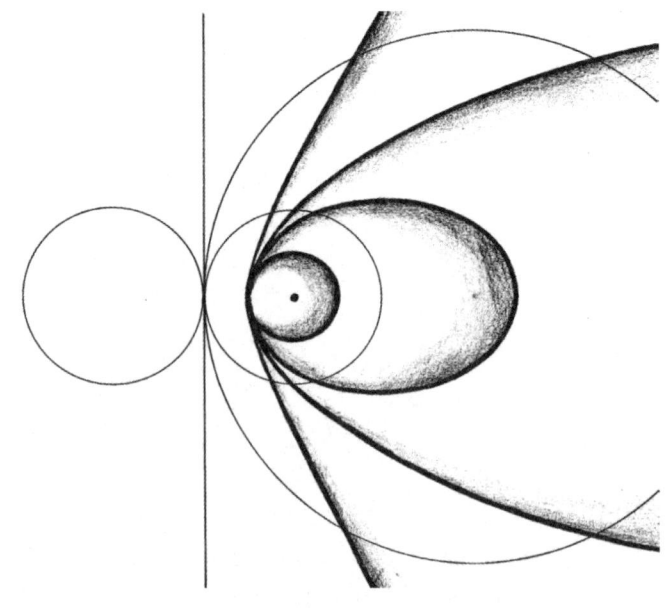

The curves of Cassini

Above, we showed that an ellipse is the locus of points such that the *sum* of the distances to the two focal points is always the same number (a constant), and that a hyperbola is the locus of points such that the *difference* of the distances to the two focal points is always the same number.

A Cassini curve is the locus of points such that the product of the distances to the two focal points is constant.

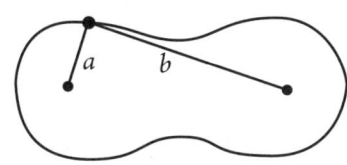

a *times* b *is always the same number*

Formulas and set-up

The goal is to have the students produce drawings that look like one of the six possibilities shown on the drawing on the next page. As the theme is transformation of the curve, we will have the students create different curves so that they can look at each other's drawings and see what happens when f (the distance between the focal points) changes. There are two things that determine what the shape of a Cassini curve will be: the distance between the two focal points, f, and the constant, C, that the product of the two distances are always equal to. In order to get the best results, we need to carefully choose values for f and C, even though a Cassini curve could be generated from any values for f and C. These values will depend upon the size of the paper.

For A4 paper, I recommend using a C value (the constant product) of 64 (for all the drawings), from which all the variations of the Cassini curves can be nicely created by using f values (the distance between the focal points in cm) of 8, 11.3, 15, 16, 17 and 20. But it is probably better for the students to use larger paper (from a standard main lesson book), in which case I recommend using a C value of 100, from which all the variations of the Cassini curves can be created by using f values (in cm) of 10, 14.14, 19, 20, 21 and 25. Either way, the whole class uses the same C value.

By using different f values, we are, in effect, allowing the two focal points to drift apart. The result is a sequence of six stages, each one clearly seen in the drawing on the next page, in which the Cassini curve transforms itself from a round oval (not exactly an ellipse), into a flat oval, into an indented oval, into a lemniscate and finally into two egg-like curves (which is mathematically still one curve). As the focal points drift further apart, these two eggs become smaller and rounder. Amazingly, this transformation looks like the biological process of cell division.

It is helpful to know (but difficult to prove) each of these things:

- The two key transition points of the Cassini curve (the flat oval and the lemniscate) occur at the instant when $f = \sqrt{2C}$ and when $f = 2\sqrt{C}$, respectively.
- The distance X_{out}, which is measured from a

focal point to the neighbouring outermost point of the curve, is given by this formula:

$$X_{out} = \frac{\sqrt{f^2 + 4c} - f}{2}$$

In the case that the curve is two eggs, the distance X_{in}, which is measured from a focal point to the innermost point of the egg, is given by this formula:

$$X_{in} = \frac{f - \sqrt{f^2 - 4c}}{2}$$

It is up to the discretion of the teacher to decide whether the students should use these formulas themselves to calculate the X_{out} and X_{in} values, or whether the teacher should simply give the resulting values to the students. Either way, these formulas can help the students to appreciate the power that formulas have to aid engineers and scientists.

The transformation of a Cassini curve
Note: f is the distance between the focal points, and C is the constant product. Drawings are reduced from the original size.

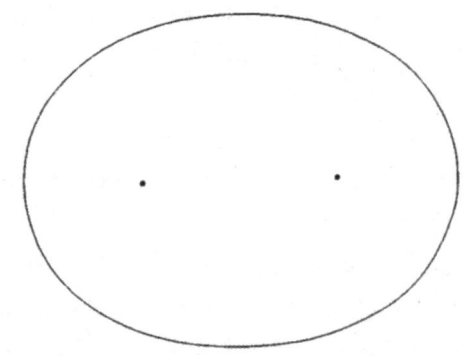

$f = 10$ cm; $C = 100$

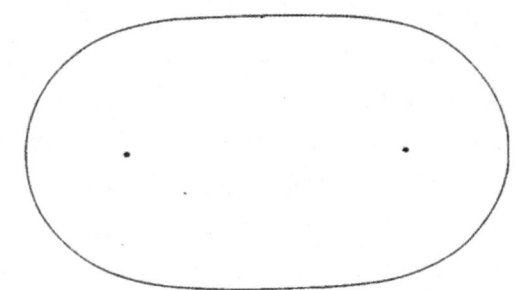

$f \approx 14.14$ cm ($f = \sqrt{2C}$); $C = 100$

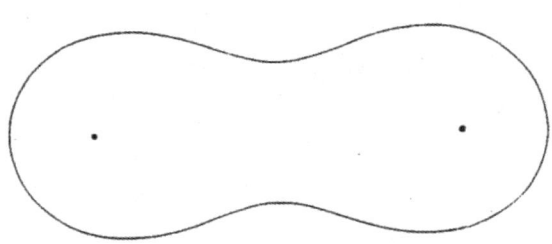

$f = 19$ cm; $C = 100$

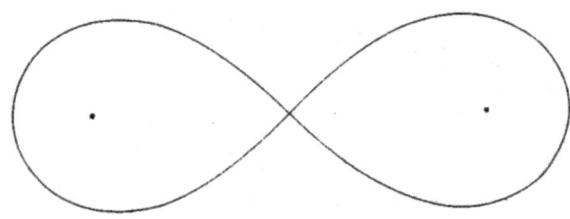

$f = 20$ cm ($f = 2\sqrt{C}$); $C = 100$

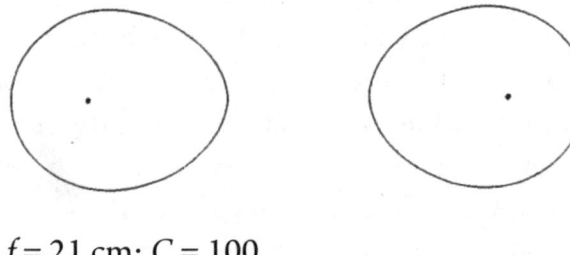

$f = 21$ cm; $C = 100$

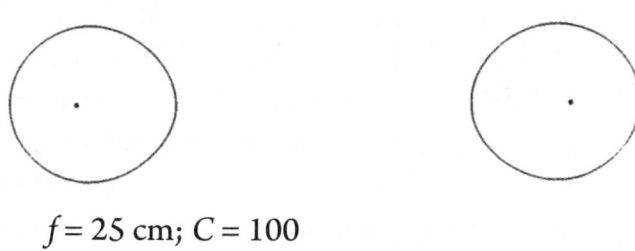

$f = 25$ cm; $C = 100$

Construction of a Cassini curve

I will now explain, in detail, how to construct one particular Cassini curve. We start by choosing (for 22 x 35 cm paper) the values $C=100$ and $f = 19$ cm, which turns out to be an *indented oval* (see the table following). We then use the above formulas to find out that $X_{out} \approx 4.29$ cm, and for X_{in}, we see that what's inside the square root sign ($f^2 - 4C$) turns out to be negative, which is not possible. Therefore, there is no value for X_{in}. (Recall that X_{in} is only valid for the case when the Cassini curve has the shape of two eggs.)

Now, we carefully place the focal points (A and B), so that they are centred horizontally on the paper 19 cm apart. Our first point (P_1) on the curve is found (as given by X_{out}) by going 4.29 cm to the left of focal point A.

The next two points on the Cassini curve are found by knowing that since the product of the distances to the two focal points must always be 100, there should be a point that is 10 cm from each of the focal points. So we set our compass exactly to a width of 10 cm, and, by placing the needle, in turn, on each of the two focal points, we draw two arcs. Since each point on an arc is 10 cm away from one focal point, we can say that the two points of intersection (P_2 and P_3 in the drawing below) of these two arcs are 10 cm away from *each* of the two focal points. (Notice that these two points will not exist if the Cassini curve is *two eggs*; the two drawn arcs will not cross one another.)

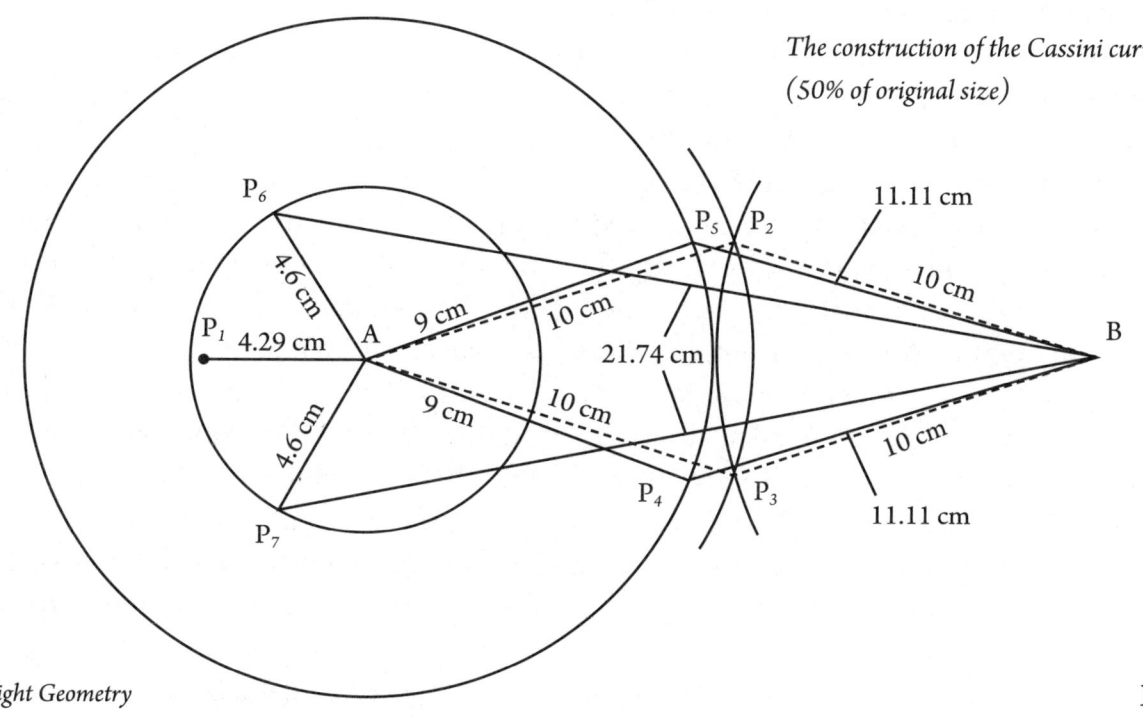

The construction of the Cassini curve (50% of original size)

Class Eight Geometry

We can now locate additional points on our curve by choosing any distance that we please between 4.29 cm (X_{out}) and 10 cm. We simply draw a circle using the distance we have chosen as the circle's radius, and with the focal point A as its centre. The points on the Cassini curve are those two points on this circle that are the proper distance away from the other focal point (B). For example, in the diagram below, we have chosen to draw a circle (the larger one) a distance of 9 cm away from focal point A. The question is now, 'What must the distance to the other focal point be such that the product of the two distances will be equal to 100?' We find this desired distance by dividing 100 by 9, which gives us approximately 11.11 cm. (Notice that 9 times 11.11 is (approximately) equal to 100.) By using a ruler, we then locate the two points on the circle (P_4 and P_5) that are a distance of 11.11 cm to the focal point B.

Similarly, we can choose *any other distance* between 4.29 and 10 cm for the radius of the circle around focal point A. In the above diagram, we have chosen a distance of 4.6 cm away from focal point A, resulting in the smaller circle. Dividing 100 by 4.6 gives us 21.74. We now find the points P_6 and P_7 by locating the two places on this circle that are 21.74 cm away from focal point B. We continue finding more pairs of points by drawing circles a certain distance away from focal point A, calculating what the distance from focal point B must be, and then using our ruler to find where the desired points occur on each circle. Of course, we need to find points that occur around focal point B as well, by drawing circles around the focal point B, and using our ruler to find the calculated distances to focal point A. So we draw the same-sized circles around B as we did around A, and then imagine there is a line of reflection (passing through the points P_2 and P_3) that reflects all the points around focal point A (P_1, P_6, P_7, P_4, P_5) to locations around focal point B.

After locating several points by using the method described above, we should be able to clearly see the path of the whole curve. We then carefully draw the curve by connecting the dots. I have used a French curve to assist me in drawing the curve shown here, but the students should do this free-hand, as best as they can.

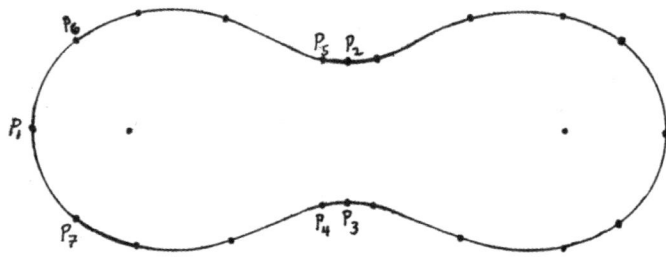

The process for drawing any other Cassini curve is basically the same as described above. In the above example, we just happened to have chosen values for f (equal to 19) and C (equal to 100) that resulted in the Cassini curve having the shape of an indented oval (shown above). The table below summarises the characteristics of various Cassini curves given certain values of f and a value of C equal to 100 (the whole class should use this value for C). Notice that there is only one specific instant that the curve becomes a 'flat oval', namely when the distance between the focal points is approximately 14.14 cm. Likewise, there is only one specific instant that the curve becomes a lemniscate, namely when the distance between the focal points is exactly 20 cm. These two values (14.14 and 20) are given to us by the formulas $f = \sqrt{2C}$ and $f = 2\sqrt{C}$ with the assumption that C is 100. The f values for the other curves in the table (below) were chosen somewhat arbitrarily. In other words, an oval occurs with any f value less than 14.14; an indented oval occurs with any f value between 14.14 and 20; and two eggs are the result of an f value that is greater than 20. I have chosen to put the f values of 19 and 21 into the table because they nicely show what is happening near the magical transition point of the lemniscate, which is when f equals 20.

As a final note regarding Cassini curves, I should mention that this is a great opportunity to integrate two disciplines by having the class do this 6-step transformation of the Cassini curve in eurythmy class. In my school, the eurythmy teacher does the Cassini curves in Class Four or Five, but tells the children they will learn about the mathematical significance of these curves in a Class Eight geometry main lesson. In Class Eight, the eurythmy exercise is revisited, but this time the focal points are included. Two of the children, representing the two focal points, stand close together while the rest of the class moves around them in a circular path. The two focal points then move slowly apart, or back together, thereby changing the path the rest of the class must now walk. This creates a process of transformation equivalent to what they experienced in their drawings.

C (constant product)	f (distance between focal points, cm)	Shape of curve	$X_{out} = \dfrac{\sqrt{f^2 + 4c} - f}{2}$ (Focal point to outside of curve)	$X_{in} = \dfrac{f - \sqrt{f^2 - 4c}}{2}$ (Focal point to inside of curve)	Range (of distances from curve to focal point)
100	10 cm	oval	6.18 cm	n/a	6.18 – 16.18
100	14.14 ($f = \sqrt{2C}$)	flat oval	5.18	n/a	5.18 – 19.32
100	19	indented oval	4.29	n/a	4.29 – 23.29
100	20 ($f = 2\sqrt{C}$)	lemniscate	4.14	10 cm	4.14 – 24.14
100	21	two eggs	4	7.30 cm	4 – 7.30 and 13.70 – 25
100	25	two eggs	3.51	5	3.51 – 5 and 20 – 28.51

Class Eight Geometry

Appendix

Drawings

Equiangular spirals
Formed with inscribed regular polygons

Joining the midpoints of the sides of the polygons

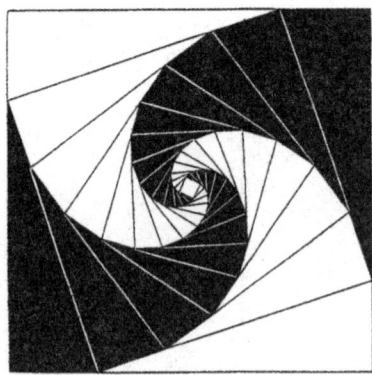

Joining the quarter-points of the sides of squares

A Teacher's Source Book for Mathematics in Classes 6 to 8

Rotations of circles
Showing the constructions and the final shaded-in drawings

197

The metamorphosis of a limaçon

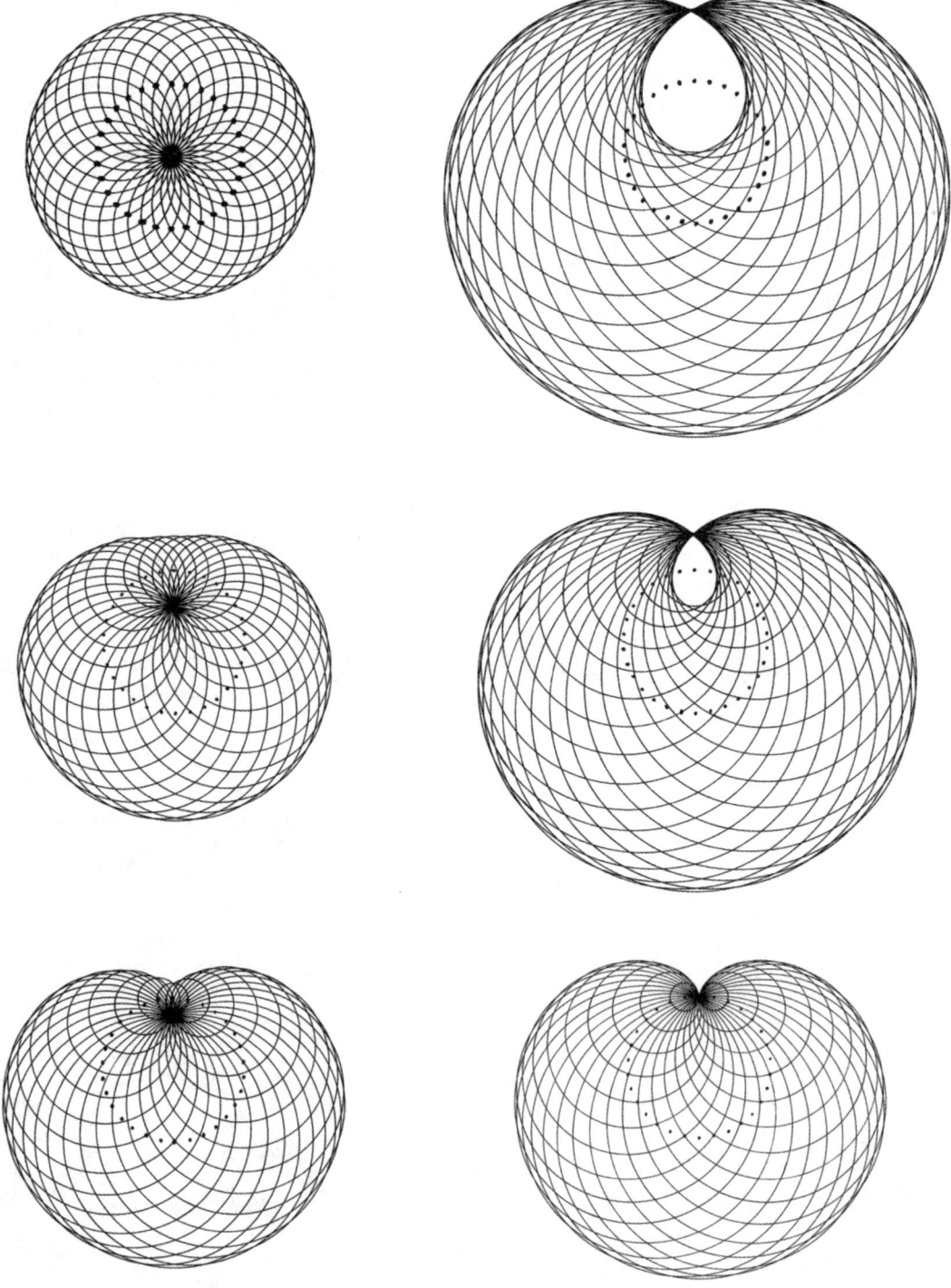

The hierarchy of quadrilaterals

Start with any *quadrilateral*. Connect the midpoints to form a *parallelogram*. Bisect the parallelogram to get a *rectangle*. Bisect these angles to get a *square*.

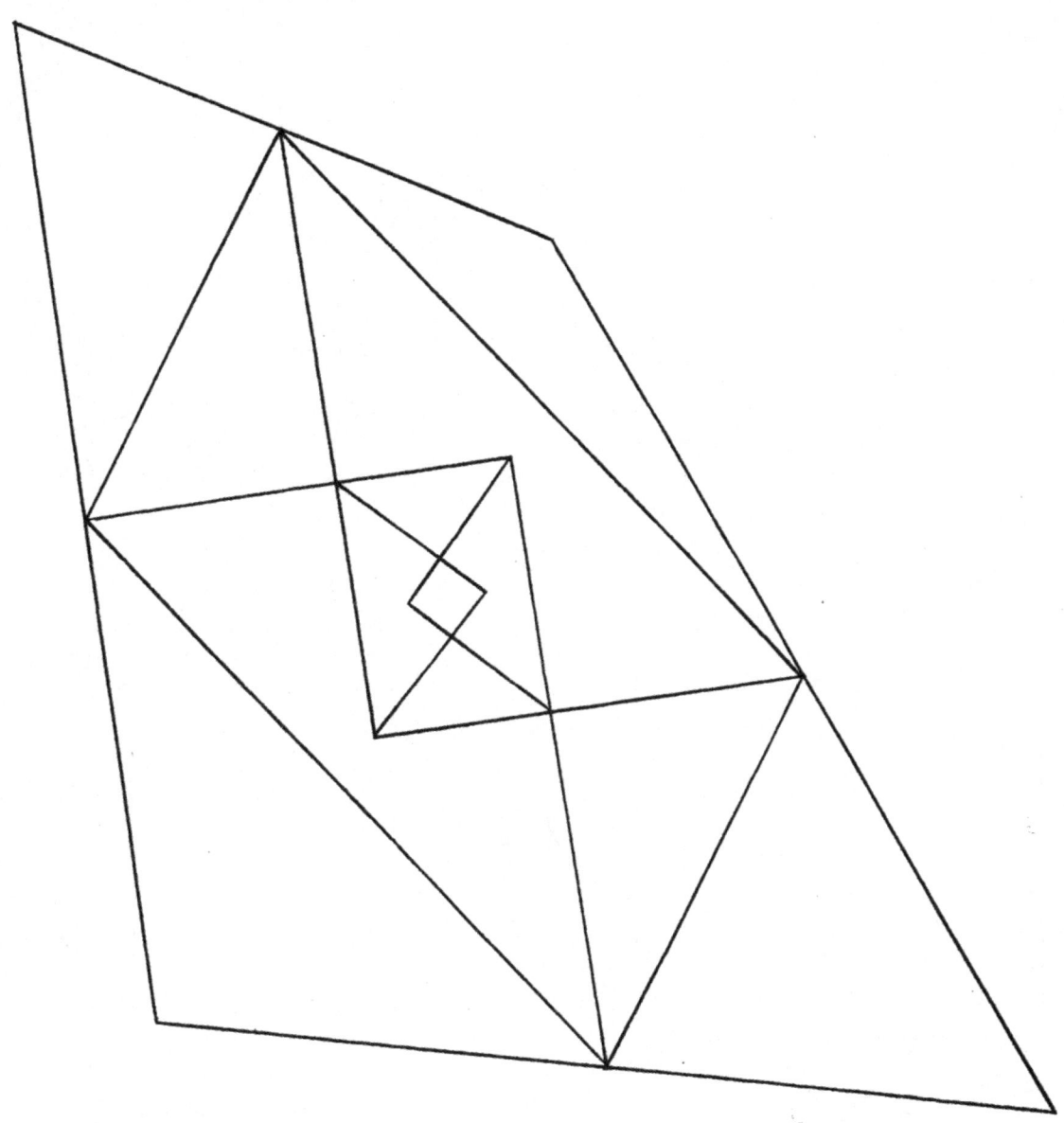

Appendix

Knots and interpenetrating polygons
Using the 8-division and the 12-division of the circle

The 24-division with all of its diagonals

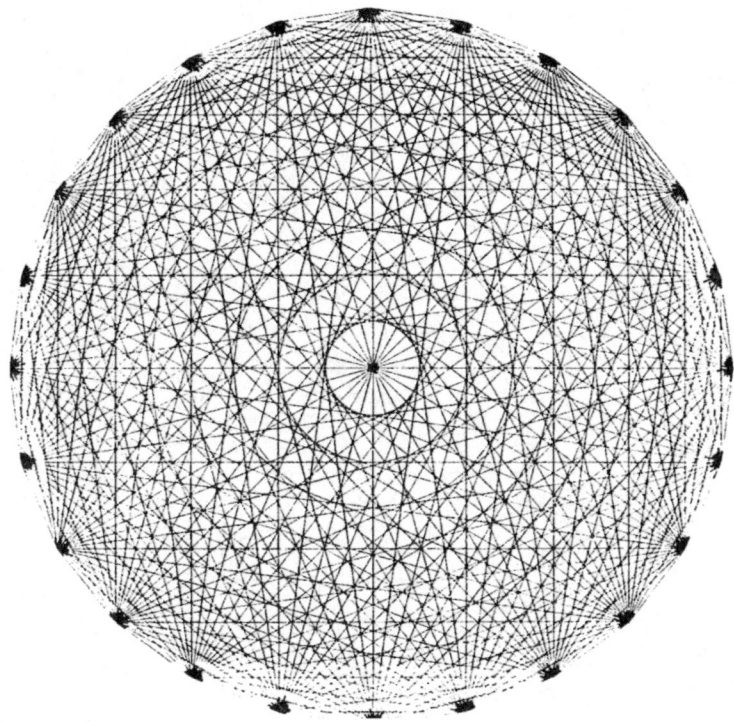

The king's crown

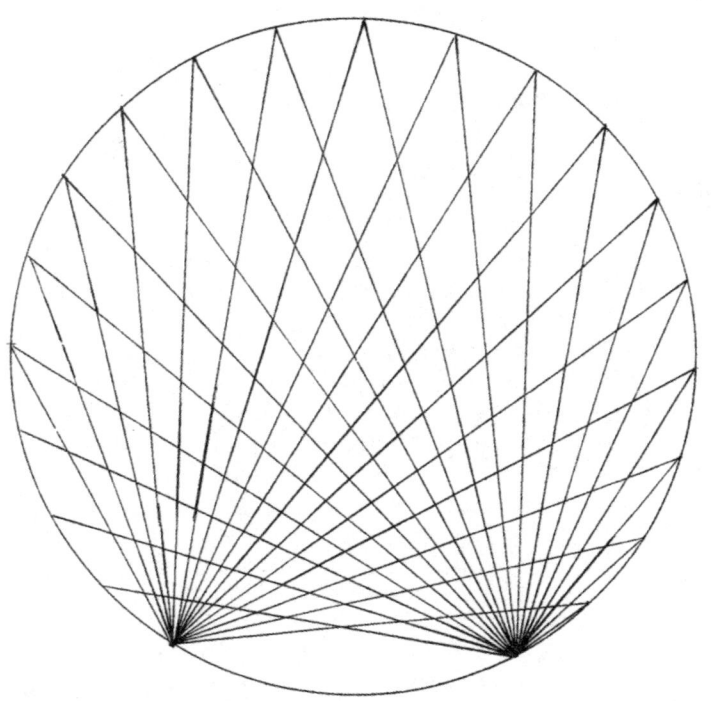

Appendix

Star patterns with geometric division

Morley's theorem
The 6 angle trisectors of any triangle meet to form an equilateral triangle

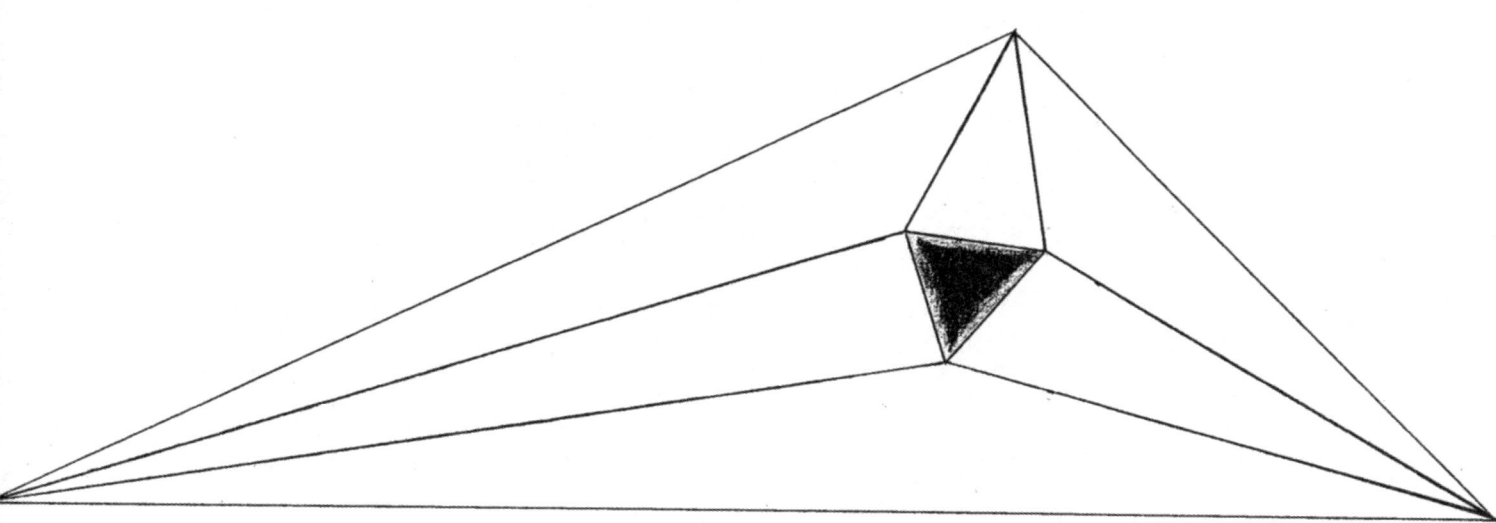

Appendix

The perspective reduction of a figure

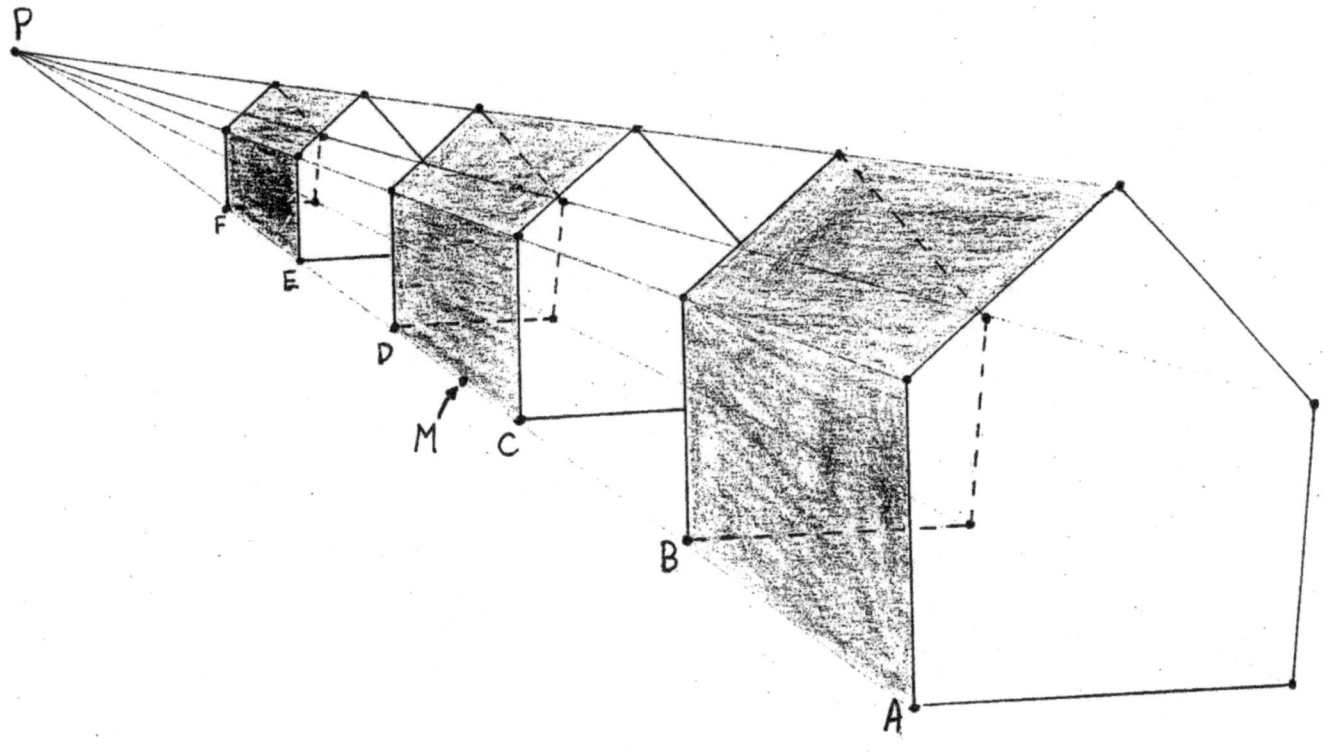

There are six pentagons in this drawing, including those hidden on the back of the 'houses'. The drawing has been done so that each pentagon is 75% of the size of the previous one. This also means that the second pentagon (which has point B at its lower left corner) is 75% as far from the point of perspective (P) as the first pentagon. In order to do this we 'double-bisect' the line segment AP by first finding the midpoint (M) of the line segment PA, and then bisecting the resulting line segment MA, thereby locating point B. We use this same method to 'bring in' the other four corners of the first pentagon to the other four points of the second pentagon. Similarly, the third pentagon is 75% of the size of the second pentagon, which means that the length of line segment PC is 75% of the length of PB. Likewise, the points D, E and F are each another step of 25% of the distance toward P. Notice that reductions like 25%, 50% or 75% are relatively easy, but something random (e.g. 37%) would be quite difficult with just a compass and straightedge.

Advanced Topics
Questions regarding repeating decimals

This is an investigation of the mathematical laws that arise when a fraction is converted into a decimal, which may repeat.

With each of the questions below, we are converting a fraction into a decimal by dividing the numerator by the denominator. We assume that we are starting with a *reduced fraction*.

What are the denominators of the fractions that don't become repeating decimals?

If the denominator is a 2, 4, 5, 8, 10, 16, 20, 25, 32, 40, 50, 64, 80, 100, 125, etc., then the decimal doesn't repeat.

What are the rules for when a fraction (or division problem), expressed as a decimal, repeats and when it just ends?

If we look at the denominators from the question above, then we see that they are all powers of two (e.g. 2, 4, 8, 16, 32, etc.) or powers of five (e.g. 5, 25, 125, 625, etc.) perhaps with zeros added on to the end. Another way of looking at this, is that their factor trees have only 2s and 5s in them. *Fractions with a denominator having a factor that is anything other than a 2 or a 5 will repeat.* For example, $^{11}/_{60}$ as a decimal repeats because its prime factorisation ($2^2 \times 3 \times 5$) has a three in it. On the other hand, $^{11}/_{80}$ doesn't repeat because its prime factorisation is $2^4 \times 5$, which contains only twos and fives.

What is the most number of digits that can possibly appear under the repeat bar when a fraction is converted into a decimal?

The number of digits under the repeat bar can be at most one less than the number in the denominator. The explanation is as follows: Using the example of $^4/_7$ we divide 7 into 4. We keep going with the division until it ends (giving a remainder of zero) or until it repeats (giving a remainder that we have already seen). There are only seven possible remainders when dividing by seven, and a remainder of zero would mean that it doesn't repeat at all, which isn't the case. Therefore, we must get a remainder that we have already seen after, at most, 6 digits.

Indeed $^4/_7 = 0.\overline{571428}$, and we can see that it repeats every six digits. Of course it is possible to get a repeated remainder earlier. For example, any fraction with a denominator of 13 ($^5/_{13} = 0.\overline{384615}$) doesn't repeat every 12 digits (that would be the most possible for a denominator of 13), but it happens to repeat after every 6 digits. Likewise, any fraction with a denominator of 11 ($^7/_{11} = 0.\overline{63}$) repeats every two digits instead of every ten digits (which would be the most we could expect). We might expect that $^{19}/_{54}$ repeats every 53 digits, but it repeats only every 3 digits ($^{19}/_{54} = 0.3\overline{518}$). Denominators that 'go the maximum distance' before repeating include 17 ($^5/_{17} = 0.\overline{2941176470588235}$), and 19 ($^3/_{19} = 0.\overline{157894736842105263}$).

For those denominators that go the maximum distance before repeating, what patterns do we notice by using different numbers in the numerator? (For example, find the decimal values of 1/7, 2/7, 3/7, etc. What patterns do you see?)

The digits under the repeat bar are always the same! They also appear in the same order, but start off at a different place depending on what the numerator is. For example, $5/7 = 0.\overline{714285}$, and $3/7 = 0.\overline{428571}$. With both of these, we can imagine that the same 6 digits (under the repeat bar) are repeating again and again, forever. Alternatively, we can rewrite the two as: $5/7 = 0.7142\overline{857142}$, and $3/7 = 0.42\overline{857142}$. In both cases we see the digits 857142 repeating. 1/7, 2/7, 4/7 and 6/7 can also be expressed with the digits 857142 repeating. Similarly, other denominators that go the maximum distance (e.g. 17, 19, etc.) follow this same law. For example, 13/17 and 9/17 can both be expressed with the same digits in the same order under the repeat bar.

Give an example of a fraction for which there is no equivalent repeating or ending decimal?

There is no such fraction. *Every fraction either repeats or ends.* This is a very important result in order to understand irrational numbers.

The square root algorithm

The following is an outline of a lesson plan for Class Seven that takes about 10 classroom hours to execute. The goal is to teach the students how to efficiently calculate square roots of large numbers (e.g. 223,729), and to teach it in such a way that the students gain an understanding of why the square root algorithm works.

Method 1: The guess and check method

This method is simple in concept, but very tedious in practice.

Guess an approximate value of the answer, then check how good your guess is by squaring it. If your guess squared is bigger (or smaller) than the original problem then the guess was too big (or small). Guess again, by adjusting your guess accordingly, and continue until the guess turns out to be exact, or you have a satisfactory amount of accuracy (e.g. two decimal places).

Practise these kind of problems, but don't spend too much time on it. The idea is largely for the students to come to the realisation that we need to find a quicker, more efficient, method.

Large square roots that work out to be whole numbers

$\sqrt{90{,}000} = 300$
$\sqrt{25{,}000{,}000} = 5{,}000$
$\sqrt{123{,}201} = 351$
$\sqrt{7{,}569} = 87$
$\sqrt{223{,}729} = 473$

Square roots that don't work out to be whole numbers
See how far they can go with each one.
$\sqrt{263} \approx 16.2172747$
$\sqrt{2} \approx 1.41421356237309504880168872420 97$

How can we find a better method?
Make a table of squares

x	x^2
5	25
9	81
10	100
23	529
38	1,444
75	5,625
99	9,801
100	10,000
216	46,656
347	120,409
521	271,441
999	998,001
1,000	1,000,000
2,012	4,048,144
5,204	27,081,616
9,999	99,980,001
10,000	100,000,000

Have the students work in groups and fill out the right column.

Make sure that they understand that our goal is to *go in the other direction* (from the right column to the left) in order to calculate the square root of a number.

By looking at the table that has now been filled out, the students should try to answer the three questions below, while keeping in mind that we are really taking the square root of some number. We are given a number from the right column and we need to figure out its square root, which is given in the left column.

When calculating a square root that works out evenly:
What can we say about the square root of a number that:
has 1 digit?   (Its square root has 1 digit.)
has 2 digits?   (Its square root has 1 digit.)
has 3 digits?   (Its square root has 2 digits.)
has 4 digits?   (Its square root has 2 digits.)
has 5 digits?   (Its square root has 3 digits.)
has 6 digits?   (Its square root has 3 digits.)
has 7 digits?   (Its square root has 4 digits.)
has 8 digits?   (Its square root has 4 digits.)
has 9 digits?   (Its square root has 5 digits.)

What can we say about the square root of a number if the number:
ends in a 1? (Its square root ends in a 1 or a 9.)
ends in a 4? (Its square root ends in a 2 or a 8.)
ends in a 5? (Its square root ends in a 5.)
ends in a 6? (Its square root ends in a 4 or a 6.)
ends in a 9? (Its square root ends in a 3 or a 7.)
ends in a 0? (Its square root ends in a 0.)
ends in a 2, 3, 7 or 8?   (its square root can't be exact!)

Appendix

Given a certain number, how can we know exactly what the first digit of its square root is?

Start from the right and move left while grouping the digits in pairs. The left-most 'pair' will be just a single digit if the whole number has an odd number of digits (e.g. 840,889 has 84 as its left-most pair, and 54,756 has 5 as its left-most pair.) Now, while looking at this left-most pair, ask yourself, 'the square root of this left-most pair sits between what two whole numbers?' The lower of these two whole numbers is our desired answer – the first digit of the square root of the entire original number.

Example: For $\sqrt{393{,}129}$, we ask ourselves, '$\sqrt{39}$ sits between what two whole numbers?' The answer to this question is 'between 6 and 7', which leads us to the conclusion that $\sqrt{393{,}129}$ has 6 as its first digit.

What have these three questions taught us?
This should clear up any confusion. Let's use the example of $\sqrt{54{,}756}$. Since 54,756 has '5' as its left-most pair, we know that $\sqrt{5}$ is between 2 and 3. Therefore, $\sqrt{54{,}756}$ *has 2 as its first digit*. We also know that since the number of digits in the number (54,756) is 5, then the number of digits in its square root is 3 (from question 1). Therefore the $\sqrt{54{,}756}$ is two-hundred-and-something. We now have to figure out what the last two digits are (the tens' place and the ones' place). We also know that because the number (54,756) ends in a 6, its square root (if it works out evenly) ends in either a 6 or a 4 (from question 2).

Practice problems (for the concepts given above)
For each problem, give the number of digits that its square root will have (assuming that the answer works out evenly), state what the first digit is and what the possibilities are for the last digit.

$\sqrt{529}$ (The answer has 2 digits; the first digit is 2; the last digit is 3 or 7, if exact.)

$\sqrt{695{,}556}$ (The answer has 3 digits; the first digit is 8; the last digit is 4 or 6, if exact.)

$\sqrt{45{,}589{,}504}$ (The answer has 4 digits; the first digit is 6; the last digit is 2 or 8, if exact.)

$\sqrt{3{,}750{,}950{,}025}$ (The answer has 5 digits; the first digit is 6; the last digit is 5, if exact.)

$\sqrt{94{,}352}$ (The answer has 3 digits; the first digit is 3; the answer can't be exact.)

An identity needed for doing square roots
An identity is a type of equation that states a relationship that is true for all numbers. We are going to use a special identity in order to help us calculate the rest of the digits of a square root.

The first step is to start with something that we will call the *squaring formula*:

$$(a+b)^2 = a^2 + b(2a+b)$$

Use the above identity for squaring numbers, in order to show students that it works for all numbers:

Example: 73^2 ($a = 70$; $b = 3$) → $70^2 + 3(2 \times 70+3)$ → $4{,}900 + 3(143)$ → $5{,}329$

Stress to students that we need to find a new identity that is more useful for square roots.

We start by calling the number that is being square rooted, n. We then say that $\sqrt{n}$ can be broken down into the sum of two numbers a and b. For example, we can say that $\sqrt{64}$ (which is 8) is equal to $5 + 3$. This may seem to be strange, but we can see how it leads to our desired identity, shown below:

$n = a + b$ and then squaring both sides
$n = (a + b)^2$ and now using the above identity
$n = a^2 + b(2a+b)$
    and now subtracting a^2 from both sides
$-a^2 \quad -a^2$ we get...
$n - a^2 = b(2a+b)$

We will call this the *square root identity*

This identity works for any n, as long as we start with the relationship that $\sqrt{n} = a + b$.

Example: Using $\sqrt{64} = 5 + 3$, we have $n = 64$, $a = 5$ and $b = 3$, and we can see that the identity works because $64 - 5^2 = 3(2 \times 5 + 3)$. Give several examples of this, such as:

$n = 64, a = 6, b = 2$
$n = 64, a = 7, b = 1$
$n = 676, a = 18, b = 8$
$n = 676, a = 20, b = 6$

The important thing with this identity is that the students can *see that it works*, not that they can understand yet how it will be useful in calculating square roots.

Mention that with square roots that have a two-digit answer, we will intentionally set a and b to the two digits of the answer. For example, because $\sqrt{169} = 13$, we will set a equal to 10 and set b equal to 3. Similarly with $\sqrt{676}$ we will set a to 20 and b equal to 6.

Mention that our identity is also valid for square roots that don't work out evenly.

Method 2: The long algebraic method
Calculating square roots with 2-digit answers
Have the students practise a good number of these.

Example: Calculate $\sqrt{6{,}889}$.

Here $n = 6{,}889$. We know that its square root has 2 digits, that the first digit is 8 (because 68 is between 8 and 9) and that the last number is a 3 or a 7. We call our first estimate of the answer a, and in this case $a = 80$. The second digit we call b. Here is the procedure, using the square root identity $n - a^2 = b(2a + b)$ which is derived from $\sqrt{n} = a + b$:

$n - a^2 = b(2a+b)$
    and putting in $n = 6{,}889$ and $a = 80$ we get:
$6{,}889 - 6{,}400 = b(160 + b)$
$489 = b(160 + b)$

Here we try to figure out b (the second digit of the answer).

We try different single digit values for b to see what works. For example, if $b = 2$, then we try 162×2; if $b = 5$, then we try 165×5, hoping that one of them will be equal to (or just under) 489. It turns out that $b = 3$ works ($163 \times 3 = 489$). Therefore, our answer (which is exact) is **83**.

Of course, the students should show themselves that the answer is correct: that $83^2 = 6{,}889$.

Calculating answers with more than 2 digits

We now need to do the same procedure as above, but repeat the process a number of times.

Keep in mind that the a values are the digits that we are certain of at a given point, and the b values are the next digit that we are trying to figure out.

Notation: We will use a_1 to mean the value of a for the first time through the process, and therefore with only one correct digit a_3 would then represent the value of a the third time through the process, and therefore has three correct digits. The values of b are similarly given as b_1, b_2, etc.

The students should practise several examples, of course doing all the calculations neatly by hand, and keeping the work well organised so that it is easy to follow, building up to something like this example:

Calculate $\sqrt{7{,}203{,}856}$.

Step 1: We know that the answer has 4 digits, and the first digit is 2 (because $\sqrt{7}$ is between 2 and 3), so $a_1 = 2{,}000$, and we use the identity $n - a_1^2 = b_1(2a_1 + b_1)$, where $2a_1 = 4{,}000$.

$$\begin{array}{ll} n & 7{,}203{,}856 \\ a_1^2 & -\,4{,}000{,}000 \\ n - a_1^2 & 3{,}203{,}856 = b_1(4{,}000 + b_1), \end{array}$$ (because $2{,}000^2 = 4{,}000{,}000$)

where b_1 is the 100s place (e.g. 300, 400, etc.)
$b_1 = 600$ because 700 is too big, which means $b_1(2a_1 + b_1) = 2{,}760{,}000$

Step 2: We now know that the first two digits are 2 and 6, so $a^2 = 2{,}600$, and we use the identity $n - a_2^2 = b_2(2a_2 + b_2)$, where $2a_2 = 5{,}200$.

$$\begin{array}{ll} n & 7{,}203{,}856 \\ a_2^2 & -\,6{,}760{,}000 \\ n - a_2^2 & 443{,}856 = b_2(5{,}200 + b^2), \end{array}$$ (because $2{,}600^2 = 6{,}760{,}000$)

where b_2 is the tens' place (e.g. 30, 40, etc.)
$b_2 = 80$ because 90 is too big, which means $b_2(2a_2 + b_2) = 422{,}400$.

Step 3: We now know that the first three digits are 2, 6 and 8, so $a_3 = 2{,}680$, and we use the identity $n - a_3^2 = b_3(2a_3 + b_3)$, where $2a_3 = 5{,}360$.

$$\begin{array}{ll} n & 7{,}203{,}856 \\ a_3^2 & -\,7{,}182{,}400 \\ n - a_3^2 & 21{,}456 = b_3(5{,}360 + b_3), \end{array}$$ (because $26{,}80^2 = 7{,}182{,}400$)

where b_3 is the ones' place (e.g. 3, 4, etc.)
$b_3 = 4$ because 5 is too big, which means $b_3(2a_3 + b_3) = 21{,}456$, which means that our final answer is *exactly* **2,684**.

Method 3: The short algebraic method

This method is the most difficult one, but it is not as crucial for students to understand as the long algebraic method serves only as a bridge to seeing why the square root algorithm works. Don't get bogged down.

The long algebraic method described above requires some tedious, and unnecessary, calculations, which can be eliminated.

Look at the steps from the long algebraic method shown on the previous page. Looking at the left side of each step, we see, for step 1: $n - a_1^2$, and then for step 2: $n - a_2^2$, etc.

Since $a_2 = a_1 + b_1$, we can use the *squaring formula* $(a + b)^2 = a^2 + b(2a + b)$ to get:

$$a_2^2 = (a_1 + b_1)^2 = a_1^2 + b_1(2a_1 + b_1)$$

This is the key idea: In place of subtracting a_2^2 from n, we can instead subtract the whole of $\{a_1^2 + b_1(2a_1 + b_1)\}$ from n since it is equal to a_2^2. This seems like more work, but it's actually less work.

In other words, instead of doing $n - a_2^2$, we can do $n - \{a_1^2 + b_1(2a_1 + b_1)\}$, which is the same as $(n - a_1^2) - \{b_1(2a_1 + b_1)\}$*

In short: instead of doing $n - a_2^2$
we do $\quad (n - a_1^2) - \{b_1(2a_1 + b_1)\}$
Likewise, instead of doing $n - a_3^2$
we do $\quad (n - a_2^2) - \{b_2(2a_2 + b_2)\}$
Likewise, instead of doing $n - a_4^2$
we do $\quad (n - a_3^2) - \{b_3(2a_3 + b_3)\}$

* $n - \{a_1^2 + b_1(2a_1 + b_1)\}$ is the same as $(n - a_1^2) - \{b_1(2a_1 + b_1)\}$ for the same reason that $40 - (5 + 3 \times 2)$ would be the same as $(40 - 5) - (3 \times 2)$; i.e. instead of subtracting all of $5 + 3 \times 2$ from 40, we can instead subtract 5 first, and afterwards subtrack 3×2. Either way the result is the same – in this case 29.

Of course, any sane person would ask, 'Haven't we made things more complicated?' The answer to this is, quite surprisingly (and this is where the genius of this method comes in): $(n - a_2^2) - \{b_2(2a_2 + b_2)\}$ is easier to do than $n - a_3^2$ because a_3^2 requires us to square some big ugly number (e.g. 2,680), whereas we have already calculated both $(n - a_2^2)$ (which is 443,856 on the example on the previous page) and $\{b_2(2a_2 + b_2)\}$ (which is 422,400 on the example on the previous page).

Subtracting 443,856 – 422,400, is easier than squaring 2,680.

Much of the above may be confusing. So the following example should hopefully clarify things.

In short the whole procedure looks like this (again for $\sqrt{7{,}203{,}856}$):

	n	7,203,856	our first estimate (a_1) is 2,000.
	a_1^2	$-\,4{,}000{,}000$	
step 1	$n - a_1^2$	3,203,856	$= b_1(4{,}000 + b_1) \rightarrow b_1 = 600$
	$b_1(2a_1 + b_1)$	$-\,2{,}760{,}000$	
step 2	$n - a_2^2$	443,856	$= b_2(5{,}200 + b_2) \rightarrow b_2 = 80$
	$b_2(2a_2 + b_2)$	$-\,422{,}400$	
step 3	$n - a_3^2$	21,456	$= b_3(5{,}360 + b_3) \rightarrow b_3 = 4$
	$b_3(2a_3 + b_3)$	$-\,21{,}456$	
		0	which tells us our answer is exactly **2,684**

Appendix

Method 4: The square root algorithm (with zeros)

This method is basically identical to the *short algebraic method*, but it cuts out all the unnecessary writing, and there is an added shortcut that aids us in determining the values for $2a_1$, $2a_2$, $2a_3$, etc. This new shortcut is as follows.

With our example of $\sqrt{7{,}203{,}856}$, the values for $2a_1$, $2a_2$, $2a_3$ are 4,000, 5,200, 5,360. The first of these values is found simply by doubling a_1, which is $2{,}000 \times 2 = 4{,}000$. The rest of these values are found by taking the previous value and adding the new b value to it, *two times*. So from 4,000, we add b_1, which is 600, giving us 4,600, and then add 600 again, giving us our next value, 5,200. From 5,200, we add b_2, which is 80, giving us 5,280, and then adding 80 again, gives us our next value, 5,360.

Here is the whole process:

Step 1

We know that $a_1 = 2{,}000$, so we write down 2,000 twice. Multiplying the two 2,000's gives us the 4,000,000 that is written under 7,203,856, and subtracting, we get 3,203,856. Then we add 2,000 plus 2,000 to get 4,000, but we put a box in place of the zeros, and another box underneath the first box. So at this point, everything looks like this:

```
2,000      7,203,856
2,000   -  4,000,000
4,□        3,203,856
 □
```

It is important to understand that the boxes represent b_1. So at this point, with both the short and long algebraic method, we had had this equation: $3{,}203{,}856 = b_1(4{,}000 + b_1)$, and we asked ourselves, 'What must b_1 be so that $b_1(4{,}000 + b_1)$ is less than 3,203,856?' Here, with the above situation, we are asking essentially the same thing. We need to fill in the two boxes with the same value (i.e. the value for b_1). And this value must be a certain number of hundreds – resulting in a product of $4{,}100 \times 100$, or $4{,}200 \times 200$, or $4{,}300 \times 300$, etc. Since $4{,}700 \times 700$ is bigger than 3,203,856, we put 600 in the two boxes, and write the product of $4{,}600 \times 600$, which is 2,760,000, under 3,203,856.

Step 2

We now add the left column (4,600+600), which gives us 5,200, and subtract the right column (3,203,856−2,760,000), which is 443,856. Once again, we write a box in place of the zeros of 5,200, and another box under that one. Everything now looks like this:

```
2,000      7,203,856
2,000   -  4,000,000
4,600      3,203,856
  600   -  2,760,000
5,2□         443,856
  □
```

Similarly to step 1, we need to put the same number (which is the tens' place of our final answer) into both boxes so that the resulting product is less than 443,856. The possibilities are $5{,}210 \times 10$, or $5{,}220 \times 20$, or $5{,}230 \times 30$, etc. Since $5{,}290 \times 90$ is a bit too big, we put 80 into both boxes, and write the product of $5{,}280 \times 80$, which is 422,400, under 443,856.

Step 3

We add the left column and subtract the right column, resulting in 5,360 and 21,456, respectively. We put a box in place of the zero in 5,360, and a box below it (which is not shown below). 4 can be put into both boxes, resulting in 5,364 × 4, which is *exactly* 21,456. The end result, is that all our work looks like this (quite short, actually!):

```
 2,000     7,203,856
 2,000    -4,000,000
 4,600     3,203,856
   600    -2,760,000
 5,280       443,856
    80      -422,400
 5,364        21,456
     4       -21,456
                   0
```

The answer, **2,684**, comes from the underlined digits.

A remainder of zero tells us that our answer is exact.

This method of the square root algorithm is slightly different from what is done in Class Eight. (**See Class Eight**, *Square root algorithm without zeros*, p. 213.)

Calculating square roots that don't work out evenly (e.g. $\sqrt{30}$) should be delayed until Class Eight.

The square root algorithm (without zeros)

This algorithm is written in the style of a computer program, Class Eight.

Note: As you follow the algorithm below you will need to carefully keep track of the following variables:

r, x, y, difference, sum, product

Enclose the number in a 'house' as you would enclose a long division problem. Starting at the decimal point, and working out in both directions, draw short vertical lines that separate the number into pairs of two digits. Make sure that there are at least as many digit-pairs after the decimal place as the number of decimal places that are needed in the answer. Add ending zeros, if needed (e.g. in order to calculate 45 to three decimals, we would need to add three pairs of ending zeros and do $\sqrt{45.00\ 00\ 00}$.)

Let *r* be equal to the left-most digit-pair (which may be a single digit) that is inside the 'house'. Circle it. Draw a small box, large enough to hold one digit, well to the left of *r*.

Let *x* be a single digit (somewhere from 0 to 9), such that it is as large as possible, but x^2 is still less than or equal to *r*. Write *x* both in the box, and immediately below the box.

Underneath the digit that is below the box, write down the *sum* of *x* plus *x*. Write the result of squaring *x* below *r*, and below that, write the *difference* of *r* minus the square of *x*.

If there are no more digit pairs to bring down, then go to step 11.

Bring down the next digit-pair, combining it with, and writing it next to, the *difference* (that was just found) This now forms the new value for *r*. Circle it.

Draw a small box to the right of the *sum*. If the digit-pair just brought down is the first one

Appendix

after the decimal place, then write a decimal point above this box.

We must now choose a special single digit (somewhere between 0 and 9) that will be written both in the box and directly below the box. This special digit below the box will be called *y*, and the new value for *x* will be the result of taking the *sum* (found to the left of the box), and attaching to the end of it, the special digit in the box. (This means that *y* will be equal to the last digit of the new value for *x*.) This special digit is chosen such that the result of *x* times *y* is as large as possible, but still less than or equal to *r*. Write the correct choice for this special digit both in the box and below the box.

Underneath *r*, write the *product* of *x* times *y*, and then subtract it from *r*, writing this new *difference* underneath it all.

Underneath *x* and *y*, write the *sum* of *x* plus *y*. Go to step 5.

The answer to the square root problem is found by reading the digits in the boxes from top to bottom, with the decimal point possibly in the middle. If the *difference* is zero, then the answer is exact; otherwise it is an approximation.

Example: Calculate √780.0849

The work is shown below. The values for *r* are circled. The *y* values (2, 7, 9, 3) are the single digits immediately below the boxes. The *x* values (2, 47, 549, 5,583) are the numbers ending with the digit in the box. Each step number corresponds to the step number in the above algorithm.

Step 1: The number is divided into 4 digit-pairs.
Step 2: *r* = 7.
Step 3: *x* = 2.
Step 4: Sum = 4, difference = 3.
Step 6: *r* = 380.
Step 8: Trying different 'special' digits, we see that 48 × **8** is bigger than *r*, and 47 × **7** is less than *r*. The correct special digit is therefore 7, which we write both in the box and below the box.
Step 9: The product of 47 × 7 (329) is written below *r*. The *difference* is 51.
Step 10: The *sum* of 47 + 7 (54) is written below. We go back up to step 5.
Step 6: *r* = 5,108.
Step 7: We write a decimal point above the box.
Step 8: The special digit is 9, making *x* = 549 and *y* = 9.
Step 9: Difference = 167.
Step 10: Sum = 558. Go back to step 5.
Step 6: *r*=16,749.
Step 8: *x* = 5,583, Y=3.
Step 9: Difference = 0.
Step 10: Sum = 5,586, go to step 5.
Step 5: Go to step 11.
Step 11: **Our final answer is 27.93** (exactly).

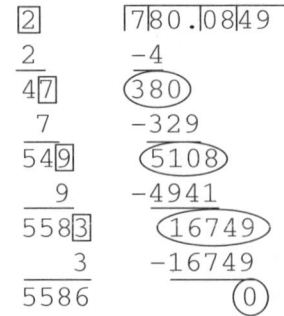

The volume of an octahedron and tetrahedron

The volume of an octahedron

What is the volume of an octahedron that has a 10 cm long edge?

The octahedron can be sliced into two square pyramids. First we will find the height of one of the triangular faces (which is different from the height of the pyramid). We will see why this height is useful in a moment. We find this height (x) by dividing the equilateral triangle in half, thereby creating a right triangle with legs of length 5 and x, and a hypotenuse of length 10. By using the *leg formula*, we find x to be $\sqrt{75}$.

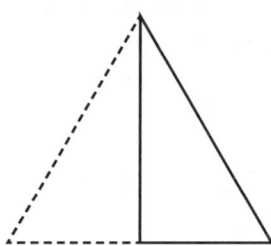

To find the volume of one of the pyramids, use the same method as explained in *Mensuration practice problems* (pp. 160f) where the volume of a pyramid is found. The trick is to find the height of the pyramid. This can be found by imagining a triangle sitting inside the pyramid that, when traced, goes from the apex of the pyramid straight down through the centre of the pyramid to the centre of the base (a square), then goes out to the midpoint of one of the edges of the base and returns back to the apex by moving up along the middle of a triangular face. This triangle's hypotenuse has a length of $\sqrt{75}$ (from above), and one leg has a length of 5. The missing side of this triangle is the desired height (h) of the whole pyramid. Using the *leg formula*, we can see that h^2 is equal to $\sqrt{75}^2 - 5^2$, which makes h equal to $\sqrt{50}$, which is approximately 7.07.

The volume of the pyramid is therefore $V = \frac{1}{3} A_{Base} \times h$, and since the area of the square base is 100, this gives a volume of $\frac{1}{3} \times 100 \times \sqrt{50}$, which is $\frac{100\sqrt{50}}{3}$ or approximately 235.67 cm³.

Since the original octahedron consists of two of these pyramids, we can say that its volume is approximately equal to 2 × 235.67, which is 471.33 cm³.

The volume of a tetrahedron

What is the volume of a tetrahedron that has a 10 cm long edge?

Again, we will imagine a right triangle sitting inside the tetrahedron that goes from the apex of the tetrahedron, down to the centre of its triangular base, then out to the midpoint of the base's edge, and finally back up to the apex of the tetrahedron. What makes this tricky is determining the length of the leg of the right triangle that goes from the midpoint of the base's edge to the centre of the base (shown as a dark line in the drawing overleaf).

If we draw all three of the angle bisectors of the base triangle, then we can see where the centre of this triangle is, and we can see that we have created six 30°, 60°, 90° triangles.

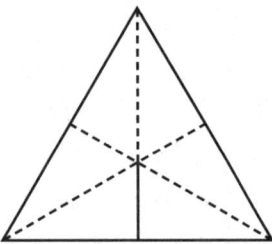

Since the hypotenuse of a 30°, 60°, 90° triangle is twice the length of the shorter leg, we can say by looking at the drawing that *the distance from the centre of the entire base triangle to a vertex of that triangle is twice the distance from the triangle's centre to the midpoint of an edge.*

Realising that one of these angle bisectors is the same as the height (or altitude) of the triangle, and is equal to $\sqrt{75}$ (see *Volume of an octahedron,* above), we can finally conclude that the distance from the midpoint of the triangular base's edge to the centre of that triangle is ⅓ the height of the triangle, which is therefore equal to ⅓ $\sqrt{75}$.

Remember the triangle that we initially 'imagined' sitting inside the tetrahedron? We now know the length of its hypotenuse, which is $\sqrt{75}$, and we know that the length of the short leg is ⅓ $\sqrt{75}$. We can use the leg formula of the Pythagorean Theorem to find the longer leg, which is equal to the height (h) of the whole tetrahedron. We get:

$$h^2 = \sqrt{75}^2 - (⅓\sqrt{75})^2$$
$$h^2 = 75 - \frac{75}{9}$$
$$h^2 = \frac{600}{9}$$
$$h = \frac{\sqrt{600}}{3}$$

Now we calculate the area of the base as $A_{Base} = ½ × 10 × \sqrt{75} = 5\sqrt{75}$ and lastly we use the volume formula $V = ⅓ A_{Base} × h$ in order to finally get the volume of the whole tetrahedron:

$$⅓(5\sqrt{75})\frac{\sqrt{600}}{3} = \frac{5\sqrt{45000}}{9} \approx 117.85 \text{ cm}^3,$$

which is exactly ¼ the volume of the octahedron.

Proof that there exists only five Platonic solids

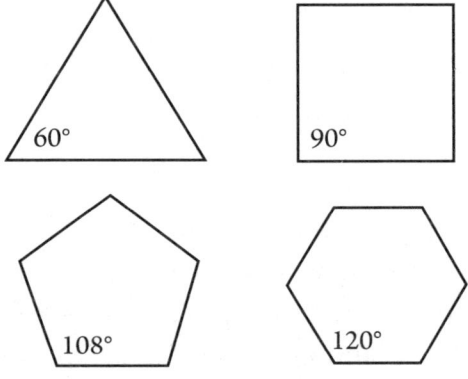

The number of degrees in each angle of the regular polygons.

Any polyhedron can be made from a *net* on paper, where each of the faces are laid out side by side and then this net is cut out and folded together, all in such a way that the desired three-dimensional solid is formed. We can then see that *every vertex* in any polyhedron has *two properties*:

Each *vertex* must be surrounded by *at least three faces*.

The *sum of the angles* (of the corners of the faces) coming together at each vertex must be *less than 360°*.

For example, the five triangular faces of an icosahedron can be placed flat on a piece of paper in such a way that they all share a common point, which is the vertex of the solid. When we do this, we notice that there is a 'gap'. When this gap and the whole net are cut out, and all the folds are made along the edges, this gap is closed in by having the two neighbouring edges come together (see arrow, in drawing). This forces the vertex (which is the point where the five triangles come together) to rise up, essentially allowing the form to become three-dimensional. If the vertex is surrounded by angles adding to exactly 360° (e.g. six triangles), then there would be no gap, and the form, when cut out, would not become three-dimensional.

By definition, a Platonic solid must have *regular* polygonal faces (e.g. equilateral triangle, square, pentagon, hexagon, etc.)

If a Platonic solid has *equilateral triangles* for faces, then there are three possibilities:

There could be three triangles at each vertex (*tetrahedron*)

There could be four triangles at each vertex (*octahedron*)

Or there could be five triangles at each vertex (*icosahedron*).

Six triangles at a point is not possible because that would make in the sum of the angles at a vertex 6 × 60°, or exactly 360°, which is not allowed according to the second property given above.

If a Platonic solid has *squares* for faces, then there is only one possibility, namely, three squares at each vertex, which is a *cube*. Four squares at a point is not possible because that would result in the sum of the angles at a vertex to be 4 × 90°, or exactly 360°, which is not allowed according to the second property given above.

If a Platonic solid has regular *pentagons* for faces, then there is only one possibility, namely, three pentagons at each vertex, which is a *dodecahedron*. Four regular pentagons at a point is not possible because that would result in the sum of the angles at a vertex to be 4 × 108°, or 432°, which is greater than 360°, and not allowed according to the second property given above.

A Platonic solid cannot have regular *hexagons* for faces because if three hexagons formed a vertex, the sum of the angles at that vertex would be 3 × 120°, which is exactly 360°, and is therefore not allowed according to the second property given above. Likewise, polygons with more than six sides (a 7-gon with angles of about 129°; an octagon with angles of 135°, etc.) are also not possible.

We have, therefore, exhausted all the possibilities for creating Platonic solids, *so there exist only five Platonic solids.*

The wonder of number

Square numbers

The square numbers are 1, 4, 9, 16, etc. They are found by squaring each integer: 1^2, 2^2, 3^2, 4^2, etc.

They can be geometrically made into squares by placing bowling pins into square shapes: three rows of three make 9, four rows of four make 16, etc.

They can also be found by adding sequences of odd numbers. For example, the fourth square number can be found by adding the first four odd numbers: 1 + 3 + 5 + 7, which is 16. Similarly, the sixth square number can be found by adding the first six odd numbers: 1 + 3 + 5 + 7 + 9 + 11, which is 36.

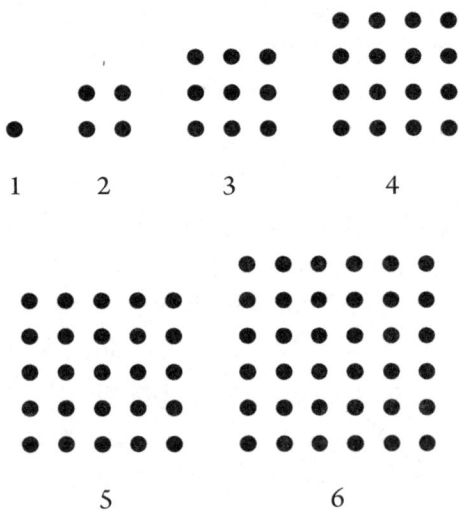

The first 100 square numbers

1^2	=	1	34^2	=	1,156
2^2	=	4	35^2	=	1,225
3^2	=	9	36^2	=	1,296
4^2	=	16	37^2	=	1,369
5^2	=	25	38^2	=	1,444
6^2	=	36	39^2	=	1,521
7^2	=	49	40^2	=	1,600
8^2	=	64	41^2	=	1,681
9^2	=	81	42^2	=	1,764
10^2	=	100	43^2	=	1,849
11^2	=	121	44^2	=	1,936
12^2	=	144	45^2	=	2,025
13^2	=	169	46^2	=	2,116
14^2	=	196	47^2	=	2,209
15^2	=	225	48^2	=	2,304
16^2	=	256	49^2	=	2,401
17^2	=	289	50^2	=	2,500
18^2	=	324	51^2	=	2,601
19^2	=	361	52^2	=	2,704
20^2	=	400	53^2	=	2,809
21^2	=	441	54^2	=	2,916
22^2	=	484	55^2	=	3,025
23^2	=	529	56^2	=	3,136
24^2	=	576	57^2	=	3,249
25^2	=	625	58^2	=	3,364
26^2	=	676	59^2	=	3,481
27^2	=	729	60^2	=	3,600
28^2	=	784	61^2	=	3,721
29^2	=	841	62^2	=	3,844
30^2	=	900	63^2	=	3,969
31^2	=	961	64^2	=	4,096
32^2	=	1,024	65^2	=	4,225
33^2	=	1,089	66^2	=	4,356

67²	=	4,489	84²	=	7,056
68²	=	4,624	85²	=	7,225
69²	=	4,761	86²	=	7,396
70²	=	4,900	87²	=	7,569
71²	=	5,041	88²	=	7,744
72²	=	5,184	89²	=	7,921
73²	=	5,329	90²	=	8,100
74²	=	5,476	91²	=	8,281
75²	=	5,625	92²	=	8,464
76²	=	5,776	93²	=	8,649
77²	=	5,929	94²	=	8,836
78²	=	6,084	95²	=	9,025
79²	=	6,241	96²	=	9,216
80²	=	6,400	97²	=	9,409
81²	=	6,561	98²	=	9,604
82²	=	6,724	99²	=	9,801
83²	=	6,889	100²	=	10,000

Triangular numbers

The triangular numbers are 1, 3, 6, 10, 15, 21, 28, 36, etc.

The reason that they are called triangular can be explained by looking at the way that the dots are placed in a triangular form, as shown below.

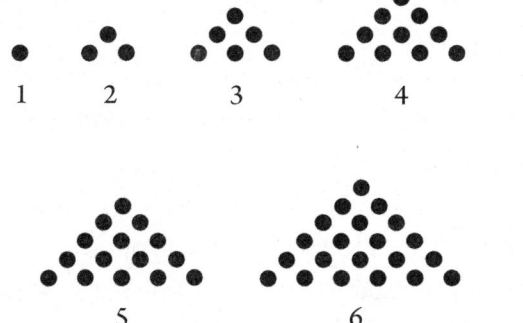

The triangular numbers can be found by adding a sequence of numbers. For example, the fourth triangular number is found by adding 1 + 2 + 3 + 4, which is 10, and, similarly, the sixth triangular number is found by adding 1 + 2 + 3 + 4 + 5 + 6, which is 21.

The sum of two consecutive triangular numbers is a square number! (Can you see why this is so?) This can be quite a thrill for students to discover this on their own!

There are only seven numbers below 2 billion that are *both* square and triangular. They are 1; 36; 1,225; 41,616; 1,413,721; 48,024,900; 1,631,432,881.

The first 75 triangular numbers

1	1	19	190
2	3	20	210
3	6	21	231
4	10	22	253
5	15	23	276
6	21	24	300
7	28	25	325
8	36	26	351
9	45	27	378
10	55	28	406
11	66	29	435
12	78	30	465
13	91	31	496
14	105	32	528
15	120	33	561
16	136	34	595
17	153	35	630
18	171	36	666

37	703	57	1,653
38	741	58	1,711
39	780	59	1,770
40	820	60	1,830
41	861	61	1,891
42	903	62	1,953
43	946	63	2,016
44	990	64	2,080
45	1,035	65	2,145
46	1,081	66	2,211
47	1,128	67	2,278
48	1,176	68	2,346
49	1,225	69	2,415
50	1,275	70	2,485
51	1,326	71	2,556
52	1,378	72	2,628
53	1,431	73	2,701
54	1,485	74	2,775
55	1,540	75	2,850
56	1,596		

Perfect, abundant and deficient numbers

What are perfect, abundant and deficient numbers? In general, a whole number is categorised as abundant, deficient or perfect based upon the sum of its factors. In order to determine whether a given whole number is perfect, abundant or deficient, we first list all the number's factors, except for the number itself. Then we sum up the numbers in that list.

If this sum is *equal* to the number itself, then we say that the number is *perfect*.

If this sum is *less* than the number itself, then we say that the number is *deficient*.

If the sum is *greater* than the number itself, then we say that the number is *abundant*.

Note that one is not considered to be a perfect number for the same reason that it isn't considered to be a prime number: it is the basis of all numbers. Also our list of factors isn't supposed to include the number itself, so the number 1 doesn't have any numbers in its list of factors.

More about perfect, abundant and deficient numbers (for the teacher)
Perfect numbers are extremely rare. There are only three perfect numbers below 5,000.

The first 7 perfect numbers are 6; 28; 496; 8,128; 33,550,336; 8,589,869,056; 137,438,691,328.

There are 21 even abundant numbers under 100, and 231 even abundant numbers that occur before 945, which is the first odd abundant number.

The Greeks (especially the Pythagoreans) believed that certain numbers had special meaning and significance. They studied perfect, abundant and deficient numbers in detail.

Early on, the Greeks knew that the first three perfect numbers were 6, 28 and 496. They had troubles finding perfect numbers beyond that because the numbers were getting too large to list and add all the factors. They wanted to find an easier method for determining perfect numbers.

Around 300 BC, Euclid discovered a formula for calculating even perfect numbers. This formula (a great topic for Class Seven or Eight algebra) made it possible to discover the next few perfect numbers (perhaps up to the seventh one). In the 1600s, Jean Prestet found the eighth perfect number: 2,305,843,008,139,952,128.

There are no known odd perfect numbers, and it is one of the great mysteries of mathematics whether or not an odd perfect number could possibly exist.

Discovering perfect numbers
Show the students that 10 is a *deficient number* because the sum of its factors (1, 2, 5) is less than 10. Then show the students that 20 is an *abundant number* because the sum of its factors (1, 2, 4, 5, 10) is greater than 20. Then tell the students that there are only two perfect numbers under 100, and let try to find them. (These are 6 and 28.)

More perfect numbers?
The students now know that the first two perfect numbers are 6 and 28, and that the next perfect number is greater than 100. Tell them that they will have to wait until Class Seven to learn how to calculate the next perfect numbers by using algebra. (A bit of drama never hurts!)

The abundance quotient
This is the quotient that results when the sum of factors (without the number itself) is divided by the number itself.
Example: Determine whether the number 10 is perfect, abundant or deficient, and calculate its abundance quotient.

The list of factors for 10 is 1, 2, 5. The sum of these factors is 8, which is less than the number itself (10), so the number is *deficient*. The abundance quotient is 8 ÷ 10, which is 0.8.

Example: Determine whether the number 20 is perfect, abundant or deficient, and calculate its abundance quotient.

The list of factors for 20 is 1, 2, 4, 5, 10. The sum of these factors is 22, which is greater than the number itself (20), so the number is *abundant*. The abundance quotient is 22 ÷ 20, which is 1.1.

Example: Determine whether the number 28 is perfect, abundant or deficient, and calculate its abundance quotient.

The list of factors for 28 is 1, 2, 4, 7, 14. The sum of these factors is 28, which is equal to the number itself (28), so the number is *perfect*. The abundance quotient (for all perfect numbers) is 1.

The first nine perfect numbers
6
28
496
8,128
33,550,336
8,589,869,056
137,438,691,328
2,305,843,008,139,952,128
2,658,455,991,569,831,744,654,692,615,953,842,176.

The tenth perfect number has 54 digits! It is still unknown if any odd perfect number exists.

Abundant numbers

Interestingly, the first 231 abundant numbers are all even numbers. The first odd-numbered abundant number is 945 (quotient = 1.032), and the second one is 1,575 (quotient = 1.047). The *abundance quotients* of each of the 'biggest' abundant numbers (i.e. having an abundance quotient greater than any previous number) from 6 up to 30,000 are listed below.

12 is abundant with a quotient of 1.333
24 is abundant with a quotient of 1.500
36 is abundant with a quotient of 1.528
48 is abundant with a quotient of 1.583
60 is abundant with a quotient of 1.800
120 is abundant with a quotient of 2.000
180 is abundant with a quotient of 2.033
240 is abundant with a quotient of 2.100
360 is abundant with a quotient of 2.25
720 is abundant with a quotient of 2.358
840 is abundant with a quotient of 2.429
1,260 is abundant with a quotient of 2.467
1,680 is abundant with a quotient of 2.543
2,520 is abundant with a quotient of 2.714
5,040 is abundant with a quotient of 2.838
1,0080 is abundant with a quotient of 2.900
1,5120 is abundant with a quotient of 2.937
2,5200 is abundant with a quotient of 2.966
2,7720 is abundant with a quotient of 3.052

The abundance quotients for the abundant numbers up to 150

12 has a quotient of 1.333
18 has a quotient of 1.167
20 has a quotient of 1.100
24 has a quotient of 1.500
28 has a quotient of 1.000
30 has a quotient of 1.400
36 has a quotient of 1.528
40 has a quotient of 1.250
42 has a quotient of 1.286
48 has a quotient of 1.583
54 has a quotient of 1.222
56 has a quotient of 1.143
60 has a quotient of 1.800
66 has a quotient of 1.182
70 has a quotient of 1.057
72 has a quotient of 1.708
78 has a quotient of 1.154
80 has a quotient of 1.325
84 has a quotient of 1.667
88 has a quotient of 1.045
90 has a quotient of 1.600
96 has a quotient of 1.625
100 has a quotient of 1.170
102 has a quotient of 1.118
104 has a quotient of 1.019
108 has a quotient of 1.593
112 has a quotient of 1.214
114 has a quotient of 1.105
120 has a quotient of 2.000
126 has a quotient of 1.476
132 has a quotient of 1.545
138 has a quotient of 1.087
140 has a quotient of 1.400

Euclid's formula for perfect numbers
$$P = (2^n - 1) \times (2^n - 1)$$
Where n is a whole number. Beginning with $n = 2$, this formula produces all the even perfect numbers (P) with the condition that $(2^n - 1)$ is a prime number.

The first ten perfect numbers*:
1. For $n = 2$ we get the perfect number 6, because $(2^n - 1) = 3$ is prime.
2. For $n = 3$ we get the perfect number 28, because $(2^n - 1) = 7$ is prime.

For $n = 4$ we don't get a perfect number, because $(2^n - 1) = 15$ is not prime.

3. For $n = 5$ we get the perfect number 496, because $(2^n - 1) = 31$ is prime.

For $n = 6$ we don't get a perfect number, because $(2^n - 1) = 63$ is not prime.

4. For $n = 7$ we get the perfect number 8,128, because $(2^n - 1) = 127$ is prime.

For $n = 8$ we don't get a perfect number, because $(2^n - 1) = 255$ is not prime.

For $n = 9$ we don't get a perfect number, because $(2^n - 1) = 511$ is divisible by 7.

For $n = 10$ we don't get a perfect number, because $(2^n - 1) = 1,023$ is divisible by 3.

For $n = 11$ we don't get a perfect number, because $(2^n - 1) = 2,047$ is divisible by 23.

For $n = 12$ we don't get a perfect number, because $(2^n - 1) = 4,095$ is divisible by 5.

5. For $n = 13$ we get the perfect number 33,550,336, because $(2^n - 1) = 8,191$ is prime.

* From Heath's translation of *The Elements*, vol. 2, p. 426; Dover Publications, 1956

For $n = 14$ we don't get a perfect number, because $(2^n - 1) = 16,383$ is divisible by 3.

For $n = 15$ we don't get a perfect number, because $(2^n - 1) = 32,767$ is divisible by 7.

For $n = 16$ we don't get a perfect number, because $(2^n - 1) = 65,535$ is divisible by 5.

6. For $n = 17$ we get the perfect number 8,589,869,056, because $(2^n - 1) = 131,071$ is prime.

For $n = 18$ we don't get a perfect number, because $(2^n - 1) = 262,143$ is divisible by 3.

7. For $n = 19$ we get the perfect number 137,438,691,328, because $(2^n - 1) = 524,287$ is prime.

For $n = 20$ we don't get a perfect number, because $(2^n - 1) = 1,048,575$ is divisible by 5.

For $n = 21$ we don't get a perfect number, because $(2^n - 1) = 2,097,151$ is divisible by 7.

For $n = 22$ we don't get a perfect number, because $(2^n - 1) = 4,194,303$ is divisible by 3.

For $n = 23$ we don't get a perfect number, because $(2^n - 1) = 8,388,607$ is divisible by 47.

For $n = 24$ we don't get a perfect number, because $(2^n - 1) = 16,777,215$ is divisible by 5.

For $n = 25$ we don't get a perfect number, because $(2^n - 1) = 33,554,431$ is divisible by 31.

For $n = 26$ we don't get a perfect number, because $(2^n - 1) = 67,108,863$ is divisible by 3.

For $n = 27$ we don't get a perfect number, because $(2^n - 1) = 134,217,727$ is divisible by 7.

For $n = 28$ we don't get a perfect number, because $(2^n - 1) = 268,435,455$ is divisible by 5.

For $n = 29$ we don't get a perfect number, because $(2^n - 1) = 536,870,911$ is divisible by 233.

For $n = 30$ we don't get a perfect number, because $(2^n - 1) = 1{,}073{,}741{,}823$ is divisible by 3.

8. For $n = 31$ we get the perfect number 2,305,843,008,139,952,128, because 2,147,483,647 is prime.
...
9. For $n = 61$ we get the perfect number 2,658,455,991,569,831,744,654,692,615,953,842,176.
10. For $n = 89$ we get the perfect number $\approx 1.916 \times 10^{53}$ (54 digits long).

Sums and differences theorems

Each of the theorems below express some rather surprising law about the relationship of numbers. If brought to the children properly, they can engender a real sense of wonder with numbers.

It is not required to cover these theorems; they should only be brought to the children if the teacher has developed a good connection to it.

The challenge is to not make it too abstract. Try to make it playful. For example, simply ask the children how many ways they can find to express 90 as the sum of two prime numbers. Have them list the different possibilities that they have found on the board. They will be amazed to see that there are nine ways to express 90 as the sum of two primes, but only two ways to express 68 as the sum of two primes.

Goldbach's theorem
Every even number can be expressed as the sum of two prime numbers.

This has not yet been proven, but is believed to be true.

Once we get past the first few even numbers, most all of them can be expressed as the sum of two prime numbers in multiple ways, yet the number of possible ways varies greatly. For example, 68 can only be expressed in two ways, either as 7 + 61 or 31 + 37, whereas 90 can be expressed in nine different ways (7 + 83; 11 + 79; 17 + 73; 19 + 71; 23 + 67; 29 + 61; 31 + 59; 37 + 53; 43 + 47).

Even numbers as the sum of two primes
4 = 2+2
6 = 3+3
8 = 3+5
10 = 3+7; 5+5
12 = 5+7
14 = 3+11; 7+7
16 = 3+13; 5+11
18 = 5+13; 7+11
20 = 3+17; 7+13
22 = 3+19; 5+17; 11+11
24 = 5+19; 7+17; 11+13
26 = 3+23; 7+19; 13+13
28 = 5+23; 11+17
30 = 7+23; 11+19; 13+17
32 = 3+29; 13+19
34 = 3+31; 5+29; 11+23; 17+17
36 = 5+31; 7+29; 13+23; 17+19
38 = 7+31; 19+19
40 = 3+37; 11+29; 17+23

42 = 5+37; 11+31; 13+29; 19+23
44 = 3+41; 7+37; 13+31
46 = 3+43; 5+41; 17+29; 23+23
48 = 5+43; 7+41; 11+37; 17+31; 19+29
50 = 3+47; 7+43; 13+37; 19+31
52 = 5+47; 11+41; 23+29
54 = 7+47; 11+43; 13+41; 17+37; 23+31
56 = 3+53; 13+43; 19+37
58 = 5+53; 11+47; 17+41; 29+29
60 = 7+53; 13+47; 17+43; 19+41; 23+37; 29+31
62 = 3+59; 19+43; 31+31
64 = 3+61; 5+59; 11+53; 17+47; 23+41
66 = 5+61; 7+59; 13+53; 19+47; 23+43; 29+37
68 = 7+61; 31+37
70 = 3+67; 11+59; 17+53; 23+47; 29+41
72 = 5+67; 11+61; 13+59; 19+53; 29+43; 31+41
74 = 3+71; 7+67; 13+61; 31+43; 37+37
76 = 3+73; 5+71; 17+59; 23+53; 29+47
78 = 5+73; 7+71; 11+67; 17+61; 19+59; 31+47; 37+41
80 = 7+73; 13+67; 19+61; 37+43
82 = 3+79; 11+71; 23+59; 29+53; 41+41
84 = 5+79; 11+73; 13+71; 17+67; 23+61; 31+53; 37+47; 41+43
86 = 3+83; 7+79; 13+73; 19+67; 43+43
88 = 5+83; 17+71; 29+59; 41+47
90 = 7+83; 11+79; 17+73; 19+71; 23+67; 29+61; 31+59; 37+53; 43+47
92 = 3+89; 13+79; 19+73; 31+61
94 = 5+89; 11+83; 23+71; 41+53; 47+47
96 = 7+89; 13+83; 17+79; 23+73; 29+67; 37+59; 43+53
98 = 19+79; 31+67; 37+61
100 = 3+97; 11+89; 17+83; 29+71; 41+59; 47+53
102 = 5+97; 13+89; 19+83; 23+79; 29+73; 31+71; 41+61; 43+59
104 = 3+101; 7+97; 31+73; 37+67; 43+61
106 = 3+103; 5+101; 17+89; 23+83; 47+59; 53+53
108 = 5+103; 7+101; 11+97; 19+89; 29+79; 37+71; 41+67; 47+61
110 = 3+107; 7+103; 13+97; 31+79; 37+73; 43+67

Appendix

112 = 3+109; 5+107; 11+101; 23+89; 29+83; 41+71; 53+59

114 = 5+109; 7+107; 11+103; 13+101; 17+97; 31+83; 41+73; 43+71; 47+67; 53+61

116 = 3+113; 7+109; 13+103; 19+97; 37+79; 43+73

118 = 5+113; 11+107; 17+101; 29+89; 47+71; 59+59

120 = 7+113; 11+109; 13+107; 17+103; 19+101; 23+97; 31+89; 37+83; 41+79; 47+73; 53+67; 59+61

122 = 13+109; 19+103; 43+79; 61+61

124 = 11+113; 17+107; 23+101; 41+83; 53+71

126 = 13+113; 17+109; 19+107; 23+103; 29+97; 37+89; 43+83; 47+79; 53+73; 59+67

128 = 19+109; 31+97; 61+67

130 = 3+127; 17+113; 23+107; 29+101; 41+89; 47+83; 59+71

132 = 5+127; 19+113; 23+109; 29+103; 31+101; 43+89; 53+79; 59+73; 61+71

134 = 3+131; 7+127; 31+103; 37+97; 61+73; 67+67

136 = 5+131; 23+113; 29+107; 47+89; 53+83

138 = 7+131; 11+127; 29+109; 31+107; 37+101; 41+97; 59+79; 67+71

140 = 3+137; 13+127; 31+109; 37+103; 43+97; 61+79; 67+73

142 = 3+139; 5+137; 11+131; 29+113; 41+101; 53+89; 59+83; 71+71

144 = 5+139; 7+137; 13+131; 17+127; 31+113; 37+107; 41+103; 43+101; 47+97; 61+83; 71+73

146 = 7+139; 19+127; 37+109; 43+103; 67+79; 73+73

148 = 11+137; 17+131; 41+107; 47+101; 59+89

150 = 11+139; 13+137; 19+131; 23+127; 37+113; 41+109; 43+107; 47+103; 53+97; 61+89; 67+83; 71+79

Fermat's theorem

The Greeks were very interested in how numbers could be expressed as the sum or difference of other special numbers (e.g. prime numbers or square numbers). It was the famous French mathematician, Pierre de Fermat, who, around 1640, came up with the following theorems:

Every prime number, except for 2, can be expressed as the difference of two square numbers in one and only one way.

The students should first make a list of consecutive square numbers and write the differences between neighbours below.

1 4 9 16 25 36…

  3 5 7 9 11…

We see that the differences/distances between them grows.

Given that the above differences between neighbours form the list of odd numbers, we can easily see *how any odd number can be expressed as the difference of two squares*. For example, we can express 7 as 16−9 (which is

$4^2 - 3^2$). Similarly, we can express 15 as $64 - 49$ (which is $8^2 - 7^2$).

The real surprise with the above theorem is that it says that if the odd number is a prime number then it can be expressed as a difference of two squares in *only one way*. For example, 15 can be expressed as the difference of two squares in *two ways*: either as $8^2 - 7^2$ or as $4^2 - 1^2$. This does not contradict our theorem because 15 is not a prime number. 7, on the other hand, is prime, therefore we know that it can only be expressed as $4^2 - 3^2$.

Odd numbers as the difference of two squares

$3 = 2^2 - 1^2$
$5 = 3^2 - 2^2$
$7 = 4^2 - 3^2$
$9 = 5^2 - 4^2$
$11 = 6^2 - 5^2$
$13 = 7^2 - 6^2$
$15 = 4^2 - 1^2; 8^2 - 7^2$
$17 = 9^2 - 8^2$
$19 = 10^2 - 9^2$
$21 = 5^2 - 2^2; 11^2 - 10^2$
$23 = 12^2 - 11^2$
$25 = 13^2 - 12^2$
$27 = 6^2 - 3^2; 14^2 - 13^2$
$29 = 15^2 - 14^2$
$31 = 16^2 - 15^2$
$33 = 7^2 - 4^2; 17^2 - 16^2$
$35 = 6^2 - 1^2; 18^2 - 17^2$
$37 = 19^2 - 18^2$
$39 = 8^2 - 5^2; 20^2 - 19^2$
$41 = 21^2 - 20^2$
$43 = 22^2 - 21^2$

$45 = 7^2 - 2^2; 9^2 - 6^2; 23^2 - 22^2$
$47 = 24^2 - 23^2$
$49 = 25^2 - 24^2$
$51 = 10^2 - 7^2; 26^2 - 25^2$
$53 = 27^2 - 26^2$
$55 = 8^2 - 3^2; 28^2 - 27^2$
$57 = 11^2 - 8^2; 29^2 - 28^2$
$59 = 30^2 - 29^2$
$61 = 31^2 - 30^2$
$63 = 8^2 - 1^2; 12^2 - 9^2; 32^2 - 31^2$
$65 = 9^2 - 4^2; 33^2 - 32^2$
$67 = 34^2 - 33^2$
$69 = 13^2 - 10^2; 35^2 - 34^2$
$71 = 36^2 - 35^2$
$73 = 37^2 - 36^2$
$75 = 10^2 - 5^2; 14^2 - 11^2; 38^2 - 37^2$
$77 = 9^2 - 2^2; 39^2 - 38^2$
$79 = 40^2 - 39^2$
$81 = 15^2 - 12^2; 41^2 - 40^2$
$83 = 42^2 - 41^2$
$85 = 11^2 - 6^2; 43^2 - 42^2$
$87 = 16^2 - 13^2; 44^2 - 43^2$
$89 = 45^2 - 44^2$
$91 = 10^2 - 3^2; 46^2 - 45^2$
$93 = 17^2 - 14^2; 47^2 - 46^2$
$95 = 12^2 - 7^2; 48^2 - 47^2$
$97 = 49^2 - 48^2$
$99 = 10^2 - 1^2; 18^2 - 15^2; 50^2 - 49^2$
$101 = 51^2 - 50^2$
$103 = 52^2 - 51^2$
$105 = 11^2 - 4^2; 13^2 - 8^2; 19^2 - 16^2; 53^2 - 52^2$
$107 = 54^2 - 53^2$
$109 = 55^2 - 54^2$
$111 = 20^2 - 17^2; 56^2 - 55^2$
$113 = 57^2 - 56^2$

Appendix

115 = $14^2 - 9^2$; $58^2 - 57^2$
117 = $11^2 - 2^2$; $21^2 - 18^2$; $59^2 - 58^2$
119 = $12^2 - 5^2$; $60^2 - 59^2$
121 = $61^2 - 60^2$
123 = $22^2 - 19^2$; $62^2 - 61^2$
125 = $15^2 - 10^2$; $63^2 - 62^2$
127 = $64^2 - 63^2$
129 = $23^2 - 20^2$; $65^2 - 64^2$
131 = $66^2 - 65^2$
133 = $13^2 - 6^2$; $67^2 - 66^2$
135 = $12^2 - 3^2$; $16^2 - 11^2$; $24^2 - 21^2$; $68^2 - 67^2$
137 = $69^2 - 68^2$
139 = $70^2 - 69^2$
141 = $25^2 - 22^2$; $71^2 - 70^2$
143 = $12^2 - 1^2$; $72^2 - 71^2$
145 = $17^2 - 12^2$; $73^2 - 72^2$
147 = $14^2 - 7^2$; $26^2 - 23^2$; $74^2 - 73^2$
149 = $75^2 - 74^2$
151 = $76^2 - 75^2$
153 = $13^2 - 4^2$; $27^2 - 24^2$; $77^2 - 76^2$
155 = $18^2 - 13^2$; $78^2 - 77^2$
157 = $79^2 - 78^2$
159 = $28^2 - 25^2$; $80^2 - 79^2$
161 = $15^2 - 8^2$; $81^2 - 80^2$
163 = $82^2 - 81^2$
165 = $13^2 - 2^2$; $19^2 - 14^2$; $29^2 - 26^2$; $83^2 - 82^2$
167 = $84^2 - 83^2$
169 = $85^2 - 84^2$
171 = $14^2 - 5^2$; $30^2 - 27^2$; $86^2 - 85^2$
173 = $87^2 - 86^2$
175 = $16^2 - 9^2$; $20^2 - 15^2$; $88^2 - 87^2$
177 = $31^2 - 28^2$; $89^2 - 88^2$
179 = $90^2 - 89^2$
181 = $91^2 - 90^2$
183 = $32^2 - 29^2$; $92^2 - 91^2$

185 = $21^2 - 16^2$; $93^2 - 92^2$
187 = $14^2 - 3^2$; $94^2 - 93^2$
189 = $15^2 - 6^2$; $17^2 - 10^2$; $33^2 - 30^2$; $95^2 - 94^2$
191 = $96^2 - 95^2$
193 = $97^2 - 96^2$
195 = $14^2 - 1^2$; $22^2 - 17^2$; $34^2 - 31^2$; $98^2 - 97^2$
197 = $99^2 - 98^2$
199 = $100^2 - 99^2$

Theorems that deal with the sum of two square numbers

See the list below of all the ways that the numbers from 2 to 442 can be expressed as the *sum of two squares*.

If a number is prime and has a remainder of 1 after dividing it by 4, then it can be expressed as the sum of two square numbers in one and only one way.

The number 73 is both prime and has a remainder of 1 when divided by 4. This theorem tells us that there must be exactly one way to express 73 as the sum of two squares. Looking at the list overleaf, we see that 73 can be expressed as $8^2 + 3^2$.

If a number is prime and has a remainder of 3 after dividing it by 4, then it is not possible to express it as a sum of two square numbers.

The numbers 43 is both prime and has a remainder of 3 when divided by 4. This theorem tells us that it must be impossible to express 43 as the sum of two squares. Looking at the list overleaf, we can see that 43 can't be expressed as the sum of two squares.

If a number is not prime then there are a variety of possibilities – it may be that the number can be expressed as the sum of two square numbers in one way, in multiple ways, or not at all.

Looking at the table below, we can see the following:

45 can be expressed as the sum of two squares in exactly one way: $6^2 + 3^2$.

48 can't be expressed as the sum of two squares in any way.

50 is the first number that can be expressed as the sum of two squares in 2 ways: $5^2 + 5^2$ or $7^2 + 1^2$

325 is the first number that can be expressed as the sum of two squares in 3 ways: $1^2 + 18^2$; $6^2 + 17^2$; $10^2 + 15^2$

1,105 is the first number that can be expressed as the sum of two squares in 4 ways: $4^2 + 33^2$; $9^2 + 32^2$; $12^2 + 31^2$; $23^2 + 24^2$

Numbers as the sum of two squares
Numbers that are missing cannot be expressed as the sum of two squares.

$2 = 1^2 + 1^2$
$5 = 1^2 + 2^2$
$8 = 2^2 + 2^2$
$10 = 1^2 + 3^2$
$13 = 2^2 + 3^2$
$17 = 1^2 + 4^2$
$18 = 3^2 + 3^2$
$20 = 2^2 + 4^2$
$25 = 3^2 + 4^2$
$26 = 1^2 + 5^2$
$29 = 2^2 + 5^2$
$32 = 4^2 + 4^2$
$34 = 3^2 + 5^2$
$37 = 1^2 + 6^2$
$40 = 2^2 + 6^2$
$41 = 4^2 + 5^2$
$45 = 3^2 + 6^2$
$50 = 1^2 + 7^2$; $5^2 + 5^2$
$52 = 4^2 + 6^2$
$53 = 2^2 + 7^2$
$58 = 3^2 + 7^2$
$61 = 5^2 + 6^2$
$65 = 1^2 + 8^2$; $4^2 + 7^2$
$68 = 2^2 + 8^2$
$72 = 6^2 + 6^2$
$73 = 3^2 + 8^2$
$74 = 5^2 + 7^2$
$80 = 4^2 + 8^2$
$82 = 1^2 + 9^2$
$85 = 2^2 + 9^2$; $6^2 + 7^2$
$89 = 5^2 + 8^2$
$90 = 3^2 + 9^2$
$97 = 4^2 + 9^2$
$98 = 7^2 + 7^2$
$100 = 6^2 + 8^2$
$101 = 1^2 + 10^2$
$104 = 2^2 + 10^2$
$106 = 5^2 + 9^2$
$109 = 3^2 + 10^2$
$113 = 7^2 + 8^2$
$116 = 4^2 + 10^2$
$117 = 6^2 + 9^2$
$122 = 1^2 + 11^2$
$125 = 2^2 + 11^2$; $5^2 + 10^2$
$128 = 8^2 + 8^2$

Appendix

$130 = 3^2 + 11^2; 7^2 + 9^2$
$136 = 6^2 + 10^2$
$137 = 4^2 + 11^2$
$145 = 1^2 + 12^2; 8^2 + 9^2$
$146 = 5^2 + 11^2$
$148 = 2^2 + 12^2$
$149 = 7^2 + 10^2$
$153 = 3^2 + 12^2$
$157 = 6^2 + 11^2$
$160 = 4^2 + 12^2$
$162 = 9^2 + 9^2$
$164 = 8^2 + 10^2$
$169 = 5^2 + 12^2$
$170 = 1^2 + 13^2; 7^2 + 11^2$
$173 = 2^2 + 13^2$
$178 = 3^2 + 13^2$
$180 = 6^2 + 12^2$
$181 = 9^2 + 10^2$
$185 = 4^2 + 13^2; 8^2 + 11^2$
$193 = 7^2 + 12^2$
$194 = 5^2 + 13^2$
$197 = 1^2 + 14^2$
$200 = 2^2 + 14^2; 10^2 + 10^2$
$202 = 9^2 + 11^2$
$205 = 3^2 + 14^2; 6^2 + 13^2$
$208 = 8^2 + 12^2$
$212 = 4^2 + 14^2$
$218 = 7^2 + 13^2$
$221 = 5^2 + 14^2; 10^2 + 11^2$
$225 = 9^2 + 12^2$
$226 = 1^2 + 15^2$
$229 = 2^2 + 15^2$
$232 = 6^2 + 14^2$
$233 = 8^2 + 13^2$
$234 = 3^2 + 15^2$

$241 = 4^2 + 15^2$
$242 = 11^2 + 11^2$
$244 = 10^2 + 12^2$
$245 = 7^2 + 14^2$
$250 = 5^2 + 15^2; 9^2 + 13^2$
$257 = 1^2 + 16^2$
$260 = 2^2 + 16^2; 8^2 + 14^2$
$261 = 6^2 + 15^2$
$265 = 3^2 + 16^2; 11^2 + 12^2$
$269 = 10^2 + 13^2$
$272 = 4^2 + 16^2$
$274 = 7^2 + 15^2$
$277 = 9^2 + 14^2$
$281 = 5^2 + 16^2$
$288 = 12^2 + 12^2$
$289 = 8^2 + 15^2$
$290 = 1^2 + 17^2; 11^2 + 13^2$
$292 = 6^2 + 16^2$
$293 = 2^2 + 17^2$
$296 = 10^2 + 14^2$
$298 = 3^2 + 17^2$
$305 = 4^2 + 17^2; 7^2 + 16^2$
$306 = 9^2 + 15^2$
$313 = 12^2 + 13^2$
$314 = 5^2 + 17^2$
$317 = 11^2 + 14^2$
$320 = 8^2 + 16^2$
$325 = 1^2 + 18^2; 6^2 + 17^2; 10^2 + 15^2$
$328 = 2^2 + 18^2$
$333 = 3^2 + 18^2$
$337 = 9^2 + 16^2$
$338 = 7^2 + 17^2; 13^2 + 13^2$
$340 = 4^2 + 18^2; 12^2 + 14^2$
$346 = 11^2 + 15^2$
$349 = 5^2 + 18^2$

353 = $8^2 + 17^2$
356 = $10^2 + 16^2$
360 = $6^2 + 18^2$
362 = $1^2 + 19^2$
365 = $2^2 + 19^2$; $13^2 + 14^2$
369 = $12^2 + 15^2$
370 = $3^2 + 19^2$; $9^2 + 17^2$
373 = $7^2 + 18^2$
377 = $4^2 + 19^2$; $11^2 + 16^2$
386 = $5^2 + 19^2$
388 = $8^2 + 18^2$
389 = $10^2 + 17^2$
392 = $14^2 + 14^2$
394 = $13^2 + 15^2$
397 = $6^2 + 19^2$
400 = $12^2 + 16^2$
401 = $1^2 + 20^2$
404 = $2^2 + 20^2$
405 = $9^2 + 18^2$
409 = $3^2 + 20^2$
410 = $7^2 + 19^2$; $11^2 + 17^2$
416 = $4^2 + 20^2$
421 = $14^2 + 15^2$
424 = $10^2 + 18^2$
425 = $5^2 + 20^2$; $8^2 + 19^2$; $13^2 + 16^2$
433 = $12^2 + 17^2$
436 = $6^2 + 20^2$
442 = $1^2 + 21^2$; $9^2 + 19^2$

The first number that can be expressed in 4 ways is…
1,105 = $4^2 + 33^2$; $9^2 + 32^2$; $12^2 + 31^2$; $23^2 + 24^2$

Powers of two table

2 to the 1 is 2
2 to the 2 is 4
2 to the 3 is 8
2 to the 4 is 16
2 to the 5 is 32
2 to the 6 is 64
2 to the 7 is 128
2 to the 8 is 256
2 to the 9 is 512
2 to the 10 is 1,024
2 to the 11 is 2,048
2 to the 12 is 4,096
2 to the 13 is 8,192
2 to the 14 is 16,384
2 to the 15 is 32,768
2 to the 16 is 65,536
2 to the 17 is 131,072
2 to the 18 is 262,144
2 to the 19 is 524,288
2 to the 20 is 1,048,576
2 to the 21 is 2,097,152
2 to the 22 is 4,194,304
2 to the 23 is 8,388,608
2 to the 24 is 16,777,216
2 to the 25 is 33,554,432
2 to the 26 is 67,108,864
2 to the 27 is 134,217,728
2 to the 28 is 268,435,456
2 to the 29 is 536,870,912
2 to the 30 is 1,073,741,824
2 to the 31 is 2,147,483,648
2 to the 32 is 4,294,967,296
2 to the 33 is 8,589,934,592

Appendix

2 to the 34 is 17,179,869,184
2 to the 35 is 34,359,738,368
2 to the 36 is 68,719,476,736
2 to the 37 is 137,438,953,472
2 to the 38 is 274,877,906,944
2 to the 39 is 549,755,813,888
2 to the 40 is 1,099,511,627,776
2 to the 41 is 2,199,023,255,552
2 to the 42 is 4,398,046,511,104
2 to the 43 is 8,796,093,022,208
2 to the 44 is 17,592,186,044,416
2 to the 45 is 35,184,372,088,832
2 to the 46 is 70,368,744,177,664
2 to the 47 is 140,737,488,355,328
2 to the 48 is 281,474,976,710,656
2 to the 49 is 562,949,953,421,312
2 to the 50 is 1,125,899,906,842,624
2 to the 51 is 2,251,799,813,685,248
2 to the 52 is 4,503,599,627,370,496
2 to the 53 is 9,007,199,254,740,992
2 to the 54 is 18,014,398,509,481,984
2 to the 55 is 36,028,797,018,963,968
2 to the 56 is 72,057,594,037,927,936
2 to the 57 is 144,115,188,075,855,872
2 to the 58 is 288,230,376,151,711,744
2 to the 59 is 576,460,752,303,423,488
2 to the 60 is 1,152,921,504,606,846,976
2 to the 61 is 2,305,843,009,213,693,952
2 to the 62 is 4,611,686,018,427,387,904
2 to the 63 is 9,223,372,036,854,775,808
2 to the 64 is 18,446,744,073,709,551,616
2 to the 65 is 36,893,488,147,419,103,232
2 to the 66 is 73,786,976,294,838,206,464
2 to the 67 is 147,573,952,589,676,412,928
2 to the 68 is 295,147,905,179,352,825,856

2 to the 69 is 590,295,810,358,705,651,712
2 to the 70 is 1,180,591,620,717,411,303,424
2 to the 71 is 2,361,183,241,434,822,606,848
2 to the 72 is 4,722,366,482,869,645,213,696
2 to the 73 is 9,444,732,965,739,290,427,392
2 to the 74 is
18,889,465,931,478,580,854,784
2 to the 75 is
37,778,931,862,957,161,709,568
2 to the 76 is
75,557,863,725,914,323,419,136
2 to the 77 is
151,115,727,451,828,646,838,272
2 to the 78 is
302,231,454,903,657,293,676,544
2 to the 79 is
604,462,909,807,314,587,353,088
2 to the 80 is
1,208,925,819,614,629,174,706,176
2 to the 81 is
2,417,851,639,229,258,349,412,352
2 to the 82 is
4,835,703,278,458,516,698,824,704
2 to the 83 is
9,671,406,556,917,033,397,649,408
2 to the 84 is
19,342,813,113,834,066,795,298,816
2 to the 85 is
38,685,626,227,668,133,590,597,632
2 to the 86 is
77,371,252,455,336,267,181,195,264
2 to the 87 is
154,742,504,910,672,534,362,390,528
2 to the 88 is
309,485,009,821,345,068,724,781,056

2 to the 89 is
618,970,019,642,690,137,449,562,112
2 to the 90 is
1,237,940,039,285,380,274,899,124,224
2 to the 91 is
2,475,880,078,570,760,549,798,248,448
2 to the 92 is
4,951,760,157,141,521,099,596,496,896
2 to the 93 is
9,903,520,314,283,042,199,192,993,792
2 to the 94 is
19,807,040,628,566,084,398,385,987,584

2 to the 95 is
39,614,081,257,132,168,796,771,975,168
2 to the 96 is
79,228,162,514,264,337,593,543,950,336
2 to the 97 is
158,456,325,028,528,675,187,087,900,672
2 to the 98 is
316,912,650,057,057,350,374,175,801,344
2 to the 99 is
633,825,300,114,114,700,748,351,602,688
2 to the 100 is
1,267,650,600,228,229,401,496,703,205,376

Appendix

Prime numbers up to 2,000

2	137	313	509	727	947	1,171
3	139	317	521	733	953	1,181
5	149	331	523	739	967	1,187
7	151	337	541	743	971	1,193
11	157	347	547	751	977	1,201
13	163	349	557	757	983	1,213
17	167	353	563	761	991	1,217
19	173	359	569	769	997	1,223
23	179	367	571	773	1,009	1,229
29	181	373	577	787	1,013	1,231
31	191	379	587	797	1,019	1,237
37	193	383	593	809	1,021	1,249
41	197	389	599	811	1,031	1,259
43	199	397	601	821	1,033	1,277
47	211	401	607	823	1,039	1,279
53	223	409	613	827	1,049	1,283
59	227	419	617	829	1,051	1,289
61	229	421	619	839	1,061	1,291
67	233	431	631	853	1,063	1,297
71	239	433	641	857	1,069	1,301
73	241	439	643	859	1,087	1,303
79	251	443	647	863	1,091	1,307
83	257	449	653	877	1,093	1,319
89	263	457	659	881	1,097	1,321
97	269	461	661	883	1,103	1,327
101	271	463	673	887	1,109	1,361
103	277	467	677	907	1,117	1,367
107	281	479	683	911	1,123	1,373
109	283	487	691	919	1,129	1,381
113	293	491	701	929	1,151	1,399
127	307	499	709	937	1,153	1,409
131	311	503	719	941	1,163	1,423

1,427	1,489	1,579	1,663	1,753	1,867	1,951
1,429	1,493	1,583	1,667	1,759	1,871	1,973
1,433	1,499	1,597	1,669	1,777	1,873	1,979
1,439	1,511	1,601	1,693	1,783	1,877	1,987
1,447	1,523	1,607	1,697	1,787	1,879	1,993
1,451	1,531	1,609	1,699	1,789	1,889	1,997
1,453	1,543	1,613	1,709	1,801	1,901	1,999
1,459	1,549	1,619	1,721	1,811	1,907	
1,471	1,553	1,621	1,723	1,823	1,913	
1,481	1,559	1,627	1,733	1,831	1,931	
1,483	1,567	1,637	1,741	1,847	1,933	
1,487	1,571	1,657	1,747	1,861	1,949	

Tables and handouts
Class Six maths tricks

1. Multiplication and zeros. When multiplying two numbers, ignore all ending zeros, do the multiplication and then add the zeros back onto the answer.

   Example: For 4,000 × 300, we multiply 4 times 3, and then add on the 5 zeros giving a result of 1,200,000.

2. Division and zeros. When dividing two numbers that both end in zeros, cancel the same number of ending zeros from each of the two numbers, then do the division problem.

   Example: For 24,000 ÷ 600, we cancel two zeros from both numbers, and then divide 240 by 6 to get 40.

3. Multiplying and dividing by 10, 100, 1000, etc. Simply move the decimal point!

   Example: 634.6 ÷ 100 = 6.346. We move the decimal point 2 places because there are 2 zeros in 100.

   Example: 48.37 × 1,000 = 48,370. The decimal point gets moved 3 places since there are 3 zeros in 1,000.

4. Adding numbers by grouping. Search for digits that add up to 10 or 20.

   Example: For 97 + 86 + 13 + 42 + 54, we see that with the ones' digits we can add 7 + 3 and 6 + 4 to make ten twice, leaving the 2 (from the 42) left over. The sum of the ones' column is therefore 22. In the tens' column, the carry of 2 combines with the 8 to form 10, as does the 9 and the 1. We are left with the 4 and 5. The tens' column is therefore 29. Our answer is 292.

5. Multiplying by 4. You can instead double the number two times.

   Example: For 4 × 35, we double 35 to get 70, and double again to get a result of 140.

6. Multiplying a 2-digit number by 11. Separate the digits, and then insert the sum of the digits in-between.

   Example: For 62 × 11, 6 plus 2 is 8, so we place the 8 between the 6 and the 2, giving a result of 682.

   Example: For 75 × 11, 7 plus 5 is 12, so we place the 2 between the 7 and 5 and carry the 1, giving 825.

7. Multiplying two numbers that are just over 100. First write down a 1, then next to the one we write down the sum of how far above 100 the two numbers are, and then the product of how far above 100 the two numbers are. Both the sum and the product must be two digits.

   Example: For 105 × 102, add 5 plus 2 (to get 7), and then multiply 5 times 2 (to get 10), giving 10,710.

   Example: For 112 × 107, we do 12 + 7 (19) and then 12 × 7 (84), which leads to an answer of 11,984.

8. Dividing by 4. You can instead cut the number in half, two times.

Example: For 64 ÷ 4, we take half of 64 to get 32, and then take half of that for a result of 16.

9. Subtraction by adding distances. Pick an 'easy' number between the two numbers, and add the distances from each of the numbers to the easy number.

Example: For 532−497, choose 500 as the easy number. The distance from 532 to 500 is 32 and the distance from 497 to 500 is 3. The answer is therefore 32 + 3, which is 35.

10. Division by nines. When dividing two numbers where the divisor's digits are all nines, we get a decimal where the dividend repeats, but the number of repeating digits must be equal to the number of nines.

Example: 38 ÷ 99 = $0.\overline{38}$

Example: 417 ÷ 999 = $0.\overline{417}$

Example: 62 ÷ 999 = $0.\overline{062}$

11. Multiplying by nines.

Method 1: Multiply by 10, 100 or 1,000, and then subtract the original number.

Example: For 47 × 99, we do 100 × 47 − 47, which is 4,700−47, giving an answer of 4,653.

Method 2 (for single digits): Multiply the single digit by 9, which gives us a two-digit answer. Then separate these two digits and insert one less nine than what was in the original problem.

Example: For 8 × 9,999, we multiply 8 times 9, which gives us 72. Then we insert three nines between the 7 and the 2, giving a final answer of 79,992.

12. Reducing before dividing. Any division problem is viewed as a fraction that can often be reduced.

Example: For 3,500 ÷ 2,800, we reduce the fraction to 5/4, which is 1¼ or 1.25.

13. Multiplying by 5. You take half the number, and then add a zero, or move the decimal point.

Example: For 5 × 26, we take half of 26 to get 13, and then add a zero, giving us a result of 130.

Example: For 5 × 4.18, half of 4.18 is 2.09, and moving the decimal point to the right one place gives 20.9.

14. Dividing by 5. Double the number, and then divide by ten (move the decimal one place to the left).

Example: For 80 ÷ 5, we double 80 and then chop off a zero, giving a result of 16.

Example: For 93 ÷ 5, we double 93 and then move the decimal point one place to the left to get 18.6.

Appendix

Class Seven maths tricks

1. Multiplying two numbers that are just one above and below a number that is easy to square. The answer is one less than the square of the 'easy' number between them.
Example: For 29 × 31, we square 30, and then subtract 1, giving a result of 899.

2. Multiplying by 25. You can instead take half the number, two times, and then add two zeros.
Example: For 25 × 48, take half of 48 to get 24, and half again to get 12. Adding two zeros gives 1,200.

3. Squaring a number ending in 5. Multiply the tens' digit by the next whole number, then place 25 at the end.
Example: For 65^2, you multiply 6 times 7, which is 42, and then add 25 at the end to get 4,225 as a result.

4. Dividing by 25. Instead, double the number two times, then divide by 100 (move decimal left two places).
Example: For 108 ÷ 25, we double 108 to get 216, and then double it again to get 432. Our answer is 4.32.

5. Multiplying a number by 15 (or 15%). Multiply the number by ten, then add that product to half of itself.
Example: For 32 × 15, we add 320 with 160 (which is ½ of 320), giving a result of 480.
Example: For 15% of 420, we add 10% of 420 (which is 42) to half of that (which is 21), resulting in 63.

6. Multiplying an even number by a number ending in 5. Cut the even number in half, and double the number ending in 5. Multiply the results.
Example: For 14 × 45, half of 14 is 7, and twice 45 is 90, giving a result of 7 times 90, which is 630.

7. Dividing by a number ending in 5. Double both numbers, then divide.
Example: For 180 ÷ 45, we double both numbers, giving 360 ÷ 90, which is 4.

8. Multiplying two numbers that have the same tens' digits and have ones' digits that add to 10. Multiply the tens' digit by the next whole number, and then place the product of the ones' digits at the end, as two digits.
Example: For 47 × 43, we do 4 times 5 (= 20), and then 7 times 3 (= 21), giving a result of 2,021.

9. Squaring a two-digit number beginning in 5. Add 25 to the ones' digit, then place the square of the ones' digit (as two digits) at the end.
Example: For 53^2, we add 25 + 3 (which is 28), then we square 3 (which is 09), giving a result of 2,809.

10. Multiplying two numbers that are an equal distance from a number that is easy to

square. Subtract the square of the distance from the square of the easy number.

Example: For 34 × 26, we notice that the numbers are both 4 from 30. The result is $30^2 - 4^2 = 884$.

11. Squaring a two-digit number ending in 1. Write down a 1. Add the tens' digit to itself, and write down the ones' digit of that answer to the left of the 1 that was first written down, and carry a 1 if it was greater than ten. Now multiply the tens' digit by itself, and add 1 if you had a carry, and write down the result to the left of all that was previously written down. It's easier than you think!

Example: For 71^2, we write down a 1, add 7 plus 7, write down the 4 (to the left of the original 1) and carry the 1. Lastly we multiply 7 times 7, and add the 1 that was carried. The answer is 5,041.

12. Multiplying by an 'almost easy' number. Do the multiplication with the easy number, and then adjust.

Example: For 12 × 39, we see that 39 is almost 40, so we multiply 12 times 40 (which is 480), and then we adjust by subtracting 12 (because 480 is one 12 too much), giving 468 as our result.

Example: For 25 × 31, we see that 31 is almost 30, so we multiply 25 times 30 (which is 750), and then add another 25, giving us a result of 775.

13. Cross multiplying when multiplying two 2-digit numbers. Multiply the 2 ones' digits to get the answer's ones' digit. Carry, if necessary. Cross-multiply to get the tens' digit (see example below). Carry, if necessary. Multiply the 2 numbers' tens' digits in order to get the hundreds' place in the answer.

Example (without carrying): For 12 × 23, the answer has a ones' digit of 2 times 3 = 6 Now we cross-multiply to get the answer's tens' digit, which is 2 times 2, plus 1 times 3, which is 7. The answer's hundreds' place is just 1 times 2, which is 2. Our final answer (see underlined digits) is then 276.

Example (with carrying): For 47 × 28, we first multiply 7 times 8 (which is 56), which means the answer's ones' digit is 6 with a carry of 5.

Then, we cross multiply for the tens' digit (see work at right), doing 7 times 2, plus 4 times 8, plus 5 (the carry), to get 51. This means that the answer's tens' place is 1, with a carry of 5. Finally, we multiply 4 times 2 and add 5 (the carry), which gives 13. The final answer (see underlined digits, above) is 1,316.

```
  4 7
 ×2 8
 ____
 1316
```

Appendix

The Archimedean solids...

Truncated tetrahedron

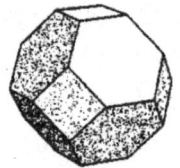

Truncated octahedron

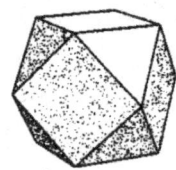

Cuboctahedron

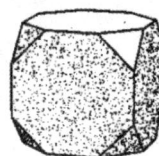

Truncated cube

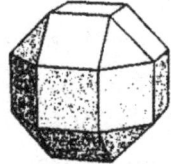

Rhombicubotahedron

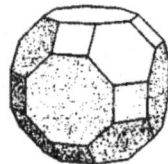

Great rhombicuboctahedron

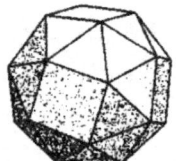

Snub cube

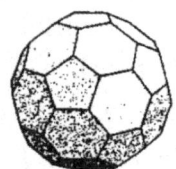

Truncated icosahedron

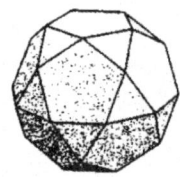

Isocidodecahedron

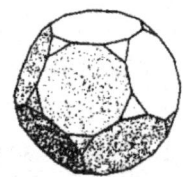

Truncated dodecahedron

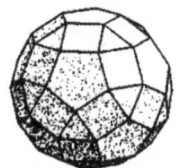

Rhombicosidodecahedron

Great rhombicosidodecahedron

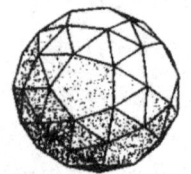

Snub dodecahedron

and their duals

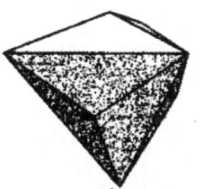
Triakistetrahedron

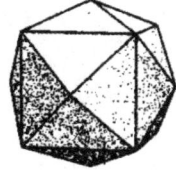
Tetrakishexahedron

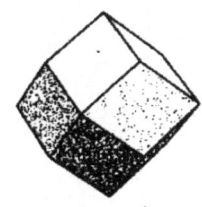
Rhombic dodecahedron

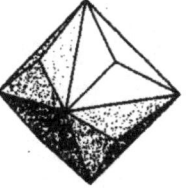
Triakisoctahedron

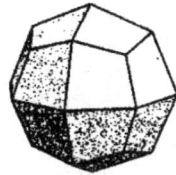
Trapezoidal iscositerahedron

Hexakisoctahedron

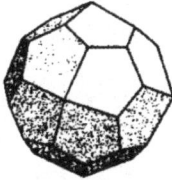
Pentagonal icositetrahedron

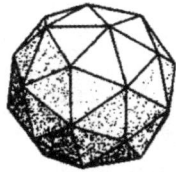
Pentakisdodecahedron

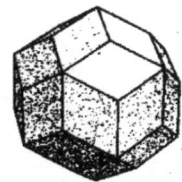
Rhombic triacontahedron

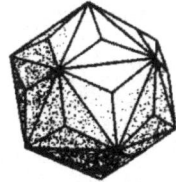
Triakisicosahedron

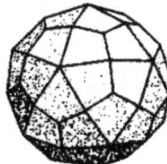
Trapezoidal hexecontrahedron

Great Hexakisicosahedron

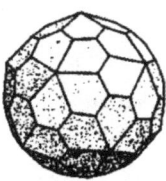
Pentagonal hexecontrahedron

Polyhedron nets

Note: Some of the nets below are *not* drawn exactly to scale.

 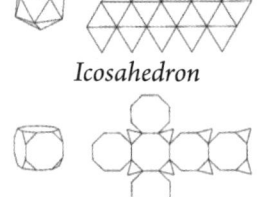

Dodecahedron *Icosahedron*

    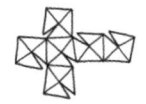  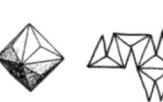

Truncated tetrahedron *Truncated octahedron* *Cuboctahedron* *Truncated cube*

 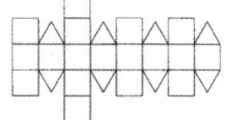      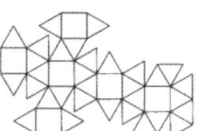

Triakistetrahedron *Tetrakishexahedron* *Rhombic dodecahedron* *Triakisoctahedron*

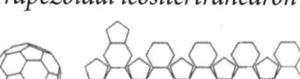    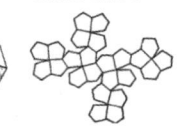

Rhombicuboctahedron *Great rhombicuboctahedron* *Snub cube*

 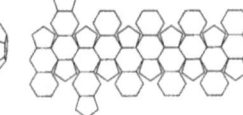  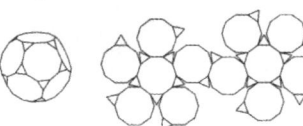

Trapezoidal icositetrahedron *Hexakisoctahedron* *Pentagonal icositetrahedron*

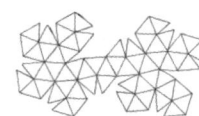 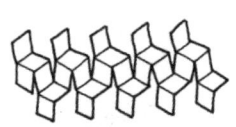   

Truncated icosahedron *Icosidodecahedron* *Truncated dodecahedron*

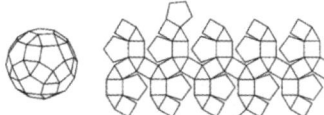 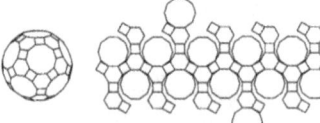 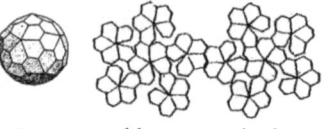

Pentakisdodecahedron *Rhombic triacontahedron* *Triakisicosahedron*

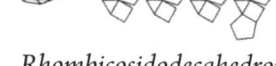 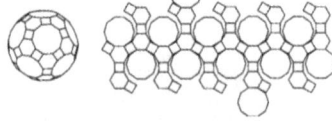 

Rhombicosidodecahedron *Great rhombicosidodecahedron* *Snub dodecahedron*

Trapezoidal hexecontahedron *Hexakisicosahedron* *Pentagonal hexecontahedron*

Patterns for the Archimedean duals (and some of the Archimedean solids)
Note: The number in the parenthesis indicates the number of faces on the solid.

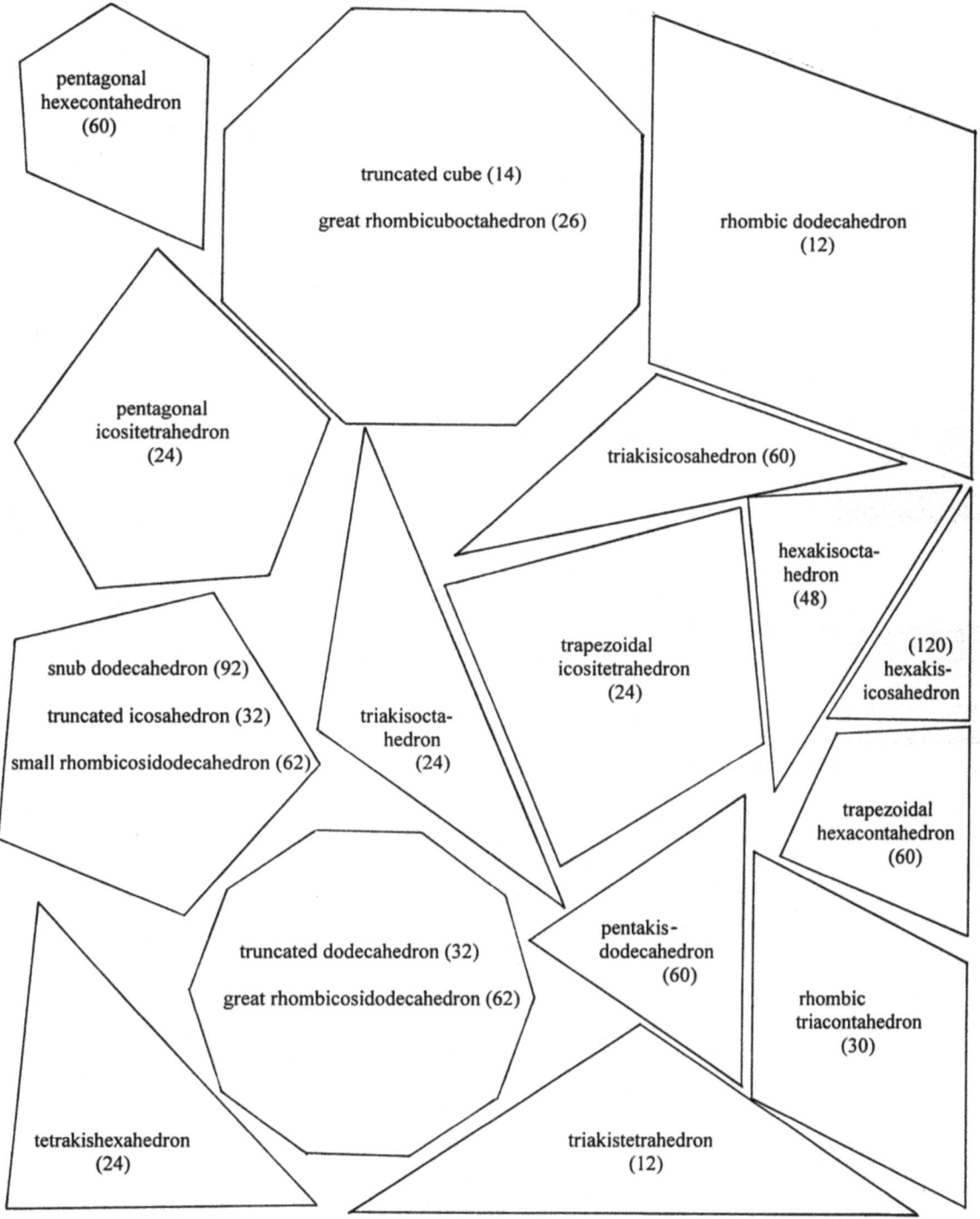

Appendix 243

Multiplication Tables for Number Bases

Binary table

	0	1
0	0	0
1	0	1

Base-five table

	0	1	2	3	4
0	0	0	0	0	0
1	0	1	2	3	4
2	0	2	4	11	13
3	0	3	11	14	22
4	0	4	13	22	31

Base-eight table

	0	1	2	3	4	5	6	7
0	0	0	0	0	0	0	0	0
1	0	1	2	3	4	5	6	7
2	0	2	4	6	10	12	14	16
3	0	3	6	11	14	17	22	25
4	0	4	10	14	20	24	30	34
5	0	5	12	17	24	31	36	42
6	0	6	14	22	30	36	44	52
7	0	7	16	25	34	42	52	61

Hexadecimal times table

	0	1	2	3	4	5	6	7	8	9	A	B	C	D	E	F
0	0	0	0	0	0	0	0	0	0	0	0	0	0	0	0	0
1	0	1	2	3	4	5	6	7	8	9	A	B	C	D	E	F
2	0	2	4	6	8	A	C	E	10	12	14	16	18	1A	1C	1E
3	0	3	6	9	C	F	12	15	18	1B	1E	21	24	27	2A	2D
4	0	4	8	C	10	14	18	1C	20	24	28	2C	30	34	38	3C
5	0	5	A	F	14	19	1E	23	28	2D	32	37	3C	41	46	4B
6	0	6	C	12	18	1E	24	2A	30	36	3C	42	48	4E	54	5A
7	0	7	E	15	1C	23	2A	31	38	3F	46	4D	54	5B	62	69
8	0	8	10	18	20	28	30	38	40	48	50	58	60	68	70	78
9	0	9	12	1B	24	2D	36	3F	48	51	5A	63	6C	75	7E	87
A	0	A	14	1E	28	32	3C	46	50	5A	64	6E	78	82	8C	96
B	0	B	16	21	2C	37	42	4D	58	63	6E	79	84	8F	9A	A5
C	0	C	18	24	30	3C	48	54	60	6C	78	84	90	9C	A8	B4
D	0	D	1A	27	34	41	4E	5B	68	75	82	8F	9C	A9	B6	C3
E	0	E	1C	2A	38	46	54	62	70	7E	8C	9A	A8	B6	C4	D2
F	0	F	1E	2D	3C	4B	5A	69	78	87	96	A5	B4	C3	D2	E1

Place Value (exponent) Table

10	9	8	7	6	5	4	3	2	1	0	BASE
1024	512	256	128	64	32	16	8	4	2	1	2
					3125	625	125	25	5	1	5
					32768	4096	512	64	8	1	8
					100,000	10,000	1,000	100	10	1	10
						65536	4096	256	16	1	16

Appendix

ASCII Code Table

Note: All codes are given in hexadecimal. Each hexadecimal digit can easily be converted to binary by using the table at the bottom of the page. For example, the character 'n' has an ASCII hexadecimal code 6E. Looking at the bottom of the page, we see that 6 is 0110 and that E is 1110. Therefore, the binary ASCII code for 'n' is 01101110. Note, also, that this table is incomplete. A full ASCII code table includes 256 codes, since there are 256 possible codes for one byte, which is an 8-digit binary code.

Hex	Char	Hex	Char	Hex	Char	Hex	Char	Hex	Char	Hex	Char
20	space	30	0	40	@	50	P	60	`	70	p
21	!	31	1	41	A	51	Q	61	a	71	q
22	"	32	2	42	B	52	R	62	b	72	r
23	#	33	3	43	C	53	S	63	c	73	s
24	$	34	4	44	D	54	T	64	d	74	t
25	%	35	5	45	E	55	U	65	e	75	u
26	&	36	6	46	F	56	V	66	f	76	v
27	'	37	7	47	G	57	W	67	g	77	w
28	(	38	8	48	H	58	x	68	h	78	x
29	)	39	9	49	I	59	y	69	i	79	y
2A	*	3A	:	4A	J	5A	z	6A	j	7A	z
2B	+	3B	;	4B	K	5B	[	6B	k	7B	{
2C	,	3C	<	4C	L	5C	\	6C	l	7C	|
2D	-	3D	=	4D	M	5D	]	6D	m	7D	}
2E	.	3E	>	4E	N	5E	^	6E	n	7E	~
2F	/	3F	?	4F	O	5F	_	6F	o	7F	del

Binary/Hexadecimal Conversion Table

Binary	Hexadecimal	Binary	Hexadecimal	Binary	Hexadecimal
0000	0	0110	6	1011	B
0001	1	0111	7	1100	C
0010	2	1000	8	1101	D
0011	3	1001	9	1110	E
0100	4	1010	A	1111	F
0101	5				

Algorithims

An algorithm for addition

This algorithm is for the addition of two whole numbers.

1. Write the smaller number under the larger number, right justified. Put a '+' sign to the left of the smaller number, and draw a horizontal line under the smaller number.
2. Start with the right-most column of digits.
3. Add together the digits in the current column (assume 0 for any missing digit), including any carry.
4. Write the last digit of the sum under the two digits just added together. If the sum was greater than 10, then carry a one by writing a '1' at the top of the next column.
5. Move to the next column.
6. If there is anything in the column (digits or carry), then go to step 3.
7. The answer (sum of the two numbers) is given below the line.

An algorithm for long division

This algorithm assumes that both the divisor and the dividend are integers greater than zero, and that the dividend is larger than the divisor. If there is a remainder, the answer is written as a mixed number.

1. Draw a short vertical line and write the divisor to the left of it, and the dividend to the right of it. Draw another line starting from the top of the first line, so that it goes over the top of the dividend.
2. Put a small x and a dot just to the left of the left-most digit of the dividend.
3. Move the dot one digit to the right.
4. The number formed by the digits between the dot and the x is called R. If R forms a number that is smaller than the divisor, go to step 3.
5. Above the horizontal line, and directly over the digit just to the left of the dot, write the largest digit that can be multiplied by the divisor giving a product less than R.
6. Write this product under R such that it is right justified with R.
7. Subtract the product from R, and write this difference down underneath the product, right justified. This is the new value for R.
8. If there are more digits to the right of the dot:
   a) Write the next digit of the dividend (the digit just to the right of the dot) at the end R.
   b) Move the dot one place to the right.
   c) Go to step 5.
9. If R is not equal to zero, then to the right of the digits on top of the horizontal line add a fraction that has R as its numerator, and the divisor as its denominator.
10. The final answer (dividend ÷ divisor) is above the horizontal line.

The square root algorithm (without zeros)

This algorithm is written in the style of a computer program, Class Eight. See p. 213.

An algorithm for prime numbers

Follow the directions carefully in order to find all the prime numbers up to 500. Those who want a bit more of a challenge should go up to 1,000 (which involves less than 50 multiplications).

1. How far are you going up to? This is n.
2. Find the square root of n This number without the decimal places is m (e.g. If n is 500, then m is 22. If n is 1,000, then m is 31.)
3. Write down 2 and the odd numbers up to n in a grid (To save time, the grid is given below. Cross out all the numbers that are larger than n, if n is less than 1,000.) Circle 2, which is the first number in the grid.
4. b is the first non-circled, non-crossed-out number. If b is greater than m, then go to step 9.
5. Circle b.
6. If b is less than 12, then cross out multiples of b, starting at b^2 and continuing until you have gone past n. Look for patterns! (This step saves *us* time compared with step 7, but is tough for computers. Why?)
7. If b is greater than 12, then multiply b by all non-crossed numbers starting with b itself (giving b^2) and working up. Cross out each product that you find. (Note: This step needs adjustment if $n \geq 13^3$, which is 2,197. This is because this algorithm is not designed to cross out cubes, or larger powers, of primes.)
8. Go to step 4.
9. Circle all non-crossed-out numbers The numbers that are circled are the prime numbers.

```
  2   3   5   7   9  11  13  15  17  19  21  23  25  27  29  31  33  35  37  39
 41  43  45  47  49  51  53  55  57  59  61  63  65  67  69  71  73  75  77  79
 81  83  85  87  89  91  93  95  97  99 101 103 105 107 109 111 113 115 117 119
121 123 125 127 129 131 133 135 137 139 141 143 145 147 149 151 153 155 157 159
161 163 165 167 169 171 173 175 177 179 181 183 185 187 189 191 193 195 197 199
201 203 205 207 209 211 213 215 217 219 221 223 225 227 229 231 233 235 237 239
241 243 245 247 249 251 253 255 257 259 261 263 265 267 269 271 273 275 277 279
281 283 285 287 289 291 293 295 297 299 301 303 305 307 309 311 313 315 317 319
321 323 325 327 329 331 333 335 337 339 341 343 345 347 349 351 353 355 357 359
361 363 365 367 369 371 373 375 377 379 381 383 385 387 389 391 393 395 397 399
401 403 405 407 409 411 413 415 417 419 421 423 425 427 429 431 433 435 437 439
441 443 445 447 449 451 453 455 457 459 461 463 465 467 469 471 473 475 477 479
481 483 485 487 489 491 493 495 497 499 501 503 505 507 509 511 513 515 517 519
521 523 525 527 529 531 533 535 537 539 541 543 545 547 549 551 553 555 557 559
561 563 565 567 569 571 573 575 577 579 581 583 585 587 589 591 593 595 597 599
601 603 605 607 609 611 613 615 617 619 621 623 625 627 629 631 633 635 637 639
641 643 645 647 649 651 653 655 657 659 661 663 665 667 669 671 673 675 677 679
681 683 685 687 689 691 693 695 697 699 701 703 705 707 709 711 713 715 717 719
721 723 725 727 729 731 733 735 737 739 741 743 745 747 749 751 753 755 757 759
761 763 765 767 769 771 773 775 777 779 781 783 785 787 789 791 793 795 797 799
801 803 805 807 809 811 813 815 817 819 821 823 825 827 829 831 833 835 837 839
841 843 845 847 849 851 853 855 857 859 861 863 865 867 869 871 873 875 877 879
881 883 885 887 889 891 893 895 897 899 901 903 905 907 909 911 913 915 917 919
921 923 925 927 929 931 933 935 937 939 941 943 945 947 949 951 953 955 957 959
961 963 965 967 969 971 973 975 977 979 981 983 985 987 989 991 993 995 997 999
```

Table of Square Roots

$\sqrt{1} = 1.000$	$\sqrt{27} = 5.196$	$\sqrt{53} = 7.280$	$\sqrt{79} = 8.888$
$\sqrt{2} = 1.414$	$\sqrt{28} = 5.292$	$\sqrt{54} = 7.348$	$\sqrt{80} = 8.944$
$\sqrt{3} = 1.732$	$\sqrt{29} = 5.385$	$\sqrt{55} = 7.416$	$\sqrt{81} = 9.000$
$\sqrt{4} = 2.000$	$\sqrt{30} = 5.477$	$\sqrt{56} = 7.483$	$\sqrt{82} = 9.055$
$\sqrt{5} = 2.236$	$\sqrt{31} = 5.568$	$\sqrt{57} = 7.550$	$\sqrt{83} = 9.110$
$\sqrt{6} = 2.449$	$\sqrt{32} = 5.657$	$\sqrt{58} = 7.616$	$\sqrt{84} = 9.165$
$\sqrt{7} = 2.646$	$\sqrt{33} = 5.745$	$\sqrt{59} = 7.681$	$\sqrt{85} = 9.220$
$\sqrt{8} = 2.828$	$\sqrt{34} = 5.831$	$\sqrt{60} = 7.746$	$\sqrt{86} = 9.274$
$\sqrt{9} = 3.000$	$\sqrt{35} = 5.916$	$\sqrt{61} = 7.810$	$\sqrt{87} = 9.327$
$\sqrt{10} = 3.162$	$\sqrt{36} = 6.000$	$\sqrt{62} = 7.874$	$\sqrt{88} = 9.381$
$\sqrt{11} = 3.317$	$\sqrt{37} = 6.083$	$\sqrt{63} = 7.937$	$\sqrt{89} = 9.434$
$\sqrt{12} = 3.464$	$\sqrt{38} = 6.164$	$\sqrt{64} = 8.000$	$\sqrt{90} = 9.487$
$\sqrt{13} = 3.606$	$\sqrt{39} = 6.245$	$\sqrt{65} = 8.062$	$\sqrt{91} = 9.539$
$\sqrt{14} = 3.742$	$\sqrt{40} = 6.325$	$\sqrt{66} = 8.124$	$\sqrt{92} = 9.592$
$\sqrt{15} = 3.873$	$\sqrt{41} = 6.403$	$\sqrt{67} = 8.185$	$\sqrt{93} = 9.644$
$\sqrt{16} = 4.000$	$\sqrt{42} = 6.481$	$\sqrt{68} = 8.246$	$\sqrt{94} = 9.695$
$\sqrt{17} = 4.123$	$\sqrt{43} = 6.557$	$\sqrt{69} = 8.307$	$\sqrt{95} = 9.747$
$\sqrt{18} = 4.243$	$\sqrt{44} = 6.633$	$\sqrt{70} = 8.367$	$\sqrt{96} = 9.798$
$\sqrt{19} = 4.359$	$\sqrt{45} = 6.708$	$\sqrt{71} = 8.426$	$\sqrt{97} = 9.849$
$\sqrt{20} = 4.472$	$\sqrt{46} = 6.782$	$\sqrt{72} = 8.485$	$\sqrt{98} = 9.899$
$\sqrt{21} = 4.583$	$\sqrt{47} = 6.856$	$\sqrt{73} = 8.544$	$\sqrt{99} = 9.950$
$\sqrt{22} = 4.690$	$\sqrt{48} = 6.928$	$\sqrt{74} = 8.602$	$\sqrt{100} = 10.000$
$\sqrt{23} = 4.796$	$\sqrt{49} = 7.000$	$\sqrt{75} = 8.660$	
$\sqrt{24} = 4.899$	$\sqrt{50} = 7.071$	$\sqrt{76} = 8.718$	
$\sqrt{25} = 5.000$	$\sqrt{51} = 7.141$	$\sqrt{77} = 8.775$	
$\sqrt{26} = 5.099$	$\sqrt{52} = 7.211$	$\sqrt{78} = 8.832$	

Appendix

Note: If there are ending zeros inside the square root, then you can remove an even number of zeros from inside, which will result in half as many zeros (or moving the decimal place half as many places) in your answer.

Examples:

With $\sqrt{25{,}000{,}000}$ we remove 6 zeros, then adding 3 zeros to $\sqrt{25}$, gives an answer of 5,000.

With $\sqrt{60{,}000}$ we remove 4 zeros. Since $\sqrt{6}$ is 2.449, we move 2 decimal places to get 244.9.

With $\sqrt{600{,}000}$ we remove 4 zeros. Since $\sqrt{60}$ is 7.746, we move 2 decimal places to get 774.6.

Note: This table should not be used if, after removing an *even* number of zeros, there are more than two digits inside the square root. For example, it *can* be used for $\sqrt{58{,}000{,}000}$, but *cannot* be used for $\sqrt{58{,}700}$ or for $\sqrt{580}$ or for $\sqrt{5{,}800{,}000}$.

Pythagorean triples

3, 4, 5	11, 60, 61
5, 12, 13	16, 63, 65
8, 15, 17	33, 56, 65
7, 24, 25	48, 55, 73
20, 21, 29	13, 84, 85
12, 35, 37	36, 77, 85
9, 40, 41	39, 80, 89
28, 45, 53	65, 72, 97

Growth Rate Table giving values for $(1+r)^t$ from the formula $P = P_0(1+r)^t$

t	$(1+r)$ 1.01	1.02	1.025	1.03	1.035	1.04	1.05	1.06	1.07	1.08	1.09	1.1	1.15	1.2	1.25	1.3	1.4	1.5	2
2	1.0201	1.0404	1.05063	1.0609	1.07123	1.0816	1.1025	1.1236	1.1449	1.1664	1.1881	1.21	1.3225	1.44	1.5625	1.69	1.96	2.25	4
3	1.0303	1.06121	1.07689	1.09273	1.10872	1.12486	1.15763	1.19102	1.22504	1.25971	1.29503	1.331	1.52088	1.728	1.95313	2.197	2.744	3.375	8
4	1.0406	1.08243	1.10381	1.12551	1.14752	1.16986	1.21551	1.26248	1.3108	1.36049	1.41158	1.4641	1.74901	2.0736	2.44141	2.8561	3.8416	5.0625	16
5	1.05101	1.10408	1.13141	1.15927	1.18769	1.21665	1.27628	1.33823	1.40255	1.46933	1.53862	1.61051	2.01136	2.48832	3.05176	3.71293	5.37824	7.59375	32
6	1.06152	1.12616	1.15969	1.19405	1.22926	1.26532	1.3401	1.41852	1.50073	1.58687	1.6771	1.77156	2.31306	2.98598	3.8147	4.82681	7.52954	11.3906	64
7	1.07214	1.14869	1.18869	1.22987	1.27228	1.31593	1.4071	1.50363	1.60578	1.71382	1.82804	1.94872	2.66002	3.58318	4.76837	6.27485	10.5414	17.0859	128
8	1.08286	1.17166	1.2184	1.26677	1.31681	1.36857	1.47746	1.59385	1.71819	1.85093	1.99256	2.14359	3.05902	4.29982	5.96046	8.15731	14.7579	25.6289	256
9	1.09369	1.19509	1.24886	1.30477	1.3629	1.42331	1.55133	1.68948	1.83846	1.999	2.17189	2.35795	3.51788	5.15978	7.45058	10.6045	20.661	38.4434	512
10	1.10462	1.21899	1.28008	1.34392	1.4106	1.48024	1.62889	1.79085	1.96715	2.15892	2.36736	2.59374	4.04556	6.19174	9.31323	13.7858	28.9255	57.665	1024
11	1.11567	1.24337	1.31209	1.38423	1.45997	1.53945	1.71034	1.8983	2.10485	2.33164	2.58043	2.85312	4.65239	7.43008	11.6415	17.9216	40.4957	86.4976	2048
12	1.12683	1.26824	1.34489	1.42576	1.51107	1.60103	1.79586	2.0122	2.25219	2.51817	2.81266	3.13843	5.35025	8.9161	14.5519	23.2981	56.6939	129.746	4096
13	1.13809	1.29361	1.37851	1.46853	1.56396	1.66507	1.88565	2.13293	2.40985	2.71962	3.0658	3.45227	6.15279	10.6993	18.1899	30.2875	79.3715	194.62	8192
14	1.14947	1.31948	1.41297	1.51259	1.61869	1.73168	1.97993	2.2609	2.57853	2.93719	3.34173	3.7975	7.07571	12.8392	22.7374	39.3738	111.12	291.929	16384
15	1.16097	1.34587	1.4483	1.55797	1.67535	1.80094	2.07893	2.39656	2.75903	3.17217	3.64248	4.17725	8.13706	15.407	28.4217	51.1859	155.568	437.894	32768
16	1.17258	1.37279	1.48451	1.60471	1.73399	1.87298	2.18287	2.54035	2.95216	3.42594	3.97031	4.59497	9.35762	18.4884	35.5271	66.5417	217.795	656.841	65536
17	1.1843	1.4002	1.52162	1.65285	1.79468	1.9479	2.29202	2.69277	3.15882	3.70002	4.32763	5.0544	10.7613	22.1861	44.4089	86.5042	304.913	985.261	131072
18	1.19615	1.42825	1.55966	1.70243	1.85749	2.02582	2.40662	2.85434	3.37993	3.99602	4.71712	5.55992	12.3755	26.6233	55.5112	112.455	426.879	1477.89	262144
19	1.20811	1.45681	1.59865	1.75351	1.9225	2.10685	2.52695	3.0256	3.61653	4.3157	5.14166	6.11591	14.2318	31.948	69.3889	146.192	597.63	2216.84	524288
20	1.22019	1.48595	1.63862	1.80611	1.98979	2.19112	2.6533	3.20714	3.86968	4.66096	5.60441	6.7275	16.3665	38.3376	86.7362	190.05	836.683	3325.26	1048576
25	1.28243	1.64061	1.85394	2.09378	2.36324	2.66584	3.38635	4.29187	5.42743	6.84848	8.62308	10.8347	32.919	95.3962	264.698	705.641	4499.88	25251.2	3.4E+07
30	1.34785	1.81136	2.09757	2.42726	2.80679	3.2434	4.32194	5.74349	7.61226	10.0627	13.2677	17.4494	66.2118	237.376	807.794	2620	24201.4	191751	1.1E+09
40	1.48886	2.20804	2.68506	3.26204	3.95926	4.80102	7.03999	10.2857	14.9745	21.7245	31.4094	45.2593	267.864	1469.77	7523.16	36118.9	700038	1.1E+07	1.1E+12
50	1.64463	2.69159	3.43711	4.38391	5.58493	7.10668	11.4674	18.4202	29.457	46.9016	74.3575	117.391	1083.66	9100.44	70064.9	497929	2E+07	6.4E+08	1.1E+15
60	1.8167	3.28103	4.39979	5.8916	7.87809	10.5196	18.6792	32.9877	57.9464	101.257	176.031	304.482	4384	56347.5	652530	6864377	5.9E+08	3.7E+10	1.2E+18
80	2.21672	4.87544	7.20957	10.6409	15.6757	23.0498	49.5614	105.796	224.234	471.955	986.552	2048.4	71750.9	2160228	5.7E+07	1.3E+09	4.9E+11	1.2E+14	1.2E+24
100	2.70481	7.24465	11.8137	19.2186	31.1914	50.5049	131.501	339.302	867.716	2199.76	5529.04	13780.6	1174313	8.3E+07	4.9E+09	2.5E+11	1.1E+14	4.1E+17	1.3E+30
150	4.44842	19.4996	40.605	84.2527	174.202	358.923	1507.98	6250	25560.3	103172	411126	1617718	1.3E+09	7.5E+11	3.4E+14	1.2E+17	8.3E+21	2.6E+26	1.4E+45
200	7.31602	52.4849	139.564	369.356	972.904	2550.75	17292.6	115126	752932	4836850	3.1E+07	1.9E+08	1.4E+12	6.9E+15	2.4E+19	6.1E+22	1.7E+29	1.7E+35	1.6E+60

Note: The cell on the bottom right (1.6E + 60) means 1.6×10^{60} in scientific notation. The last column is where $(r + 1)$ is 2, or $r = 1$, which means 100% annual growth, or doubling.

Appendix

Useful distances

Average radius of the earth:	6,371 km (3,960 mi)
Polar circumference of earth:	40,005 km (24,859 mi)
Equatorial circum. of earth:	40,076 km 24,902 mi
Surface area of the earth:	510,000,000 km² (197,000,000 mi²)
Total land area of the earth:	149,000,000 km² (57,500,000 mi²)
Radius of the sun:	696,000 km (432,000 mi)
Radius of the moon:	1,738 km (1,080 mi)
Distance to the moon:	384,400 km (239,000 mi)
Distance to the sun:	150,000,000 km (93,000,000 mi)
One light year:	9.46 × 1,012 km (5.8784 × 1,012 mi)
Distance to the nearest star:	4.07 × 1,013 km (2.53 × 1,013 mi)

Conversion Table

Measure and conversion tables

Metric system

Weight
1 tonne = 1,000 kilograms (kg)
1 kg = 1,000 grams (g)
1 g = 1,000 milligrams (mg)

Length
1 kilometre (km) = 1,000 metres (m)
1 m = 100 centimetres (cm)
1 m = 1,000 millimetres (mm)

Area
1 km² = 100 hectares (ha)
1 ha = 10,000 m² (100 × 100 m)
1 m² = 10,000 cm²
1 cm² = 100 mm²

Volume
1 m³ = 1,000,000 cm³
1 m³ = 1,000 litres (ℓ)
1 ℓ = 1,000 cm³ (10 × 10 × 10 cm)
1 ℓ = 1,000 mℓ cm³ (10 × 10 × 10 cm)
1 mℓ = 1 cm³

Speed
1 km/h ≈ 0.278 m/s
1 m/s = 3.6 km/h

Density
1 g/cm³ = 1 kg/ℓ = 1,000 kg/m³

Imperial system

Weight
1 stone (st) = 14 pounds (lb)
1 lb = 16 ounces (oz)

Length
1 mile (mi) = 1,760 yards (yd)
1 mi = 5,280 feet (ft)
1 yd = 3 ft
1 ft = 12 inches (in)

Area
1 mi^2 = 640 acres
1 acre = 4,840 yd^2
1 yd^2 = 9 ft^2
1 ft^2 = 144 in^2

Volume
1 gallon (gal) = 8 pints (pt)
1 pt = 20 fluid ounces (fl oz)*
1 ft^3 = 1,728 in^3

Speed
1 mph ≈ 1.467 ft/s
1 ft/s ≈ 0.682 mph

Density
1 oz/in^3 = 108 lb/ft^3

Conversion to metric
Weight
1 st ≈ 6.35 kg
1 lb ≈ 454 g
1 oz ≈ 28.35 g

Length
{List no b}1 mi ≈ 1.6093 km
1 yd ≈ 91.44 cm
1 ft ≈ 30.48 cm
1 in ≈ 2.54 cm

Area

1 mi^2 ≈ 2.59 km^2
1 acre ≈ 0.405 ha
1 yd^2 ≈ 0.836 m^2
1 ft^2 ≈ 0.0929 m ≈ 929 cm^2
1 in^2 ≈ 6.452 cm^2

Volume
1 (imp) gal ≈ 4.546 ℓ
1 pt ≈ 568.25 mℓ
1 fl oz ≈ 28.41 mℓ
1 ft^3 ≈ 0.0283 m^3
1 in^3 ≈ 16.387 cm^3

Speed
1 mph ≈ 1.6093 km/h ≈ 0.4470 m/s
1 ft/s ≈ 0.3048 m/s ≈ 1.097 km/h

Density
1 oz/in^3 ≈ 1.73 g/cm^3
1 lb/ft^3 ≈ 16.02 kg/m^3

Temperature
C = 5/9(F − 32)

Conversion to imperial
Weight
1 kg ≈ 2.2046 (2.2) lb
1 g ≈ .0353 oz

Length
1 km ≈ 0.6214 mi
1 m ≈ 1.094 yd
1 m ≈ 3.281 ft
1 cm ≈ 0.39370 in

---

* The US pint is only 16 fl oz, so a US pint and gallon is smaller than imperial. The US gallon is about 3.785 ℓ. (The imperial and US fl oz is also not exactly the same.)

Area
1 km² ≈ 0.386 mi²
1 ha ≈ 2.471 acre
1 m² ≈ 1.196 yd²
1 m² ≈ 10.764 ft²
1 cm² ≈ 0.155 in²

Volume
1 ℓ ≈ 0.220 (imp) gal
1 ℓ ≈ 1.76 pt
1 ℓ ≈ 35.2 fl oz
1 m³ ≈ 35.314 ft³
1 cm³ ≈ 0.0610 in³

Speed
1 km/h ≈ 0.6214 mph ≈ 0.9114 ft/s
1 m/s ≈ 3.281 ft/s ≈ 2.237 mph

Density
1 g/cm³ ≈ 0.578 oz/in³
1 kg/m³ ≈ 62.43 lb/ft³

Temperature
$F = \frac{9}{5}(C + 32)$

Density of some materials
Water (at a maximum density of 4°C)
    1 g/cm³ = 1 kg/ℓ = 1,000 kg/m³ (0.578 oz/in³, 62.43 lb/ft³)
Air 1.29 kg/m³ 1.29 oz/ft³ – coincidentally!)
Aluminium 2.70 g/cm³ (169 lb/ft³)
Iron 7.10 g/cm³ (443 lb/ft³)
Mercury 13.5 g/cm³ (843 lb/ft³)
Gold 19.3 g/cm³ (1,204 lb/ft³)

Assessment tests and maths skills
Class Four assessment test

About this test:

This test should be given at the end of Class Four.

This test does not represent the typical level of difficulty of maths problems for Class Four. It should be quite easy for most of the students.

The primary purpose of this test is to assess the basic skill level of the whole class, and to determine which students have weak basic skills.

After this test has been given, parents should receive a report regarding the progress of their child.

It is best for the remedial or resource teacher to administer this test to the students on a one-to-one basis. This will allow the teacher to make important observations of the student during the work, which includes answers to questions such as:

- Has the student learned the arithmetic facts (e.g. $15 - 8$ or 9×7) by heart, or do they have to figure it out?
- Do they think of $61 - 57$ as a borrowing problem?
- Do they recognise that 5×4 is the same as 4×5?
- Is $600 \div 3$ harder than it should be?
- Do they seem to have a good sense of number?

The student should be instructed that if a problem is too hard, then they should skip it and come back to it later.

The 'mental maths' problems should be done with a pencil, but without showing work.

Estimating, measurement and sense of number

These questions should be asked orally by the teacher.

1) Hold your hands about 30 cm apart.
2) Hold your fingers about 2 cm apart.
3) About how many metres do you think it is between here and the wall?
4) How much does this bucket of water weigh (in kg)?
5) How much do you think I weigh?

Mental arithmetic

6) $8 + 5 = $ _____
7) $7 + 4 = $ _____
8) $12 + 5 + 6 = $ _____
9) $69 + 3 = $ _____
10) $80 + 70 = $ _____

11) $5 \times 4 = $ _____
12) $4 \times 5 = $ _____
13) $11 \times 6 = $ _____
14) $9 \times 7 = $ _____
15) $8 \times 6 = $ _____
16) $7 \times 8 = $ _____
17) $3 \times 9 = $ _____

18) $15 - 8 = $ _____
19) $11 - 7 = $ _____
20) $61 - 57 = $ _____
21) $30 - 4 = $ _____
22) $52 - 8 = $ _____
23) $100 - 40 = $ _____
24) $100 - 25 = $ _____
25) $300 - 52 = $ _____

26) 18 ÷ 2 = _____
27) 600 ÷ 3 = _____
28) 54 ÷ 9 = _____

Written arithmetic
29) 725 + 439
30) 459 − 183
31) 36 × 7

Class Six assessment test

Notes for the teacher:

This test should be given at the end of Class Six.

This test does not represent the typical level of difficulty of maths problems for Class Six.

It should be quite easy for most of the students.

The primary purpose of this test is to assess the basic skill level of the whole class, and to determine which students have weak basic skills.

After this test has been given, parents should receive a report regarding the progress of their child.

It may be best to give the first half of this test on one day, and then the second half on the following day.

The first 23 problems are intended to be mental maths and should be read orally by the teacher. For each of these problems, the students should write down only the final answer. The time interval between questions should be about five seconds per question for the easiest questions, and ten seconds per question for the hardest ones.

Mental arithmetic
1) 8 + 5
2) 7 + 7
3) 38 + 7
4) 12 + 28
5) 11 − 7
6) 60 − 3
7) 53 − 5
8) 72 − 68
9) 700 − 8
10) 304 − 298
11) 6 × 9
12) 8 × 7
13) 40 × 6
14) 200 × 40
15) 21 ÷ 3
16) 600 ÷ 3
17) 8,000 ÷ 200
18) What is ½ of 50?
19) What is ¼ of 240?
20) What is ⅔ of 21?

Word problems
21) A three metre long string is cut into six equally long pieces. How long is each piece?
22) If Sally earns £60 per day in her job, how much does she earn in 6 days?
23) At a bakery, 4 large loaves of bread cost £12. What would then be the cost of 5 loaves of bread?

Class Six written assessment test
Addition and subtraction
24) 284 + 349

25) 67 + 24 + 8 + 43

26) 728 − 253

27) 3,604 − 764

Multiplication and division
28) 624 × 3

29) 83 × 25

30) 749 × 286

31) 430 × 200

32) Use short or long division: 2,718 ÷ 6

33) Use long division: 8,242 ÷ 26

Fraction and decimals
34) $\frac{5}{8} + \frac{2}{8}$

35) $\frac{1}{4} + \frac{2}{3}$

36) $\frac{7}{8} - \frac{5}{11}$

37) $\frac{5}{8} \times \frac{2}{8}$

38) $\frac{8}{9} \times \frac{7}{8}$

39) $\frac{8}{25} \times \frac{35}{48}$

40) $8 \div \frac{1}{3}$

41) $\frac{2}{3} \div \frac{4}{5}$

42) $5\frac{3}{5} + 1\frac{6}{7}$

43) $2\frac{1}{2} \times 3\frac{2}{5}$

44) 74.1 + 9.24

45) 30.8 – 4.37

46) 1.23 × 0.07

47) 39.2 × 1.84

48) 265.8 ÷ 0.06

49) What is 0.71 as a fraction?

50) What is 0.025 as a reduced fraction?

51) What is $\frac{19}{1000}$ as a decimal?

52) What is $\frac{37}{400}$ as a decimal?

Summary of maths skills for Class One through Eight

Often parents worry that their child is behind. They can become alarmed if their child isn't proficient with a skill that is being covered in school. Part of the problem can be an assumption that students should learn every skill quickly, and then never forget it. In practice, however, the development of an important skill often follows a three-year progression from introduction to practice/review to mastery. Certainly, we want all of our students to have solid maths skills for their future education and career. Waldorf students should have an advantage!

This document shows when each particular skill is introduced, practised and then mastered.

There is much more to maths class than what is shown with this summary of maths skills.

The examples are not class specific (e.g. under 'fractions' we are not saying when 3½ ÷ 5 is covered).

Skill	Introduced?	Practised?	Mastered?	Example of skill
Counting to 100	Class 1	Class 1 – 2	Class 2	…37, 38, 39, 40, 41…
Times tables	Class 1	Class 1 – 3	Class 3	2, 4, 6, 8, 10… 7, 14, 21, 28, 35…
Arithmetic facts	Class 1	Class 2 – 4	Class 4	$8 \times 7 =$ $13 - 8 =$
Mental arithmetic	Class 1	Class 1 – 8	Class 2 – 8	$62 - 55 =$ $480 + 30 =$
Basic measurement	Class 3	Class 4 – 5	Class 5	How tall is that tree? 2 m = 200 cm
Vertical adding & subtracting (carrying/borrowing)	Class 3	Class 4 – 5	Class 5	607 – 438
Vertical (long) multiplication	Class 3	Class 4 – 5	Class 5	538 × 357
Vertical (long) division	Class 4	Class 5 – 6	Class 6	$47 \overline{)7990}$
Fractions	Class 4	Class 5 – 6	Class 6	¾ + ⅔ 3½ ÷ 5
Decimals	Class 5	Class 5 – 6	Class 6	$2.6 - 0.17$ 0.34×2.83
Measurement conversions	Class 5	Class 6 – 8	Class 7 – 8	9 miles = _____ km
Advanced mental maths	Class 5	Class 5 – 8	Class 7 – 8	$25 \times 18 =$ 15% of 260 =
Percents	Class 6	Class 7 – 8	Class 8	37% of 2000 25 is what % of 60?
Speeds/ratios/proportions	Class 6 – 7	Class 7 – 10	Class 8 – 10	similar triangles fuel consumption
Areas and volumes	Class 6	Class 7 – 10	Class 8 – 10	area of a triangle volume of a sphere
Basic equations	Class 7	Class 7 – 9	Class 9	$3x - 7 = 8x + 23$
Signed numbers	Class 7	Class 7 – 9	Class 9	$-5 + 9 - 3 + 10 =$ $(-6)(-9) =$

Appendix

Suggested reading

Allen, Jon, *Drawing Geometery*, Floris Books, 2007
—, *Making Geometery: Exploring Three-Dimensional Forms*, Floris Books, 2012
Baravalle, Hermann von, *Geometric Drawing and the Waldorf Plan*, Rudolf Steiner College Press, 1991
—, *The Waldorf Approach to Arithmetic*, Parker Courtney Press, 1996
—, *Perspective Drawing*. Rudolf Steiner College Press, 2000
Diggins, Julia, *String, Straightedge, and Shadow – The Story of Geometry*. Jamie York Press, 2003
Franceschelli, Amos, *Algebra, Mathematics for Grades 6, 7, and 8*, Mercury Press, 1995
Holden, Alan, *Shapes, Space and Symmetry*, Dover Publications, 1992
Jarman, Ron, *Teaching Mathematics in Rudolf Steiner Schools for Classes I – VIII*, Hawthorn Press, 1998
Julius, Edward H., *Rapid Math Tricks and Tips*, John Wiley & Sons, 1992
Kretz, Harry, *Solid Geometry*, AWSNA, 1997
Lockwood, E. H., *A Book of Curves*, Cambridge University Press, 2002
Lundy, Miranda, *Sacred Geometry*, Wooden Books, 2000
Schuberth, Ernst, *Introduction of Advanced Arithmetical Operations for Waldorf School 7th Grades*, AWSNA, 1999
—, *Mathematics Lessons for the Class Six*, AWSNA, 2002
Sheen, Renwick, *Geometry and the Imagination*, AWSNA, 2002
Stockmeyer, Karl, *Rudolph Steiner's Curriculum for Steiner-Waldorf Schools*, Floris Books, 2015
Sutton, Daud, *Platonic and Archimedean Solids*, Wooden Books, 2005
Swanson, Herbert, *Geometry for the Waldorf High School*, AWSNA, 1987
(Also quite useful for middle school.)
Ulin, Bengt, *Finding The Path*, AWSNA, 1991
Williams, Robert, *The Geometric Foundation of Natural Structure*, Dover Publications, 1979

Glossary

abundance quotient	The sum of a number's factors divided by the number itself.
abundant number	A number that has its sum of factors greater than itself.
acute angle	An angle that is less than 90°.
acute triangle	A triangle that has all acute angles.
algorithm	Step-by-step instructions usually associated with computer programming.
al-Khwarizmi (780–850)	The Father of Algebra.
alternate interior angles	When two parallel lines are crossed by a transversal, two angles that are both inside the parallel lines, but on opposite sides of the transversal.
arc	A part of a circle's circumference.
Archimedean dual	A solid where all the faces and the dihedral angles are the same.
Archimedean solid	A solid with regular (but different) faces, where all the vertices are the same.
Archimedes (c. 287 – 212 BC)	Great Greek mathemetician. Discovered many things, including formula for the volume of a sphere, Archimedes' principle (hydraulics), the law of the lever, method for calculating π and made the first steps toward calculus.
ASCII code	Computer codes for storing characters, (e.g. from the keyboard).
binary (numbers)	Another word for *base-two*.
bisect	To cut something into two equal parts.
bit	The smallest unit of storage in a computer's memory. It is either 0 (off) or 1 (on).
cardioid	A heart-shaped curve, and a specific case of a limaçon.
Cassini curve	A loci curve that can either be an oval, an indented oval, a lemniscate or two eggs.
casting out nines	The process of 'throwing out' all digits that add to nine.
chord	A line that connects two points on a circle.
circumscribe	To draw a figure on the outside of another one, so that it passed through its vertices.
coefficient	A number that occurs before, and is multiplied by, a variable, (e.g. The '4' in $4 \times 2 + 5$).
commensurable	The notion that two lengths can be expressed *exactly* as a ratio in whole number form.
complementary angles	Two angles that add to 90°.

compound fraction	A fraction that has one, or more, fractions in the numerator or denominator.
compound interest	Interest that is calculated on both the initial deposit and the accruing interest.
concentric circles	Circles that have the same centre.
congruent	Another word for equal. Congruent figures are exactly the same shape and size.
conic section	A curve that results from taking the cross section of a double cone. There are three types of conic sections: ellipse, parabola and hyperbola.
constant	Usually a whole number or fraction that is separate from the variable term, (e.g. The '5' in $4 \times 2 + 5$).
corresponding angles	Angles that are in the same relative location of the two 'intersections' created when two parallel lines are crossed by a transversal.
deficient number	A number that has its sum of factors less than itself.
denominator	The bottom part of a fraction.
density	The weight of a material per unit of volume. Density = weight ÷ volume.
dihedral angle	The angle at which two planes meet along an edge.
dimensional analysis	The study of units of measurement.
dividend	The number that is being divided by the divisor. It is 'inside' the house when doing long division.
divisor	The number that divides into the dividend. It is 'outside' the house when doing long division.
dodecahedron	A Platonic solid that has twelve equilateral pentagons for faces.
ellipse	A conic section curve that resembles an oval.
equiangular polygon	A polygon that has all equal angles.
equilateral polygon	A polygon with all equal sides.
Eratosthenes (276 – 194 BC)	A Greek mathematician and astronomer who accurately calculated the circumference of the earth.
Euclid (*c.* 300 BC)	A Greek who gathered all known mathematics into one book, *The Elements*.
Eurythmy	A type of body movement art (somewhat resembling a form of dance) that results in 'visible speech'. Eurythmy is taught in most Waldorf schools.
evenly divisible	When one number divides into another without leaving a remainder.

exponential growth	Growth that is based on a geometric progression. Also 'constant percentage growth.'
GCF	Greatest common factor, (e.g. The GCF of 48 and 36 is 12).
geometric progression	A progression where each number is a given percentage larger than the previous one.
golden ratio/mean	The ratio of the lengths of the diagonal and side of a regular pentagon.
golden rectangle	A rectangle where the ratio of its base and height is equal to the golden ratio.
half-wheel theorem	The theorem stating that the angles in a triangle add to 180°, so named because the proof resembles a 'half-wheel'.
hexadecimal	Another word for *base-sixteen*.
hexahedron	Another word for 'cube'. A Platonic solid that has six squares for faces.
hyperbola	A conic section curve that has two branches, where each branch approaches the lines of an 'X'.
hypotenuse	The longest side, and the side opposite the right angle, of a right triangle.
hypotenuse formula	The version of the Pythagorean Theorem that allows us to calculate the length of the hypotenuse of a right triangle, if the other two sides are given. The formula is: $c^2 = a^2 + b^2$. (See also *leg formula*.)
icosahedron	A Platonic solid that has twenty equilateral triangles for faces.
improper fraction	A fraction where the numerator is greater than the denominator, (e.g. 7/3).
inscribe	To draw a figure inside another one so that it is barely touching it.
integer	A positive or negative whole number (…-3, -2, -1, 0, 1, 2, 3…)
inversely proportional	If we say that two things are inversely proportional, then we mean that if one goes up (or down), then the other does the opposite, (e.g. 'The amount of time you spend getting somewhere is inversely proportional to your speed.').
irrational number	A number that cannot be expressed as a whole-number fraction, (e.g. π, $\sqrt{20}$, etc.).
isosceles triangle	A triangle with two equal sides, and two equal angles.
kite	A quadrilateral with two pairs of equal adjacent sides.
LCM	Least common multiple, (e.g. the LCM of 12 and 8 is 24).
leg	One of the two shorter sides of a right triangle.

leg formula	The version of the Pythagorean Theorem that allows us to calculate the length of a right triangle's leg (i.e. one of the two shorter sides of the triangle), if the other two sides are given. The formula is: $a^2 = c^2 - b^2$. (See also *hypotenuse formula*.)
lemniscate	A figure-eight curve.
limaçon	A variation of a cardioid, or heart-shaped curve.
loci	The study of curves on a plane.
mensuration	The study of measurement, especially area and volume.
mixed number	A whole number combined with a *proper* (or *simple*) fraction (e.g., $3½$, or $5^4/_7$).
net	A two-dimensional pattern that folds up into a three-dimensional shape.
number bases	The study of number systems that use a base other than ten.
numerator	The top part of the fraction.
obtuse angle	An angle that is more than 90°.
obtuse triangle	A triangle that has an obtuse angle in it.
octahedron	A Platonic solid that has eight equilateral triangles for faces.
octal (numbers)	Another word for *base-eight*.
parabola	A conic section curve that has the shape of the path followed by a rock thrown in the air.
parallelogram	A quadrilateral with opposite sides that are both parallel and equal.
pentagram	A five-pointed star.
perfect number	A number that has its sum of factors equal to itself.
perpendicular bisector	A line that bisects another line and meets it at a right angle.
perpendicular lines	Two lines that cross at 90° angles.
platonic solid	A regular and 'perfectly symmetrical' three-dimensional solid.
polygon	A closed figure that is bounded by three or more straight lines.
polyhedron	A solid that is bounded by four or more faces that are flat polygons.
prime factorisation	A breakdown of a number into a product of its prime factors.
prime number	A whole number that can be divided evenly only by itself and one.
prism	A solid that has rectangles for sides and a top and bottom that are the same.
progression	A sequence of numbers where each one gets progressively bigger than the previous one.
proportion	(1) Meaning 'fraction', (e.g. 'What *proportion* of the class is boys?'). (2) An equation where there is *one* fraction on each side.

proportional	If we say that two things are proportional, then we mean that if one goes up (or down), then the other does the same, (e.g. 'How far you drive is directly proportional to the amount of time.').
protractor	A small tool that allows one to measure the numbers of degrees in an angle.
Pythagoras (c. 570 – 495 BC)	The first great Greek mathematician and philosopher. His secret brotherhood or school discovered the Pythagorean Theorem and proved the existence of irrational numbers.
quadrilateral	A polygon with four sides.
quotient	The answer to a division problem. The number of times that the divisor goes into the dividend.
rational number	A number that can be expressed as a whole-number fraction, including decimals.
reciprocal	To find the reciprocal of a fraction, we flip it. With decimals, we divide the number into 1.
rectangle	A quadrilateral with four right angles, where opposite sides are equal.
regular	Means that all sides, angles, and faces are equal, (e.g. equilateral triangle, square).
repeating decimal	A decimal where a pattern repeats forever, (e.g. $5.3\overline{72}$ means $5.372727272\ldots$).
rhombic dodecahedron	An Archimedean dual solid that has 12 rhombuses for faces.
rhombus	A quadrilateral with four equal sides and with equal opposite angles. It is commonly called a diamond.
right angle	An angle equal to 90°.
right triangle	A triangle that has a right angle in it.
same-side interior angles	When two parallel lines are crossed by a transversal, the two angles that are both inside the parallel lines, and on the same sides of the transversal.
secant	A line that crosses a circle in two places.
segment of a circle	A 'piece of pie' from a circle.
scalene triangle	A triangle that has all three sides with different lengths.
shear and stretch	The process of slicing something into thin strips or sheets, and then shifting it so that the area or volume is kept the same.
similar figures	Two figures that have the same shape, but (probably) different sizes.
simple interest	Interest that is based upon only the initial deposit, as opposed to compound interest.

square root algorithm the	A procedure, similar to long division, which allows for calculating decimal value of the square root of a number.
supplementary angles	Two angles that together form a straight line, or 180°.
tangent	When a line (or curve) touches, but does not cross a curve.
tetrahedron	A Platonic solid that has four equilateral triangles for faces.
transversal	A line that crosses two parallel lines.
trapezium	A quadrilateral with one pair of parallel sides (trapeziod in North America).
truncate	With solid geometry, it means that we cut off the vertices (corners).
variable	A letter representing an unknown number or quantity, (e.g. the 'x' in $4x^2 + 5$).
vertex	The corner of a polygon or polyhedron (solid), or the point of an angle.
vertices	Plural of vertex.
vertical angles	Two angles that are opposite one another when two lines intersect.

Special symbols used in this book

- $\approx$ means 'approximately'.
- $=$ means 'equal to'.
- $\equiv$ means 'equivalent to'.
- $\neq$ means 'not equal to'.
- $\angle B$ means 'angle B'.
- 7 m^2 means '7 square metres' (area), and the 7 is not being squared
- $5.468\overline{1}$ means 'five point 4 six-eight-one repeating', is equal to $5.4681681681\overline{681}\ldots$

Index

AAS (angle-angle-side) triangle 105
abundance quotient 221
abundant numbers 220–22
acute triangle 60
addition, algorithm for 247
algebra, Class 7 93–100
—, Class 8 144–47
—, how much 21
algebraic word problems 100
algorithm (for computers) 149f
— for addition 247
— for long division 247
—, prime number 150, 248
—, square root 89f, 129f, 206–16
—, square root without zeroes 150
al-Khwarizmi, Muhammad ibn Musa 93f
angle(s)
—, alternate interior 114
—, bisecting 63
—, copying 62
—, corresponding 113
—, dihedral 163
— in polygons 115
— puzzles 115
—, same side interior 114
— theorems and proofs 113–15
— in triangle 114
anti-prism 164
arc 60
Archimedean duals 164, 174
—, drawing 241
—, patterns for 243
Archimedean solids 164, 172
—, drawing 240
—, patterns for 243
Archimedean spiral 70

Archimedes' principle (density) 140f
Archimedes' ratio of volumes 157
area 72f, 101f, 151–54
—, converting metric and imperial 139
—, surface *see* surface area
arithmetic facts 24
arithmetic mean 56
arithmetical progression 69
ASA (angle-side-angle) triangle 103
ASCII code 148, 246
assessment test, Class 4 255
—, Class 6 256
average 56

Baravalle's proof of Pythagorean theorem 151
base-eight 121
— times table 244
base-five 123
— times table 244
base-sixteen (hexadecimal) 124
— times table 245
binary (base-two) 125f
— code (computers) 148
— times table 244
binary/hexadecimal conversion table 246
bipyramid 164
bisector, perpendicular 63
bit (from computers) 148
business maths 47
byte (from computers) 148f

calculators, use of 24f, 131
cardioid 71f
Cassini curve 191–95

casting out nines 33
Celsius/Fahrenheit conversion 52
chord 60
circle 187, 190
—, area of 153f
—, area of segment 154
—, ratio of 86f
—, terminology 60
circumscribed 166
close-packing 177
coefficient (in algebra) 94
commission 50
compound rate problems 91
computers, main lesson block 25, 148–50
cone, surface area of 158
—, volume of 156f
congruent figures 59
conic sections 186
constant (in algebra) 94
constructions (geometric) 106f
— by guess and check 106
—, approximate 107
—, compass and straightedge 106
—, Euclidean 106
—, measurement 106
conversion table 252–54
converting metric and imperial systems 76
cross multiplying 142
cube, nets for 175
—, snub 173
—, transforming into a dodecahedron 168
—, transforming into a rhombic dodecahedron 169
—, transforming into a tetrahedron 168

—, transforming into an
    octahedron 167
—, truncated 172
cuboctahedron 172
currency exchange rates 57f
curves from network of lines 119
cylinder, volume of 155

decimals 43–47
— and fractions 42
—, converting from fractions 43, 46
—, converting to fractions 44
—, repeating 44–47
deficient numbers 221
density, converting metric and
    imperial 139–41
depreciation 135
dihedral angle 163
dimensional analysis 136
dimensions, three 60f
directrix 181
discount 51
distributive property 146
dividend 37
divisibility rules 34, 74
division 36
—, algorithm for long 247
—, geometric 107
—, long 37
— rules for signed numbers 97
—, short 39
divisor 37
dodecagon, construction of 67
dodecahedron, snub 173
dodecahedron, transforming into
    an icosahedron 169
dodecahedron, truncated 172
duality 171f

earth, dimensions of 252
—, population of 162
edge (in stereometry) 163

ellipse 182f, 185, 187, 188–90
enlarging/reducing drawings 119
equation (in algebra) 94, 145
—, golden rule 99
—, solving 98
—, with fractions 146
equiangular figure 59
equilateral figure 59
equilateral triangle 60
—, construction of 65
estimating by rounding 38
Euclid's perfect number formula
    96, 224
Euclidean constructions 106
Euler's formula 177
even numbers as the sum of two
    primes 225
exchange rates 57f
expanded notation 121
exponential growth 69, 134
— formula 134
exponents 34
—, laws of 145
expressions (in algebra) 97, 144f
—, evaluating 144f
—, simplifying 97

Fahrenheit/Celsius conversion
    52
Fermat's theorem 226
Fibonacci sequence 111
focus 181
formulas (in algebra) 94
fractions 40
— and decimals 42
— and negatives 145
—, compound 42
—, converting from decimals 44
—, converting from percents 48
—, converting to decimals 43
—, improper 41
—, in equations 146
—, reducing 40

—, simplifying 40
frequency & string length 84
fuel consumption 138

Galileo's law of falling bodies 95
Gauss, Carl Friedrich 94
Gauss's formula 94
geometric division 107
geometric drawing 61–72, 102–9
geometric progressions 69
glossary 261
Goldbach's theorem 225
golden ratio (phi, ϕ) 109–13
golden rectangle 112
golden spiral 112
golden triangle 113
graphs 53
greatest common factors (GCF)
    36
group work 22
growth 131
growth rate table 251
growth, exponential 134

half-wheel theorem 114
Heron's formula (area of triangle)
    152
hexadecimal (base-sixteen) 124
— times table 245
hexagon, construction of 66
homework 23
hyperbola 183f, 186f, 188–90

icosahedron, truncated 172
icosidodecahedron 172
imperial system 54
imperial to metric conversions
    136–41
inner-tube problem 178
interest 50f
—, compound 50f, 78
—, simple 50f
—, simple, formula 52

irrational numbers 85–89
Islamic art 119
isosceles triangle 60

Kepler, Johannes 165
king's crown 72
—, drawing 202
kite 60
knots and interpenetrating
     polygons 72
—, drawing 201

learning support 20
least common multiples (LCM)
     36
lever, law of 85
limaçon 71f
—, metamorphosis of 198
line segment, bisecting 62
—, copying 62
—, dividing into equal parts 64
linear growth 134
loci 178–95
logarithmic (equiangular)
     spiral 68–70
—, drawing 197
loss 51

map scales 142f
maths main lesson blocks
—, Class 6 29
—, Class 7 30
—, Class 8 31
maths tricks 33, 236–39
maths skills, summary 258f
mean 56
median 56
mensuration (area and volume)
     151–63
mental arithmetic 22f, 33
metric system 54, 75
metric to imperial conversions
     136–41

mixed numbers 40
mode 56
moon, size and distance to 252
Morley, theorem of 116, 204
multiplication rules for
     signed numbers 97
multiplication tables for
     number bases 244f

navigation 119
negative numbers 96
nested pentagons and
     pentagrams 109
nines, casting out 33
number bases 121–29
—, multiplication tables 244f
numbers, mixed 40

obtuse triangle 60
octagon in circle, construction
     of 67
octagons, nested 70
octahedron, nets for 175
—, volume of 162, 216
octahedron, truncated 172
octal 121
— times table 244
odd numbers as difference of
     two squares 227
operations, order of 144
orienteering 119
orthogonal views 170

parabola 181f, 187, 189f
parallel lines, construction of 64
parallelogram 60
—, area of 101f
pay, rate of 51
—, formula 52
pentagon 109f
pentagram 109f
percent, percentages 47–51,
     76–79, 131

—, converting to fractions 48
—, increase and decrease 49f,
     78, 132
percent, increase and decrease
perfect number 220f, 223
—, Euclid's formula 96, 223
perimeter 59
perpendicular line, construction
     of 63
perspective drawing 119
—, reduction 205
phi (ϕ), (golden ratio) 109–13
pi (π) 86f
—, Archimedes calculation of
     87
place value (exponent) table for
     number bases 245
Plato's Academy 165
Platonic solids 164–66
—, proof of only five 217f
polygons, interpenetrating,
     and knots 72
—, drawing 201
polyhedron 163
— nets 242
—, types of 164
Prestet, Jean 222
prime factorisation 35, 45
prime number(s)
— algorithm 150, 248
— up to 2000 234
—, difference of two 227
—, sum of two 224
prism 164
—, volume of 155, 160
profit 50
proportions, direct and
     inverse 84
— in recipes 142
—, word problems 142
pyramid 164
—, height of 161
—, surface area of 160f

Index

—, three tilting pyramids in a cube 156f
—, volume of 156f
Pythagorean crisis of irrational numbers 85
Pythagorean theorem 116f, 130
—, hypotenuse formula 130
—, leg formula 130
—, proof 116f
—, proof of Baravalle 151
Pythagorean triples 117, 250
—, Arabian formula 118
—, Plato's formula 118
—, Pythagoras' formula 118

quadrilaterals, hierarchy of 72, 199
—, types of 60
quotient 37

ratios 56, 80
—, decimal form 81
—, reciprocals of 82
— and similar figures 83
—, three thoughts of 80
—, two forms of 81
—, whole number form 81
rectangle 60
— of whirling squares 112
reducing fractions 40
reducing/enlarging drawings 119
reflections, drawing 119
regular figure 59
repeating decimals 88f, 205
—, converting to fractions 147
—, laws of 89, 205
rhombic dodecahedron 169
rhombicosidodecahedron, great 173
rhombicosidodecahedron, small 173
rhombicuboctahedron, great 173

rhombicuboctahedron, small 172
rhombus 60
rice problem, grains of 139
right triangle 60
roots 34
rotations of circles 71
—, drawing 197
rule of 72 135

SAS (side-angle-side) triangle 103
scalene triangle 60
scientific notation 121
secant 60
sections of a cone 186
shadows, drawing 119
shear and stretch 101
shear and stretch, in 3-D 155f
significant digits 57
similar figures 59
solids, constructing paper models 174–77
speed 55, 90
—, average 91
sphere, surface area of 158
—, volume of 158
spirals 68–71
spiral of Archimedes 70
spiral, equiangular (logarithmic) 68–70
—, drawing 197
square 60
— in circle, construction of 66
—, ratio of 85f
—, construction of 65
square numbers 218
—, sum of two 228f
square root(s) 34
— algorithm 89f, 129f, 206–14
— algorithm (without zeros) 150
square root table 249

SSA (side-side-angle) triangle 104
SSS (side-side-side) triangle 102
star patterns 109
—, drawing 203
statistics 56
stereometry 163–78
string length & frequency 84
sums and differences of square numbers 227
sun, size and distance to 252
supplementary angles 59
surface area 158f
symbols 266

tangent 60
tax 50
temperature conversion formulas 52, 94
tetrahedron, truncated 172
tetrahedron, volume of 162, 216f
Thales, theorem of 115
transformation of solids 166–70
trapezium 60
—, area of 152
trapezohedron 164
triangle(s)
—, acute 60
—, area of 102, 152f
— in circle, construction of 66
—, constructions 102
—, construction of equilateral 65
—, equilateral 60
—, isosceles 60
—, obtuse 60
—, right 60
—, types of 60
triangular numbers 219
24-division with all diagonals 72, 202
24-gon, construction of 68
two, powers of 231f

unit conversions 136
unit cost 51f, 138
unitary method 51f

variable (in algebra) 94
vertex 163
vertical angles 59
volume of solids 155–58

volume, converting metric and imperial 139

word problems, algebraic 100

MAKING MATHS MEANINGFUL

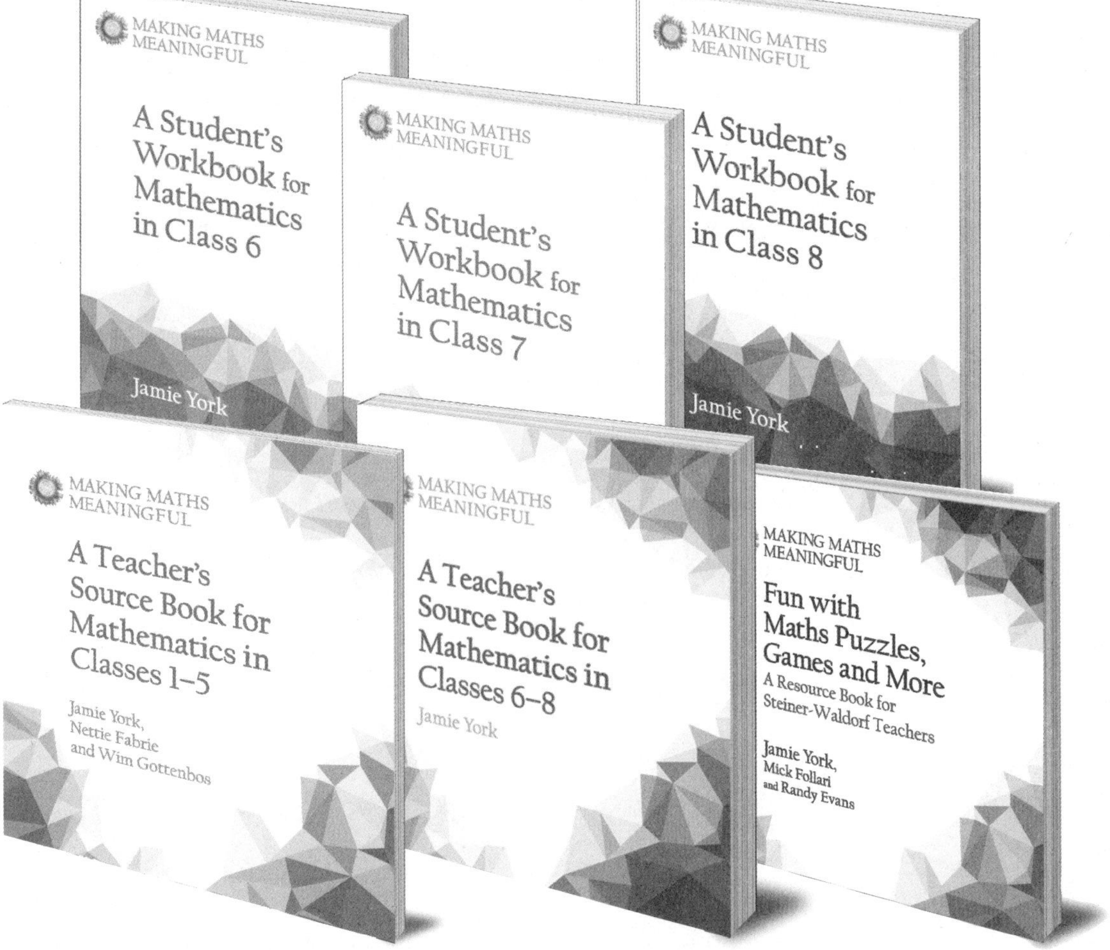

Jamie York's unique maths books are available for Classes 1 to 8, with two comprehensive teacher's source books plus separate student workbooks for Classes 6, 7 and 8. Workbooks are available individually or in classroom packs with a teacher's answer booklet.

"Jamie York has helped me develop students who are on the path to becoming imaginative, analytical thinkers in high school."
– Waldorf teacher, Portland, Oregon

florisbooks.co.uk